The UK Economy
A Manual of Applied Economics

CONTRIBUTORS

Chapter 1
> M.C. Kennedy *B.Sc. (Econ.) (London)*
> *Lecturer in Economics, University of Manchester*

Chapter 2
> N.J. Gibson *B.Sc. (Econ.), Ph.D. (Belfast)*
> *Professor of Economics, The New University of Ulster*

Chapter 3
> J.S. Metcalfe *B.A. (Econ.), M.Sc. (Manchester)*
> *Professor of Economics, University of Manchester*

Chapter 4
> J.R. Cable *B.A. (Nottingham), M.A. (Econ.) (Manchester)*
> *Senior Lecturer in Economics, University of Warwick*

Chapter 5
> David Metcalf *M.A. (Econ.) (Manchester), Ph.D. (London)*
> *Professor of Economics, University of Kent*
> and
> Ray Richardson *B.Sc. (Econ.) (London), Ph.D. (Columbia)*
> *Reader in Industrial Relations, London School of Economics*

The UK Economy
A Manual of
Applied Economics

Ninth Edition

Edited by
A. R. Prest M.A. Ph.D.
Professor of Economics, London School of Economics

and

D. J. Coppock B.A. (Econ.)
Emeritus Professor of Economics, University of Manchester

Weidenfeld and Nicolson

London

First published in Great Britain by
George Weidenfeld and Nicolson Limited
91 Clapham High St London SW4

ISBN 0 297 78180 4 cased
ISBN 0 297 78181 2 paperback

Text set in 10/11 pt IBM Press Roman, printed and bound
in Great Britain at The Pitman Press, Bath

Contents

TABLES

Chapter 4

Chapter 5

FIGURES

Chapter 1

STATISTICAL APPENDIX

ABBREVIATIONS

(1) Economic Terms

BOF	Balance for Official Financing
CAP	Common Agricultural Policy
CET	Common External Tariff
c.i.f.	Cost including Insurance and Freight
DCE	Domestic Credit Expansion
ECU	European Currency Unit
FIS	Family Income Supplement
f.o.b.	Free on Board
GDP	Gross Domestic Product
GNP	Gross National Product
MCA	Monetary Compensation Amounts
MLH	Minimum List Headings
NSA	Non Sterling Area
NS	North Sea
OSA	Overseas Sterling Area
PAYE	Pay as you Earn
PDI	Personal Disposable Income
PRT	Petroleum Revenue Tax
PSBR	Public Sector Borrowing Requirement
R and D	Research and Development
RPM	Resale Price Maintenance
SDRs	Special Drawing Rights
SIC	Standard Industrial Classification
SITC	Standard Industrial Trade Classification
TFE	Total Final Expenditure at Market Prices
VAT	Value Added Tax

(2) Organizations, etc.

CBI	Confederation of British Industry
CSO	Central Statistical Office (UK)
DE	Department of Employment
DI	Department of Industry
ECE	Economic Commission for Europe
ECSC	European Coal and Steel Community
EEA	Exchange Equalization Account
EEC	European Economic Community
EFTA	European Free Trade Area
FAO	Food and Agriculture Organization
GATT	General Agreement on Tariffs and Trade
IFC	International Finance Corporation
IMF	International Monetary Fund
MC	Monopolies and Mergers Commission
NBPI	National Board for Prices and Incomes

NEB	National Enterprise Board
NEDC(O)	National Economic Development Council (Office)
NIESR	National Institute of Economic and Social Research
NRDC	National Research and Development Corporation
OECD	Organization for Economic Cooperation and Development
OPCS	Office of Population Census and Surveys
OPEC	Organization of Petroleum Exporting Countries
PC	Price Commission
TUC	Trades Union Congress
UN	United Nations
UNCTAD	United Nations Commission for Trade and Development
WB	World Bank

(3) Journals, etc.

AAS	*Annual Abstract of Statistics* (HMSO)
AER	*American Economic Review*
BB	*British Business* (formerly *Trade and Industry*)
BEQB	*Bank of England Quarterly Bulletin*
BJIR	*British Journal of Industrial Relations*
BLS	*British Labour Statistics, Historical Abstract* (HMSO)
BTJ	*Board of Trade Journal* (HMSO)
DEG	*Department of Employment Gazette* (HMSO)
EC	*Economica*
EJ	*Economic Journal*
ET(AS)	*Economic Trends (Annual Supplement)* (HMSO)
FES	*Family Expenditure Survey* (HMSO)
FS	*Financial Statistics* (HMSO)
IFS	*International Financial Statistics*
JIE	*Journal of Industrial Economics*
JPE	*Journal of Political Economy*
JRSS	*Journal of Royal Statistical Society*
LBR	*Lloyds Bank Review*
LCES	*London and Cambridge Economic Service*
MBR	*Midland Bank Review*
MDS	*Monthly Digest of Statistics* (HMSO)
MS	*The Manchester School of Economic and Social Studies*
NIBB	*National Income Blue Book* (HMSO)
NIER	*National Institute Economic Review*
NWBQR	*National Westminster Bank Quarterly Review*
OEP	*Oxford Economic Papers*
QJE	*Quarterly Journal of Economics*
RES	*Review of Economic Studies*
REST	*Review of Economics and Statistics*
SJPE	*Scottish Journal of Political Economy*
ST	*Social Trends* (HMSO)
TBR	*Three Banks Review*
TER	*Treasury Economic Report* (HMSO)
TI	*Trade and Industry* (HMSO)

Foreword to the Ninth Edition

In 1966, when the first edition of this book was published, the foreword began as follows:

> The central idea behind this book is to give an account of the main features and problems of the UK economy today. The hope is that it will fulfil two functions simultaneously, in that it will be as up to date as possible and yet will not be simply a bare catalogue of facts and figures. There are many sources of information, official and otherwise, about the structure and progress of the UK economy. There are also many authors to whom one can turn for subtle analyses of the problems before us. Our effort here is based on the belief that there is both room and need for an attempt to combine the functions of chronicler and analyst in the confines of a single book.
>
> The contributors to these pages subscribe rather firmly to the belief that economists should practise, as well as preach, the principle of the division of labour. The complexity of a modern economy is such that, whether one likes it or not, it is no longer possible for any individual to be authoritative on all its aspects; so it is inevitable that the burden of producing work of this kind should be spread among a number of people, each a specialist in his or her particular field. Such a division carries with it obvious dangers of overlap and inconsistency. It is hoped that some of the worst pitfalls of this kind have been avoided and there is reasonable unity of purpose, treatment and layout. At the same time, it is wholly undesirable to impose a monolithic structure and it is just as apparent to the authors that there are differences in outlook and emphasis among them as it will be to the readers.
>
> The general intention was to base exposition on the assumption that the reader would have some elementary knowledge of economics — say a student in the latter part of a typical first year course in economics in a British university. At the same time, it is hoped that most of the text will be intelligible to those without this degree of expertise. We may not have succeeded in this; if not, we shall try to do better in the future.

Despite the usual extensive re-writing, we should still regard this as an accurate description of our intentions.

Chapter 1, 'The Economy as a Whole', is concerned with questions of applied macroeconomics: fluctuations in output and expenditure, the determinants and management of demand, inflation and economic growth. The chapter ends with a section on the economic prospects in the near future. Chapter 2, The Monetary, Financial and Fiscal Systems', starts with a brief discussion of the general theoretical background and then analyses in detail the theory and practices of monetary, financial and fiscal policies in the UK in recent years. The final section discusses the policy record and some prospects, and implications of membership of the EEC. Chapter 3, 'Foreign Trade and the Balance of Payments', deals with the importance of foreign trade and payments to the UK economy and assesses UK balance of payments performance over the last two decades or so. It then looks at current problems and policies in this field and ends with a discussion of the reform of the international monetary system. Chapter 4, 'Industry', starts with a summary of

UK industrial performance between 1960 and 1980 and then looks briefly at agriculture. Nationalized industries, competition policy and regional policy are examined at length. The final section is on industrial policy. Due regard is paid to the implications of EEC membership throughout. The last chapter, 'Labour', analyses employment and unemployment among the UK labourforce, and then discusses problems of wealth, income distribution and pay. The final sections are concerned with trade unions, wage inflation and related policy issues.

Whilst we try to minimize unnecessary overlapping between chapters, we quite deliberately aim at complementary treatment of some topics. Thus Chapter 1 is a more Keynesian approach to macroeconomic problems whereas Chapter 2 is more monetarist-oriented. Wage inflation is looked at from different angles in Chapters 1 and 5. Aspects of EEC membership come up in Chapters 2, 3 and 4. The implications of North Sea oil are very wide-ranging both domestically and internationally, and so receive discussion in all the first four chapters. Most aspects of government revenue are the province of Chapter 2, but national insurance contributions are covered in Chapter 5. Regional policy in partly a concern of Chapter 2 (fiscal aspects), partly Chapter 4 (industrial structure) and partly Chapter 5 (employment aspects).

To minimize the use of space, factual material or definitions appearing in one chapter but relevant to another are not always duplicated and so it must be understood that to this extent any one chapter may not be self-contained.

Each chapter is accompanied by a list of references and further reading. The Statistical Appendix has seven tables dealing with different aspects of the UK economy. There is an index as well as the detailed list of headings and sub-headings given in the Contents pages.

We acknowledge the great help given to us by all those who have rendered secretarial or computing assistance.

London School of Economics   A.R. PREST
University of Manchester   D.J. COPPOCK

April 1982

1

The economy as a whole
M.C. Kennedy

I   INTRODUCTION
I.1   Methodological Approach

This chapter is an introduction to applied macroeconomics. It begins with a brief description of the national income accounts, and goes on to discuss the multiplier, the determination of national expenditure and output in the short run, the policy problems of maintaining full employment, the causes of inflation and of economic growth. It cannot claim to give all the answers to the questions raised, but aims to provide the reader with a basis for further and deeper study.

In principle there is no essential difference between applied economics and economic theory. The object of applied economics is to explain the way in which economic units work. It is just as much concerned with questions of causation (such as what determines total consumption or the level of prices) as the theory which is found in most elementary textbooks. The difference between theoretical and applied economics is largely one of emphasis, with theory tending to stress logical connections between assumptions and conclusions, and applied economics the connections between theories and evidence. Applied economics does not seek description for its own sake, but it needs facts for the light they shed on the applicability of economic theory.

At one time it used to be thought that scientific theories were derived from factual information by a method of inference known as *induction*.[1] Thus it was supposed that general laws about nature could be deduced from knowledge of a limited number of facts. From the logical point of view, however, induction is an invalid procedure. For example, the fact that ten men have been observed to save one-tenth of their income does not entail the conclusion that the next man will do so. The conclusion may be true or false, but it does not rest validly on the assumptions. Inductive conclusions of this kind simply have the status of conjectures and require further empirical investigation.

More recently it has come to be accepted that scientific method is not inductive but *hypothetico-deductive*. A hypothesis may be proposed to explain a certain class of event. It will generally be of the conditional form 'if p then q', from which the inference is that any particular instance of p must be accompanied by an instance of q. Thus the hypothesis is tested by all observations of p; it is corroborated whenever p and q are observed together; and falsified if p occurs in the absence of q.

---

1   For a highly readable introduction to the problems of scientific method the reader is referred to P.B. Medawar, *Induction and Intuition in Scientific Thought*, Methuen, 1969, and the more serious student to K.R. Popper, *The Logic of Scientific Discovery*, Hutchinson, 1959, and *Conjectures and Refutations*, Routledge and Kegan Paul, 1963. For a treatment of methodological problems in economics, see I.M.T. Stewart, *Reasoning and Method in Economics*, McGraw-Hill, 1979, and M. Blaug, *The Methodology of Economics*, Cambridge University Press, 1980.

It will be clear that this concept of scientific inference places the role of factual information in a different light from the inductive approach. Facts, instead of being the foundation on which to build economic or scientific theories, become the basis for testing them. If a theory is able to survive a determined but unsuccessful attempt to refute it by factual evidence, it is regarded as well tested. But the discovery of evidence which is inconsistent with the theory will stimulate its modification or the development of a new theory altogether. One of the purposes of studying applied economics is to acquaint the theoretically equipped economist with the limitations of the theory he has studied. Applied economics is not an attempt to bolster up existing theory or, as its name might seem to imply, to demonstrate dogmatically that all the factual evidence is a neat application of textbook theory. Its aim is to understand the workings of the economy, and this means that it will sometimes expose the shortcomings of existing theory and go on to suggest improvements.

The discovery that a theory is falsified by factual observations need not mean that it must be rejected out of hand or relegated to total oblivion. Economists, as well as natural scientists, frequently have to work with theories that are inadequate in one way or another. Theories that explain part but not all of the evidence are often retained until some new theory is found which fits a wider range of evidence. Frequently the theory will turn out to have been incomplete rather than just wrong, and when modified by the addition of some new variable (or a more careful specification of the *ceteris paribus* clause), the theory may regain its status. The reader who notices inconsistencies between theory and facts need not take the line that the theory is total nonsense, for the theory may still hold enough grains of truth to become the basis for something better.

It is often argued that our ability to test economic theories by reference to factual observations is sufficient to liberate economics from value judgements, i.e. to turn it into a *positive* subject. This position has more than an element of truth in it: when there is clear evidence against a theory it stands a fair chance of being dropped even by its most bigoted adherents. Nevertheless, it would be wrong to forget that a great deal of what passes for factual evidence in economics is infirm in character (e.g. the statistics of gross domestic product or personal saving), so that it is often possible for evidence to be viewed more sceptically by some than by others.

The discussion of economic policy which also figures in this chapter is partly normative in scope, and partly positive. The normative content of policy discussion consists in the evaluation of goals and priorities. But the means for attaining such goals derive from the positive hypotheses of economics. They involve questions of cause and effect, the hypothetical answers to which are appraisable by reference to evidence. In making recommendations for the achieve-ment of policy goals, however, the economist treads on thin ice. This is partly because his positive knowledge is not inevitably correct, but also because it is seldom possible for him to foresee and properly appraise all the side-effects of his recommendations, some of which have implications for other policy goals. When economists differ in their advice on policy questions it is not always clear how much the difference is due on the one hand to diagnostic disagreements, or, on the other, to differences in value judgements. Indeed it is seldom possible for an economic adviser to reveal all the normative preferences which lie behind a policy recommendation. Thus policy judgements have to be scrutinized carefully for hidden normative assumptions. It follows that the reader of this chapter must be on his guard against the author's personal value judgements.

I.2   Gross Domestic Product

Most of the topics discussed in this chapter make some use of the national accounts statistics. A complete explanation of what these are and of how they are put together is available elsewhere.[1] It will be useful, however, in the next few pages to remind the reader of the main national accounting categories in so far as they affect this chapter.

The most important concept of all is gross domestic product (GDP). This is the value of the total output of the whole economy. Its significance can be most readily appreciated by imagining that the economy is like some simple productive enterprise, such as a farm. Suppose that a farm produces only wheat, the total production during a single year being 100 bushels and the price £1. The value of total production is therefore £100. Total output is equated to total expenditure on the output, under the accounting convention that any part of the year's output which is not sold is recorded as an addition to stocks, and as such regarded as investment expenditure by the farmer. Total expenditure, moreover, is equated to total income because the proceeds from the sale of output are divided between money profits, rent and wages, whilst all unsold output is deemed to be profit in kind. Thus the income and output of the farm and the expenditure on its output are evaluated so as to make them identically equal to each other.

The GDP of the UK, by analogy with the simple production unit, can also be added up in three different ways: from the sides of income, output and expenditure. The first of these, total *income*, measures the sum of all incomes of the residents of the UK earned in the production of goods and services in the UK during a stated period. It divides into income from employment, income from self-employment and profit, and income from rent. These are factor incomes earned in the process of production and are to be distinguished from *transfer incomes*, such as pensions and sickness benefits, which are not earned from production and which, therefore, are excluded from the total. The breakdown of factor incomes for 1980 is illustrated in table 1.1 on page 4.

As with the simple production unit, the value of *output* accruing in the form of unsold stocks is included in total factor output. But a problem arises when the prices at which stocks are valued in the national accounts vary during the course of the accounting period. When this happens, the value of stocks held at the beginning and end of the period will have been reported at two different prices, and it is then necessary to make a special valuation adjustment known as the adjustment for *stock appreciation*. A firm holding stocks of wood, for example, may increase its holding from 100 tons on 1 January to 200 tons on 31 December. If the price of wood was £1.00 per ton at the beginning of the year and £1.10 at the end of the year, the increase in the monetary value of stocks will show up as $(£1.10 \times 200) - (£1.00 \times 100)$, which equals £120. This figure is inflated by the amount of the price increase and fails, therefore, to give an adequate record of what the Central Statistical Office (CSO) calls 'the value of the physical increase in stocks'. In order to rectify this, the CSO attempts to value the physical change in

---

1   See, for example, S. Hays, *National Income and Expenditure in Britain and the OECD Countries*, Heinemann, 1971; R. and G. Stone, *National Income and Expenditure*, 9th edition, Bowes and Bowes, 1972; H.C. Edey and others, *National Income and Social Accounting*, 3rd edition, Hutchinson, 1967; or the official publications, *National Accounts Statistics, Sources and Methods*, HMSO, 1968, and *The National Accounts, A Short Guide*, HMSO, 1981.

TABLE 1.1
GDP and GNP at Current Prices, UK, 1980

FROM INCOME

	£m	% of domestic income[1]
Income from employment	137,083	67.9
Income from self-employment	18,394	9.1
Income from rent	13,231	6.5
Gross trading profits of companies	24,979	12.4
Gross trading surplus of public corporations and other public enterprises	6,185	3.1
Imputed charge for consumption of non-trading capital	2,138	1.1
Total domestic income (before providing for stock appreciation)	202,010	100.0
less Stock appreciation	−6,477	
Gross domestic product at factor cost (from income)	195,553	
Residual error	−2,065	
Gross domestic product at factor cost (from expenditure)	193,488	

BY INDUSTRY

	£m	% of total[1]
Agriculture, forestry and fishing	4,296	2.1
Petroleum and natural gas	7,649	3.7
Other mining and quarrying	3,222	1.6
Manufacturing	48,060	23.4
Construction	13,025	6.5
Services and distribution	129,013	62.8
Total (after providing for stock appreciation)	205,265	100.0
Adjustment for financial services[2]	−9,732	
Gross domestic product at factor cost (from income)	195,553	

FROM EXPENDITURE

	£m	% of TFE[1]
Consumers' expenditure	135,403	47.8
General government final consumption	48,337	17.1
Gross domestic fixed investment	40,050	14.1
Investment in stocks	−3,596	−1.3
Export of goods and services	63,198	22.3
Total final expenditure at market prices	283,392	100.0
less Imports of goods and services	−57,832	
less Adjustment to factor cost	−32,072	
Gross domestic product at factor cost	193,488	
Net property income from abroad	−38	
Gross national product at factor cost	193,450	

Source: NIBB, 1981, tables 1.1, 1.2 and 1.9.
1 Percentage figures may not add up to 100.0 because of rounding.
2 Deduction of net receipts of interest by financial companies.

stocks at the average price level prevailing during the period. If, in the example, the price averaged £1.05 over the period, then the value of the physical increase in stocks would be shown as £1.05 (200–100), which equals £105. The difference of £15 between this and the increase in monetary value is the adjustment for stock appreciation. It must be deducted from the reported value of factor incomes in order to reach an estimate of gross domestic income.

GDP measured from the income side can be rearranged in terms of the factor incomes earned in each industry. This breakdown is available annually, and gives an up-to-date picture of the industrial composition of GDP. It is shown in table 1.1.

An alternative, and independent, estimate of current price GDP can be assembled from data on production, although this is possible only when a Census of Production is taken. The procedure of adding up the output of individual firms to arrive at GDP is complicated by the existence of *intermediate output*, whereby one firm's output is used as raw material in the output of another. Wheat produced on a farm, for example, may be used by a bakery to make bread, and there is a danger here of double-counting. To surmount this difficulty, the distinction is drawn between the total or gross output of a firm and its *value added*, the difference between them being the value of intermediate input. Imports are a special case of intermediate input, in that they are produced by enterprises outside the UK.

GDP can also be measured from the side of *expenditure*. Conceptually this total is identical to the income and output totals; but in practice the expenditure statistics are collected from independent sources and do not lead to exactly the same figure. The difference between the income and expenditure estimates is known as the residual error and is sometimes quite large. In 1980 it was £2,065m, or 1.1% of GDP.

The breakdown of the expenditure total is especially important in the analysis of aggregate demand. Expenditures are undertaken by four types of spending unit: persons, public authorities, firms and foreign residents.[1] Purchases by persons are described as consumers' expenditure, or, more loosely, as consumption. The latter description, however, may be slightly misleading when applied to expenditure on durable goods such as motorcars and refrigerators, the services of which are consumed over several years and not solely in the year in which they are purchased. One form of personal expenditure which is not classed as such is the purchase of new houses. These are deemed to have been sold initially to 'firms' and included under the broad heading of domestic capital formation or gross investment. Fixed investment, other than housing, represents the purchases by firms of physical assets that are not used up in current production, but which accrue as additions or replacements to the nation's capital stock. The preface 'gross' warns us that a year's gross investment does not measure the change in the size of the capital stock during the year because it does not allow for withdrawals from the capital stock due to scrapping, or for wear and tear. The concept of gross capital formation is also carried through into the definition of domestic product itself. Net domestic product is not easily measured, but attempts to include only that investment which adds to the total stock of capital. It is less relevant to the level of employment than gross output.

---

1   The distinctions between types of spending units are not always clear-cut, e.g. expenditure by self-employed persons is partly consumers' expenditure and partly investment.

The sum of exports, consumers' expenditure, government final consumption and gross investment is known as total final expenditure at market prices, or TFE for short. Each of the four components contains two elements which must be deducted before arriving at GDP at factor cost. The first is the import content of the expenditure which must, of course, be classified as foreign rather than domestically produced output. The simplest way of removing imports is to take the global import total as given by the balance of payments accounts and subtract it from TFE, and this is the usual method. Estimates do exist, however, for the import content of the separate components of final expenditure in the input-output tables, but they are drawn up much less frequently than the national accounts. The second element of total final expenditure which must be deducted to obtain the factor cost value of GDP is the indirect tax content (net of subsidies) of the various expenditures. This is present for the simple reason that the most readily available valuation of any commodity is the price at which it sells in the market. This price, however, will overstate the factor incomes earned from producing the commodity if it contains an element of indirect tax; and it will understate factor income if the price is subsidized. The deduction of indirect taxes (less subsidies) is known as the *factor cost adjustment*, and is most conveniently made globally since it can be found from the government's records of tax proceeds and subsidy payments. Estimates of its incidence on the individual components of TFE are available annually in the National Income *Blue Book*.[1]

Gross domestic product from the expenditure side is thus obtained by adding up the components of TFE at market prices, and by subtracting imports of goods and services together with the factor cost adjustment. It relates to expenditure on the total production in the UK of the residents of the United Kingdom. It differs from the other aggregate concept, gross national product (GNP), in that it does not include receipts of interest, profits and dividends by UK residents from productive assets owned overseas; nor does it exclude the profits of foreign-owned enterprises producing in the UK. The balance of these two amounts is known as net property income from abroad and must be added or subtracted from GDP in order to obtain GNP. In most years it is positive, but in 1980 it was a small negative amount.

I.3   Gross Domestic Product at Constant Prices

Table 1.1 summarizes the national accounts for 1980 at the prices obtaining in 1980. As such it is a useful source of information as to the way in which domestic income, output and expenditure were divided in a particular year. If, however, we wish to compare the *volume* of goods produced in different periods we must use a different set of figures. These are the estimates of GDP at constant prices, the expenditure side of which is presented in the Statistical Appendix, table A-1. They show the value of GDP for each year in terms of the prices ruling in 1975. Similar estimates are available for the output total of GDP together with its main industrial components. These totals are derived almost entirely from movements in quantities, the various quantities for each year being added together by means of the value weights obtaining for 1975.

There are only two direct estimates of GDP at constant prices: the expenditure- and the output-based estimates, both of which may be broken down into constant-

---

1   *NIBB*, 1981, table 1.1.

price components. But an income estimate of constant-price GDP may be obtained by dividing the current-price total by the implied-price index (or 'deflator') for GDP. This index is simply the result of dividing GDP at current prices by GDP at constant prices (both on the expenditure basis). This means that for GDP as a whole there are, altogether, three independent estimates of the constant-price total. There are often sizeable discrepancies between the three estimates, and this implies that it is unwise to be too precise about the level of constant-price GDP. In 1980, for example, GDP in constant prices was put by the income estimate at 109.2% of the 1975 level, whereas the output and expenditure estimates made it 107.3 and 107.2% respectively. These discrepancies in the level of GDP also mean that the annual rate of change is not known unambiguously. The decline in GDP from 1979 to 1980, for example, was put at 1.6% by the expenditure estimate and at 2.8% by the output figure, with the income figure falling between the two. An inspection of annual changes in GDP since 1970 shows that, on average, the spread between the highest and lowest estimates was 1.6%; in three years it was 2.0% or slightly higher; and in only one year was it less than 1.0%.

Gross domestic product is an important entity in its own right and changes in its real amount are the best estimates available of changes in total UK production. Even so, it must be remembered that it leaves a good deal out of the picture by excluding practically all productive work which is not sold for money. The national income statistics neglect, for example, the activities of the housewife, the do-it-yourself enthusiast and the so-called 'black economy', even though they must add millions of hours to UK production of goods and services. It is also important to recognize that GDP stands for the production of UK residents, not their expenditure. As an expenditure total it measures the spending of all persons, resident or foreign, on the goods and services produced by the residents of the UK. Thus if national welfare is conceived as spending by UK residents, it is incorrect to represent it by GDP. The total appropriate for this purpose is GDP *plus* imports *minus* exports. This total is referred to as total domestic expenditure, and is equal to the UK's total use of resources, which is the sum of consumption, government expenditure and gross investment. It is an amount which can diminish quite substantially when there is a sharp improvement in the balance of payments.

II   FLUCTUATIONS IN TOTAL OUTPUT AND EXPENDITURE
II.1   Fluctuations in Output and Employment

The British economy has experienced cyclical fluctuations since the time of the industrial revolution. During the nineteenth century these appeared to follow a fairly uniform pattern, with a peak-to-peak duration of seven to ten years and a tendency for 'full employment' (roughly defined) to reappear at each cyclical peak. After the First World War this pattern ceased, and for nearly twenty years there were well over one million unemployed. Unemployment reached nearly 9% of the workforce in the recession of 1926 and nearly 16% in 1932.

The period after the Second World War until the early 1970s was one of continuously high employment, with only the mildest fluctuations in GDP, employment and unemployment. The unemployment rate (UK, excluding school-leavers) never exceeded an annual figure of 2.5%, and, during peak periods of activity, was as little as 1 or 1½% of the employed labourforce. During this period, real GDP never declined by more than 1.0% during the downturn phase of the cycle, and in most 'recessions' it simply rose at a slower-than-average rate of increase. This period of high and stable employment was also characterized by a much lower average rate of inflation than has been experienced since 1970.

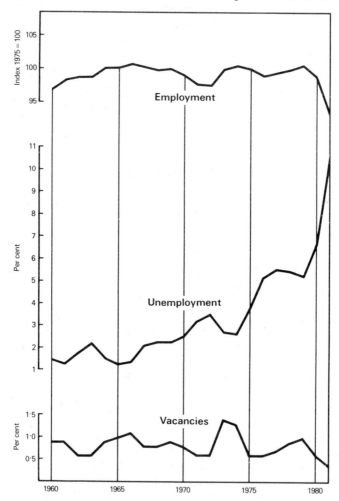

Figure 1.1   Employment, unemployment and vacancies, UK, 1960-81

It was not until the 1970s that the business cycle threatened to return on the scale of the prewar era (see figure 1.1). A mild recession in 1970-72 was followed in 1973-6 by a doubling of unemployment to 5.6% of the labourforce. Finally, in 1979-81, the UK economy experienced a depression which was fully commensurate with that of 1929-33. By early 1982 unemployment had reached 3 million, or about 12% of the employed labourforce, whilst the rate for young people aged between 16 and 19 was over 20%. The recession was most severe in Northern Ireland, Scotland, Wales and the industrial centres of England.

A comparison of the 1979-81 depression with that of 1929-32 is given in table 1.2, where it can be seen that unemployment in 1981 was not quite as high as it had been in 1932, but that the declines in employment, industrial production and estimated GDP were very similar in the two depressions. The most important difference concerned the behaviour of wages and prices, both of which were falling in 1929-32, whereas in 1979-81 they were increasing rapidly. This created a dilemma for economic policy-making which was not present in the 1930s.

II.2   Expenditures in the Cycle

Business recessions occur because of a decline in total spending. In the United States' depression of 1929-32, when real GNP fell by almost one-third, the mainspring of the recession was a decline in fixed investment which spread, through falling incomes, to personal consumption. The accompanying decline in US imports led to falling world trade and production, and thus to depression in the export industries of other countries.

In the United Kingdom in 1929-32, the decline in GDP was very largely confined to exports. These fell by 32%, which in absolute amount was enough to account for the whole of the decline in total final expenditure. There were mild declines in fixed investment and stock-building and offsetting increases in consumers' and government expenditure (see table 1.3).

TABLE 1.2

Comparison of Three Recessions, UK, 1929-81

		Percentages	
	1929-32	1973-5	1979-81
Unemployment rate: peak year	7.3	2.6	5.4
trough year	15.6	5.3	10.6
Change in employment	−3.6	−0.4	−6.8
Change in GDP (average estimate)	−5.1	−2.8	−4.6
Change in industrial production	−10.8	−8.6	−11.5
Change in wage rates, per annum	−1.9	+23.9	+14.0
Change in prices, per annum	−6.8	+20.0	+15.0

Sources: C.H. Feinstein, *National Income, Expenditure and Output in the United Kingdom, 1855-1965* (Cambridge University Press, 1972); *Economic Trends Annual Supplement 1982*; *National Institute Economic Review, February 1982*; *Financial Statement and Budget Report 1982*.

If 1929-32 was an export-led recession, those of 1973-5 and 1979-81 were predominantly stock recessions, with most of the decline in TFE being accounted for by large swings from stock accumulation to stock declines. Exports fell in 1979-81, partly because of the worldwide depression and partly because the exchange rate was allowed to rise: expenditure fell in 1973-5 but held up in 1979-81. In both recessions there were sizeable declines in fixed investment, which by 1981 was running at its lowest level in 13 years. Nevertheless, the large decline in stocks offered some prospect of recovery since even a fall in the rate of decline of stocks acts as a stimulus to total output and employment. The prospects for the economy are discussed more fully in section VI of this chapter.

Periods of recovery have usually been led by a revival of fixed investment, but in 1975-9 the main stimuli came from exports, consumption and stockbuilding (see table 1.4). Recovery, moreover, was somewhat less than complete with unemployment in 1979 at 1.3 million, or 5.4% of total employees. Unfilled vacancies in 1979 numbered only 241,000 compared with the 1973 peak level of 307,000.[1] There are grounds, therefore, for saying that the recession of 1979-81 started from an initial level of activity which was already somewhat depressed. Part of the difficulty, however, appeared to be an occupational or local mismatching of unemployment and vacancies.[1]

TABLE 1.3

Expenditures in Three Recessions, UK, 1929-81

	Level in 1929	Change 1929-32	Level in 1973	Change 1973-5	Level in 1979	Change 1979-81
	£bn at 1938 prices		£bn at 1975 prices		£bn at 1975 prices	
Consumers' expenditure	3.77	+0.07	66.3	−1.6	71.4	+0.2
Government consumption	0.44	+0.03	21.5	+1.5	23.9	+0.7
Fixed investment	0.46	−0.06	21.2	−0.8	20.9	−1.6
Investment in stocks	0.03	−0.03	2.5	−4.0	1.5	−3.6
Exports of goods and services	0.99	−0.32	26.0	+1.2	33.0	−0.4
TFE	5.69	−0.32	137.5	−3.6	150.7	−4.8

Sources: Feinstein, op. cit.; *ET(AS)* 1982; *FSBR* 1982.

II.3   The Determinants of Demand

The proximity of national output to its full-employment potential is determined by the levels of total expenditure, which, in the simplest terms, can be divided into two main categories of spending: the 'exogenous' items, which are not affected by the current level of national income, and the 'endogenous' expenditures, which depend on current or lagged income. In the simplest textbook accounts, the former category is represented as investment, and is said to be determined by the stock of unexploited technological potential, by business expectations of the rate of return, and the rate of interest. Consumption, on the other hand, is taken as dependent on income itself, so that the line of causation runs from investment to income to consumption, with investment acting as the principle cause of movements in total output.

This simple model of income determination is of clear relevance to the way in which GDP is determined in the 'real world'. But, as we have seen, there are various complications. The exogenous component of total expenditure has to include,

---

1 See section IV for a fuller discussion of unemployment and vacancies in relation to the pressure of demand.

TABLE 1.4

Growth Rates of Expenditures (at constant prices) During the Main Cyclical Phases, UK, 1959-81
(Percentage increases per annum)

	1959-61	1961-3	1963-5	1965-72	1972-3	1973-5	1975-9	1979-81
Fixed investment	9.4	0.7	10.7	2.9	6.9	-1.9	0.6	-4.0
Investment in stocks (expressed as % of TFE)	0.1	-0.2	0.3	-0.1	1.8	-1.5	0.6	-2.5
Exports	4.4	3.2	4.2	5.9	11.6	2.2	5.4	-0.6
Government consumption	2.7	2.3	2.1	2.2	4.7	3.7	0.9	1.5
Consumers' expenditure on goods and services	3.1	3.2	2.4	2.8	4.8	-1.2	2.6	1.0
Imports	5.4	3.3	5.5	5.7	11.7	-3.1	5.4	-2.8
GDP (average estimate)	4.0	2.5	4.2	2.4	7.2	-1.4	2.6	-2.3

Sources: ET(AS) 1982, FSBR 1982.

besides fixed investment, exports, government expenditure and investment in stocks, whilst the endogenous items must include imports as well as consumption. A large area of macroeconomics and applied econometrics is devoted to the attempt to explain in some detail how those various expenditures are determined. These explanations are essential if we are to understand economic fluctuations and to be able to forecast and control them.

II.4   Consumers' Expenditure

Consumers' expenditure is the largest single element in aggregate demand. It accounts for nearly half of TFE (see table 1.1) and, after the removal of its import and indirect-tax content, for about the same fraction of GDP at factor cost. Consumption is one of the more stable elements of demand, and it held up well in the recession of 1979-81. But its total amount is so large in relation to GDP that even quite small percentage variations in it can have important repercussions for output and employment. An understanding of consumption behaviour, therefore, as well as an ability to predict it, are important objectives for economic analysis. A great deal of attention has been given to consumption, both in theory and statistically, although this work has been more heavily concentrated upon consumption in the US where the relevant statistical data are available for a longer period than for the UK.

The starting point for the early studies of consumer behaviour was the well-known statement by Keynes:[1] 'The fundamental psychological law upon which we are entitled to depend with great confidence both *a priori* from our knowledge of human nature and from the detailed facts of experience, is that men are disposed, as a rule and on the average, to increase their consumption as their income increases, but not by as much as the increase in their income.' Keynes was suggesting that current income was the principal, although not the only, determinant of consumers' expenditure in the short run, and that the marginal propensity to consume (the ratio of additional consumption to additional income) was positive, fractional and reasonably stable.

If we focus attention upon savings rather than consumption, it can be seen (figure 1.2) that the ratio of personal savings to personal disposable income has shown a strong upward trend over the postwar period, with deviations from trend which are associated with cyclical fluctuations. The savings ratio was above trend in the peak years of 1961, 1965 and 1971, and below trend in the intervening recessions. In the recession of 1973-5 and in 1980, however, the savings ratio was on the high side.

Cyclical movements in the savings ratio can be accounted for in various ways. One possible explanation is that consumer behaviour is driven partly by habit and convention, so that when income declines the individual attempts to maintain his expenditure at its previous level with the consequence that the average propensity to consume (APC) rises and the savings ratio declines. A related explanation can be found in the ideas of the normal-income theorists.[1]

---

1   J.M. Keynes, *General Theory*, p. 96.

2   For an examination of these theories, see M.J. Farrell, 'The New Theories of the Consumption Function', *EJ*, December 1959 (reprinted in Klein and Gordon (eds.), *Readings in Business Cycles*, Allen and Unwin, 1966). The classic reference is F. Modigliani and R. Brumberg, 'Utility Analysis and the Consumption Function', in K. Kurihara, *Post-Keynesian Economics*, Allen and Unwin, 1955.

Their main proposition is that consumption does not depend upon current income but on normal income, a concept which can be defined either precisely as the expected lifetime income of the consumer or much more vaguely as his notion of average income over some ill-defined future period. Thus it is changes in the level of expected income which are likely to change consumption. If current income increases, then it will raise consumption only in so far as it raises normal income, and the amount by which it does so will depend upon the expected persistence of the income change. Cyclical changes in income are (by definition) not persistent, and the likelihood is that some consumers, perhaps a majority, will recognize them as such. Thus the APC will tend to be high in depressions and low at the peaks, whilst the savings ratio (see figure 1.2) will do the reverse.

The UK savings ratio has shown a pronounced increase over recent years, rising from about 8% in 1971 to an apparent 15% in 1980. The causes of the increase are not known with certainty, but one factor has been the erosion in the value of consumers' assets due to inflation. This may have led to attempts to replenish real wealth by saving more out of current income.[1] It is also possible that the slowing down of real income growth, higher unemployment and fears of anti-inflationary policies have all combined to make consumers less optimistic about their future incomes than they were in the 1960s, and to save more for that reason.

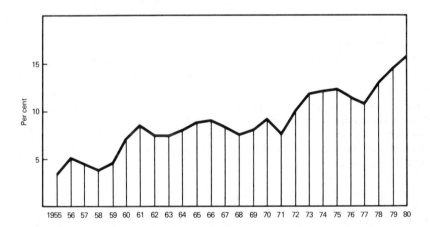

Figure 1.2   Personal saving as a percentage of personal disposable income, UK, 1955–80

An important influence upon consumers' expenditure is the availability and cost of credit and particularly of credit for financing purchases of durable goods.[2] These goods, which constitute 9% of total consumption, are more in the nature of capital equipment than consumption in that they yield a flow of utility over time. It is

1   For a discussion see K. Cuthbertson, 'The Measurement and Behaviour of the UK Savings Ratio', *NIER*, February 1982. It should be noted that figures for the savings ratio are prone to substantial revision: that for 1976 was put at 14.6% in 1980, but is now (*ET(AS)*, 1982) revised down to 11.6%.

2   It should be noted that the *Blue Book* definition of durable goods includes cars, motorcycles, furniture, carpets, and electrical goods, but, perhaps arbitrarily, does not include clothing, curtains, pots and pans, or books.

natural where income is generally rising that such goods should be bought extensively on credit, and something like one half of their total is financed by hire-purchase. The availability of HP finance used to be regulated through government controls on the minimum percentage downpayment and the maximum repayment period. But these controls have not been used since 1971, and it is now interest rates rather than direct controls which tend to regulate HP borrowing.

The marginal propensity to consume: The marginal propensity to consume (MPC) is the increase in spending which, *ceteris paribus*, an individual plans to undertake on the assumption of a unit rise in his disposable income. The aggregate MPC, likewise, is the weighted average of all individual MPCs.

An insight into the possible size of the aggregate MPC can be obtained by application of the life-cycle hypothesis, which assumes that the object of saving is to finance consumption during retirement.[1] An individual of representative age (say 38) who receives an increase in his income of £1 a year will plan to save just enough to maintain a constant annual addition to his spending. If he expects to go on receiving the extra income until he retires at age 65 and if he also expects to live for a further 12 years after retirement (the life expectation of a 65-year-old man), then his extra £1 will be earned for a further 27 years, but will be needed for spending over a period of 39 years. These two periods are the key to his MPC, which will be 27/39 = 0.69, whilst his marginal propensity to save will be 0.31. The calculation assumes that he disregards the interest on his savings, that the increases in income had not been previously anticipated, and that he expects it to be a permanent addition to his income. It also assumes that he is not interested in leaving any further bequests to his children, and that he is prepared to make calculations of the kind suggested. These, no doubt, are stringent assumptions, but they do enable us to deduce that a 'representative' increase in aggregate income (i.e. one which is spread evenly across ages and income levels) might involve an MPC in the region of 0.7. This is lower than the recorded ratio of consumption to income, which was 0.85 in 1980, and well below the life-cycle theory's hypothetical APC, which is unity since individuals are assumed to consume all of their life-time income.

An empirical estimate of the MPC may be found either by econometric methods or by direct inspection of the data. Early econometric studies of consumption were in general agreement that the MPC deduced from short-term time series data was in the region of 0.6 to 0.8.[2] These results, which relate mainly to the United States, accord with the *a priori* estimates gleaned from the life-cycle hypothesis. An inspection of the data for the UK shows that the annual change in consumption, measured at current prices, has over 30 years varied between 0.5 and 1.2 times the increase in disposable income. Over the last five years the figures were:

	1975-6	1976-7	1977-8	1978-9	1979-80
change in consumption (£bn)	10.2	11.0	12.9	17.8	18.7
change in personal disposable income (£bn)	11.0	11.5	17.4	23.1	24.0
estimated MPC	.93	.96	.74	.77	.78

---

1   Modigliani and Brumberg, op. cit.

2   See G. Ackley, *Macroeconomic Theory*, Macmillan, New York, 1961 and R. Ferber, 'Research on Household Behaviour', *AER*, 52, 1962, for surveys of these studies.

These still show a fairly wide range in the MPC, but in the calculation of the multiplier in section II.8 below we shall assume that the MPC is 0.75, which is roughly its estimated value for the last three years. There is no certainty that this is exactly the right figure, and some estimates go very much lower.[1]

II.5   Gross Fixed Investment

Fixed investment or gross domestic fixed capital formation is a heterogeneous total, comprising housing and business investment in both the public and the private sectors. Its breakdown by industry and sector in 1980 is shown in table 1.5. Of the three main components, it is manufacturing investment which is the most volatile. But all three sectors vary enough from year to year to have important effects upon output and employment.

TABLE 1.5

Gross Domestic Fixed Capital Formation, UK, 1980 (£bn)

	Private sector	*Public sector*	*Total*
Dwellings	3.5	2.6	6.0
Manufacturing	6.7	0.3	7.0
Other fixed investment	17.5	9.4	27.0
Total	27.7	12.3	40.1

Source: NIBB, 1981, p. 130; current prices. Detail does not add to totals because of rounding.

Gross investment consists of net additions to the capital stock plus the replacement of worn-out or obsolete capital. It is undertaken in anticipation of future profit, and is heavily dependent, therefore, upon expected sales in future years. A hypothesis which goes some way towards explaining the behaviour of manufacturing investment is the capital-stock-adjustment principle. This states that the level of investment is related positively to the level of output and negatively to the existing capital stock (of land, buildings and machinery in productive use). The principle may be expressed as

$$I_t = aY_{t-1} - bK_{t-1}$$

or, in ratio form, as

---

1   For example, the estimate implied by the Treasury's model is not much above 0.3 for durable and non-durable goods spending. This seems to have been due to the introduction of a price variable which tends to lower the implied explanatory power of income. The variable was introduced in the attempt to account for the rise in the savings ratio in the 1970s, and is assumed to be a proxy for wealth. See H.M. Treasury, *Macroeconomic Model Technical Manual*, 1979.

$$\frac{I_t}{Y_{t-1}} = a - b \frac{K_{t-1}}{Y_{t-1}}$$

Here I_t stands for gross investment in the current year. Y_{t-1} for last year's level of output, K_{t-1} for the capital stock at the end of the preceding year; and a and b are constant coefficients. The principle may be interpreted in various ways, one of which is to assume (not too implausibly) that technology dictates a fixed proportional relationship between the stock of capital equipment and the level of output. It follows, since net investment is an increase in the capital stock, that its amount will be planned in relation both to the expected volume of production and to the current size of the capital stock. If it is assumed as an approximation that the expected volume of output is equal to the level most recently experienced, then the expressions above may be seen to hold.[1]

Figure 1.3 illustrates the relationship between the investment ratio and capital-output ratio for manufacturing industry. It shows a fairly close correspondence between peaks in one ratio and troughs in the other in a period running from 1955 to about 1970. This suggests that the capital-stock-adjustment principle may well have been at work during this period. Since 1970, however, the relationship has largely disappeared, and this is probably because capacity has been less fully utilized. Figures published by the CBI, for example, show that the percentage of businessmen who believed their output was constrained by capacity shortages fell from about 48%, on average, in 1960-9 to 37% in 1970-81.[2] Investment will be undertaken by private firms only if it is expected to be more profitable than meeting the same demand from existing capacity.

Economic theory suggests that there are a number of relevant considerations ignored by the stock-adjustment principle. One of these is the expected profitability of the investment, which, although related to the volume of expected sales and output, is dependent on other factors too. Expected profitability is likely to be guided by actual profitability which, in recent years, has been exceptionally low. Thus the National Institute has calculated that the real rate of return on capital to industrial and commercial companies (excluding North Sea activities) has fallen from over 9% a year in the 1960s to 6% or less in the period since 1974

1   The equations are derived by denoting K_t^* as the desired capital stock, Y_t^* as expected output, R_t^* as desired replacement investment, I_t^* as desired gross investment and I_t as actual gross investment. Then, by definition,

$I_t^* = K_t^* - K_{t-1} + R_t^*$

and by assumption:

$I_t = bI_t^* = b(K_t^* - K_{t-1} + R_t^*)$

$K_t^* = a_1 Y_t^*$

$R_t^* = a_2 Y_t^*$

$Y_t^* = Y_{t-1}$

$\therefore \ I_t = b(a_1 Y_{t-1} - K_{t-1} + a_2 Y_{t-1})$

$= b(a_1 + a_2) Y_{t-1} - bK_{t-1}$

$= aY_{t-1} - bK_{t-1}$ where $a = b(a_1 + a_2)$

which is the first of the equations in the text.

2   For details and further discussion, see 'The British Economy in the Medium Term', *NIER*, November 1981, pp. 13-14.

and to a mere 2% in 1980.[1] The ratio of profits to domestic output has fallen from over 19% in the 1960s to 15% in 1980. These trends, which are less pronounced when North Sea oil is included, go some way to explaining the low level of investment in the 1970s.

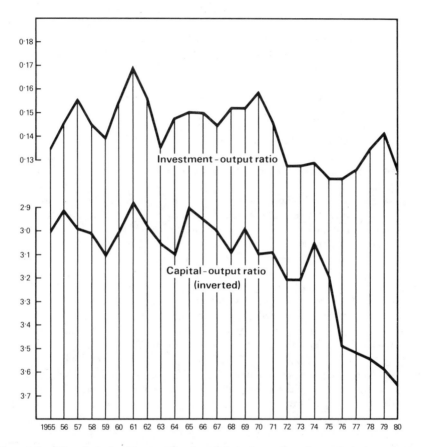

Figure 1.3   Manufacturing investment and capital stock as ratios of manufacturing output, UK, 1955–80

A further factor is the rate of interest which, as the cost of borrowing, can never be completely ignored as an influence upon the level of investment. Interest must be paid on all funds that are borrowed from outside the firm and it must be forgone on internal funds which could have been lent at interest but which, instead, are used to finance the firm's own investment projects. If interest rates had fluctuated violently, it would have been necessary to include them as an additional variable in the determination of investment in the UK. But for many years they showed only rather modest movements, never rising, for example, by more than 2% in a year over the period 1958-73.[2] In 1973-4, however, the debenture rate

1   *NIER*, February 1982, pp. 23-5.

2   This may explain why so few econometric studies have found interest rates to be an important influence on investment in Britain. See D. Savage, 'The Channels of Monetary Influence', *NIER*, February 1978.

rose from 11.4% to 16.4% as a result of faster inflation and this almost certainly affected investment. It has remained high ever since.

Another factor which must surely be taken into account in any general explanation of investment behaviour is the availability of funds for investment and the constraints that from time to time have been imposed by credit policy. Investment is financed predominantly from internal sources and only partly from outside credit institutions. As far as internal sources are concerned it must be accepted that company profits, besides acting as a guide to future profitability, will also act as a financial constraint upon investment. As for external sources of credit, there seems little doubt that a tight control of the money supply will constrain the total amount of investment.

Other business fixed investment does not appear to conform with the capital-stock-adjustment principle anything like as readily as manufacturing investment. This may be because the assumption of a fixed relationship between capital and output does not hold well in non-manufacturing industries. It is less easy, therefore, to explain investment in these industries, although it must still be the case that expected sales, profits, interest rates and credit availability are relevant influences. Econometric studies have claimed a role for lagged changes in domestic output,[1] whilst short-term forecasts can be made on the basis of investment intentions' surveys such as those carried out by the Department of Trade and Industry, the CBI and the *Financial Times*.

Housing investment needs to be divided between the public and private sectors and examined in relation to demand and supply influences in both sectors. The demand for public-sector building comes indirectly from population trends and directly from the policies of the public authorities. The demand for private-sector building depends both upon population characteristics (family formation and size) and also upon expected lifetime income, the cost of mortgage credit, the prices of new houses and of substitute accommodation. It is subject to the important and highly variable constraints set by the availability of mortgage credit which in turn are determined partly by general credit policy and partly by the policies of the building societies. Among the main influences on the side of supply are the size of the building industry and the number of building workers, the price and availability of building land, and stocks of bricks and other building materials. With such a variety of factors at work it is not easy to construct or present a satisfactory model of the determination of housing investment, and we do not attempt the task in this chapter. The problem of predicting housing investment is eased, however, by the statistics of new houses started, which, with an assumption about completion times, makes it possible to forecast housing for at least a short period ahead.

II.6   Stocks and Stockbuilding

Stockbuilding or investment in stocks is the change in a level — the level of all stocks held at the beginning of the period. In any one year, stock investment can be positive or negative, whilst the change in stock investment between successive years can exert an important influence upon GDP. The increase in stock investment

---

1 For example M.J.C. Surrey, *The Analysis and Forecasting of the British Economy*, NIESR and Cambridge University Press, 1971, p. 32, and HM Treasury, *Macroeconomic Forecasting Model, Technical Manual*, 1979.

in 1975-7, for example, was equivalent to 2.8% of GDP, whilst the decline in 1979-81 was equivalent to 3.2% of GDP.

At the end of 1980 the total value of stocks held in all industries was approximately £67bn or 30% of the value of GDP in a year. Stocks held by manufacturing industry amounted to nearly £37bn, or about 77% of the annual value of manufacturing output. Manufacturers' stocks divide into materials and fuel (£12.6bn), work in progress (£13.2bn) and stocks of finished products (£11.3bn).[1]

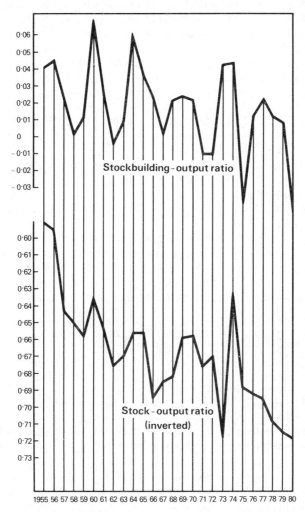

Figure 1.4   Manufacturers' stockbuilding and stock levels as ratios of manufacturing output, UK, 1955–80

---

1   *NIBB*, 1982, table 12.1. The other main holders of stocks are wholesale and retail business.

Stocks of work in progress are held because they are a technical necessity of production, whilst stocks of materials and finished goods are held mainly out of a precautionary motive. They are required as a 'buffer' between deliveries and production; or, more precisely, because manufacturers are wise enough to know that they cannot expect an exact correspondence between the amount of materials delivered each day and the amount taken into production, or between completed production and deliveries to customers.

For these reasons it seems plausible to assume that manufacturers carry in their minds the notion of a certain optimum ratio between stocks on the one hand and output on the other. If stocks fall below the optimum ratio they will need to be replenished; if they rise above it they will be run down. The reasoning here is the same as that of the stock-adjustment principle which we have already considered in connection with fixed investment. The principle holds moderately well for manufacturers' stockbuilding, which is by far the most volatile part of stock investment in the UK. Its application is illustrated in figure 1.4, where it can be seen, for example, that the stock investment peaks of 1960, 1964, 1969 and 1973-4 all coincided with low values of the stock-output ratio. The correlation is rather less satisfactory for the later 1970s.

The stock-adjustment principle is only the beginning of a complete explanation of investment in stocks. It relates only to planned stockbuilding, and it makes no allowance for the level of interest rates, price expectations and the uncertainty of sales forecasts. Nor can it account for unplanned movements in stocks, which will occur for finished goods whenever sales deviate from their expected levels. Involuntary stock accumulation will take place whenever sales turn out lower than expected, and involuntary rundowns when sales are higher than expected.

II.7   Government Spending, Exports, Imports and Indirect Taxes

Of the two remaining components of TFE, government expenditure is primarily determined by the social and military objectives of the central and local authorities, and partly by macroeconomic and financial policy. Until recently, it was unusual for government spending to be affected by macroeconomic policy, the preferred instrument of control being changes in tax rates. But the advent of financial targets for the PSBR (see section VI) and of expenditure control by cash limits represents a change of regime which could be significant in future years. Already there has been a substantial drop in public-sector investment (by 39% in 1979-81) although government expenditure as a whole has fallen only slightly.

Exports of goods and services are determined by two principal factors: by the level of overseas income and by export prices, measured in terms of foreign currency, which, in turn, are influenced by the exchange rate for sterling. UK exports correlate quite closely with the volume of world trade in manufactures, and exports to particular countries are linked to national GNP. The influence of prices is measured by the price elasticity of demand, which according to some econometric models is not too high: the range suggested by the National Institute, Bank of England and Treasury models is -0.6 to -0.8.[1] The 3% drop in exports between the last quarter of 1979 and 1980, for example, was associated with a rise

---

1   S. Brooks, 'Systematic econometric comparisons: exports of manufactured goods', *NIER*, August 1981, p. 70.

of 9% in the effective rate of exchange and by a decline of about 1½% in the volume of world trade in manufactures. The effective exchange rate fell back during 1981, and exports had recovered by the last quarter to about the same level as two years earlier. Export trends are discussed in more detail in chapter 3.

TFE is the sum total of exports of goods and services, government expenditure, fixed investment, stockbuilding and consumption. These elements are normally measured at market prices and they all contain a substantial content of imported components and materials. To proceed, therefore, from TFE at market prices to GDP at factor cost it is necessary to remove the indirect-tax and import contents of the various expenditure items. The indirect-tax content (net of subsidies) is known annually for the various expenditure items, whereas the import content is known annually only for TFE. Estimates of the import content for individual expenditures can be worked out by input-output methods, and are shown, together with the indirect-tax contents, in table 1.6 below.

TABLE 1.6

Domestic Output Content of Total Final Expenditure at Market Prices

		Percentages of market price totals			
	Consumers' expenditure	*Government current expenditure*	*Gross domestic fixed investment*	*Exports of goods and services*	*Total final expenditure*
Indirect taxes (less subsidies)	16	8	18	5	11
Imports of goods and services	21	10	27	23	20
Domestic output content	63	82	55	72	69

Sources: NIBB, 1981, table 1.1; 'Summary Input-Output Tables for 1973', *ET*, June 1978.

The main determinants of imports are the level of income, stocks of materials and competitive factors. It is probably this last group which is responsible for the upward trend (see chapter 3) in the ratio of imports of goods and services (at constant 1975 prices) to TFE:

1950-54	16.2%
1955-9	16.9%
1960-64	18.1%
1965-9	19.2%
1970-74	21.8%
1975-9	22.1%
1980	23.1%

It is possible that this trend can be broken down and explained in terms of price competitiveness, trade policy and other variables, but many forecasting equations for imports have simply extrapolated the trend at its recent rate of increase.

The influence of stocks upon the volume of imports has been recognized for many years and at one time it was thought that every £100m of stockbuilding would add about £50m to the import bill.[1] More recently, however, the influence of stocks appears to have weakened. Some estimates suggest an import content of stockbuilding of 0.3 rather than 0.5.[2] The reason for the decline in the coefficients is probably the increased weight of finished manufactures in the import total (see chapter 3).

The underlying explanation of the import content of stockbuilding is to be sought in terms of the stock-adjustment principle which, as suggested above, has a useful part to play in determining stockbuilding and fixed investment. If imports are found to vary directly with stockbuilding, and if stockbuilding follows the stock-adjustment principle, then imports will vary with the level of income and the initial level of stocks. Thus equations in terms of income and stockbuilding can be recast in terms of income and initial stock levels.[3] The more general point is that approximately one-third of total imports of goods and services consists of items which are used as inputs in the process of production. These are classified in chapter 3 as imports of basic materials, mineral fuels and lubricants, and semi-manufactures. They enter into stocks in the same way as domestically produced coal or iron-ore, and they are subject to similar laws of behaviour.

II.8   Personal Income and the Multiplier

Any increase in GDP will normally give rise to a multiplier process, since the initial rise in personal income leads to higher consumption, and thus to higher GDP. Successive rounds of higher income and consumption will lead to the eventual establishment of an 'equilibrium' level of GDP, this being the level which GDP finally settles at. The multiplier process is the succession of income changes, and the 'multiplier' itself is the ratio of the total or cumulative increase in GDP to its initial or 'first round' increase.

In elementary models, the multiplier may be found quite simply because no distinctions are made between GDP and personal income, and because taxation, undistributed profits and the import contents of expenditure are ignored. On these lines, it can be seen that an initial increase in GDP of 100 units, combined with a marginal propensity to consume of, say, 0.5, will lead to an eventual increase in GDP of 200 units. This is because the initial rise in GDP due, for example, to investment expenditure, will cause personal incomes to rise by the same amount, so that consumption will then increase (after a time-lag) by 50 units. This, in turn, raises personal incomes in the consumer-goods industries by 50 units so that consumption in the third round of the multiplier will increase by 25 units. Each increase in income leads to a rise in consumption half as large, so that the sequence of increases in GDP from period to period will be:

$$100, 50, 25, 12.5, 6.25, 3.125, \ldots \ldots \text{etc.}$$

---

1   See 'Forecasting Imports' by W.A.H. Godley and J.R. Shepherd, *NIER*, August 1965.

2   M.J.C. Surrey, *Analysis and Forecasting of the British Economy*, op. cit.

3   If M = mY + nI (where M, Y and I are imports, income and stockbuilding respectively, m, the marginal propensity to import and n, the import content of stockbuilding), and if I = aY − bK, then M = (m + na)Y − nbK. The import ratio is now expressible in terms of the stock-output ratio.

It is not difficult to see that if all the terms are added together they sum to 200, which is the equilibrium increase in GDP. Since this is twice the original increase of 100 units, the multiplier is 2. This value may also be found from the formula:

$$\frac{\Delta Y}{\Delta I} = \frac{1}{1 - \text{MPC}} = \frac{1}{1 - 0.5}$$

where ΔY is the final increase in GDP and ΔI the initial increase, which in this example was investment-goods output.[1]

The multiplier for the UK follows the same principles as the simple model. But its calculation is complicated by a number of factors, one of which is the distinction which must be drawn between GDP and personal income. This may be illustrated by a direct comparison for 1980:

GDP (£195.5bn)	equals	Income from employment and self-employment (£155.5bn)	plus	Rent, total profits and trading surpluses, and imputed change in capital consumption (£46.4bn)	minus	Stock appreciation (£6.5bn)
Personal income (£201.0bn)	equals	Income from employment and self-employment (£155.5bn)	plus	Personal receipts of rent, dividends and interest (£19.6bn)	plus	Transfer incomes (£25.9bn)

The main points here are that although income from employment and self-employment is shared by both totals, the personal sector's receipts of rent, dividend and interest are considerably smaller than those accruing to the nation as a whole. Personal income also includes a substantial transfer element — mainly pensions and social-security benefits — which do not figure in GDP because they are not payments for productive services.

To arrive at an estimate of the UK multiplier we may begin by assuming an initial increase in GDP of £100m. This is the domestic output content of a larger increase in TFE at market prices, the difference being due to the import and indirect-tax contents of the expenditure. The coefficients in table 1.6, for example, suggest that £100m of GDP would typically correspond to an increase in government expenditure of £122m or fixed investment of £182m.

A series of assumptions must now be made as to the size of various 'withdrawals' or leakages between an increase in GDP and the ensuing increase in the 'consumption', the latter being conceived as *consumers' expenditure on new domestic product* and not simply as consumers' expenditure at market prices. The first stage in the calculation concerns the likely increase in personal income. This will depend on the way in which new GDP is divided between employment incomes and profits, on how much of the latter is distributed to the personal sector

---

1 The formula assumes that ΔI is a sustained increase in the level of investment expenditure. An unsustained or 'one-shot' injection of new investment would lead only to a temporary rise in GDP in which the series of period-to-period changes in GDP would be +100, −50, −25, −12.5, −6.25, etc.

as dividend income, and also on how much transfer incomes decline as a result of lower unemployment and other national insurance benefits. It can be assumed that the increase in GDP is divided between employment income and profits in its usual ratio of about 4:1, so that £80m will go directly into personal income in the form of income from employment. To this we may add about £6m for higher dividends, since most of the £20m rise in profits will find its way into undistributed profits and corporate taxes. But we also have to allow for a reduction in transfer incomes arising from lower unemployment benefits, and this would be of the order of £4m.[1] Thus the total increase in personal income will be £80 + 6 − 4 = £82 million, which gives us the first in a series of coefficients needed to derive the multiplier (see table 1.7).

TABLE 1.7

Stages in the Multiplier Estimate

	£m	*Assumed marginal relationships*
1st round increase in GDP	100	
Increase in personal income	82	$b_1 = .82$
Increase in personal disposable income	56	$b_2 = .68$
Increase (after a time-lag) in consumers' expenditure at market prices	42	$b_3 = .75$
Increase in consumers' expenditure at factor cost	34	$b_4 = .81$
Increase in domestically produced consumption at factor cost (equals 2nd round increase in GDP)	26	$b_5 = .76$

The remaining stages of the calculation involve the marginal rate of direct taxation (including higher pension and national insurance payments) which is taken to be about 32%, the marginal propensity to consume, which we have already estimated in section II.4 above to be about 0.75, and the marginal import and indirect-tax contents of consumption. The latter are taken from the average contents given in table 1.6 (but note that the import content of *factor cost* consumption will be higher, at 0.24, than the import content of market price consumption). It is, of course, arguable that the marginal import content is higher than the average import content but we have not allowed for this possibility.

The upshot of the calculation is that the second-round increase in GDP is only £26m, or 0.26 times the initial increase. It follows that the third, fourth and later increases will all be 0.26 times the previous rise, so that the sequence of period-to-period changes in GDP can be represented as follows:

£100, 26, 6.8, 1.8, 0.5, 0.1 . . . . 0 million

This series sums to a cumulative increase of £135m, so that the multiplier is 1.35. Its value may also be found from the expression:

$$\frac{1}{1 - 0.26} = 1.35$$

---

1 Derived by assuming that every 1% rise in GDP leads to a 0.5% increase in employment, and from official estimates of unemployment benefits. See *Treasury Economic Progress Report*, February 1981.

where 0.26 can be described as the marginal propensity to purchase new domestic output. It represents the five coefficients b_1, b_2, b_3, b_4 and b_5 all multiplied together.[1]

It should be noted that we have defined the multiplier as the ratio of the eventual increase in GDP to the initial increase in GDP, and not to the initial increase in market price expenditure. This is in order to keep the numerator and denominator in the same domestic output terms. The multiplier so defined applies much more directly to domestic employment than the alternative ratio of the final GDP increase to the rise in the market price value of expenditure with imports and indirect taxes included.[2]

These calculations help to indicate orders of magnitude only, and are not meant to be precise estimates. In practice, there are other effects of an increase in GDP besides the multiplier which also have to be taken into account. The most basic of these is the effect on stockbuilding, since any increase in demand will be met initially from stock, so that there will be some involuntary stock decline at the start of the process, and this will be reversed later as production is stepped up to replenish stocks and to meet the higher level of demand.[3] The National Institute's econometric model, for example, shows negative stock investment in the first quarter of an increase in total final expenditure, followed by stock accumulation in the third and fourth quarters.

The main econometric models can be simulated to provide estimates of the effect of changes in expenditure on GDP quarter by quarter. According to one study, they show that the ratio of the 4th quarter is in the region of 1.1 to 1.3.[4] This is lower than our own estimate of the multiplier value of 1.35. But the figures are not strictly comparable since the econometric models attempt to estimate a variety of other relationships, the most important of which are the stock-adjustment effects on stockbuilding and fixed investment. The value of the multiplier is increased with variable exchange rates, because rising imports lead to a lower exchange rate and hence to higher demand for UK exports. Any increase in wage rates due to the higher pressure of demand also raises the multiplier value, whereas rising interest rates due to pressure in the money market act in the opposite direction.[4]

III   BUDGETARY POLICY AND DEMAND MANAGEMENT
III.1   Objectives and Instruments

The period since the Second World War has been characterized by two rather different approaches to macroeconomic policy. The first of these was the demand

---

1 Thus $0.26 = \dfrac{82}{100} \cdot \dfrac{56}{82} \cdot \dfrac{42}{56} \cdot \dfrac{34}{42} \cdot \dfrac{26}{34} = b_1 b_2 b_3 b_4 b_5$ and the multiplier is $\dfrac{1}{1 - b_1 b_2 b_3 b_4 b_5}$.

2 This discussion has followed an early estimate of the multiplier in W.A.B. Hopkin and W.A.H. Godley, 'An Analysis of Tax Changes', *NIER*, May 1965.

3 In extreme cases there may be severe oscillations in GDP or even an explosive time-path. On this the classic reference is L.A. Metzler, 'The Nature and Stability of Inventory Cycles' in R.A. Gordon and L. R. Klein (eds.), *Readings in Business Cycles*.

4 See J.S.E. Laury, G.R. Lewis and P.A. Ormerod, 'Properties of Macroeconomic Models of the UK Economy: A Comparative Study', *NIER*, February 1978.

management approach, whereby governments sought to influence the level of demand in the economy with the intention of maintaining or restoring an acceptable level of employment. The second approach was directed more towards the restoration of price stability, with a high level of employment taking a lower priority than hitherto. This approach reached its fullest manifestation under the Conservative government elected in 1979, and is discussed in section VI.

The demand management approach was inaugurated by the White Paper on *Employment Policy* (Cmd. 6527) issued in 1944 by the wartime coalition government. The White Paper stated that:

> The Government believe that, once the war has been won, we can make a fresh approach, with better chances of success than ever before, to the task of maintaining a high and stable level of employment without sacrificing the essential liberties of a free society.

The White Paper recommended that there should be a permanent staff of statisticians and economists in the Civil Service with responsibility for interpreting economic trends and advising on policy. The execution of employment policy was to be examined annually by Parliament in the debate on the Budget. The White Paper foresaw that high levels of employment were likely to endanger price stability, and it pointed out the need for 'moderation in wage matters by employers and employees' as the essential condition for the success of the policy.

For nearly 30 years the task of maintaining a high level of employment proved to be less difficult than had been expected. The White Paper had not laid down any precise target for the level of employment. But the levels attained in nearly every postwar year until 1975 were higher than the authors of the White Paper had hoped. It became apparent at the time that high levels of employment were compatible with a fairly moderate rate of inflation. The average rate of retail price inflation in the 1950s, for example, was about 4% per year whilst unemployment averaged as little as 1½% of the labourforce.

As we observed in section II (above), however, the postwar economy passed through a series of fluctuations with the annual unemployment rate varying within a narrow range. Part of the reason for these fluctuations could be found in the different views taken by successive governments (or sometimes by the same government at different times) as to the most desirable pressure of demand. The aim of high employment was always in some measure of conflict with the objectives of both balance of payments equilibrium and price stability. A conflict with the balance of payments was also present in so far as governments were unwilling to make use of instruments of policy, such as exchange-rate devaluation or import controls, for dealing with the external balance. Thus fiscal measures, which act upon the level of employment, were at times directed towards the required balance of payments, with the consequence that the employment objective took second place. This conflict of objectives was particularly noticeable in two periods: from 1956 to early 1959 when the Conservative government was aiming at price stability and a long-term balance of payments surplus, and preferred to deflate employment rather than depreciate sterling to achieve it; and also in the period of eighteen months preceding the devaluation of sterling in November 1967.

The employment objective was also in conflict with that of price stability. Here there is no independent instrument of control to parallel the variability of the exchange rate. Incomes policy, in the sense of voluntary or compulsory guidelines for the rate of increase in wages and prices, was seldom found to be particularly successful and certainly not successful enough to permit nice percentage variations in the permitted rate of inflation. Thus the absence of an independent instrument for controlling inflation implied a genuine conflict of aims. This, together with the balance of payments, helps to explain why the target level of employment was not wholly stable, but tended to fluctuate according to the priorities of the government of the day.

It follows that the decision on what level of employment to aim for was normally made on the basis of a compromise with the objectives of price stability and the balance of payments. But once the employment target was settled, the problem of how to attain it became a technical issue.

One elementary point concerns the existence of time-lags between the detection of a policy problem and its remedy. This means that it is not sound strategy to wait until unemployment has reached some intolerably high figure before acting or thinking about action to correct it. The unemployment statistics are about a month behindhand; civil servants may take up to six months to advise the appropriate action; Parliament may take three months to enact it; and even after the policy is put into force, the full economic effects may not appear for some months afterwards. Thus a strategy based solely upon the observation of recent performance can involve a significantly long time-lag (of twelve months or longer) between the observed need for a change in policy and the effects of that change upon the level of employment.

It is partly for this reason that economic management in the UK was based upon a strategy of looking ahead rather than on response to observed performance. This means that the policy-maker relies heavily upon the use of economic forecasts. If he can *correctly* foresee the emergence of a policy problem, then the problem of the delay between the need for intervention and its effects is removed.

There is another reason, too, for relying upon forecasts. This is the need to tailor the amount of intervention to the future size of the problem rather than to what is currently observed. The mere observation of high unemployment or excessive inflation in no way guarantees that it will continue in the same degree of seriousness. The problem may get worse or it may get better. Quite clearly it is essential to form some view of what will happen in the future before deciding the degree and the direction of policy intervention required. Failure to produce a correct forecast of the course of employment over the next twelve to eighteen months could result in an *inadequate* degree of corrective policy action. Or it could be *destabilizing*,[1] in the sense that the effect of intervention is to remove the level of output still further from target than it would have been without it.

The last four decades have seen a very considerable advance in the various branches of knowledge which bear upon the problems of forecasting and managing the economy. The chief of these have comprised: (i) an enormous improvement, attributable to the CSO, in economic statistics, and particularly the development of quarterly, seasonally adjusted, constant-price, national expenditure figures; (ii) the development of a conceptual framework and quantitative model for forecasting the levels of GDP and employment over a period of about eighteen months; (iii) the development of a conceptual framework and quantitative model for estimating the effects on GDP of tax changes and other instruments of demand management.

---

1 A more accurate term would be 'perverse', since policy does not necessarily aim to stabilize anything.

III.2   The Effects of Policy Instruments

If fiscal intervention is to achieve targets for employment and output, it is necessary for the policy-makers to make fairly precise quantitative assessments of the effects of their policy instruments upon the level of domestic output. In this section we shall concentrate upon the effects of three such instruments: changes in government expenditure on goods and services, changes in indirect taxation and changes in personal income tax.

In the case of a change in government expenditure, the effects can be estimated by removing the import and indirect-tax contents (see table 1.6) and by applying the multiplier estimate of 1.35 derived in section II.8 above. The effects of a typical increase, say, of £100m, will be as follows:

	£m
increase in government expenditure at market prices	+100
increase in government expenditure at factor cost	+92
initial increase in GDP	+82
multiplied increase in GDP	+111

Less typical expenditures, such as the purchase of foreign missiles and military aircraft, will have larger import contents than the figure in table 1.6, and will sometimes involve no significant increase in domestic output and employment.

In point of fact government expenditure was seldom used as an instrument for influencing employment during the era of demand management. This was because its level was determined by political and social objectives of a different order, and also because it was difficult to organize changes in its amount with much hope of precision.[1] The more usual instruments of demand management were changes in tax rates, particularly income and indirect taxes.

The effect on GDP of a change in income tax may be illustrated by reference to the increase in the single and married allowances introduced in the Budget of March 1982. These were estimated by the Inland Revenue to reduce tax payments by £1,815m in a full year.[2] Personal disposable income would be raised by an equal amount, so that the *initial*, or multiplicand, effect upon GDP can be found using the coefficients in table 1.7:

	£m
increase in personal disposable income	+1,815
increase in consumers' expenditure at market prices	+1,361
increase in consumers' expenditure at factor cost	+1,103
initial increase in GDP	+838
multiplied increase in GDP	+1,115

The initial increase in GDP of £838m is simply the change in tax revenue multiplied by the marginal propensity to consume (b_3 in table 1.7), along with the

---

1   J.C.R. Dow, *The Management of the British Economy 1945-60*, Cambridge University Press, 1964, pp. 180-1.

2   *Financial Statement and Budget Report 1982-83*, p. 10.

coefficients b_4 and b_5 which remove the indirect-tax and import contents of the increase in consumers' expenditure. The multiplier effect raises this by 1.35 to a figure which, with current price GDP at about £220bn, is equivalent to a gain in total output of approximately 0.5%. This is the deviation in GDP from what it would have been in the absence of the tax reduction, and is not affected by the primary justification of the change which was to adjust the allowances in line with inflation. There were, of course, a number of other changes in the 1982 Budget, and these are discussed in section VI.

In estimating the effects of changes in indirect taxes, the initial effect can be found by taking the additional revenue (as estimated by the Board of Customs and Excise) and applying the relevant coefficients. As an example, we may take the increase in VAT from 8 to 15% introduced in the Budget of June 1979. This was estimated to add £4,175m to the revenue in a full year.[1] With no initial change in personal disposable income on consumers' expenditure at market prices, this must imply the following:

	£m
decrease in consumers' expenditure at factor cost	−4,175
initial decrease in GDP	−3,173
multiplied decrease in GDP	−4,284

Here the initial change in GDP is found by applying the coefficient b_5 of table 1.6 so as to remove the import content of the change in factor cost consumption. The multiplier effect raises the initial effect by 1.35 to give an eventual reduction of about 2.6% of current price GDP in 1979 − a fairly large change.[2]

We may sum up this discussion by noting that the effects of revenue changes are much smaller for income taxes than for indirect taxes. If we consider a reduction in income tax of £100m, it leads to an initial increase in GDP of only £26m, since £74m of the increase in personal disposable income finds its way into personal savings, indirect taxes and imports. With a reduction of indirect taxes, however, consumers' expenditure at market prices is unaffected and the only leakage is into imports, which, at £24m, gives an initial increase in GDP − the domestic content of the additional factor cost consumption − of £76m. Thus the effect of a change in indirect taxation is about three times as large as an increase in direct taxation yielding the same initial revenue.[3]

When discussing the effects of tax changes it is advisable to remember that all changes in the budget balance have to be financed either by borrowing from the

1 *Financial Statement and Budget Report, 1979-80*, p. 31.

2 An alternative way of estimating the effect of indirect-tax changes is to work out the increase in consumer prices and real disposable income. The consumption and GDP effects may then be calculated in an analogous way to those of a change in income tax.

3 The algebraic representation of the two *initial* changes in GDP is $-b_3\, b_4\, b_5\, \Delta TI$ and $-b_5\, \Delta TC$, where ΔTI and ΔTC stand, respectively, for the change in income-tax and consumption-tax revenues, and where the coefficients b_3, b_4 and b_5 are the marginal propensities listed in table 1.7. The multiplied changes in GDP are these amounts times a multiplier of $\dfrac{1}{1 - b_1\, b_2\, b_3\, b_4\, b_5}$. Strictly speaking, new tax rates involve changes in b_2 and b_4, but these are small enough to be disregarded for practical purposes.

public or by increasing the money supply. Strictly speaking, the effects described above must assume that the method of financing is an expansion of the money supply. This invites the claim that we have not been describing fiscal policy *per se* but a mixed policy of fiscal changes with monetary accommodation. But the name does not matter since the Chancellor of the Exchequer is responsible both for fiscal and monetary policy, and is therefore able to ensure that budget deficits are financed in ways which do not subvert the objectives of policy. It should be noted, however, that if fiscal changes are financed by borrowing from the public there will be consequential increases in interest rates which will tend to inhibit consumer purchases of durable goods and investment by firms. Furthermore, if the rise in interest rates spreads to mortgage rates, the effect could be similar to a rise in taxation since every mortgage-holder will find that his take-home pay, after tax and mortgage payments, is less than it was before. It follows that reductions in taxation which are financed by borrowing will be somewhat less expansionary than those financed through increases in the quantity of money.

The alternative to fiscal policy is often taken to be monetary policy, although, as we have seen, fiscal expansion may be financed by an increase in the money stock. Debt management may be used to accomplish a change in interest rates without any marked alteration in the budget balance. The effects of interest changes on investment are likely to be delayed for many months and their main impact will fall outside the normal forecasting horizon of twelve to eighteen months. But the effects on consumers' expenditure through higher mortgage rates and HP payments may operate more swiftly. Monetary policy can also affect spending by altering the availability of credit.

III.3   Economic Forecasts

The Treasury's forecasts have to be published by Act of Parliament, and they were originally developed as an aid to demand management. This was because it was not found satisfactory to decide fiscal changes solely by reference to the current performance of the economy. To have done this would have been to run the risk of delayed, and possibly destabilizing, adjustments to the levels of demand and employment. Thus the difference between the government's preferred level of GDP and a *forecast* level is likely to be a better guide to the requisite scale of fiscal action than the difference between preferred and *actual* GDP. This must be true if the forecasts are accurate.

National income forecasts used to be prepared in the Treasury three times a year, with their timing geared to the Budget. They are now made to a timetable which depends on all major policy decisions, and the need, under the 1975 Industry Act, to publish at least twice a year. The published forecasts extend about 15 months ahead; that for March 1982, for example, goes forward to the first half of 1983.[1]

One of the first problems encountered in any economic forecast is that of establishing GDP estimates for the period extending from the last known figures to the month in which the forecast is assembled. The February forecast, for example, has to be made with the benefit of quarterly GDP figures which do not go beyond September of the previous year. A GDP estimate has to be put together for the

---

1   *Financial Statement and Budget Report 1982-83.*

October-December quarter on the basis of monthly information which includes exports, imports, retail sales and industrial production. This can be difficult because of various gaps in coverage, and because different indicators frequently tell conflicting stories, as, for example, when the employment and industrial production figures move in different directions.

Once the base period is established, the forecast proper (i.e. the part relating to the future) can be started. The methods by which this is done need not be described in detail. But for 6 months to a year ahead the task is made easier by the presence of a number of forward indicators which provide fairly direct information on the prospects for particular sectors of demand. The CBI, for example, conducts regular inquiries into whether its members intend to invest more or less in the next 12 months than in the previous period. The Department of Industry has its own inquiry, in which business is asked to estimate the percentage change in prospective investment. There are new-order series for engineering, machine tools and shipbuilding, which provide a forward view of production (for investment or export) in these industries. There are also figures for new orders received by contractors for private construction work, whilst in the field of housing investment figures are collected for orders received by contractors, for new houses started, and Building Society commitments and advances on new dwellings.[1] Government current expenditure and the government component of fixed investment can be predicted from information provided by government departments and the nationalized industries. Direct information, therefore, covers a fairly significant proportion of the autonomous element in total demand, and can be processed to provide forecasts for 6 to 12 months ahead. Some help towards the personal income and consumption forecast is available from the knowledge of recent wage settlements which helps to establish the wage, although not the employment, dimension of total wage income; and the government will also have estimates of the pay and employment of its own employees.

For longer-term forecasts, and for the more obviously endogenous components of GDP, the forecaster must have an integrated model, in which the relationships are either estimated econometrically or arrived at in some systematic way. The Treasury has for several years had a large econometric model in which there are over 700 economic relationships at its disposal. At the risk of some simplification this may be described as a highly complex and disaggregated multiplier model, with stock-adjustment equations for the main investment items, and with exports linked to world production and relative prices. The model includes links between wages, prices and the exchange rate, and it also makes some use of interest rates as a determinant of investment, although here the coefficients are imposed and not estimated by regression methods. Imports are determined by GDP, stockbuilding and competitive factors.[2]

---

1 These figures are all published in *Economic Trends*.

2 A non-technical account of Treasury forecasting is given in 'Forecasting in the Treasury', *Economic Progress Report*, June 1981, and a highly technical account in HM Treasury, *Macroeconomic Forecasting Model, Technical Manual*, HMSO, 1979. Some of the individual equations are discussed in Ch. 2 of K.A. Chrystal, *Controversies in British Macroeconomics*, Philip Allan, Oxford, 1979. Earlier accounts of Treasury methods can be found in A.D. Roy, 'Short-term Forecasting for Central Economic Management', in K. Hilton and D.F. Heathfield (eds.), *The Econometric Study of the United Kingdom*, Macmillan, 1970; J.R. Shepherd, 'Short-term Forecasting for the UK Economy', in Sir Alec Cairncross (ed.), *The Managed Economy*, Blackwell, 1970; and J.R. Shepherd, H.P. Evans and C.J. Riley, 'The Treasury Short-term Forecasting Model', Government Economic Service Occasional Papers (HMSO).

The Treasury's model is in a constant state of revision, if only because there are many different ways of formulating consumption and investment functions, and it is not an easy matter to judge which of them is best. Thus although the model is in constant use, it may be assumed that parts of it will be questioned by those responsible for getting the forecast right. The model, therefore, does not dictate the forecast to the exclusion of all argument and discussion. Furthermore, as every forecaster knows, there are always events which a model is not able to handle (strikes and fuel shortages, for example) and which necessitate judgmental estimation of their effects upon economic activity.

The main upshot of the government forecasting work is a table in considerable detail of the course of GDP and its components, quarter by quarter, over a period of two to three years. The published version of the forecast normally provides estimates by half-years.

III.4   Criticisms of Demand Management

Demand management came in for a great deal of criticism even during the period when employment was held high with comparatively little inflation. There were business objections to the frequency of tax changes, although these were heard more frequently when taxes were raised than when they were lowered. Much of the criticism came from journalists who were under contract to write regular columns in the newspapers. Opposition spokesmen in Parliament (of either main political party) were reluctant to concede the need for tax cuts because of their electoral advantage to the other side. There were complaints of 'stop-go' and, latterly, of 'too much fine tuning' although these terms were never very carefully defined. Amidst all the clamour it was difficult to distinguish criticisms of the technical proficiency of demand management from differences about the objectives which it was seeking to attain.

The criticisms divide into four main groups: (i) that the economy fluctuated considerably despite the advocacy of 'stable' employment in the 1944 White Paper; (ii) that the technical apparatus of demand management was inadequate to its task; (iii) that economic policy was in some sense destabilizing; (iv) that errors in demand management were responsible for, or connected with, the rapid inflation of the 1970s.

(i) On the first of these points there is no doubt that the course of the economy was not perfectly stable for most of the period when demand management was practised. This phenomenon (which was sometimes labelled the 'stop-go' cycle) has been described and charted in section II of this chapter. What is not so clear, however, is the extent to which this instability reflected changes in economic objectives, or failures to achieve a constant objective. For an unstable and highly cyclical time-path for the economy may represent a series of changes of mind by successive governments about the best level of employment at which to run the economy. The conflicts or presumed conflicts between economic objectives are sufficiently obvious to make it doubtful whether the target pressure of demand has always been the same. Indeed, in so far as the facts can be ascertained, the target appears to have fluctuated quite significantly.

The extent by which targeted GDP fluctuated from year to year may be detected from the available information on Treasury forecasts. These forecasts, after allowance for the effects of tax changes introduced at the time, represent the increase in GDP which the government finds acceptable at the time they are made. As such they are tantamount to target increases in output. For the period 1955-68 these target rates of increase may be related to the level of *potential output* (the level of GDP in a specific period which could have been produced with employment at some standard percentage of the labourforce). A series for the target use of potential output is given in table 1.8. It shows a fall of about 4% between 1955 and 1959, increases in 1960 and 1964, which was an election year, and a fairly steady target from then until 1968. Unfortunately, this procedure cannot be continued after 1968 because of the breakdown in the relationship between unemployment and vacancies. The best that can be done is to relate target changes in actual output to the growth rate of output (2.1% per annum) which would have maintained unfilled vacancies at a constant percentage of the labourforce. The main feature of this series is the sharp increase in the intended pressure of demand between 1971 and 1973, the sharp contraction in 1975, and the acceptance of slump conditions in 1980-82, by which time demand management had been abandoned. The principal conclusion is that there were, quite definitely, fluctuations in the level of productive potential at which governments sought to run the economy. Whether these can be traced to electoral ambitions is less clear, since not all the election years were years of high targeted demand pressure. But it is, perhaps, disputable whether a government gets more votes from tax give-aways in a year of depression than it does from high employment and a neutral budget. The other explanation offered is that years of high demand led to balance of payments difficulties and inflation, to which the Chancellor responded with phases of demand deflation until such time as they changed their priorities once again. Whether this was really true is disputable, but it is not established by the mere existence of fluctuations.

(ii) As regards the technical apparatus of demand management the key question is whether, and by how much, it has failed to achieve the target levels of employment and GDP which governments were aiming for. Since the target levels of GDP are equivalent to the government forecasts after allowance has been made for the effects of each Budget, this question is essentially a matter of the accuracy of forecasts.[1] If the Treasury forecasts the increase in GDP incorrectly, then it will be led into taking the wrong measures. The result will be that the target level of GDP will be missed by the same amount as the forecast is in error.

The question of the accuracy of Treasury forecasts can only be answered satisfactorily for those forecasts which have been published or described with sufficient clarity to permit comparisons with the outcome. For 1968 and after, the forecasts have been published as part of the *Financial Statement and Budget Report*. But before this date the information is not always as good, and must be assembled from official documents or even from forecasts made by other bodies at the same time. Nevertheless, the task is worth attempting even though the results (see table 1.8) cannot be sacrosanct.[2]

---

1 Forecasting accuracy is not always simple to interpret: there may be strikes or other events of an unforeseeable nature which affect the accuracy of the forecasts without necessarily discrediting the methods by which they are derived.

2 The same qualifications carry through to the series for the Target Use of Potential Output.

TABLE 1.8

Short-term Targets and Forecast Errors, UK, 1955-82

		Target use of potential output or target pressure of demand[1] %	Forecast (and target) change in GDP from year earlier[2] %	Actual change in GDP from year earlier[3] %	Error (forecast less actual) %
1955	(year)	99	2.9	3.8	−0.9
1956	"	98	1.1	1.2	−0.1
1957	"	97	1.3	1.7	−0.4
1958	"	95	−0.4	−0.3	−0.1
1959	(4th qtr)	94	2.8	6.5	−3.7
1960	"	98	3.1	3.8	−0.7
1961	"	94	1.8	1.9	−0.1
1962	"	98	3.9	0.8	3.1
1963	"	97	4.6	6.7	−2.1
1964	"	101	5.4	3.9	1.5
1965	"	99	2.7	2.5	0.2
1966	"	98	2.0	1.5	0.5
1967	"	97	3.1	1.9	1.2
1968	(2nd half)	97	3.6	5.0	−1.4
1969	"	97	1.9	2.4	−0.5
1970	"	99	3.6	2.0	1.6
1971	"	97	1.1	1.7	−0.6
1972	"	101	5.5	3.1	2.4
1973	"	102	6.0	5.7	0.3
1974	"	102	2.6	−1.1	3.7
1975	"	97	0.0	−1.4	1.4
1976	"	97	3.9	3.7	0.2
1977	"	96	1.5	1.6	−0.1
1978	"	97	3.0	3.4	−0.4
1979	"	95	−0.5	1.2	−1.7
1980	"	92	−3.1	−3.9	0.8
1981	"	88	−0.2	−0.5	0.3
1982	"	85	1.5	−	−

Notes and Sources:

1 Potential output for 1955-68 is the level of GDP which is estimated to be attainable with a 1.0% rate of unemployment: source M.C. Kennedy, 'Employment Policy − What Went Wrong?' in Joan Robinson (ed.), *After Keynes*. For 1968-82 the level of GDP required to maintain a constant vacancy rate is assumed to have grown at 2.1% per annum, i.e. the actual growth rate for 1968-79.

2 Kennedy, op. cit., and *Financial Statement and Budget Reports* (HMSO).

3 Average estimate of GDP, *ET(AS)*, 1982.

The main point to emerge from an assessment of Treasury forecasts over the period since 1955 is that, whilst they have not been as accurate as might have been hoped, they have led policy seriously astray on only four or five occasions. There is not much doubt that the 1959 forecast, when the error was 4%, was one of the worst. It meant that an unforeseen recovery in total output was coupled with an expansionary Budget, and the result was a much higher level of employment at the end of the year than the government had actually intended. By contrast, the forecasting error in 1962 went the other way, with the result that there was a recession despite the policy aim of a roughly 4% rise in output (implying high employment). The error was put right in 1963, although the recovery went further than intended. The worst forecast of recent years appears to have been 1974, when the Treasury was much too optimistic (by 3.7% of GDP) about the economic outlook.

Taking the whole period from 1955-81, the average error in Treasury forecasts (regardless of sign) was about 1.1% of GDP. This implies an average deviation of about 0.4% between the actual and desired unemployment rate, and is equivalent to an error between the appropriate rate of income tax and the actual rate of about 3p in the £. The size of the forecast errors must be seen, however, against the background of conflicting and by no means accurate estimates of GDP itself. There is not much evidence that the forecasts have become any more accurate with the passage of time.[1]

(iii) A number of writers have sought to show or to deny that demand management has been destabilizing, which implies that policy intervention removed the economy further from target than it would have been if it had been left alone.[2] To do this it is necessary to make assumptions as to the target level of output and the level which output would have attained in the absence of discretionary intervention. Some of these assumptions have been questionable. Thus one writer has claimed that policy was destabilizing because it was demonstrable that 'policy-off' changes in GDP (i.e. after deducting the effects of changes in taxation and government spending) were less widely scattered round the average annual increase in GDP than policy-on (i.e. actual) changes in GDP.[3] It is arbitrary, however, to measure failures of policy in terms of dispersion around an average annual increase in GDP. For there is no presumption, as we can see from table 1.8, that governments were aiming each year at a constant rise in GDP; there is every reason (in times of depression or boom) to suppose that they would aim at changes in GDP of different magnitudes and sometimes of a different sign from the average annual increase.

The stabilizing effectiveness of short-term policy was also investigated in terms of the stability of GDP around its trend. It was shown by Artis[4] that for the 1958-70 period the dispersion of quarterly levels of observed GDP from their time-trend was larger than the dispersion of estimated 'policy-off' GDP (i.e. after deducting the cumulative effects of all tax changes introduced after a particular base year) from their (different) time-trend. This result indicates that policy was 'destabilizing' in the sense of this particular method of measurement. But, as the author made clear, there was never any presumption that the course of target GDP coincided with trend GDP. It is also questionable whether 'policy-off' GDP should be arrived at by subtracting from actual GDP the cumulative effect of measures taken over several years rather than the effect of those measures taken in the particular year.

---

1 For an official assessment of forecasting errors since 1976, see 'Forecasting in the Treasury', op. cit.

2 For reviews of these and other studies of short-term policies, see G.D.N. Worswick, 'Fiscal Policy and Stabilization in Britain' in A.K. Cairncross (ed.), *Britain's Economic Progress Reconsidered* and M.C. Kennedy, ibid.

3 B. Hansen, *Fiscal Policy in Seven Countries, 1955-65*, OECD, Paris, 1969.

4 M.J. Artis, 'Fiscal Policy for Stabilization', in W. Beckerman (ed.), *The Labour Government's Economic Record, 1964-70*, Duckworth, 1972.

The main conclusion seems to be that there has not, as yet, been any convincing demonstration that demand management was destabilizing. Such a demonstration would have to make acceptable assumptions about both the objectives of economic policy and the effects of policy instruments. It is not difficult to accept that policy was destabilizing in particular years: in 1959, for example, the economy might well have remained nearer to target if an expansionary budget had not coincided with an investment boom which the Treasury had probably failed to predict. But this was an example of exceptionally poor economic forecasting in one particular year. The general picture was one of fairly close proximity between actual GDP and target, with an average forecast error of only 1.1%, and this implies that *on average* the degree to which policy might have been destabilizing (assuming that it was) would have been very minor. It would hardly matter, for example, if the average gap between target and policy-off GDP was a hypothetical 0.9% when the average gap between target and actual GDP was 1.1%. The economy would have been mildly better off without discretionary fiscal policy, but the amount of harm done by it would have been too small to worry about.

The associated criticism that there was 'too much fine tuning' may also be discussed briefly. If this means simply that the economy would have held very nearly as close to target levels of output during the demand management period (1944-74) without the intrusion of minor alterations in tax rates, then the point must be taken. For there is not much doubt that the effects of these tax changes were quite small in terms of their effects on GDP. A possible objection, however, is that the mere ritual of changing taxes up and down in response to the declared needs of the economic situation engendered a degree of confidence in the economic future which was beneficial for business confidence and investment. There is no way in which this hypothesis can be very satisfactorily tested, and the fact that the ritual of demand management coincided with the most sustained period of high employment ever known cannot, unfortunately, settle the issue. But it remains a point of view to be set against the complaint that there was an excess of small-scale intervention.

(iv) During the period of fast inflation in the 1970s demand management came in for some further criticisms. One of these was that the very fast expansion of demand during 1973, together with the high pressure of demand in 1974, were responsible for the acceleration in the rate of inflation. This criticism, however, attributes to demand management an inflation which was mainly, although not entirely, due to independent factors. We discuss these in section IV, where the main elements in the inflation are seen as a really exceptional rise in import prices — 100% in 3 years — together with some element of wage-pushfulness. Nevertheless, the inflation of 1973 and 1974 (the so-called 'Barber boom') cannot be dissociated entirely from demand factors or demand management. The pressure of demand was on some indications higher in these two years than it had been in any year since 1955, and the sheer speed of the expansion may have created its own special pressures. (The annual rate of increase in GDP between the first quarter of 1972 and 1973 was 10.1%.) As a rough estimate we can probably attribute about one-quarter of the 16% rise in retail prices in 1974 to the abnormally high pressure of demand. This leaves most of the inflation to be explained in other ways.

It has also been suggested[1] that 'the whole intellectual basis of postwar

---

1   M. Friedman and D. Laidler, 'Unemployment *versus* Inflation', IEA, 1975 Occasional Paper 44, p. 45.

"demand management" by government is undermined if the natural unemployment rate hypothesis is true'. The hypothesis in question postulates that there is some level of the unemployment rate, the *natural* rate, which is compatible with a zero rate of price inflation provided that the expected rate of price inflation is also zero. If unemployment falls below the natural rate, then rising inflation will be the consequence. Wage increases will generate price increases which lead to expected price increases and hence to further wage increases. But there is no reason why this version of the hypothesis should undermine the basis of demand management. Governments which sought to avoid inflation would simply set target unemployment at or above the natural rate of unemployment. They would seek to achieve their target by exactly the same combination of forecasts and instruments which we have described. Far from destroying the basis of demand management, the natural-rate hypothesis simply underlines its importance.[1]

III.5 Demand Management and the PSBR

Demand management can, and has, been described without reference to the Budget deficit or the public-sector-borrowing requirement (PSBR), which is the combined deficit of the central government, local authorities and public corporations. This was deliberate. For if tax rates are to be decided according to the government's target level of GDP, and if the government's expenditure is set according to its social or political objectives, then the government deficit will be a *consequence* of demand management and not an independent target on its own. At given tax rates, the size of the deficit will also vary with the state of the economy, since the tax base (predominantly incomes and expenditure) will vary with the level of economic activity and prices, as will certain transfer payments, notably unemployment benefits.

In the 1960s the PSBR was never more than £2bn a year, but in the 1970s it rose well above this figure, reaching £10.5bn in 1975 and £8.4bn in 1978 (calendar years). This was approximately 5% of GDP at market prices.

The significance of this figure needs to be examined. What it means is that the public authorities have to borrow this sum of money from the banking system, private residents or overseas lenders. If the money is borrowed from overseas, the interest paid will constitute a transfer of national income abroad. If it is borrowed from the private sector, it will lead to a competition for funds and a rise in interest rates. This will mean higher monthly payments for anyone buying his house with a mortgage; it also leads to falling security values, including those of ordinary shares. Thus the only alternative is to finance the deficit by the issue of new money, and this may be done without any undesirable effects on mortgage payments or property values. This last course, however, is frequently resisted in the belief that any increase in the money stock *necessarily* involves an increase in the level of prices. This hypothesis, which is a generalization of the quantity theory of money to circumstances where real output is not necessarily fixed, is arguably false (see section IV) but very widely held in certain quarters, particularly in the City of London. Since it implies that there is no method of financing a public-sector deficit which does not have serious economic consequences, it forms the basis of a view that the PSBR should gradually be reduced. This objective, pursued with determination, implies the end of demand management.

---

1 The hypothesis is sometimes taken to include the view that the natural rate represents supply and demand equilibrium in all labour markets. We discuss this view in section VI.

IV   **INFLATION**
IV.1   **Inflation and its Causes**

Inflation is defined variously as *any* increase in the general level of prices or as any
sustained increase. In this chapter we shall use the wider definition since it enables
us to include short-lived increases in the general price level, such as those of 1920,
1940 and 1951-2, within the sphere of discussion without raising the further
definitional question of whether they were sufficiently 'sustained' to be called
inflations.

In measuring the rate of inflation we have a choice of index numbers. The
appropriate index of the prices charged for all goods produced in the UK economy
is the implied deflator for GDP, so called because it is obtained by dividing the
value of GDP at current prices by GDP at constant (1975) prices. The GDP
deflator includes export prices. If an index is required to measure the prices of
goods purchased by UK residents, the best general measure is the implied deflator
for total domestic expenditure, since this is an average of the prices paid for
consumption and investment goods, both privately and publicly purchased. If we
are chiefly interested in the prices paid for consumer goods and services we have a
choice between the implied deflator for consumers' expenditure and the index of
retail prices. The former, like all implicit indices, is not compiled directly from
price data but is found by dividing the current value of consumers' expenditure by
the volume estimate as measured at constant prices.[1] By contrast, the index of
retail prices (the cost-of-living index) is compiled directly from price data. It
registers the prices of a collection of goods and services entering a typical shopping
basket. The composition of the basket has been revised from time to time so as to
keep up with changes in the pattern of expenditure. Being a base-weighted index it
gradually becomes outdated in coverage. In periods of inflation, it will tend to
exaggerate the increase in the cost of living because consumers will switch their
expenditure patterns towards those goods which are rising less rapidly in price.
Nevertheless, it is accurate enough for most purposes.

The 1970s are now well established as the most inflationary decade of the
twentieth century. The index of retail prices trebled between 1970 and 1979. The
average rise in retail prices was 12.7% a year in the 1970s compared with 3.3% in
1953-69, 2.1% in 1934-9 and declining prices in 1925-33.

Any general explanation of inflation in an open economy like the UK needs to
take account of at least three independent types of inflationary impulse:
(i)   increases in world prices and UK import prices
(ii)   excess demand in the home economy
(iii)   wage-push.
An economy which is engaged in overseas trade is exposed to inflationary impulses
from the world outside. In the UK, where such a large part of our food and raw
materials are imported from overseas, the effects of world inflation are felt
primarily through higher prices paid for imported primary commodities and
consequential increases in production costs and food prices. Nor can the UK
insulate itself from higher world prices for those primary commodities, like oil,
which it produces at home. Many of our most violent changes in prices, both up
and down, can be traced to changes in the world prices of primary commodities.

The second main element in our model of inflation is the degree of excess
demand (i.e. demand less supply at going prices) in the markets for goods and

---

1   The volume or constant price estimates are derived from base-weighted quantity indices.

labour. Wages and prices in individual markets may be expected to increase whenever demand runs ahead of supply. The rate at which they increase, moreover, will probably be related to the degree of excess demand in the market. And in markets where there is excess supply there will be a tendency for prices, and perhaps wages too, to decline. Or, in the case of wages, they may increase less rapidly than the general price level, with a consequential fall in the real wage. In the economy as a whole these tendencies will manifest themselves in terms of the overall balance of excess demands and excess supplies for particular commodities and types of labour. This balance used to be measurable for the labour market by the rates of unemployment and unfilled vacancies. But in the last decade or so these two series have lost their old relationship to each other, so that there is now some ambiguity about the pressure of demand. (See section IV.3 below.)

The third ingredient in our model of inflation is more controversial, and is the potentially independent force of wage-pushfulness. It is necessary to include this as a separate factor because wages are widely fixed by bargaining between the representatives of powerful groups, the union and the firm or employers' federation, each of which has the ability to influence the bargain by threatening to interrupt production and employment. Whilst there are reasons to expect that the pressure of demand for labour will normally be an influence in the bargaining process, we cannot exclude the possibility that alterations in the strength of the union, in the loyalty of its members and in its preparedness to strike may act as an independent force (i.e. independent of market forces) in determining wage increases.

We can combine these three main causes of inflation into a more complete model by relating them to expected price increases and the exchange rate in the manner illustrated in figure 1.5. The model assumes that the *process* by which excess demand leads to price inflation is through the rate of increase in wages. Higher wages mean higher average costs of production and these lead after a time-lag to higher prices. This will happen either because business firms tend to set prices by a constant markup over variable costs or because they seek to maximize profits. Higher prices lead, again after a time-lag, to higher wages since trade unions will tend to claim compensation for increases in the cost of living, or in other words to restore the real wages of their members. Thus the central ingredient of our model is a wage-price spiral which is superimposed upon the excess demand for labour. But besides excess demand, the spiral may also be set in motion by exogenous increases in wages coming from wage-push, or by increases in import prices as a consequence of movements in world commodity prices.

A possible objection to this manner of looking at the inflationary process is that it does not allow for a direct influence of excess demand upon the rate of price increase. This omission is forced upon us mainly by the dearth of statistical indicators of excess demand in the goods market and partly, too, by the fact that a number of studies have attempted to find evidence of this relationship and have not been successful.[1] However, we do not wish to pretend that there is never a direct effect of excess demand upon prices — only that the main sequence to have been identified runs from excess demand to wage increases and then to prices. A second

---

1 For example, L.A. Dicks-Mireaux, 'The Inter-Relationship between Cost and Price Changes, 1945-1959', *OEP* (NS), Vol. 13(3), reprinted in R.J. Ball and P. Doyle, *Inflation*, Penguin, 1969. The model of figure 1.5 is an extension of the relationships investigated by Dicks-Mireaux.

objection to the model might be that there is no reference to the quantity of money. This lack of an explicit reference, however, does not rule out monetary causation of inflation since additions to the quantity of money will lead to increases in wages and raise prices through the medium of excess demand, and excess demand has a prominent place in the model. This amounts to saying that monetary inflation is a branch of demand-pull inflation. An increase in the money supply will act through interest-rate reductions or more directly through credit availability to increase the demand for goods and services, and hence create excess demand. There is no place in our model, or in economic theory in general, for an influence of money upon prices which is not transmitted through the medium of excess demand.

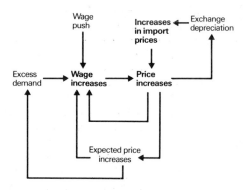

Figure 1.5   Inflationary processes

Besides excess demand and the wage-price spiral, figure 1.5 allows for two other possible interactions between wages and prices, both of them operating through the effect of rising prices upon expected future prices. The first of these is the possibility that expectations of future price changes, rather than compensation for past increases, may be a major factor in wage bargaining. It has been suggested by some writers[1] that the expectation of a price increase of, say, 10% in the next twelve months will induce trade unions and employers to settle for increases in nominal wages of as much as 10% more than would have occurred if prices had been expected to be stable. The hypothesis assumes a degree of sophistication in the process of wage bargaining which may not be characteristic of many trade unions. It is certainly arguable that their wage claims are more likely to be based on the actual rather than the expected rise in the cost of living. But the employers' side must not be neglected, and here there may be something in the idea that the propensity of firms to grant wage increases is influenced by their expectations of price increases on the part of their competitors. Price expectations, therefore, cannot be ignored in a model of the inflationary process, and they become increasingly important as people learn to live with inflation.

The second additional link between wages and prices runs from expectations of higher prices to the level of excess demand. As consumers become aware that prices

---

1   For example, M. Friedman, 'The Role of Monetary Policy', *AER*, Vol. 58(1), pp. 1-17, and *Unemployment versus Inflation*, op. cit.

are going to rise rapidly in the future they may seek to protect themselves from an erosion of the value of their money by switching out of money and financial assets into goods. The effects of this form of behaviour will be manifested in a tendency for the savings ratio to decline (which has not happened in the UK) and for the velocity of circulation of money to rise (which has also not happened). We have included it in the figure, along with the link between price expectations and wage bargaining, because it is a mode of behaviour which has been observed in other countries in periods of hyperinflation.[1] It is a form of behaviour which, along with expectational wage bargaining, is likely to develop as inflation gathers pace and as people learn from experience how money can lose its value. The fact that such behaviour can become general adds greatly to the danger of inflation getting out of hand and provides an extremely powerful case for stopping it as early as possible.

A third linkage in the system is that running from domestic prices through to the exchange rate and back to import prices. As domestic costs and prices rise, exporters have to increase their prices too. If the foreign demand for exports (or the home demand for imports) is elastic, this leads to a deterioration in the balance of payments which leads, in turn, to a decline in the exchange rate. When this happens the sterling price of imports increases, and domestic costs and prices go up further.

One further point which will not be clear from the scheme in figure 1.5 is that increases in the price level always tend to raise the demand for money. If the quantity of money is kept unchanged the effect will be to raise interest rates, thus lowering the levels of real output and employment, and causing a reduction in excess demand which will ultimately check the inflation. This check will be removed, however, if the central bank is aiming to hold interest rates at a steady level. It will then have to *increase* the money supply as the demand for money rises. Thus although inflationary processes may be initiated by excess demand, by wage-push or by increased import prices, they may be supported through permissive increases in the supply of money.

IV.2   Imported Inflation

There is a real sense in which the UK takes its price level from the world outside. Nearly every major increase or decrease in the price level has been associated with a major change in import prices (see table 1.9). Import prices were very volatile in the early 1920s; they rose rapidly in 1940 at the beginning of the Second World War; and again in 1951 with the Korean War. Between 1972 and 1974 they rose by 87% as a result of a very fast rise in fuel prices (260% in the two years) together with price increases for basic materials (up 100%) and food, beverages and tobacco (70%). There are strong grounds for believing that this was the main factor responsible for the protracted spiral of price and wage increases in the 1970s.

The main effect of a rise in import prices is to increase costs of production which, in turn, means higher final prices. Imports of goods and services comprise some 20% of TFE, so that, as a rough rule of thumb, a rise of 10% in import prices will lead to an initial rise in final prices of 2%; and these will be raised further by

1   See, for example, A.J. Brown, *The Great Inflation*, London, 1955 and P. Cagan, 'The Monetary Dynamics of Hyperinflation' in M. Friedman, *Studies in the Quantity Theory of Money*, Chicago, 1956.

TABLE 1.9

Changes in Import and Retail Prices, UK, Selected Years

	Change in import prices (%)	Change in retail prices (%)
1920	19.0	15.8
1921	−33.3	−9.2
1922	−19.6	−19.0
1940	38.5	16.5
1951	33.0	9.1
1973	27.9	9.2
1974	46.2	16.1
1976	22.2	16.5
1977	15.0	15.8
1980	15.0	18.0

Sources: retail prices *BLS, DEG*; import prices 1920-40 *LCES* (average value index for merchandise imports); 1951-80 *ET(AS), AAS* (unit value index).

the response of wages. An additional effect occurs in the case of imports in inelastic demand such as foodstuffs and materials. Here the difficulty of substituting domestic output for imports means that the import bill rises and the exchange rate, assuming this to be flexible, declines. When this happens the sterling price of imports rises further and there is an additional increase in final prices. The average elasticity of demand for UK imports has been increasing as a result of a growing proportion of finished manufactured goods, the demand for which is relatively elastic. But even in 1980 the bulk of merchandise imports, some 58%, consisted of food, beverages, tobacco, fuel and industrial materials, the demand for which is very inelastic.

Imported inflation is not readily curable because there is not much prospect of offsetting the effect on final prices other than by inducing large reductions in total demand and employment. It is only when the balance of payments is in surplus that a rise in import prices can be offset by an appreciation of the exchange rate.

IV.3   Excess Demand, Unemployment and Vacancies

Whilst external influences have been responsible for most, if not all, the major inflationary episodes in UK economic history, there is not much doubt that the pressure of demand on internal resources has been an important influence too. The measurement of this pressure is not without difficulties. For many years it was taken for granted that a reasonably reliable measure of demand pressure was given by the unemployment percentage. Involuntary unemployment in a particular labour market is identically equal to the excess of supply over demand at the going rate of pay. The degree of excess supply is measured by unemployment as a percentage of employment, and for the economy as a whole by the national unemployment percentage. This percentage, however, because it measures *excess supply* rather than excess demand, will register movements in the average pressure of demand only if demand movements are spread equiproportionately across all individual labour markets. When this is the case, it is possible to interpret the unemployment rate as an inverse indicator of the pressure of demand.

It might be thought that a more direct index of excess demand is given by the number of unfilled vacant jobs. But the figures here are much less complete than those for unemployment. The unemployed have an incentive to register because, as a rule, they are entitled to unemployment benefit. Unfilled vacancies, however, are recorded by employers only if they believe it worth their while to notify them. They may prefer to recruit through the local newspapers rather than through job centres. And an employer who has already notified the job centre of vacancies for a particular kind of worker will not need to register new vacancies because the original notice will be sufficient to attract applicants. Thus the vacancy statistics are bound to be incomplete, and it is officially recognized that only a part, perhaps one-third, of all new vacancies are notified to the Department of Employment.[1]

For many years the unemployment and vacancy statistics moved in a close, consistent relationship to each other. A given unemployment percentage was always observed against a given vacancy rate, and changes in the two percentages were the same in absolute magnitude. It was possible, therefore, to regard the unemployment percentage as a measure of *both* the degree of social distress caused by lack of work *and* of the degree of inflationary pressure in the economy.

In the last fifteen years, however, the measurement of excess demand has become problematical because of a major change in the relationship between the unemployment and vacancy statistics. A given level of vacancies is now associated with a much higher level of unemployment than it used to be. The extent of the change can be seen from the following comparisons:

	Unfilled vacancies, GB		*Unemployment, GB*	
	(000s, percentages in brackets)			
1965-6 (average)	262	(1.1)	315	(1.4)
1973-4 (average)	297	(1.3)	576	(2.6)
1978-9 (average)	241	(1.3)	1,248	(5.2)
1962-3 (average)	145	(0.6)	461	(2.0)
1971-2 (average)	137	(0.6)	777	(3.5)
1975-6 (average)	145	(0.6)	1,055	(4.6)
1980	143	(0.6)	1,596	(6.7)

The figures illustrate a continuing tendency for unemployment to rise relative to vacancies. Between 1962-3 and 1971-2 the unemployment rate to be associated with a given rate for unfilled vacancies had increased by 75%; by 1975-6 it had more than doubled; and by 1980 it was nearly 3 times what it had been in the early 1960s.

There are a number of possible reasons for this dramatic increase in unemployment relative to vacancies:

(i) First, there is a purely statistical reason. There was some evidence in the Census sample of 1971 that unemployment was being more completely recorded than in the earlier Censuses. Officially registered male unemployment was 71% of the Census figures in 1971 compared with 56% in 1966 and 44% in 1961. It is not clear, however, whether this was partly or entirely a cyclical phenomenon since the 1971 Census, unlike those earlier, was taken in a recession year. There is some regional evidence to suggest that the reporting rate varies with unemployment.

---

1 *DEG*, February 1980, footnote to chart.

(ii)   A second hypothesis is that better compensation for unemployment could
        have encouraged workers to spend longer on the unemployment register
        whilst looking for new jobs, thus raising the unemployment level for any
        given pressure of demand for labour. It may be significant that the shift
        in the U-V relationship has been almost totally confined to male workers,
        a high proportion of whom are entitled to unemployment benefit.
        There has been practically no shift for female workers, large numbers of
        whom do not qualify for benefit when they lose their jobs. The benefits
        explanation, however, cannot extend much beyond the early 1970s since
        most indicators of the benefit-earnings ratio have been level or falling
        since then.

(iii)   A third hypothesis is the shake-out theory, which rests on the
        supposition that during the 1960s employers were in the habit of holding
        on to labour during periods of business recession in the expectation of a
        quick return of boom conditions. This expectation, it is argued, has been
        gradually removed by the withdrawal of interest in demand management
        since the 1960s, so that hoarding labour has been seen as increasingly
        wasteful. This explanation, which originated in connection with a sharp
        rise in productivity in 1968, was put in question by the absence of any
        'shake-in' during the boom of 1973. Unemployment declined in 1973, but
        not by enough to restore its previous relationship to vacancies.

(iv)   A fourth hypothesis, which seems plausible but is again not too well
        supported by independent evidence, is that there has been a growing mis-
        match in terms of skill, occupation and locality, between the demand and
        supply of labour.

(v)   Finally there are two converse factors. The vacancy rate depends on
        employers' notifications and these may have increased with the growth of
        job centres, so that a given vacancy rate now stands for a lower pressure
        of demand than formerly. It should also be recalled that the school-
        leaving age was raised in 1973, and this would result in some increase in
        vacancies relative to unemployment.

It is not easy to make sense of what has happened. The possibilities that
unemployment has become increasingly mismatched to vacant jobs and that it has
become more completely recorded, both argue against its use any longer as an index
of demand pressure. The arguments against the vacancy figures is that they are
incomplete and unrepresentative. But they have the advantage of relating to excess
demand rather than to excess supply, and it is arguable that wages are much more
responsive to the former than they are to the latter. So we should probably use the
vacancy figures as the principal index of demand pressure for the 1970s and after,
even though there may be fears that they are not a perfectly consistent indicator.[1]

---

1   There is a large volume of literature on the relationship between unemployment and
     vacancies. It includes A. Evans, 'Notes on the Changing Relationship between Registered
     Unemployment and Notified Vacancies: 1961-1966 and 1966-1971', *Economica*, May
     1977; S.J. Nickell, 'The Effect of Unemployment and Related Benefits on the Duration of
     Unemployment', *EJ*, March 1979; A.B. Atkinson and J.S. Flemming, 'Unemployment and
     Social Security and Incentives', *Midland Bank Review*, 1978; and 'The British Economy in
     the Medium Term', *NIER*, November 1981, pp. 9-13.

IV.4   Demand-pull Inflation

Whilst there is some doubt about how to measure the intensity of excess demand in recent years, there is ample evidence from earlier periods to show that excess demand was an influence upon the rate of inflation. Numerous studies in the 1950s and 1960s showed a strong negative relationship between the level of unemployment (which is inversely related to excess demand) and the rate of change of money wage rates. One of the earlier studies of this kind, and certainly the most influential, was published in 1958 by Professor A.W. Phillips.[1] This examined the relationship between unemployment rates for nearly a century, and on the basis of data for 1861-1913 suggested that the relationship was negative, as expected, and also nonlinear.[2] The wage increases to be associated with different rates of unemployment were as follows:

Unemployment rate	1.0	2.0	3.0	4.0	5.0
% change in wage rates	8.7	2.8	1.2	0.5	0.1

The relationship became known as the *Phillips Curve* and implies a nonlinear, marginal 'trade-off' between the rate of wage increase and unemployment. Thus the rate of wage increase declines by nearly 6% if the unemployment rate goes up from 1.0% to 2.0%, but by only 1.6% if it goes up from 2.0% to 3.0%. The trade-off suggested is a modest one at all but the highest pressures of demand for labour.

One of the more remarkable features of the Phillips Curve, and one which distinguishes it from most similar studies, was that it was found to be highly reliable in predicting increases in wages during much later periods of time than the years 1861-1913 which had been used to derive the equation. Thus Phillips was able to show a very close correspondence for 1948-57 between the wage changes implied by his relationship and those that actually took place. The Phillips Curve was also very accurate in predicting wage increases over the period 1958-66, which was after the study had been published. During these eight years there was not a single error in excess of 2.5% and the mean error (regardless of sign) was only 1.1%; furthermore, the positive and negative errors tended to offset each other so that the mean algebraic error was only 0.1% over this period. These predictive successes, however, have to be seen in the light of what was an exceedingly stable level of unemployment compared with the experience from which Phillips had started. In 1861-1913 unemployment rates ranged from 1 to 11% whereas in 1948-66 they were between 1 and 2.3%. Thus one could argue that postwar experience up to 1966 tested only a small part of the Phillips relation. Nevertheless, it passed this test fairly well.

---

1 A.W. Phillips, 'The Relation between Unemployment and the Rate of Change of Money Wage Rates, 1861-1957', *Economica*, November 1958, although A.J. Brown, op. cit., had illustrated the same relationship.

2 The equation for the schedule was:

$$\frac{\Delta W}{W} = -0.900 + 9.638U^{-1.394}$$

It can also be expressed in logarithmic terms as

$$\log \left\{ \frac{\Delta W}{W} + 0.9 \right\} = 0.984 - 1.394 \log U$$

where $\frac{\Delta W}{W}$ is the percentage rate of wage change and U is the unemployment rate.

(Phillips, op. cit.)

After the mid-1960s, however, the pure Phillips Curve became increasingly unreliable as a guide to the rate of wage inflation. It under-predicted by about 4.5% per annum in 1967-9, by 10-12% in 1970-3, and by more than 20% in 1974 and 1975. There is now, unlike the period 1861-1913, no recognizable relationship between statistics of the unemployment percentage and the rate of wage increase. Wage inflation and unemployment have, if anything, increased together. It is important, therefore, to ask whether the breakdown of the Phillips relationship can be explained, and here several factors come to mind.

(i)   The main factor is the omission from the pure Phillips equation of the causal influence of price changes. This would not have mattered so much in the early 1960s when inflation was moderate. But the omission is serious with inflation at the rates experienced in the 1970s.

(ii)   A connected factor is the probability that wage increases have become increasingly sensitive to price increases during the 1970s as a result of learning to live with inflation. This is not an easy matter to establish empirically, but it is nonetheless probable that a growing number of trade-union negotiators have insisted on full compensation for price changes whilst others have sought wage negotiations at more frequent intervals. There may also have been some tendency to follow the 'expectations-augmented Phillips curve', with expected rather than actual price changes being taken as the basis for wage awards.

(iii) A third factor was the change in the relationship between unemployment and vacancies. With given rates of unemployment signalling a higher pressure of demand than previously there was bound to be some increase in the associated rates of wage inflation.

(iv)   Finally, the Phillips relationship had been partly obscured by a number of attempts, notably in 1972-3 and 1975-8, to control wage increases by incomes policy.

Whilst these factors are the most likely explanations for the breakdown of the Phillips relationship in statistical terms, they do not, in our view, imply that the theoretical relationship underlying the Phillips Curve — the link between excess demand and the rate of wage inflation — should be abandoned. What we have seen is a breakdown of the unemployment series as a measure of excess demand, together with the growth and strengthening of an omitted variable, the past or expected rate of price inflation. This judgement has to be seen in the light of what was said in section I about the falsification of economic hypotheses. The Phillips relation was for many years extremely well corroborated by the test of prediction outside its measurement period; now that it has 'failed' we can interpret the failure *either* as a case of missing variables and measurement error *or* as a breakdown of the demand-pull theory of inflation. In our view the latter interpretation is not acceptable since we should then have to re-interpret the cyclical correlation between wage increases and unemployment — observed for 100 years — in some other way. It also seems to be a matter of elementary 'commonsense' that wage awards will be higher when there is a shortage of labour.

IV.5   Wage-push Inflation[1]

The question of whether wages have increased as a result of unions pushing up wages independently of market forces is controversial chiefly because of the large volume of historical evidence in favour of a demand-pull explanation. This evidence, however, need not preclude the possibility of sporadic outbursts of wage-push inflation. Nor is there any reason in principle why wage-bargaining procedures should respond precisely and consistently to the pressure of demand in the labour market.

The main evidence in favour of a wage-push contribution to recent inflation concerns the 'pay explosion' of 1970 when the rate of wage increases was about 12% faster than could be predicted by the pure Phillips Curve. It was also about 7% higher than could have been predicted from a relationship estimated by Artis in which excess demand was measured by the number of vacancies and price changes were included as an additional causal variable.[2] It can be argued that this was a consequence either of the relaxation of incomes policy in late 1969 or of direct wage-push on the part of the trade unions. The two types of explanation are not unconnected because the government was under strong pressure from the unions themselves to bring incomes policy to an end. Evidence in favour of greater union 'militancy', which we may define for our purposes as willingness to strike in order to obtain wage increases, may be seen in the very substantial increase in industrial disputes over this period. The number of days lost in industrial disputes rose very sharply (see table 1.10). They more than doubled between 1968 and 1970, whilst between the same two years the proportion of stoppages attributed to pay disputes increased from 54% to 64%. The evidence is certainly *suggestive* of a wage-push.

There is also some evidence to suggest that the whole period from 1970 to 1975 was unusual in the extent to which increases in money wages exceeded price increases by a much larger margin than in other periods of history. The most convincing evidence is to be found in the movement of 'real wage rates', where these are defined as the index of weekly wage rates for manual workers in all industries and services deflated by the retail price index. Defined in this way, real wage rates moved as follows:

1960-65	2.8%
1965-70	7.3%
1970-75	22.9%
1975-80	0.6%

---

1   See Aubrey Jones, *The New Inflation*, Penguin, 1973; D. Jackson, H.A. Turner and F. Wilkinson, *Do Trade Unions Cause Inflation?*, Cambridge University Press, 1972; P. Wiles, 'Cost Inflation and the State of Economic Theory', *EJ*, June 1973; E.H. Phelps Brown, 'The Analysis of Wage Movements under Full Employment', *SJPE*, November 1971; K. Coutts, R. Tarling and F. Wilkinson, 'Wage Bargaining and the Inflation Process', *Economic Policy Review*, No. 2, March 1976, Department of Applied Economics, University of Cambridge; M.C. Kennedy, 'Recent Inflation and the Monetarists', *Applied Economics*, June 1976.

2   M.J. Artis, 'Some Aspects of the Present Inflation', *NIER*, February 1971, reprinted in H.G. Johnson and A.R. Nobay (eds.), *The Current Inflation*, Macmillan, 1971.

TABLE 1.10

Inflation 1955-81: possible contributors

	(1) Unemployment percentage	(2) Unfilled vacancies percentage	(3) Change in wage rates (%)	(4) Change in retail prices (%)	(5) Change in import prices (%)	(6) Change in exchange rate (%)	(7) Days lost in industrial disputes (m)	(8) Change in money stock (%)
1955	1.0	1.5	6.9	4.5	3.0		3.8	
1956	1.0	1.2	8.0	2.0	1.9		2.1	
1957	1.3	0.8	5.0	3.7	0.9		8.4	
1958	1.9	0.6	3.6	3.0	-7.2		3.5	
1959	2.0	0.7	2.6	0.6	-1.0		5.3	
1960	1.5	0.9	2.6	1.0	0.0		3.0	
1961	1.3	0.9	4.2	3.4	-2.0		3.0	
1962	1.8	0.6	3.6	2.6	-1.0		5.8	
1963	2.2	0.6	3.7	2.1	4.0		1.8	
1964	1.6	0.9	4.8	3.3	3.0		2.3	5.6
1965	1.3	1.0	4.3	4.8	0.6		2.9	7.6
1966	1.4	1.1	4.6	3.9	1.5		2.4	3.4
1967	2.2	0.8	3.9	2.5	0.3		2.8	10.0
1968	2.3	0.8	6.6	4.7	12.3	-14.3	4.7	6.8
1969	2.3	0.9	5.3	5.4	3.1		6.8	2.4
1970	2.5	0.8	9.9	6.4	4.5	-1.0	11.0	9.5
1971	3.3	0.6	12.9	9.4	4.7	-0.2	13.6	13.9
1972	3.6	0.6	13.8	7.1	5.7	-3.6	23.9	24.5
1973	2.6	1.4	13.7	9.2	27.9	-9.3	7.2	26.3
1974	2.5	1.3	19.8	16.1	46.2	-3.1	14.8	10.2
1975	3.9	0.6	29.5	24.2	14.0	-7.7	6.0	6.6
1976	5.2	0.6	19.3	16.5	22.2	-14.3	3.3	9.5
1977	5.7	0.7	6.6	15.8	15.6	-5.3	10.1	10.0
1978	5.6	0.9	14.1	8.3	3.9	3.7	9.4	15.0
1979	5.3	1.0	15.0	13.4	10.1	7.1	29.5	12.7
1980	6.7	0.6	18.0	18.0	15.0	10.1	12.0	18.6
1981	10.4	0.4	10.0	11.9	9.3	-1.2	4.2	24.4

Sources: (1) GB, excluding school-leavers, *BLS*, *DEG*. (2) *DEG*, Feb. 1976, Jan. 1982; adult vacancies. (3) Weekly rates for manual workers, all industries and services, *ETAS*, 1980. (4) *ETAS*, 1980; *DEG*, February 1982. (5) *ETAS*, 1982; *AAS*. (6) 1968, parity rate; 1971-81 effective exchange rate, *ET*. (7) *BLS*, *DEG*. (8) Sterling M_3, change during year; *FS*, *BEQB* (not available before 1963-4).

This shows the 1970-75 period as quite exceptional in the behaviour of real wages.[1] Throughout this period there was not a single year when the increase in money wage rates was less than 3% ahead of the rise in prices (see table 1.10). In the period from 1975 to 1981, however, real wage rates hardly rose at all, and 1978 was the only year when wage rates outpaced prices to a significant extent.

IV.6   Inflation since 1970: a Summary

In table 1.10 we have grouped together the main factors which have been suggested as causes of or contributors to the rate of inflation. The key question is why the rate of inflation in the 1970s, which averaged 13% a year, was so much higher than in the 1960s when the annual inflation rate varied between 1 and 5%. One candidate which must be considered is the pressure of demand in the economy. But as the table shows, unemployment was very much higher in the 1970s and unfilled vacancies were much the same as they had been before. Nevertheless, there were two years − 1973 and 1974 − when the vacancy rate was higher than in any year in the 1960s. It might be argued that if the pressure of demand then had been held at, say, the 1972 level, the rate of wage increase would have been about 6% less than it actually was whilst the ensuing rate of price increase would have been less by about 4%.[2] But clearly this only accounts for a small part of the inflation actually experienced − 16% in 1974 and 24% in 1975 − so that the main onus of explanation must be sought elsewhere. And the relatively low vacancy rate in most of the 1970s confirms that excess demand could not have been the main factor responsible.

The factor which, in our view, made the largest contribution to the 1970s inflation was the quite dramatic rise in world commodity prices. This had the effect of raising UK import prices by over 100% between 1972 and 1975. With imports accounting for one-fifth of TFE, this was bound to raise final prices by about 20%. The initial effect, moreover, would have carried through into wages and back again to prices, so that the final effect would have been considerably greater.

It is true, of course, that part of the increase in import prices was a consequence of our own inflation rate being faster than that of other countries, so that the exchange rate was forced downwards. But the decline in the exchange rate in 1972-4 was not comparable in magnitude to the rise in import prices, and it was not really until 1976 that our own relative inflation rate became the cause of the falling exchange rate.

---

1   Not all measures of the real wage show the same phenomenon. See, for example, *NIER*, November 1981, where figures of the real wage are derived on a *per capita* basis from the national accounts estimates of wages and salaries and deflated by the implicit price index for GDP. These actually show a slight decline in the rate of increase between 1965-70 and 1970-75. But the GDP deflator includes the prices of exports, investment and government expenditure, and may not act as a good index to use for long-period comparisons.

2   The calculation assumes that unemployment in 1972-4 has to be reduced by 1.5% in order to indicate excess demand consistently with its performance in the 1950s. This means the unemployment rates of 3.6% and 2.5% in 1972 and 1974 respectively are adjusted to become 2.1% and 1.0%. Wage-rate changes are calculated from these levels on the basis of the original Phillips equation; see footnote 2 on p. 45.

As we have argued in section IV.5 above, a second factor in the 1970s inflation was wage-push inflation. There was evidence of this in the 'wage explosions' of the early 1970s, and the figures of days lost in industrial disputes suggest that trade-union members were more prepared to go on strike for higher pay than they had been earlier. But the 1970s pay explosion could possibly have been explained by the ending of incomes policy, whilst the high strike figures in the 1970s as a whole must be partly attributed to inflation itself. Thus the reasons behind the 'wage-push' inflation are not easy to disentangle.

Taking these various arguments together, we can rule out excess demand as the main factor in the inflation of the 1970s. Even in 1973 and 1974 it was not high enough to have added greatly to the rate of price increase. The main factors at work were the colossal rise in import prices, combined with what seems to have been a purely autonomous 'wage-push' inflation during the first half of the decade. These two factors, together with their repercussions through the wage-price spiral, were quite sufficient to explain the course of UK prices during the 1970s.

IV.7   Monetary Explanations of Inflation

The increased rate of inflation in the 1970s was accompanied by markedly faster increases in the stock of money. The money supply had been rising at about 6% a year in 1964-9 whereas in 1971-4 the rate of increase was very much faster. A number of economists, journalists and stockbrokers have interpreted the connection between the rise in the rate of monetary expansion and the faster inflation rate as cause and effect.[1] Some have attributed to money the sole blame for the inflation.

It is generally accepted in economic theory that increases in the supply of money can lead to higher real output or to higher prices. But they do so by raising the aggregate demand for goods and services, thus adding to the pressure of demand. This means that if the inflation of the 1970s had been caused by the rise in the money supply it would have been accompanied by a rise in vacancies and lower unemployment. These changes, moreover, would need to have been substantial to account for such a sharp increase in the rate of inflation. However, as we have already explained above, there was no general or sustained increase in the pressure of demand in the 1970s. Unemployment was higher than it had been, and the vacancy rate, although high in 1973 and 1974, was lower on average in the 1970s than it had been earlier. This absence of any increase, let alone any marked increase, in the pressure of demand is fairly compelling evidence against the monetarist point of view.

This conclusion, however, does not prevent us from agreeing that *if* the money supply had not been allowed to increase so fast, then inflation in the 1970s would

---

1 For example, M. Parkin, 'Where is Britain's Inflation Rate Going?', *LBR*, July 1975, W. Rees-Mogg, *The Times*, 13 July 1976, and, for an American example, M. Friedman, *Money and Economic Development*, Praeger, 1973. The monetarist case against the Keynesians is put in D. Laidler, 'Inflation in Britain: a Monetarist Perspective', *AER*, September 1976, and the Keynesian case against the monetarists in Sir John Hicks, 'What is Wrong with Monetarism?', *LBR*, October 1975 ; Lord Kahn, 'Thoughts on the Behaviour of Wages and Monetarism', *LBR*, January 1976 ; E.H. Phelps Brown, 'A Non-Monetarist View of the Pay Explosion', *TBR*, March 1975 ; M.C. Kennedy, 'Recent Inflation and the Monetarists', op. cit.

have been less severe. If, for example, the money stock had increased at only 6% per annum during the decade instead of the recorded 14%, then it is reasonable to conjecture that interest rates would have been much higher and that expenditure would have been curtailed. Thus the pressure of demand would have been lower with a consequential lowering of the rate of wage increase. But it is difficult to believe that tighter money would have had much impact upon the rise in oil and other import prices, or their consequential effects on final prices.

IV.8   Inflation and Economic Policy

In the period when inflation was merely creeping it was possible to regard it as a small price to pay for the benefit of high employment. A gently sloping trade-off between inflation and unemployment made the problem of political compromise minimal compared with the situation in the 1970s. The advocacy of an incomes policy in the 1960s was associated either with those who hoped to be able to run the economy at a pressure of demand which now seems unthinkable, or else with those who sought to use it as an instrument of income redistribution.

The arrival of fast inflation in the 1970s transformed the policy problem. It resulted in a rapid erosion of real incomes during the intervals between wage settlements, with effects that were socially divisive and disruptive. It also transformed economic behaviour. Economic units learned how to live with inflation and sought to defend their real wages either by insisting on a full compensation for past increases in the cost of living or possibly, in a few cases, by bargaining on the basis of price forecasts. This meant that there were only two ways of bringing inflation under control. One was to deflate domestic demand to such a low pressure that the effect of unemployment upon the rate of wage increase was large enough to offset that of cost-of-living compensation and/or price expectations. Given that prices in some years were increasing at rates of over 15% a year, this would have necessitated either intolerably high unemployment or an impossibly long period of correction. The other alternative was an incomes policy under which the rate of wage increase was subjected to firm quasi-statutory control. This was the main course adopted in 1975-8, although unemployment was allowed to increase as well. An incomes policy was introduced in three stages, starting in July 1975 with a maximum wage increase of £6 per week. This policy gave way to limits of £2.50-£4.00 per week in July 1976, and in July 1977 to a 10% limitation on pay increases. The winning of union agreement to the first two stages of the incomes policy was a singular act of diplomacy which may well have saved the UK economy from hyperinflation.

It was certainly the first time that an incomes policy can be said to have made a significant impact upon the rate of wage inflation. The increase in average weekly wage rates, which had been 30% in 1975, fell to 19% in 1976 and in 1977 to only 7%. But the government was not able to obtain union agreement to a continuation of incomes policy in 1978, and it was unwilling to enforce a statutory policy. Thus the rate of wage increase rose to 14-15% in 1978 and 1979.

The Conservative government which was returned in May 1979 was strongly opposed to incomes policy, and strove to contain inflation by a progressive reduction in the rate of increase in the money stock. This approach, which was formalized as a Medium Term Financial Strategy in the Budget of 1980 and reiterated in those of 1981 and 1982, is discussed at greater length in section VI of this chapter. Meanwhile, the rate of inflation rose to 13% in 1979 and 18% in 1980 as a consequence of the pay explosion in 1978/9, a new round of fuel price increases, and the raising of VAT in the 1979 Budget. The inflation rate was falling in 1981, and money wages, as we have seen, were rising much less rapidly than prices. This, however, was attributable to the massive increase in unemployment.

V   ECONOMIC GROWTH
V.1   The Growth of Productive Potential

In ordinary language it is usual enough to speak of any increase in GDP, however it comes about, as economic growth. In economic theory and applied economics it is best to reserve the term for increases in a country's productive potential. This means that demand-induced spurts of economic expansion, such as those occurring in cyclical recoveries, do not qualify as economic growth in the sense we have in mind.

TABLE 1.11

Economic Growth, UK, 1900-79

	Percentage increase per annum			
	GDP	GDP per person	Employed labour force	Capital stock excluding dwellings
1900-13	1.5	0.6	0.9	1.7
1922-38	2.3	1.2	1.1	1.7
1950-60	2.5	2.1	0.4	2.8
1960-70	2.7	2.4	0.3	4.3
1970-79	1.9	1.7	0.2	3.2

Sources: 1950-79, *ET*, October 1981; *NIBB*, 1981; *ET(AS)*; 1900-38, C.H. Feinstein, op. cit., p. T.51.

The table shows that both the growth rates of productive potential and the under-lying trend in productivity increased between the beginning of the century and the 1960s, but fell back somewhat in the 1970s.

The growth rate of productive potential can only be measured satisfactorily over very long intervals of time or between periods when the utilization of resources was closely similar. Thus the periods indicated in table 1.11, which presents estimates of the growth rate in the UK, have been chosen because they begin and end with similar rates of unemployment. The exception was 1970-79 where unemployment was considerably higher at the end of the period, so that a full use of the labourforce (assuming that this would have been possible) would have added about 0.3% to growth rate of GDP.

The concept of the growth rate of productive potential is not without its limitations. In the first place it says little or nothing about the causes of growth but simply describes a time-trend. An extrapolation of the growth rate for any period into the future could easily turn out wrong if the forces that determine full-employment output are going to be present in different amounts or combinations from those of the past.

A second reservation concerns the interpretation of growth *rates* generally and their relation to *levels*. In calculating growth from 1960 to 1970, for example, one takes the compound rate of increase which will transform the level of GDP in 1960 into that of 1970. This does not tell us anything about the intervening years, during which the level of GDP could have been above or below the suggested time-path. Thus the average *rate* of growth is, in general, no guide to the average *level* of output over the period. An allied point is that the *level of potential output* is arbitrarily defined by the unemployment rate at which it is measured. This does not necessarily represent the maximum attainable level.

One of the questions which the economics of growth must try to answer is why some countries have grown so much faster than others and why, in particular, the underlying growth rate of the UK economy has been slower in the postwar period than that of most other industrial countries (see table 1.12). The answer, if it is to be found at all, must be sought under the more general heading of the causes of economic growth. The causes of growth have been debated by economists since the time of Adam Smith. Growth must depend, in the first instance, upon the increase in the quantity and quality of the factors of production and the efficiency with which they are combined. These increases may be influenced, however, by factors on the side of demand such as the pressure of demand on resources and the degree to which it fluctuates.

The supply of labour depends primarily on the evolution of the population of working age, including net migration, the secular decline in hours worked, and the increase in the length of annual and national holidays. Changes in the pressure of demand, however, affect the size of the labourforce and the number of hours worked, and, over the longer period, may influence migration.

The quality of labour must in large degree depend upon the facilities available for education and training, the opportunities taken of them, and the degree to which they match the changing demands for skills arising out of changes in technology and the structure of aggregate demand. Measurement of these influences, however, is difficult and there is little evidence to show which way, if at all, they have affected the international comparison in table 1.12. The mobility of labour from job to job and from area to area is probably an important factor in economic growth in so far as it reflects the degree to which the labourforce can adjust to economic change. It has been argued, not without evidence, that much of the relatively fast growth of the German, Italian and French economies can be attributed to the movement of labour from the agricultural to the industrial sectors.[1] But it is still not clear how much of this mobility has been a cause and how much a consequence of the disparity in growth rates between the agricultural and industrial sectors.

One obvious influence on the growth of labour productivity is the rate of increase in the nation's stock of capital, both in quantity and in quality. Some indications of the growth of the UK capital stock are given in table 1.11, where it can be seen that the rate of increase, like that of productivity, has tended to rise during the course of this century − although it, too, fell back in the 1970s. The stock of capital, however, is extremely difficult to measure. This is because the figures of depreciation in the national accounts are based on data collected for tax purposes and cannot serve as very precise indications of the rates of scrapping and deterioration of existing capital. Moreover, the economic value of a piece of capital

---

1 A. Maddison, *Economic Growth in the West*, Allen and Unwin, 1964.

equipment is a subjective concept, depending on expectations of future returns and modified by problems of evaluating risk. Estimates of the capital stock, therefore, must be treated with a good deal of reserve.

TABLE 1.12
Rates of Growth, 1970-79

| | Annual percentage rates | |
	GDP	*GDP per capita*
Belgium	3.2	3.0
Denmark	2.9	2.4
France	3.9	3.3
Germany	2.9	2.8
Italy	3.0	2.4
Japan	5.4	4.1
Netherlands	3.1	2.3
Norway	4.4	3.9
Sweden	2.0	1.6
United Kingdom	2.2	2.1
Canada	4.4	3.2
United States	2.4	3.2

Source: National Accounts of OECD Countries

The quality of the capital stock is, perhaps, even more important and even more difficult to measure. According to one widely accepted view, the quality of capital depends, by and large, upon its age structure. This view looks upon the capital stock as a series of vintages of gross investment, each new vintage containing machines of higher quality than the previous one. Scientific and technical progress are embodied in new machines, not old ones, so that the most recent capital equipment is likely to be the most efficient. This view is the basis of the 'catching-up hypothesis' which has been advanced to explain the faster growth of some countries in the early postwar period. The argument is that those countries in which the capital stock was seriously depleted by the war were in a position to replenish it with brand-new equipment, and were thus enabled to grow faster than those countries where the bombing and destruction had been less severe. The embodied view of technical progress, together with the difficulties of measuring the quantity of capital, has led a number of economists[1] to emphasize gross rather than net capital formation as the better indicator of the extent to which capital resources have been enhanced. A high rate of gross investment, even if it is entirely for replacement purposes, will reduce the age of the capital stock and increase its quality.

Turning to influences on the side of demand, two aspects of the question need to be distinguished: the average pressure of demand and the size of fluctuations around the average. It can certainly be argued that a low average pressure of demand, such as obtained (to choose an extreme example) in the 1930s, is inimical to innovation and investment. It hinders investment because capital equipment is

---

1 For example, A. Maddison, ibid.

under-utilized and because its continuation for any length of time is likely to set an unfavourable climate for expectations. High demand, on the other hand, will generally have the opposite effect. It has also been argued that high demand encourages managers and workers to devise new and better ways of working with existing equipment, thereby making technical progress of a variety which is not embodied in new types of machine. This effect has sometimes been described as 'learning by doing', and it fits in with the view that the scale of production problems that have to be solved is itself a stimulus to their solution. Evidence has been produced, for example, to show how the time taken to assemble a prototype airframe has progressively diminished as the workforce has gained experience of repeating the same jobs over and over again. On the other hand, it has also to be borne in mind that high demand pressure may work the other way. The presence of a sellers' market with easy profits could diminish the incentive to innovate and even lead to lazy attitudes to production. An extreme pressure of work can promote mental and physical exhaustion.

Another question is whether the amplitude of fluctuations tend to impede economic growth. It seems probable that the expectation of fluctuations will retard capital formation because profitability will be held down in periods of recession. It may also be the case that expectations of cycles lead to the installation of machinery which can be adapted to use in periods of both high and low output, whereas the prospect of steady growth could enable the introduction of machinery which would be specially designed to produce a steadier level of sales. In this case it is likely that the extra adaptability will be achieved at some cost to the efficiency of capital, and growth will be slowed down. It may be no coincidence, therefore, that three countries with some of the lowest growth rates in the 1950s — the UK, US and Belgium — suffered sharper fluctuations in unemployment than the others[1] (Japan was the exception to this rule).

V.2   Economic Growth and Policy

Government prefers a fast rate of growth to a slow rate because it results in greater tax revenues from a given structure of tax rates, and thus permits tax reductions at full employment or a larger provision of public services (hospitals, schools and so forth) than would otherwise be possible. Fast growth may also render a policy of income redistribution less painful to the better-off than would be so if the growth of income was slow or non-existent. Thus it is not surprising that governments have sometimes announced a faster growth rate as a goal of economic policy.

What is not so clear, however, is whether the means of attaining faster growth are sufficiently well known and understood. There is considerable controversy among economists as to the effects on economic growth to be had from, say, a faster growth of the capital stock and from technical progress. Many would argue that neither are quantifiable, and that the attempts which have been made to quantify them are suspect in a number of ways. Thus it does not seem that growth policy is in the same category as, for example, demand-management policies, in which moderately fine calculations can be made as to the effects of changing the instruments of policy by known amounts. Probably all that can be hoped for from

---

1 On these points see A. Maddison, ibid., pp. 43-56, and R.C.O. Matthews, 'The Role of Demand Management', in Sir Alec Cairncross (ed.), *Britain's Prospects Reconsidered*, Allen and Unwin, 1970.

policy to promote growth is action, or a series of actions, designed to create a climate which is favourable to worthwhile investment, innovation and enterprise. It seems doubtful, however, if even the most determined attempt to alter the environment would show results within the lifetime of a single government. Nor does it seem likely, to judge from earlier experience, that dramatic effects can be expected from the mere announcement of a growth target. This was last done in 1965 when the government published a National Plan in which the rate of growth of GDP was to have been 4% per annum for 1964-70. In the event the growth rate turned out to be only 2.4%, and much of the public investment which had been based on the 4% growth assumption proved to be excessive. It is still debatable whether the growth rate would have been any higher if the balance of payments had been managed more adroitly than it was.

VI   INFLATIONARY DEPRESSION, PROSPECTS AND POLICIES
VI.1   The Economic Situation

The situation in early 1982 was a particularly serious example of the problem which had been facing the UK economy for several years – a combination of fast inflation with high unemployment. Retail prices in March were 10.4% higher than a year earlier while unemployment, at 2.8 million or 11.8% of the employed labour-force, had reached a level which had not been contemplated since the 1930s. More than 900,000 people had been unemployed for a year or more, and the number of young unemployed was a particular cause for concern. A minimum estimate of the amount of economic waste could be gleaned from the fact that real GDP (by output) had fallen 6½% from the spring of 1979 to the end of 1981.

The most promising aspect of the economic situation was the fall in the rate of inflation. The rate of wage increase had fallen from 16% at the end of 1980 to 8% at the end of 1981, and this was 4% less than the rate of price increase. The decline in real wage rates could be attributed to the depressed state of the labour market, or, as some would put it, to the raising of unemployment above its 'natural' or non-inflationary rate. Thus the Treasury forecast was that the rate of inflation in retail prices would decline to 9% by the fourth quarter of 1982 and 7½% by the spring of 1983. This reduction from a 21% rate in the second quarter of 1980 would, if achieved, represent a similar success to that accomplished by incomes policy in 1975-7.

VI.2   Economic Prospects and the Budget

The Treasury's forecasts for 1982-3 provided for only a very small increase in GDP – 1.5% between the second halves of 1981 and 1982, and a further rise of 1% to the first half of 1983. The main elements in the forecast were as follows:

	Level, 2nd half 1981	Change 2nd half 1981 to 1st half 1983
		(£bn at 1975 prices)
Consumers' expenditure	35.8	0.4
Government consumption	12.4	0.05
Government fixed investment	0.9	0.05
Other fixed investment	8.8	0.55
Exports of goods and services	16.7	0.6
Investment in stocks	−0.3	0.45
TFE	74.2	2.1
Imports of goods and services	17.6	1.2
Adjustment to factor cost	6.2	0.2
Statistical adjustment	−0.8	0.6
GDP	49.7	1.3

Source: Financial Statement and Budget Report, March 1982.

All such forecasts are, as we have seen, subject to some margin of error, and here the most likely sources of error could have been consumption, where Treasury forecasts had turned out low in recent years, and investment, where the forecast may have been too high given the depressed state of confidence. These uncertainties, however, could not alter the main conclusion from the forecast — namely that GDP was unlikely to increase at a sufficiently fast rate to outpace the increase in output per person and, thus, to prevent unemployment from rising still further.

VI.3   The Medium Term Financial Strategy

With unemployment at levels not experienced for 50 years it was a matter of concern that the budgets of 1981 and 1982 had made no attempt to reflate demand and employment. The reasons for this were various, but one of them was the Medium Term Financial Strategy under which target rates of increase were announced for the money stock. The original (1980) and 1982 targets were as follows:

	1981-2	*1982-3*	*1983-4*	*1984-5*
1980: % increase in money stock (£M3)	6-10	5-9	4-8	—
1982: % ranges for monetary growth	—	8-12	7-11	6-10

The reduction in monetary growth was seen as the principal instrument for controlling inflation. The theory behind the strategy was the belief that the growth rate of the money stock (rather than demand pressure, wage costs or import prices) was, itself, the principal determinant of inflation and inflationary expectations. This view, which is easily argued on the *assumptions* of fixed output and a constant velocity of circulation, has something to commend it for a closed economy at full employment — although even then a demand-induced rise in prices can take place with no change in the money stock. But its application to a depressed, open economy was much more dubious. It seems to have been accepted, however, mainly on the basis of the long-term correlations between the money stock and prices made popular by Professor Milton Friedman.[1] These have always been open to the objection that the demand (or need) for money is a function of the price level, and that, as a matter of history, the causal connection ran from prices to money rather than the other way. Rising prices due to internal demand and other factors tends to raise interest rates, and this puts pressure on the central bank to increase the money stock.

The most serious fallacy underlying the government's financial policy was the belief that any additional public borrowing would lead to a fall in private expenditure. Behind this was the mistaken assumption that an x per cent addition to the stock of money would lead inevitably to an x per cent rise in the price level. This was particularly dangerous in connection with reflationary fiscal policy, where an addition to government expenditure financed by printing money (i.e. borrowing from the Bank of England) was seen as significantly inflationary whereas the same increase financed by borrowing from the public would not be. In fact it makes no difference whether the new demand is financed by borrowing or by printing money since it is the *addition to demand*, and not its means of finance, that is the potentially inflationary factor. Furthermore, with under-utilized resources, there are good reasons for supposing that additions to demand will tend to raise output and employment rather than prices. In these circumstances, an x per cent rise in the money stock will tend to raise output, whilst the increase in prices need be nothing like x per cent.

The effect of the MTFS, however, was to make it extremely difficult to reflate the economy by fiscal action. Any increase in government spending (or tax reduction) was bound to increase borrowing from the public (thus raising interest rates) or to increase the money stock above its target and, in the government's view, to add proportionately to the rate of inflation. The objection, particularly during 1981, to all such proposals, was that they could not be 'afforded' even though there were ample resources of labour and capital not being used.

In early 1982, the government was still maintaining that its monetary policy (rather than demand policy) was its instrument for controlling inflation, whilst the aim of fiscal policy was to keep interest rates down. The MTFS still had a prominent place in the *Financial Statement and Budget Report*, although there were a few signs that it might be gradually phased out. The monetary targets had been breached in 1981, the target ranges had been made less stringent, and the definition of the money stock was altered from £M3 to the much looser concept of 'principal monetary aggregates'. Thus there was some prospect that the MTFS might not remain an obstacle to fiscal expansion for very much longer.

VI.4   The Risks of Adding to Inflation

Whilst the government's view of inflation was arguably fallacious, there were, nonetheless, quite genuine reasons for believing that a policy of fiscal expansion would add something to the rate of inflation. These consisted of the Phillips Curve

---

1   See, for example, Chapter 9 of Milton and Rose Friedman, *Free to Choose*, Secker and Warburg, 1980. The same view is repeated in the Treasury's memorandum of evidence to the 3rd Report from the Treasury and Civil Service Committee, *Monetary Policy*, Vol. III, Appendices, pp. 68-85, 24 February 1981.

effects of lower unemployment on the rate of wage increase and the effects of higher GDP on imports, the exchange rate and import prices. The first of these effects was arguably small – at least in the initial stages of reflation – because of the high level of unemployment. The original 1958 Phillips Curve was virtually horizontal for unemployment levels above 4%, and although these rates may correspond to higher demand pressure in the 1980s, there is still no certainty that a sharp addition to the rate of wage increase would follow from a gradual reduction in unemployment to somewhere in the region of 5%.

The other inflationary channel was through the effect of higher GDP on imports. Each 1% addition to GDP could be expected to add 1 to 1½% to the import volume. But the fall in the exchange rate (and consequent rise in import prices) which was needed to hold the balance of payments in equilibrium could easily be exaggerated. It depends mainly on the elasticities of demand for exports and imports, and if these are −1.5 and −0.5 respectively, the exchange-rate decline would have to be about 1-1.5% for each 1% rise in GDP.[1] Even a 10% addition to GDP would, on those assumptions, add only 10 or 15% to import prices, and, in the first instance, 2 or 3% to final prices. Subsequent rounds of the wage-price spiral would, of course, raise this amount, but the main point of this example (which is illustrative rather than precise) is that the inflationary dangers arising via the exchange rate are not too serious.

These inflationary consequences of fiscal expansion could, moreover, be offset in some degree by including reductions in indirect taxes, the national insurance surcharge, and national insurance contributions as part of the expansionary package. These would involve direct reductions in prices or in industrial costs. There would also be some amelioration of the exchange-rate effects if other countries could be persuaded to reflate at the same time as the UK. But here there would be some danger of a general increase in world demand leading to increases in import costs through a general increase in world commodity prices. There was, however, something to be said in favour of public expenditure schemes with a low import content.

Finally, there remained the problematical issue of incomes policy. If an unemployment rate of 12% was the price to be paid for controlling inflation, then an effective incomes policy, if one could be found, was an attractive alternative to the government's policies. If such a policy could not be devised then the choice was unpalatable and the outlook grim.

---

1   The reasoning is as follows: a 1% fall in the exchange rate leads to a 1% fall in UK export prices in terms of foreign currency and a 1.5% rise in their volume. The value of exports in terms of £s rises by 1.5%. At the same time, import prices (in £s) rise by 1%, whilst the import volume falls by 0.5%. The value of imports must rise, therefore, by 0.5%. Thus a 1% exchange-rate reduction improves the foreign balance by 1.5% on exports less 0.5% on imports, making a net improvement of approximately 1% of the value of imports.

REFERENCES AND FURTHER READING

C. Allsopp and V. Joshi, 'Alternative Strategies for the UK', *NIER*, February 1980.

F.T. Blackaby (ed.), *British Economic Policy 1960-74*, NIESR and Cambridge University Press, 1979.

S.T. Cook and P.M. Jackson (Eds.), *Current Issues in Fiscal Policy*, Martin Robertson, 1979.

Economic Policy Review, Department of Applied Economics, University of Cambridge.

M.K. Evans, *Macroeconomic Activity*, Harper and Row, 1969.

C.H. Feinstein, *National Income, Expenditure and Output of the United Kingdom 1855-1965*, Cambridge University Press, 1972.

J.S.E. Laury, G.R. Lewis and P.A. Ormerod, 'Properties of Macroeconomic Models of the UK Economy: A Comparative Study', *NIER*, February 1978.

D.G. Mayes, 'The Controversy Over Rational Expectations', *NIER*, May 1981.

Midland Bank Review.

National Institute Economic Review.

D. Savage, 'The Channels of Monetary Influence: A Survey of the Empirical Evidence', *NIER*, February 1978.

M.J. Stewart, *The Jekyll and Hyde Years: Politics and Economic Policy Since 1964*, Dent, 1977.

M.J.C. Surrey, *The Analysis and Forecasting of the British Economy*, NIESR and Cambridge University Press, 1971.

Treasury, *Economic Progress Report.*

Treasury, *Financial Statement and Budget Report 1982-83.*

2

The monetary, financial and fiscal systems

N.J. Gibson

I   INTRODUCTION: THE POLICY DILEMMA

The previous chapter conveys an overall picture of the UK economy, paying particular attention to fluctuations in economic activity, demand management, inflation, and economic growth. This chapter concentrates on a more restricted subject area. It describes the monetary, financial and fiscal systems and examines the monetary, credit and fiscal policies of the authorities, that is, the UK government and the Bank of England.

The term 'policy' implies the existence of goals or objectives, and a strategy or instruments to achieve them. For twenty years after the Second World War the most frequently cited policy goals in the UK were the maintenance of full employment, price stability and fixed exchange rates, the encouragement of economic growth and the achievement of a 'satisfactory' balance of payments.[1] However, since the late 1960s the emphasis on the maintenance of fixed exchange rates has all but disappeared and more flexible exchange rates have become the norm, though this does not mean that the balance of payments has become a matter of little concern. Furthermore, a reduction in the rate of inflation, rather than the maintenance of full employment, has come to dominate the policy goals of the authorities. The former is seen as a necessary means for creating conditions conducive to economic growth.

The standard policy instruments at the disposal of the authorities are monetary, credit and fiscal. That is, by varying interest rates and the availability of credit and by altering taxes and government expenditure, the authorities may hope to realize some or all of their policy goals. But in addition to the instruments mentioned, the authorities may vary exchange rates, restrict imports and impose controls on prices and incomes. They may even go beyond this and introduce rationing and other measures.

The policy problem is clearly a complex one. In dealing with it the authorities may attempt to use their policy instruments to influence what are called target variables, sometimes known as intermediate targets to distinguish them from the goals or ultimate targets described above. The belief or hope is that the instrument and target variables are causally related and that in turn there is a reasonably stable link between the target variable and the desired goal. For instance, the authorities seem to assume that by manipulating interest rates they can affect the amount of money in the system or its rate of growth and that there is, at least in the longer term, a link between the latter and the rate of inflation.

But the foregoing is evidently a somewhat idealized picture. Once a set of goals is chosen a host of questions arise. Can they be defined precisely? Are they mutually compatible within the particular economic system, given the policy

1   See chapters 3 and 5 respectively for an extensive explanation and discussion of the balance of payments and incomes controls.

instruments at the disposal of the authorities? If they are not, which goals should be sacrificed or modified? Are there alternative policy instruments that might be used to achieve one or more of the policy goals? Have the authorities, or for that matter has anyone else, the necessary knowledge about the relationships between instruments and goals? Do they know exactly when and by how much to manipulate the policy instruments or even how many instruments they need? These questions highlight what may be called the policy dilemma.

Implicit in this discussion of goals and instruments are questions concerning both value judgements and how an economic system works. Each of these questions is a recurring theme in this chapter. Section II looks briefly at the theoretical and empirical basis of monetary and fiscal policy. Section III discusses the structure of the banking and financial system, and examines some money and credit theories. The taxation system is considered in section IV, which also includes a brief discussion of taxation within the EEC. Finally, in section V policy since the 1960s is briefly surveyed and also included is a short discussion of the prospects and possible implications of economic and monetary union within the EEC.

II   SOME THEORETICAL AND EMPIRICAL BACKGROUND
II.1   Certain Keynesian and Monetarist Positions

If the policy dilemma is as difficult as the foregoing discussion suggests, what has economics got to say about it? To attempt to answer this question is to enter the highly controversial debate which has been over-simply and crudely described as Keynesianism versus Monetarism.

Keynesianism does, of course, trace its lineage from the writings of Keynes and especially *The General Theory of Employment, Interest and Money*.[1] In writing *The General Theory* Keynes had set himself the task of providing a general theory of the working of the aggregate economic system but one which allowed involuntary unemployment of labour to persist. The term 'involuntary' has the connotation that it is undesired and that unemployed workers would provide their services at the existing real wage (or even a lower one) if there were only a demand for them; the persistence of involuntary unemployment was taken to suggest that there were no automatically working market forces which would tend to eradicate the involuntary unemployment and that, in particular, a willingness of workers to accept a reduction in money wages would not solve the problem. For Keynes and his followers the answer lay in expanding aggregate demand for goods and services and so indirectly for labour.

The preferred policy instrument for influencing aggregate demand was fiscal policy, either through changing government expenditure or taxation or a combination of both. Monetary policy might also be used to influence interest rates and so aggregate demand, though for some Keynesians this approach was less reliable as they were sceptical about the impact of changes in interest rates on investment expenditure and felt that in some circumstances, such as that of a deep recession, the demand for money, if it could be relied on at all, might be so elastic that interest rates could not be made low enough to stimulate expenditure.

This approach to policy — variously called demand management or the 'neoclassical synthesis', as it stressed that so long as aggregate demand was sustained

---

1   Macmillan, 1936.

market processes could be relied upon to allocate resources more or less efficiently – dominated economic thinking in the period immediately following the Second World War. There was considerable confidence amongst economists and governments that by manipulating aggregate demand – sometimes known as fine-tuning – full employment could be maintained.

However, by the 1950s there was some concern about the ability to generate full employment and at the same time achieve price stability. This concern came eventually to be formulated in terms of the so-called 'Phillips curve', which purported to have found an inverse relationship, over a lengthy historical time-period, between the rate of unemployment and the rate of change of wages.[1] That is, as unemployment became smaller the rate of increase of wages got larger. The first may be taken as a proxy for an expanding aggregate demand and the second puts pressure on prices generally to rise. Policy-makers seemed to be posed with a fundamental dilemma; they could not have full employment and price stability at the same time. Nevertheless, many Keynesians welcomed the advent of the Phillips curve as they had been unhappy with the traditional emphasis on the downwards rigidity of nominal wages and prices.

There were, however, other Keynesians who never accepted the neoclassical synthesis and emphasized other and perhaps more radical aspects of *The General Theory*. For them wages and wage costs are basically exogenous or at any rate largely the outcome of non-economic, social and political factors, and any attempt to restrain them through controlling aggregate demand will result in falling output and rising unemployment with perhaps little or no effect on wages and prices; or indeed falling output and employment together with rising prices may occur; this combination of phenomena is commonly called stagflation. The protagonists of this approach also tend to emphasize the inherent uncertainty of economic life, stressing the importance of unpredictable expectations about the future and their impact on economic activity. If this approach is accepted it rules out, of course, any attempt to rely on the existence of reasonably stable investment and monetary relationships as a basis for economic policy. Incomes and prices policies and other forms of government intervention in the areas of finance, investment, foreign trade and exchange rates are generally suggested as the type of policy required.

In addition to the foregoing there is a less radical strand of the Keynesian tradition which also attacks the assumption of the automatic working of market processes and, in particular, the notion of general flexibility of prices and instead emphasizes that prices may be sticky and adjust at varying rates in different markets. This became known as disequilibrium analysis, and of necessity stressed the importance of quantity adjustments as well as price adjustments. They too would expect attempts to control inflation solely by restrictive fiscal and monetary policies to lead to unemployment and loss of output. However, they still consider such policies to be important but would buttress them by some form of incomes and prices policy and perhaps other types of intervention such as in the foreign exchange market. In general, however, they still place considerable reliance on market processes and their ability to allocate resources comparatively efficiently.

There were, of course, economists who never saw themselves as part of the Keynesian tradition, notably a group of University of Chicago economists under

---

1 For a more extensive discussion of the Phillips curve, see chapter 1, section IV.4.

the tutelage of Milton Friedman. In 1956 in his famous article 'The Quantity Theory of Money — a Restatement',[1] Friedman powerfully challenged those versions of Keynesianism which had tended to play down or dismiss the relevance of money to the operation of the economic system. He did this by recasting the traditional quantity theory of money as a theory of the *demand* for money; a demand that was stable and could be specified in terms of a small number of key variables. He also contended that there were factors affecting the supply of money which did not affect its demand and hence on these arguments the way was open to trace out the effects of changes in the supply of money on such key variables as nominal income. Monetarism had been born, though it was more than a decade before the label was invented.

The term seems to owe its origin to Karl Brunner, another famous monetarist, who in 1968 attached the term to three major conclusions which he claimed had emerged from intensive research work in the previous ten years or so: 'First, monetary impulses are a major factor accounting for variations in output, employment and prices. Second, movements in the money stock are the most reliable measure of the thrust of monetary impulses. Third, the behaviour of the monetary authorities dominates movements in the money stock over business cycles.'[2] These statements constituted a strong challenge to the whole Keynesian tradition, with its relative neglect and in some instances dismissal of the importance of money in the operation of the economic system.

A further forceful attack on an element in the Keynesian tradition came from Friedman in the late 1960s. He convincingly questioned the validity of a stable trade-off between inflation and unemployment; the Phillips curve thus came under strong critical pressure. Friedman argued that the Phillips curve as ordinarily understood assumed that the anticipated rate of inflation was given. His position was that this could only be a short-run phenomenon and that the experience of rising prices would lead to a revision of anticipated inflation and an upward shift in the Phillips curve. In the long term there was for him no trade-off between inflation and unemployment; indeed the long-run Phillips curve was vertical, defining what he called the 'natural rate of unemployment'. That is, the rate which in the long run emerged from the interaction of real market forces, though it was not to be seen as a constant.

Friedman felt that his criticisms of the original Phillips curve and his argument that the long-run Phillips curve was vertical carried important implications for monetary policy. In particular, any attempt to reduce unemployment below its natural rate through monetary expansion, or indeed expansionary fiscal policies, would not succeed in the long run but would lead to greater inflation and, if the attempt was maintained, to accelerating inflation. Moreover, any reduction in the rate of monetary expansion once the process is under way could be expected to be accompanied by both rising prices and rising unemployment; in other words stagflation is again observed. And more generally the effectiveness of demand management policies is seriously open to doubt.

Running through the immediately preceding account is the notion that people's adjustments to rising prices take time. This notion became formalized in terms of what is called the adaptive expectations hypothesis. Briefly this suggests that people

---

1   In Milton Friedman (ed.), *Studies in the Quantity Theory of Money*, University of Chicago Press, 1956.

2   'The Role of Money and Monetary Policy', *Review*, Federal Reserve Bank of St Louis, July 1968, p. 9.

form their expectations about future prices by extrapolating their past experience of actual prices, giving most weight to the recent past. On the face of it, if this type of lagged response does exist it would seem to allow for some element of demand management, sometimes referred to as fine-tuning. Friedman would, however, be inclined to reject this inference on a number of grounds, in particular because of the variability of the lagged adjustments and hence the extreme difficulty in following a policy which is really stabilizing in its effects.

However, the adaptive expectations hypothesis has itself come under strong criticism from what has come to be called the 'rational expectations' or 'new classical' economics. The basis of the challenge to adaptive expectations is that if people generally operate on the basis of them then they are going to be systematically in error and this is clearly not rational. On the more positive side, rational expectations require that views about the future be formulated in the light of all the available information. The implication of this is far-reaching, as it implies, for instance, that people in making their decisions will take into consideration anticipated government policy. But this in turn carries the consequence that the objectives of government policy may then be frustrated. If, for example, government hopes to encourage a growth in output and employment through expansionary monetary policies and people generally anticipate that this will result in rising prices, then on this approach they will take the latter into account in their own decision-making and the objectives of government may be undermined. In other words the rational expectations approach casts grave doubt on the possibilities for effective government demand management policies.

The approach, as indicated above, is also described as the 'new classical' economics. The reason for this term is that like the old classical economics (some would say neoclassical) the new relies heavily on market clearing processes, discounting the importance of price rigidities and so-called persistent disequilibria, and postulates optimizing behaviour on the part of economic agents, with the optimization extending to expected future events; it is the latter that is 'new'. This whole approach has, of course, encountered heavy criticism, frequently on the grounds of the lack of realism of its assumptions, especially the one relating to market clearing. The traditional retort to this criticism is that a theory is to be judged not by the so-called realism or otherwise of its assumptions but by its ability to predict. Lurking in the background of these remarks are important methodological issues but these cannot be pursued further.

It should be evident from the foregoing discussion that a highly intensive and at times conflicting debate has been and still is in progress about the operation of the economic system and what may be appropriate policy measures for governments to employ in their attempts to stabilize its operation. Nevertheless, it is possible to discern some areas of broad agreement or at least of a coming closer together. The branch of Keynesianism which has come to stress the importance of quantity as well as price adjustments in markets and also that the rates of adjustment in different markets may vary greatly, being particularly rapid for foreign exchange rates but sluggish in many labour markets, represents views which would be shared by some monetarists. Similarly there are those in the Keynesian tradition who are much more ready to concede to the monetarists that the behaviour of the money supply in terms of its rate of growth and changes therein are of basic importance to the output, employment and price behaviour of the economic system. And there is also a widespread recognition that expectations about the future are of importance to the effectiveness of policy measures. However, the areas of agreement should not be overstated and they do not necessarily imply agreement on the appropriate policy responses. Thus the task of the policy-makers remains extremely difficult. It is time to explore some of their views about these matters.

II.2   Views of the Authorities

The Bank of England has made it clear that, like many others, they were strongly influenced by Keynesian thinking for a considerable number of years after the Second World War. A Governor of the Bank has stated as regards the early part of this period that 'the doctrine of Keynes, at least as interpreted by his followers . . . had led to a totally new emphasis on fiscal policy . . . . monetary policy went into limbo. There was general scepticism about its relevance.'[1]

This scepticism would seem to have persisted, except perhaps for a brief interlude in the mid-1950s, until the late 1960s. By the latter period the Bank had come to be influenced by the rise of monetarism and especially by empirical evidence 'suggesting that there might well be a stable relationship between the demand for money and the level of income and interest rates'.[2] For the Bank, 'The identification of this function appeared to provide a sound intellectual basis for monetary policy'.[3] In particular, other things being equal, if the authorities could control the appropriate interest rates the quantity of money demanded would be given, though, of course, it was never believed that matters were as clear-cut as this statement suggests.

However, it was from around the late 1960s that the authorities paid increasing attention to the growth of what have come to be called the monetary aggregates. There are a number of these but the two most relevant to this discussion are M_1 and M_3. M_1 refers to notes and coin in circulation with the public plus sterling sight deposits held by the private sector only. M_3, which subsumes M_1, consists of notes and coin in circulation with the public, together with all deposits whether in sterling or other currencies, held by UK residents in both the public and private sectors.

Despite the increasing attention which the Bank claim they gave to monetary aggregates from the late 1960s, M_3 grew extremely rapidly in the early 1970s and it would seem that it was not until the end of 1973 that they adopted targets for the rate of growth of M_3.[4] Publication of targets, however, did not take place until 1976. The Bank saw the introduction of targets as providing 'the framework of stability within which other policy objectives [could] be more easily achieved'[5] and believed there was a 'relationship between monetary growth and inflation over the longer term'.[6]

These statements would suggest that around the mid-1970s the Bank had become converted to monetarism. This may, however, overstate the case, though it should also be noted that the Bank would seem to have begun to share the

---

1   'Monetary Management in the United Kingdom', *BEQB*, Vol. II, No. 1, March 1971, p. 41.

2   'An Account of Monetary Policy', *BEQB*, Vol. 18, No. 1, March 1978, p. 32.

3   ibid.

4   For further discussion of this period, see below, pp. 118-19.

5   'An Account of Monetary Policy', p. 34.

6   ibid., p. 35.

scepticism of many economists about frequent fiscal-policy adjustments or what has been called 'fine-tuning' as a means of demand management. Nevertheless, the Bank cannot be simply labelled as monetarist since the mid-1970s in their approach to economic policy; they are rather more eclectic and pragmatic than this would imply; the present Governor of the Bank has, however, referred with approval to the label 'practical monetarism', though even this term needs to be interpreted with caution.

It is clear that the evolution of the views of the Bank away from a Keynesian perspective to one with a monetarist emphasis has been shared by the authorities generally. The Treasury, the major economic department of government, in evidence to a House of Commons committee has stated that 'There is a clear relationship between the growth of the money stock and the rate of inflation in the medium term. This is the foundation of the Government's strategy for reducing inflation by means of monetary control.'[1]

The mention of the medium term is important because it allows that in the short term the effects of, say, a reduction in the rate of growth of the money supply may adversely affect output and employment. The Treasury took the view that the consequences for output and employment would depend crucially on price expectations and that if these were revised downwards and reflected in money wages the impact on output and employment would be reduced. Central to this revision was the commitment by government to its money supply targets. Although the Treasury was not optimistic that adverse effects on output and employment could be avoided in the short term, it saw no reason why the effects should permanently damage potential growth.

The Treasury explained the differences between the short- and medium-term effects of a restrictive monetary policy in terms of the rapidity of response of different markets. Financial markets, including foreign exchange markets, were understood to respond much more quickly than labour markets. As regards the foreign exchange markets, a restrictive policy would strengthen the exchange rate and tend to make domestic economic activity less competitive, putting pressure on output, prices and wages. In the long run it was considered that once prices and wages had adjusted there would be no effect on the real exchange rate. Thus the Treasury like the Bank has taken up a qualified monetarist approach to economic policy.

II.3   Empirical Evidence

It might have been hoped that the conflict of views on how the economy works and the appropriate policies for the authorities to follow in order to achieve their goals could have been resolved by the building and testing of macro-econometric models. However, as the introduction to this chapter implies, this hope has not so far been realized. The Treasury and Civil Service Committee referred to earlier was deeply disappointed at the dearth of empirical evidence presented to it in its enquiry into monetary policy.

---

1 'Memorandum by H.M. Treasury', Third Report from the Treasury and Civil Service Committee, Session 1980-81, *Monetary Policy*, Vol. II, Minutes of Evidence, HC, 163-II, 24 February 1981, p. 90. See also Vol. I, Report, 163-I and Vol. III, Appendices, 163-III.

One of the difficulties is, of course, that different models may suggest substantially different answers on not only how the economy works but what would be the consequences of following a carefully specified monetary or fiscal policy. Testing these matters with a model is known as simulation. Moreover, to compare different models in a meaningful way and to assess their performance in tracking, predicting and simulating economic behaviour can be a highly technical and complex matter and even with the greatest care may fail to provide definitive answers.

Notwithstanding these difficulties, there is some measure of agreement between econometric model-builders in the UK and the US that both monetary and fiscal policies have in the short run important effects on output, employment and prices, with the price effect coming about more slowly than the other two effects. The actual impact of the policies will, of course, depend in part on the initial state of the economy as well as unpredictable events which may subsequently impinge upon its operation. In the longer term there is a presumption, at least as regards the US, that 'the response of the economy to both monetary and fiscal policy is . . . consistent with the views advanced by Friedman and the monetarists'.[1] However, these conclusions are of little comfort to policy-makers acutely aware of both the costs of unemployment in the short and medium term and the inefficiencies and inequities of continuing and variable price inflation. What in some sense constitutes an optimum or best set of policies is clearly an elusive phenomenon.

III   THE MONETARY AND FINANCIAL SYSTEM
III.1   Introduction

The monetary and financial system is made up of a set of institutions which trade in or exchange financial instruments of various types and maturities. These include deposits of banks and building societies, notes and coin, loans (whose attributes may vary greatly), company and government stocks and securities, and many other kinds of instrument. The trade in instruments necessarily gives rise to a host of financial markets of varying degrees of interdependence, which are of fundamental importance to the efficient operation of the economic system and which extend outside national boundaries into the world at large. In this chapter, however, attention is concentrated on the major domestic financial institutions, beginning with a discussion of the monetary sector; other financial institutions are discussed later.

III.2   The Monetary Sector

The monetary sector has recently been officially defined to include the following institutions:[2]
    (i)   all recognized banks and licensed deposit-takers (LDTs);
    (ii) the National Girobank;

---

1   F. Modigliani, 'The Channels of Monetary Policy in the Federal Reserve-MIT-University of Pennsylvania Econometric Model of the United States', in G. A. Lenton (ed.), *Modelling the Economy*, Heinemann, 1975, p. 241.

2   'Money and Banking Figures: Forthcoming Changes', *BEQB*, Vol. 21, No. 4, December 1981, p. 531.

(iii) those listed institutions in the Channel Islands and the Isle of Man which have opted to comply with the new monetary control arrangements;

(iv) the trustee savings banks;

(v) the Banking Department of the Bank of England.

The terms 'recognized banks' and 'LDTs' are new to the UK banking system and were introduced under the 1979 Banking Act. To acquire the status of a recognized bank, an institution or parent institution has to satisfy the Bank of England that it enjoys 'a high reputation and standing in the financial community' and provides or will provide directly or through a subsidiary, 'a wide range of banking services or a highly specialized banking service' and can meet certain minimum capital and reserve requirements.[1] Under the Act 'a wide range of banking services' is defined to include both domestic and foreign banking services, though the Bank has some discretion in what it requires to satisfy the conditions.

To become LDTs institutions have also to meet requirements similar to those specified for recognized banks but without any conditions as regards the range of services they offer. In fact a number of institutions which sought recognized bank status were not granted it and had to be content with the status of a LDT; the grounds for refusal would seem often to have been the extent of the range of services offered.

In February 1982 there were some 590 recognized banks and LDTs, with the former accounting for just under 50 per cent of the total number. As might be expected, this large number of institutions covers banks — where the term is used to refer to both recognized banks and LDTs unless the text specifies otherwise — with enormous variation in size and range of activities. It includes the large London clearing banks with some 11,000 branches between them, the three Scottish clearing banks, the four Northern Ireland banks, discount houses, accepting houses and highly specialized investment banks and trust companies, finance houses, consortium banks and some literally hundreds of overseas banks with offices in London.[2]

Putting aside the National Girobank which is further discussed below, the monetary sector includes certain institutions in the Channel Islands and the Isle of Man which accepted an invitation to become part of the monetary sector, although the Banking Act does not apply to either area. In doing so they have, of course, to comply with the official monetary control provisions; the latter are examined below. Early in 1982 there were some 55 Channel Islands and Isle of Man institutions which had opted to become part of the UK monetary sector; some of the institutions concerned are branches of mainland banks. The major reason for the large number of financial institutions in the Channel Islands and the Isle of Man is that they find distinct fiscal advantages in being outside the jurisdiction of the UK fiscal authorities.

The remaining institutions that are part of the monetary sector, the trustee savings banks and the Banking Department of the Bank of England, are discussed later.

The Governor of the Bank of England recently described the UK as 'a relatively small country with a relatively very large financial centre exposed to international monetary forces acting in a turbulent world.'[3] Table 2.1 shows a highly aggregated

---

1 Quotations from the 1979 Banking Act (1979 c. 37), Schedule 2, Part I.

2 For further discussion, see below, sections III.6 and III.7.

3 'Recent Changes in the Monetary and Regulatory Framework', *BEQB*, Vol. 22, No. 1, March 1982, p. 102.

picture of the monetary sector at the end of 1981; the figures are intended to exclude double counting and to show the position of the sector *vis-à-vis* third parties. Total assets and liabilities were over £330,000m with approximately £100,000m in sterling and £230,000m in other currencies. In comparison with most other countries many of these figures are relatively large in relation to GDP and clearly do expose the UK to international monetary forces, especially those reflected in eurocurrency markets (See section III.5 *et seq*.)

TABLE 2.1

UK Monetary Sector, end-December 1981 (£m)

	Sterling	Other currencies	Total
(i) *Liabilities*			
Domestic deposits	75,563	10,552	86,115
Overseas-sector deposits	14,418	217,308	231,726
Non-deposit liabilities (net)	n.a.	n.a.	13,641
			331,482
(ii) *Assets*			
Lending:			
to public sector	22,702	1,000	23,702
to private sector	67,326	15,364	82,690
to overseas sector	11,844	213,246	225,090
	101,872	229,610	331,482

Source: BEQB.

It should be noted that there is a rough matching of sterling assets and liabilities (though some of the latter are overseas sector deposits which may at times exhibit some volatility and so affect the foreign exchange markets) and similarly for other currencies, though this does not necessarily imply a similar matching of maturity dates of liabilities and assets. Indeed one of the fundamental functions of financial institutions is to operate in ways which allow a mismatch of maturity dates to persist without any threat to the stability of the particular institution and ultimately the whole system. This function used to be called borrowing short and lending long, but is now more aptly referred to as maturity transformation. The capacity to engage in this practice hinges crucially on the ability of the institutions to pool independent risks, in the sense of, say, deposit withdrawals being offset by new deposits and similarly for transactions on the assets side of balance sheets. There are, of course, in addition other important factors at work including economies from large-scale operation and the system of prudential and supervisory controls applied by monetary authorities. The particular controls operated in the UK are discussed in relation to the activities of the Bank of England.

III.3   The Bank of England

The Bank of England acts as the main banker to the government and plays a basic role in smoothing government cash transactions between the government and the banking system and in administering and managing the national debt – broadly speaking, the debt liabilities of the state to its nationals, to its own agencies and to overseas holders. As agent of the government, the Bank helps to regulate and control foreign exchange transactions and manages the Exchange Equalization Account, which holds the official gold, foreign exchange reserves and SDRs of the UK.[1] The Bank is also banker to the banking system and has a major responsibility for the carrying out of monetary policy and for the prudential supervision of the monetary sector; in short the Bank of England is a central bank.

The Bank is divided into two parts for accounting purposes; it produces two balance sheets, one for the Issue Department and one for the Banking Department. The origin of the double-balance-sheet system is to be found in monetary controversies during the first half of the nineteenth century and was introduced under the 1844 Bank Charter Act, separating the note-issue function from all other functions of the Bank. But the two balance sheets still retain a certain, if somewhat artificial, significance in that the Issue Department is classified in the national accounts as part of the public sector whereas the Banking Department is classified for banking purposes with the banking sector. The position of the Issue Department in December 1981 is shown in Table 2.2.

The notes in circulation are necessarily held by persons, companies and financial institutions. Notes in the Banking Department would, of course, disappear from the accounts if the two balance sheets were amalgamated. The assets of the Issue Department are classified as government securities and other securities. The latter include commercial bills, local authority bills, and, on occasion, local authority deposits and bonds . . . and company securities and other miscellaneous securities.'[2]

TABLE 2.2

Issue Department (selected items), 9 December 1981 (£m)

Liabilities		*Assets*	
Notes:			
in circulation	11,001	Government securities	6,329
in Banking Dept.	24	Other securities	4,696
	11,025		11,025

Source: BEQB

'Government securities include British government and government-guaranteed securities, Treasury bills, ways and means advances to the National Loans Fund . . . and any special Treasury liability',[3] arising when the total market value of assets is less than the note issue. Any increase in the note issue implies an equal addition to holdings of securities. In other words, when the Issue Department supplies additional notes, which it does via the Banking Department, it obtains interest-earning securities in exchange, which are then held within the public sector.

---

1 See 'The Exchange Equalisation Account: Its Origins and Development', *BEQB*, Vol. 8, No. 4, December 1968.

2 'Additional Notes to the Tables', 1, *BEQB*, Vol. 22, No. 1, March 1982.

3 ibid.

The Issue Department uses its assets to facilitate the issue and redemption of the national debt; it underwrites all new issues of government stock, taking up any that are not bought by the public on the day of issue and subsequently sells them as demand appears. Similarly, it purchases stocks nearing redemption, avoiding large cash payments to the public when the actual redemption date arrives. The Issue Department may in fact be in the market as a buyer or seller of government securities, or both, almost continuously. That is, it engages extensively in open-market operations. The latter are not, of course, confined to transactions involving government securities. In particular, in its money-market operations it deals extensively in commercial bills.

The balance sheet of the Banking Department is shown in Table 2.3.

TABLE 2.3

Banking Department (selected items), 9 December 1981 (£m)

Liabilities		*Assets*	
Deposits:			
Public	40	Government securities	433
Bankers	482	Advances and other accounts	1,026
Reserves and other		Premises, equipment and	
accounts	1,503	other securities	556
Special deposits	–	Notes and coins	24
	2,025		2,039

Source: FS.
Note: The balance sheet does not exactly balance because certain subsidiary items, such as capital, have been omitted.

Public deposits are all government balances. They include those of the Exchequer, the National Loans Fund, HM Paymaster General, the National Debt Commissioners, Dividend Accounts and certain other government accounts. The total amount involved is relatively small by comparison with bankers' deposits despite the enormous scale of government transactions. The main reason for this is that government attempts to keep these balances as low as is consistent with carrying out its operations. Any so-called surplus balances are used to buy back government debt in an attempt to keep down costs. As may be seen from Table 2.3, net payments from the government to the community will have an immediate effect on bankers' deposits, increasing the cash holdings of the banking system whilst reducing public deposits. The reverse is true for net payments from the community to the government, and so smoothing-out movements of funds between public and bankers' deposits is a major preoccupation of the Bank day by day; they use the resources of both the Banking Department and the Issue Department for these operations which generally take place in the money market; this matter is returned to below.

Bankers' deposits have taken on an enhanced significance since the introduction of the new monetary control arrangements from 20 August 1981.[1] Previously bankers' deposits were mostly current accounts of banks, predominantly those of

---

1 See, 'Methods of Monetary Control', *BEQB*, Vol. 20, No. 4, December 1980, pp. 428-9; 'Monetary Control: Next Steps', ibid., March 1981, pp. 38-9; and 'Monetary Control – Provisions', ibid., September 1981, pp. 347-9.

the London clearing banks and discount houses. But since 20 August 1981 they consist of what are called operational deposits and non-operational, non-interest-bearing deposits. As their name suggests operational deposits are those held, mainly by the London clearing banks, for settling clearing transactions and the purchase of Bank notes. Non-operational, non-interest-bearing-deposits refer to those deposits held to satisfy the new cash ratio imposed by the authorities on all recognized banks and licensed deposit-takers above a minimum size (see section III.4 *et seq.* below). The deposits are designed to provide resources to the Bank and to enable it to earn income from the corresponding assets.

Reserves and other accounts include balances of overseas central banks, certain dividend accounts, local authorities' and public corporation accounts, as well as unallocated profits of the Banking Department. The accounts of the Bank's remaining private customers are also included here. These accounts are not without importance but they are not central to this chapter and so are not discussed further.

Special deposits were first introduced in April 1960. Under the initial scheme the London clearing banks and Scottish clearing banks were from time to time obliged to transfer special deposits to the Bank in support of monetary and credit policy. This scheme came to an end in September 1971 when all outstanding special deposits were repaid and was replaced by a new scheme covering a much wider range of banks. The new monetary control arrangements introduced from 20 August 1981 also involve a special-deposits scheme. Special deposits are further discussed below.

Government securities introduce the assets of the Banking Department and include Treasury bills and government and government-guaranteed securities and ways and means advances to the Exchequer.[1] These advances occur if the Exchequer finds itself short of funds at the end of the day and wishes to make up its balance; the advances are generally only overnight loans, being repaid the following day.

The Banking Department, through sales and purchases of Treasury bills and government securities, affects the volume of bankers' deposits and hence the cash holdings of the banking system. In general, government securities in the Banking Department can be used in much the same way as those in the Issue Department to facilitate debt management and monetary policy. However, the assets at the disposal of the Banking Department are rather smaller than those available to the Issue Department.

Advances and other accounts are of three main types: advances to the discount market, loans to the remaining private customers of the Bank, and what are called support loans to deposit-taking institutions. The first are discussed in the section below dealing with the discount market. The second refers to loans made by the Bank to a number of secondary banks which had got into liquidity difficulties in the early 1970s through lending to certain property companies.

---

1 A 'bill' in the sense used here is a piece of paper which is evidence of indebtedness on the part of the person or body on whom it is drawn. The bill is said to be 'discounted' when it is purchased at a price below its value on maturity. Hence Treasury bills are evidence of indebtedness of the Treasury. These bills initially have usually ninety-one days to run to maturity and might be acquired by the discount houses at, say, £97.50 per £100, which would represent a discount of approximately 10% per annum on the value at maturity and a yield to the holder of about 10.28%.

Premises, equipment and other securities and notes and coins can be dealt with briefly. Other securities are non-government securities and include commercial bills purchased by the Bank in order to keep a watch on the quality of such bills circulating in the London market. The Bank will not purchase bills of which they disapprove and this acts as a deterrent to their circulation. Other securities also include local authority bills and bonds and some holdings of equity share capital of other companies. Notes are the counterpart of the items in the Issue Department and some coin is held for ordinary business purposes.

III.4   The Discount Market

The term discount market refers to the twelve discount houses that are members of the London Discount Market Association (LDMA). The discount houses constitute a unique set of highly specialized banking institutions which are at the centre of the day-to-day money market operations of the Bank of England as it implements its monetary and credit policies. Indeed the term money market is frequently restricted to operations involving the discount houses, though it is also used to cover all markets, including interbank markets, which deal in wholesale (large) sums for same-day settlement. The Bank has gone to considerable lengths in introducing its new monetary control arrangements to preserve and sustain the significance of the discount market in the operation of the monetary system. An examination of the balance sheet of the discount market makes this clear.

TABLE 2.4

Discount Market (selected items), 9 December 1981 (£m)

	Sterling	Other currencies	Total
Liabilities: Borrowed funds			
Bank of England	20	–	20
Other UK monetary sector	4,360	157	4,517
Other UK	318	13	331
Overseas	9	49	58
TOTAL	4,707	219	4,926
(of which call and overnight)	(4,413)		
Assets			
Cash deposits with Bank of England	2	–	2
UK and NI Treasury bills	99	–	99
Local authority and other public-sector bills	229	–	229
Other bills	2,663	34	2,697
Funds lent:			
UK monetary sector	34	–	34
Certificates of deposit	642	198	840
UK local authorities	120	–	120
Other United Kingdom	24	–	24
Overseas	–	–	
Investments:			
British Government stocks	742	–	742
Local authorities	243	–	243
Other	23	22	45
Other sterling assets	9	–	9
	4,830	254	5,084

Source: BEQB.

The borrowed funds from the Bank of England pinpoint one aspect of the special relationship between the discount houses and the bank. Apart from some institutions in the gilt-edged market — the market for government and government-guaranteed securities — the discount houses are the only financial institutions which may, when they cannot obtain funds from other sources, approach the Bank for funds. The Bank is then prepared to lend to the discount houses against suitable collateral but only 'on terms designed to discourage their use'.[1] In other words, the Bank will impose stiff conditions as regards collateral, duration and interest rates for this type of assistance; it is intended to be a 'last resort' form of help and not part of the day-to-day operations of the Bank.

By far the greater amount of borrowed funds, which, of course, constitute the liabilities of the discount houses, are denominated in sterling and come from the rest of the UK monetary sector in the form of call money, that is, a deposit which is placed on a day-to-day basis and which can be withdrawn any day before noon. Under the new monetary control arrangements, what are called 'eligible banks', that is, recognized banks whose acceptances are eligible for rediscount at or sale to the Bank,[2] have undertaken to hold on any day not less than the equivalent of 4% of their eligible liabilities (ELs) as secured funds with the members of the LDMA.[3] By August 1981 there were some 96 eligible banks, including the London clearing banks and all the major accepting houses. The 4% holding is defined as an average which is to be maintained by each eligible bank over either a six- or twelve-month period, whichever is preferred, in relation to their ELs on the last but one monthly bank return day; for example, the relevant ELs for each day in banking December will be those outstanding on the make-up day in banking October.

The reason given by the Bank for introducing this requirement for eligible banks — they must also similarly hold 2% of their ELs (making 6% in total) as secured call money with money brokers and gilt-edged jobbers[4] — was to ensure that there existed 'a market in bills of the size necessary for the Bank's open market operations'.[5] The Bank feared that with the abolition of the banks' reserve assets ratio (RAR) there might not be a market of sufficient scale for its money market activities (the RAR is discussed in section III.8 below). Implicit in this new emphasis on the market in bills — Treasury bills, local authority bills and commercial bills — is a determination of the Bank to allow market forces greater

---

1 'The Role of the Bank of England in the Money Market', *BEQB*, vol. 22, no. 1, March 1982, p. 87.

2 An 'acceptance' is a commercial bill on which a reputable bank has placed its name thus undertaking to honour the bill when it matures. An acceptance is also known as a bank bill, in contrast with a trade bill which is a commercial bill that has not been accepted by a bank.

3 Eligible liabilities of the banks are defined in section III.5 dealing with the London clearing banks. It may help to think of ELs as broadly the eligible deposit liabilities of each recognized bank and licensed deposit-taker. They are the basis for the Bank's determination of the amount of cash each institution must deposit with it in fulfillment of the new cash ratio requirement. Eligible banks, on the other hand, are those particular banks whose acceptances the Bank will rediscount or buy.

4 There are six recognized money brokers; the amount of secured call money they can take is limited by the Bank. See, 'Monetary Control — Provisions', op. cit., p. 348, fn. 3.

5 'Monetary Control: Next Steps,' op. cit., p. 39.

freedom to influence the rates ruling in bill markets and to avoid as far as possible secured lending to the discount market. These developments are all part of the new approach to monetary control.

From the definition of call money and more generally the secured money discussed above, it is evident that it is a highly liquid asset from the point of view of the banks, subject, of course, to eligible banks maintaining their required percentages. If for some reason, perhaps because of large net payments to government, the banks find themselves running short of funds they may decide not to renew some of their call money with the discount houses. The latter will then generally have to find funds by offering bills to the Bank. But under the new arrangements of 1981 the Bank no longer announces rates at which it will deal in bills and may refuse the offer in whole or in part if it is not satisfied with the rates involved. By this technique it is in a strong position to influence market rates in ways it considers consistent with its overall interest-rate policy. This policy at any point of time is defined in terms of maintaining short-term rates within an *unpublished* band. Notwithstanding the wish of the Bank to operate as described, it still retains the right to lend to the discount houses at rates of its own choosing. Thus in the ultimate the banks need have no fear that funds will be forthcoming if they decline to renew some or all of their secured money with the discount houses.

Turning to the assets of the discount market, it will be noticed that they have a small holding of cash deposits with the Bank of England. These are, in fact, part of the non-operational, non-interest-bearing deposits already mentioned in the discussion of the balance sheet of the Banking Department of the Bank. The members of the LDMA, like other banks, are now required since 20 August 1981 to hold one-half of one per cent (½%) of their ELs in such deposits.[1] The deposits play no part in day-to-day money market management and are fixed in amount twice a year for a period of six months. The ELs of the discount houses constitute their sterling deposits 'other than from institutions within the monetary sector and from money brokers and gilt-edged jobbers in the Stock Exchange'.[2] Since the bulk of the borrowed funds of the discount houses come from the rest of the monetary sector, it is not surprising that their cash deposits are relatively small in amount.

The discount houses occupy a very special position in the market for UK Treasury bills though these are in quantitative terms less important than formerly. One reason for this is that the authorities in the second half of the 1970s came increasingly to concentrate on controlling the rate of growth of the money stock and in so doing found it desirable and possible to press sales of government securities on the non-bank private sector; this enabled the authorities to reduce the volume of Treasury bills on offer. Nevertheless, the long-standing arrangement remains whereby the discount houses tender week-by-week for the whole issue of Treasury bills.[3] Each discount house determines the rate or rates at which it will tender. In the past if the discount houses did not have adequate funds to take up the whole tender the Bank stood ready to help by open-market purchases which

---

1 The ½% cash ratio requirement applies only to monetary sector institutions whose ELs average £10m or more over the calculation period.

2 'Monetary Control – Provisions', op. cit., p. 347.

3 The Bank also makes from time to time special issues of Treasury bills of less than 91 days to maturity to remove funds from the market. A recent example took place in September 1981 when large VAT refunds were expected; a dispute had delayed their earlier repayment.

provided the market with the necessary additional funds to acquire the new Treasury bills. This is tantamount to the Bank lending directly to the Treasury and is clearly open to abuse by an impecunious government. It must be presumed that with a commitment to let market forces have greater influence in determining interest rates this form of assistance by the Bank will disappear or be used infrequently.

It may be seen from table 2.4 that in terms of volume Treasury bills are greatly outweighed by other bills including local authority bills and commercial bills. The Bank in its market activities now operates on a large scale in both these latter categories of bills.

The remaining asset of the discount houses which is of particular importance to the monetary management of the authorities is British government stocks. Of the total holding of £742m on 9 December 1981, £174m had up to one year to run to maturity and £533m one to five years. This concentration of short-term government securities in the ownership of the discount houses facilitates the debt management policies of the authorities, as they can generally replace the stocks on or before maturity and so avoid making large cash payments.

It is evident from the foregoing discussion that the discount market has a pivotal role in monetary management and that the authorities have gone to considerable lengths in their new monetary arrangements to see that it is sustained and even strengthened.

III.5   The London Clearing Banks

The title London clearing banks (LCBs) refers to six banks which between them 'carry out the bulk of the nation's cash distribution and money transmission activities'.[1] The six banks are Barclays, Coutts, Lloyds, Midland, National Westminster and Williams and Glyn's. Money transmission necessarily involves an enormous volume of transfers both by paper (or voucher) and electronically between banks and bank branches. The offsetting of transfers between banks is known as clearing and is carried out through the Bankers' Clearing House or Bankers' Automated Clearing Services with net balances settled through the Bank of England. The two former institutions are owned by the six banks mentioned and hence the origin of the term London clearing banks.[2] Other banks are also able to make use of these clearing arrangements and may be admitted to membership of the Bankers' Clearing House.

The total business of the six clearing banks is dominated by the big four, Barclays, Lloyds, Midland and National Westminster. Between them they control over 95% of the total deposits of the group. Moreover, Coutts is a wholly owned subsidiary of National Westminster. More generally the LCBs have extensive ownership links with other banks and financial institutions, including the Scottish clearing banks and some of the Northern Ireland banks.

A feature of the LCBs (and also of the Scottish clearing banks and Northern Ireland banks) is that, of their total deposit liabilities, by far the greater

---

1 Committee to Review the Functioning of Financial Institutions (Wilson Committee), *Report and Appendices*, Cmnd. 7937, HMSO, June 1980, p. 408.

2 The Scottish clearing banks and the Northern Ireland banks carry out in their respective countries similar activities; limitations on space do not permit their separate discussion.

proportion is denominated in sterling: on 9 December 1981 £48,500m, as compared with £18,000m in foreign currencies. This position, as may be seen below in sections III.6 and III.7, contrasts strongly with that of many other banks and especially overseas banks where foreign or eurocurrency business is the dominant activity; the term eurocurrency is now in common use and refers to transactions denominated in currencies other than that of the country or jurisdiction in which the institution is located.

TABLE 2.5

London Clearing Banks, 9 December 1981 (£m)

	Sterling	Other currencies[1]	Total
(i) *Liabilities*			
Deposits:[2]			
UK monetary sector	2,582	3,448	6,030
UK public sector	606	} 2,001	} 43,057
UK private sector	40,450		
Overseas	3,028	11,559	14,587
Certificates of deposit	1,816	960	2,776
Capital and other funds and			
items in suspense, etc.			10,459
Total liabilities			76,909
(ii) *Assets*			
Notes and Coin	976	–	976
Balances with Bank of England			
Special and cash ratio deposits	167	–	167
Other	148	–	148
Bills:			
Treasury bills	287	–	287
Eligible local authority bills	150	–	150
Eligible bank bills	728	–	728
Other	92	46	138
Market loans and advances:			
Secured money with LDMA			
(market loans)	2,163	–	2,163
Other UK monetary sector[3]	6,055	7,142	13,197
Certificates of Deposit	785	138	923
UK local authorities (market loans)	441	–	441
Other UK (market loans)	293	–	293
Overseas	3,119	9,181	12,300
UK public sector (advances)	173	75	248
UK private sector (advances)	31,239	1,101	32,340
Investments:			
British government stocks	2,284	–	2,284
Other	2,021	887	2,908
Sterling and other currencies			
miscellaneous assets	–	–	7,218
Total assets			76,909

Source: BEQB.

1   Other currency liabilities and assets are valued in sterling at the closing middle-market spot rate on reporting days.

2   Sterling sight deposits amounted to £18,564m and were 38% of total sterling deposits of £48,482m.

3   Other UK monetary sector includes unsecured sterling lending to the LDMA and, under the heading of other currencies, market loans and advances to the UK monetary sector.

The relative dominance of the LCBs in terms of holdings of sterling deposits has been declining over the years. By 9 December 1981 the LCBs accounted for only 44% of gross sterling deposits of the monthly reporting institutions; twenty years earlier it would have been closer to twice this percentage.[1] These figures, however, accentuate the relative decline of the LCBs in a number of ways. They do not allow for inter-bank transactions, which, netted out, would tend to favour the LCBs, and a number of the other banks are their subsidiaries in whole or in part. The owner-ship of the deposits of the LCBs is heavily concentrated with the UK private sector which also contrasts with the position of other British banks and overseas banks; these two groups are much more dependent on overseas deposits, especially in foreign currencies.

Putting aside the currency distinction, deposits are of two main types; sight deposits and time deposits. Sight deposits, which may or may not be interest-bearing, are transferable or withdrawable on demand without interest penalty; they include the well-known current or chequeing accounts on which no interest is paid but where an abatement in charges may be allowed, depending on the balances maintained and the scale of transmission activity. Time deposits refer to all other deposits, except certificates of deposit which are shown separately in Table 2.5. Time deposits include the traditional interest-earning 7-day deposits, that is, deposits which require 7 days' notice of withdrawal, although it is common practice to waive this requirement and to adjust interest payments in lieu of notice. In addition, time deposits include wholesale deposits; these are large deposits, usually for amounts in excess of £50,000, which carry interest at rates reflecting conditions in the money markets both at home and abroad. The time-period of the deposits may vary from as little as 8 days to 5 years and over.

The advent of wholesale deposits – they first appeared in the 1960s – has given rise to what is called liability management. The latter is said to occur when a bank is approached for a loan or loans for specific time-periods, known as term loans, and matches the loans by bidding for or seeking out in the money markets deposits of corresponding term; thus in these circumstances little in the way of maturity transformation may take place, though risk transformation may still occur. This type of development which is particularly widespread amongst other British banks and overseas banks, known as the inter-bank market, is of considerable importance for the authorities in their attempts to control the rate of growth of bank deposits as part of the money stock.

A certificate of deposit (CD) is a negotiable instrument, denominated in sterling or dollars, issued by a bank in receipt for deposits for a fixed period of time and at a fixed rate of interest. The minimum amount of a CD is usually £50,000 and with an original term to maturity of between three months and 5 years. CDs have advantages for both the issuers and the holders. Issuing banks have found them to be a useful means of raising large amounts for strictly fixed periods – unlike the so-called fixed-term deposit where payment may be requested, and be hard to refuse, before maturity. Holders of CDs, including banks, have found them highly convenient as they can sell them in the secondary market if they need immediate funds for liquidity or other purposes. The discount houses are major operators in the secondary market but there is also an extensive inter-bank market.

---

1 Monthly reporting institutions are those members of the monetary sector which report on a monthly basis other than members of the LDMA, the trustee savings banks and the Banking Department of the Bank. Such institutions generally have a total balance sheet of £100m or over or ELs of £10m or over.

The remaining liabilities entry is items in suspense and transmission and capital and other funds. The former refers to credit balances received but not yet credited to customers' accounts and to items such as standing orders and credit transfers already debited to customers' accounts but not yet paid to the receiving body. Capital and other funds are mainly capital and reserves. These are of fundamental importance as a protection against insolvency through default on loans, investment losses and foreign exchange losses. The Bank of England is paying increasing attention to the adequacy of bank capital and reserves, and it will be recalled that to acquire under the 1979 Banking Act the status of a recognized bank or a licensed deposit-taker an institution has to satisfy the Bank about the adequacy of its capital. This matter now falls under the heading of prudential control of banking activities and is discussed further in section III.8 below.

Turning to the assets of the LCBs, notes and coin are required for their ordinary day-to-day business. Special and cash ratio deposits with the Bank refer only to the latter category as at the present time (April 1982) there are no special deposits. Cash ratio deposits were defined earlier in the discussions of the Bank and the discount houses. At £167m in December 1981 they amounted to almost exactly 50% of all cash ratio deposits with the Bank on that date and at current rates of interest should earn the latter some £20m in a year and so may be considered as a substantial charge on the LCBs. However from the point of view of the LCBs it is actually an improvement on the position before 20 August 1981 when they had, in agreement with the Bank, held with it on average the equivalent of 1½% of their ELs in non-interest-bearing deposits. Indeed it was formerly through variations in these deposits that the Bank sought to affect short-term interest rates in its money market operations. For example, downward pressure on these deposits would tend to lead to increases in interest rates in the money market as the LCBs sought to replenish their balances with the Bank. This technique still exists but is operated in relation to the operational deposits (see below) of the LCBs and not their cash ratio deposits.

ELs for the LCBs and other banks are not defined in quite the same way as for the discount houses. Broadly speaking, they comprise sterling deposit liabilities, excluding deposits with an initial maturity of over two years, since these are considered as more akin to loan capital than deposits; in addition ELs include any sterling resources obtained by switching foreign currencies into sterling; finally offsets to the foregoing are allowed for inter-bank transactions, except for cash ratio and any special deposits with the Bank, and adjustments are made for items in transit. The offsets mean that in the calculation of ELs those funds lent by one institution to another in the monetary sector are deductible as well as 'money at call placed with money brokers and gilt-edged jobbers in the Stock Exchange, and secured on gilt-edged stocks, Treasury bills, local authority bills and eligible bank bills'.[1] On 9 December 1981 the ELs of the LCBs totalled £38,100m whilst their sterling deposits were £48,500m.

The other balances of the LCBs with the Bank are their operational deposits and are voluntarily held for clearing and reserve purposes. It is noticeable that on 9 December 1981 at £148m they were actually smaller in total than the compulsory cash ratio deposits, and even when the former are combined with the £976m of their notes and coin holdings their total 'cash' of £1,124m represents only

---

1 'Monetary Control – Provisions', op. cit., p. 347.

2.3% of their total sterling deposits, putting aside their foreign currency deposit liabilities. Bearing in mind that the remaining banks in the UK monetary sector, as is indicated in sections III.6 and III.7 below, hold relatively little cash resources there is clearly an enormous pyramid of credit built on a slender cash base; this is the actual fulcrum of the monetary system on which the Bank operates through its open-market operations. The slenderness of the base is not necessarily a matter for alarm but neither is it a matter that should be ignored and it is certainly relevant to the whole issue of the prudential control of the monetary sector.

Leaving aside any further discussion of bills, as these were considered in section III.4, the next major category of assets is market loans and advances. Market loans refer to loans made at rates determined in the various money markets and are often made through the agency of money brokers; the loans may be secured or unsecured, are mainly with other members of the monetary sector and may be denominated in sterling or other currencies.

The secured money with the LDMA – which is considerably in excess of the minimum requirement of 4% of ELs for eligible banks – together with most bills and other balances with the Bank, formerly constituted the major part of the reserve assets the banks were required to hold under the 1971 Competition and Credit Control (CCC) arrangements. The actual RAR was originally 12½% of ELs but in preparation for the introduction of the new monetary control arrangements was reduced to 10% in January 1981 and following a temporary reduction to 8% for most of March and April 1981 was abolished in August 1981. The CCC arrangements and the reasons for the abolition of the RAR and the alternative supervision by the authorities of liquid asset holdings of the banks are discussed below in section III.8.

Advances include all direct lending to customers, with or without collateral, and may take the form of fixed-term loans or overdrafts. With loans, the customer's account is credited in accordance with the agreed drawing arrangements, whereas the overdraft is literally an overdrawing of a current account which is correspondingly debited. In principle the overdraft is repayable on demand and its size is subject to an agreed limit which may be revised from time to time. Loans may be for different periods; from 5 to 7 years is quite common and it is possible to negotiate longer-term loans.

The interest rates charged on loans and advances vary considerably, depending on the duration as regards loans, the creditworthiness of the borrower, the purposes for which funds are required and the security provided by the borrower. At any point of time the actual rates charged will be related directly or indirectly to those ruling in the wholesale deposit and other money markets. The link may be indirect, in that each of the LCBs declares a *base rate* which is itself related to rates in the money markets and may then use its base rate to determine charges for advances; most rates are between 1% and 5% higher than base rate.

Sterling advances by the LCBs to the private sector totalled £31,200m on 9 December 1981 and are clearly of enormous importance to the operation of the economic system; they constituted some 50% of all advances of monthly reporting banks in the UK. Moreover, the sterling advances of the LCBs to the private sector have been growing extremely rapidly in the last few years; between December 1978 and December 1981 they increased by almost 100% and had grown from being 54% to 64% of sterling deposits. This development undoubtedly reflects in part the difficulties of the company sector in a period of severe economic recession.

III.6   Accepting Houses and Other British Banks

Accepting houses and other British banks are classified separately in the statistical tables of the *BEQB* but they have sufficient monetary and financial activities in common to justify discussing them together. The term 'accepting houses' as used here refers to the 17 members of the Accepting Houses Committee and certain of their banking subsidiaries in the Channel Islands and Isle of Man. But the term originally arose because of the important role the houses played and still play in accepting commercial bills on behalf of clients; for this service they receive a commission, which clients are willing to pay, as accepted bills command a lower rate of discount in the market. In December 1981 the accepting houses had £2,500m of acceptances outstanding, about 28% of the total for monthly reporting institutions; the corresponding overall balance sheet proportion was around 4%.

Accepting houses are also known as merchant banks since the banking activities of a number of them emerged as a consequence of their business as merchants, particularly in overseas trade. The accepting houses now provide a wide range of banking services, mainly for the corporate sector. Their activities encompass operations in the following areas: the wholesale deposit markets for both sterling and foreign currencies — the latter is now the larger of the two; large-scale term lending to corporate borrowers; the foreign exchange market; the gold and silver bullion markets; in the making and underwriting of new issues both in sterling and other currencies — the main accepting houses are all members of the Issuing Houses Association; advising on mergers and takeovers; managing investments on behalf of clients, including investment trusts, unit trusts, insurance companies and pension funds; and acting as trustees.

The accepting houses and other British banks as deposit-takers are subject to the requirements of the 1979 Banking Act and to the new monetary control arrangements. These requirements are, in part, reflected in the aggregate balance sheet for the two sets of institutions. It may be seen in table 2.6 that on 9 December 1981 these institutions held £64m of cash ratio deposits in fulfilment of the ½% of ELs requirement under the new monetary arrangements and £827m secured money with the LDMA; the ELs of the accepting houses and other British banks were £3,081m and £15,176m respectively (these figures are not shown in table 2.6). It should also be noted that for the two sets of institutions the distinguishable sterling and other currency assets at £35.2m and £42.6m (the totals are not shown in table 2.6) exceeded the corresponding sterling and other currency deposits; in other words there is an approximate matching of liabilities and assets according to currency. This suggests that there may be relatively little switching from, say, foreign currency assets into sterling assets, which is a matter of some significance for monetary and credit policy. Such switching could, for instance, permit an extension of domestic credit. This matter is returned to in section III.8.

Other British banks (the Bank describes them as British banks: other) refers to those monthly reporting institutions with majority UK ownership, leaving aside the London and Scottish clearing banks, the Northern Ireland banks, the accepting houses and consortium banks. The group also includes certain subsidiaries in the Channel Islands and the Isle of Man, certain UK-registered institutions which are owned by overseas residents, but which operate only in the UK domestic market, the offices in GB of the NI banks and some further subsidiaries of those banks. Before the introduction of the new monetary control arrangements the group had

TABLE 2.6

Accepting Houses and Other British Banks, 9 December 1981 (£m)

	Sterling	Other currencies[1]	Total
(i) *Liabilities*			
Deposits:[2]			
UK monetary sector	12,026	13,494	25,520
UK public sector	524	{ 2,291	{ 15,437
UK private sector	12,622		
Overseas	4,191	23,432	27,623
Certificates of deposit	1,285	2,363	3,648
Capital and other funds and items in suspense, etc.	–	–	8,786
Total liabilities			81,014
(ii) *Assets*			
Notes and Coin	36	–	36
Balances with Bank of England:			
Special and cash ratio deposits	64	–	64
Other	7	–	7
Bills:			
Treasury bills	194	–	194
Eligible local authority bills	96	–	96
Eligible bank bills	378	–	378
Other	66	30	96
Market loans and advances:			
Secured money with LDMA (market loans)	827	–	827
Other UK monetary sector[3]	8,315	8,121	16,436
Certificates of deposit	2,059	583	2,642
UK local authorities (market loans)	2,777	–	2,777
Other UK (market loans)	714	–	714
Overseas	2,669	29,216	31,885
UK public sector (advances)	414	380	794
UK private sector (advances)	14,464	2,804	17,268
Investments:			
British government stocks	953	–	953
Other	1,165	1,527	2,692
Sterling and other currencies miscellaneous assets	–	–	3,155
Total assets			81,014

Source: BEQB.

1 and 3   See corresponding footnotes to table 2.5.

2   Sterling sight deposits amounted to £5,961m and were 19% of total sterling deposits of £30,648m.

some 65 members but this will now have increased. Their composition is evidently highly varied, covering international banks which transact much of their business abroad; merchant and wholesale banking subsidiaries of the clearing banks, which operate in much the same way as the accepting houses; former finance houses and leasing companies which as deposit-takers come under the provisions of the 1979 Banking Act; domestic banks such as the Co-operative Bank and the Yorkshire

Bank, which are small relatively to the major LCBs and offer mainly retail banking services through branches and other outlets; and the National Girobank. The latter is exempt from the provisions of the Banking Act.

On 9 December 1981 their total balance sheet at £64.3m represented some 15% of the corresponding balance sheet for all monthly reporting institutions. Of their total deposits of £57.3m, some 43% were denominated in sterling and 57% in other currencies. However, the ratio of sterling deposits to other currency deposits varies widely between institutions, ranging from zero to nearly 100%.

The finance houses included in the group, whilst carrying out many typical banking functions as regards both the type and management of their liabilities and assets, employ considerable amounts of funds in instalment lending and leasing to industrial and other companies, as well as engaging in consumer instalment lending. Finance houses commonly operate through branch offices but they also offer their facilities through retailers or dealers at the point of sale. The customer of the product is generally able to arrange through the retailer or dealer an appropriate form of loan, hire-purchase or similar type of finance. The provisions of the 1974 Consumer Credit Act are central to the activities of finance houses and similar bodies. Broadly speaking the Act regulates all lending to non-corporate borrowers for amounts up to £5,000 except that under the 1979 Banking Act bank lending by way of overdrafts is exempt. The Act also provides for a system of licences relating to the consumer credit and hire-purchase industry and controls the form of credit advertisements. In addition, consumer instalment credit is regulated by hire-purchase control orders, which stipulate the minimum deposit which must be paid by the would-be purchaser and the maximum repayment period.[1]

The National Girobank is intended to provide a simple, cheap, accessible money-transmission service for those who ordinarily do not have chequeing accounts with banks. Accessibility is achieved by offering its services through some 21,000 post offices throughout the UK. Following a review of the activities of the National Giro (it was renamed the National Girobank in 1978), which had grown much more slowly than expected, it was decided in 1975 to extend the range of banking services offered. These now include both current and interest-bearing deposit accounts and certain limited lending to personal customers. But at 31 March 1980 its customers' balances were only some £500m.

The trustee savings banks (TSBs) are not formally described as other British banks in the statistical tables of the Bank and they do not come under the provisions of the 1979 Banking Act, but they are included in the new monetary sector. It is convenient to consider them in this section as they have now much in common with some of the domestic retail banks.

A trustee savings bank is an unincorporated society run by trustees and offering a range of banking services, mostly to individuals. For some 160 years until 1976 they had been obliged to invest most of their funds with the public sector. But the 1976 Trustee Savings Bank Act made provision for a gradual relaxation of government controls over their activities, and since then they have increased the banking services they offer, including lending to the general public. It is the intention that the TSBs should become fully fledged commercial banks.

---

1   There are a great many small companies and other bodies involved in consumer credit activities besides the finance houses discussed in this section; but in financial terms their activities are small.

As part of the process, the number of TSBs has been reduced from over 70 to 16 and between them they have over 1,600 branches. There is also a Central Trustee Savings Bank which was established in 1973 and is now a recognized bank under the 1979 Banking Act; it provides a comprehensive range of banking, clearing and investment services to the TSBs.

At 31 December 1981 the TSBs had sight deposits (current and savings accounts) of £1,950m and time deposits of almost £4,100m. Together these represented the equivalent of some 5.5% of the total sterling deposits of monthly reporting institutions; it is estimated that the inclusion of TSBs deposits in the sterling M_3 definition of the money stock will bring about a once-for-all increase of about 7.5%.[1] The assets of the TSBs on the same date were still heavily concentrated in public-sector debt, but this will decrease as further relaxation of government control takes place. However, advances to customers, whilst on a small scale, had reached £675m. The TSBs should become a useful source of competition for the clearing banks in the provision of retail banking services.

III.7 Overseas Banks and Consortium Banks

In the statistical tables of the Bank, overseas banks are classified into three categories; American, Japanese and others. Before the introduction of the new monetary control arrangements the numbers in each category were approximately 60, 22 and 130 respectively; the numbers may be slightly greater now. Branches as well as subsidiaries of foreign banks are included in the overseas category, as are certain branches and subsidiaries in the Channel Islands and the Isle of Man.

Consortium banks are banks 'which are owned by banks or financial institutions but in which no one bank or financial institution has a direct shareholding of more than 50%, and in which at least one shareholder is based overseas'.[2] The activities of both overseas banks and consortium banks are heavily concentrated on foreign or eurocurrency business; such banks are frequently referred to as eurobanks and the markets in which they operate as euromarkets. These markets are truly international in that they involve banks outside the UK and link together the major banking centres of the world; indeed, much of the trading in the euromarkets is inter-bank and may give rise to a chain of transactions between banks before funds end up with non-bank customers. It is evident that the activities of eurobanks and the existence of eurocurrency markets raise important issues for domestic monetary control and for the prudential supervision of banking systems.[3]

The scale of eurocurrency business undertaken by the overseas banks and consortium banks may be appreciated from table 2.7. On 9 December 1981 the foreign currency deposits of these banks totalled £227,000m (the total is not shown in the table), representing some 79% of all foreign currency deposits of monthly reporting institutions; and of the total of £227,000m over 60% were overseas deposits, mostly with overseas banks. Moreover, the foreign currency deposits of the overseas banks and consortium banks were almost ten times as large as their sterling deposits at some £24,000m. This is not intended to imply that the latter are insignificant; they constituted some 22% of sterling deposits of monthly

---

1 Sterling M_3 is defined below, p. 88.

2 *BEQB*, vol. 22, no. 1, March 1982.

3 See, 'Eurobanks and the Inter-Bank Market', *BEQB*, vol. 21, no. 3, September 1981, pp. 351-64. See also section III.8 below.

reporting institutions and were equivalent to nearly 50% of the sterling deposits of the LCBs.

TABLE 2.7

Overseas Banks and Consortium Banks, 9 December 1981 (£m)

	Sterling	*Other currencies*[1]	*Total*
(i) *Liabilities*			
Deposits:[2]			
UK monetary sector	9,044	47,027	56,071
UK public sector	64	{ 5,685	{ 11,024
UK private sector	5,275		
Overseas	6,165	137,193	143,358
Certificates of deposit	3,169	36,897	40,066
Capital and other funds and			
items in suspense, etc.	–	–	4,581
Total liabilities			255,100
(ii) *Assets*			
Notes and Coin	15	–	15
Balances with Bank of England:			
Special and cash ratio deposits	68	–	68
Other	3	–	3
Bills:			
Treasury bills	142	–	142
Eligible local authority bills	32	–	32
Eligible bank bills	273	–	273
Other	110	745	855
Market loans and advances:			
Secured money with LDMA			
(market loans)	999	–	999
Other UK monetary sector[3]	6,319	45,863	52,182
Certificates of deposit	1,179	4,720	5,899
UK local authorities (market loans)	2,053	–	2,053
Other UK (market loans)	426	–	426
Overseas	3,451	160,854	164,305
UK public sector (advances)	2,396	430	2,826
UK private sector (advances)	7,743	10,680	18,423
Investments:			
British government stocks	559	–	559
Other	480	2,882	3,362
Sterling and other currencies			
miscellaneous assets	–	–	2,673
Total assets[4]			255,095

Source: BEQB.

1 and 3   See corresponding footnotes to table 2.5.

2   Sterling sight deposits amounted to £3,529m and were 15% of total sterling deposits of £23,717m.

4   Total assets and total liabilities do not come to exactly the same amount because of rounding errors.

However, the private-sector sterling deposits of the overseas banks and consortium banks were only 22% of their total sterling deposits whereas the corresponding figure for the LCBs was 83%. But this position may not last, as the American overseas banks, in particular, are making determined efforts to move into domestic banking.

On the assets side of the balance sheet of the overseas banks and the consortium banks, the predominant foreign currency asset is overseas market loans and advances at £161,000m; these funds are mostly on loan to overseas banks. Of their sterling assets their cash ratio deposits of £68m are less than half as large as the corresponding deposits of the LCBs, again reflecting the smaller involvement of the former in domestic banking. Nevertheless, the overseas banks and the consortium banks are of major importance to the UK monetary and financial system. How the authorities attempt to influence and control that system is the subject of the next section.

III.8   The Authorities and Monetary and Prudential Control

It was mentioned in section II.2 that the Bank in its approach to monetary policy had come to espouse what the Governor termed practical monetarism. One reason was the belief that the demand for money is stable in terms of its relationship to certain income concepts and interest rates. This belief seemed to hold out the possibility that if the authorities could control the relevant interest rates for any given level of income, the short-run demand for money would be determined, except for random components, and with it the stock of money in existence. However, the confidence of the authorities that they could determine the stock of money in this way may never have been great and, at least as regards the M_3 definition of money, was severely shaken in the two years following the introduction of their CCC measures in September 1971; these measures were designed to permit and encourage greater competition in the monetary system and at the same time rely on market methods of controlling it rather than quantitative restrictions. But between the fourth quarters of 1971 and 1973 the minimum lending rate (MLR) at which the Bank then lent funds to the discount market had risen from 5% per annum to 13%, a very large increase by historical standards; and yet M_3 had increased by the extraordinary figure of 64%.

Faced with this problem the authorities had to modify their immediate commitment to the objectives of CCC, and in late 1973 they introduced the supplementary special deposits (SSD) scheme, which came to be known as the 'corset'. In broad terms, the SSD scheme, which was a form of direct control, required banks (and certain finance houses) whose interest-bearing deposits grew at more than a prescribed rate, to place non-interest-bearing deposits with the Bank. The faster the banks' interest-bearing deposits grew in excess of the prescribed rate, the more deposits the banks had to place with the Bank. In short the scheme was designed to severely penalize the banks for any 'undue' expansion of their interest-bearing deposits. But the Bank for many reasons was not happy with the SSD scheme and brought it to an end in June 1980.[1]

Meanwhile, for a number of years the authorities had concentrated their attention on the longer-run demand for money. The justification for this would

1 See 'The Supplementary Special Deposits Scheme', *BEQB*, vol. 22, no. 1, March 1982. pp. 74-85.

seem to be that, notwithstanding the experience of 1972 and 1973, there was evidence suggesting that the longer-run demand for money was reasonably stable.

It is a plausible step from this position to suggest that there should be target rates of growth of the money stock over a period of years and that it is unnecessary to be unduly concerned about temporary departures from the growth path; which is not to say it is easy to recognize what is a temporary departure.

But the question arises what monetary aggregate should be employed for target or control purposes? The preferred concept of the authorities is known as sterling M_3 ($£M_3$) and includes notes and coin in circulation with the public, together with all sterling deposits (including certificates of deposit) held by UK residents in both the public and private sectors; some allowance is made for items in transit between the banks to avoid double counting. $£M_3$ is, of course, related to M_1 and M_3 as defined earlier; in fact, $£M_3$ subsumes M_1, and M_3 equals $£M_3$ plus all deposits held by UK residents in other currencies.

The main reason why the authorities prefer $£M_3$ is that it can be related, at least in an arithmetic sense, to changes in some key credit counterparts which in turn link it to the fiscal, credit and exchange-rate policies of the authorities. The term 'credit counterparts' refers in the first instance to the assets side of the balance sheet of the monetary sector, and overall monetary policy comes to be formulated in terms of influencing the rate of growth of these assets and is sometimes referred to as a 'supply side' approach to monetary control. In other words the thrust of monetary control is not towards a direct effect on the demand for money but to influence the 'supply' of those assets which are the counterparts of the money stock and, by this means, to attempt to control its rate of growth.

It is helpful in following this argument to make use of a stylized and simplified balance sheet of the monetary sector.[1] The balance sheet on the liabilities side includes, under the heading of sterling deposits of UK residents, deposits of both the private and public sectors, the main components of $£M_3$; the other main component of the latter being notes and coin in circulation with the public.[2]

Monetary Sector Balance Sheet

Liabilities	*Assets*
Sterling deposits:	Sterling lending to:
UK residents	UK public sector
Banks abroad (net)	UK private sector
Other overseas	Overseas non-banks
Foreign currency deposits	Foreign currency assets
Non-deposit liabilities (net)	
Total liabilities	Total assets

It follows from the definition of $£M_3$ that:

the change in $£M_3$ = the change in notes and coin in circulation with the public *plus* the change in sterling deposits of UK residents

---

1 Adapted from 'Money, Credit and Liquidity', Section 7, *Financial Statistics: Explanatory Handbook*, HMSO, April 1982, p. 69.

2 It should be recalled that the Issue Department of the Bank of England and the Royal Mint are not part of the monetary sector, and so notes and coin in circulation with the public are not included in the stylized balance sheet.

It also follows from re-arranging the monetary sector balance sheet that:

the change in sterling
   deposits of UK residents   = the change in sterling lending to:

                          UK public sector
                          UK private sector
                          Overseas non-banks

                          less the increase in:
                          sterling deposits from banks abroad (net)
                          other overseas sterling deposits
                          foreign currency deposits net of foreign currency assets
                          non-deposit liabilities (net)

The next step is to consider the financing of the public sector, and in particular, the public-sector borrowing requirement (PSBR), broadly the difference between public-sector expenditure and receipts. Now the PSBR can be financed by borrowing from the private sector and the monetary sector and through transactions with the overseas sector. Alternatively whatever part of the PSBR is not financed by the private and overseas sectors is financed by the monetary sector under the heading of the change in sterling lending to the public sector. Hence it follows that:

the change in sterling lending
   to the UK public sector
   (by the monetary sector)   = the PSBR (surplus = −)
                          less
                          net purchases of public-sector debt by the UK private sector
                          less
                          external and foreign currency finance of the public sector

Thus the items on the right-hand side of the equality sign may be substituted into the re-arranged balance sheet of the monetary sector for the change in sterling lending to the public sector. This is, in fact, carried out below, making use at the same time of the definition of the change in $£M_3$ mentioned above. It may be noted that the main debt instruments involved in purchases of public-sector debt by the UK private sector are national savings, certificates of tax deposit and government securities. Each of these items is included in *net* purchases of public-sector debt by the UK private sector, but notes and coin are excluded in the presentation below. This *net* figure also does not allow for purchases of commercial bills by the Issue Department of the Bank of England which constitutes lending by the public sector to the private sector. The latter is taken account of below by including it with sterling lending to the private sector. The outcome is as follows:

the change in $£M_3$ =   (a) the PSBR
                                 less (b) *net* purchases of public-sector debt by the UK
  Domestic counterparts   private sector (excluding the change in notes and coin in
    (a), (b) and (c)   circulation with the public)
                                 plus (c) the change in sterling lending to the UK private
                                      sector by the monetary sector and the Issue Department
                                      of the Bank

(*continued*)

	plus (d) the change in sterling lending to overseas non-banks
External and foreign	*less* the increase in:
currency counterparts	(e) sterling deposits from banks abroad (net)
(d), (e), (f), (g) and	(f) other overseas sterling deposits
(h)	(g) foreign currency deposits net of foreign currency assets
	(h) external and foreign currency finance of the public sector

(i) non-deposit liabilities (net)

Thus putting aside the non-deposit liabilities of the banks, the credit counter-parts to the increase in £M$_3$ may be related to what the authorities call 'domestic counterparts' and 'external and foreign currency counterparts'.[1] Hence the supply-side approach to monetary control may be formulated in terms of policies to influence the behaviour of the domestic and external and foreign currency counterparts to £M$_3$.[2]

Broadly speaking the PSBR may be seen as related to fiscal policy, the sale of public-sector debt to debt management policy, sterling lending to credit policy, and currency flows to exchange-rate policy. This is not to say that the policies are or can be independent; a change in fiscal policy, for example, is likely to have repercussions on not only the PSBR but also public-sector debt sales, interest rates and credit conditions generally, and exchange rates.

It seems evident that approaching the problem of monetary control from the supply side is necessarily hazardous. The various credit counterparts can and do vary greatly in ways that are clearly not amenable to fine-tuning by the authorities. Furthermore, it is unlikely that there is any simple causal relationship between the major credit counterparts and £M$_3$; a change in one may be offset in whole or in part by changes in the others. In particular, there may be no systematic causal link between the PSBR and changes in £M$_3$.

Notwithstanding this, and the authorities are perfectly aware of it, they remain convinced that over the longer term it is essential to reduce the PSBR as part of the medium-term financial strategy (MTFS) for bringing down the rate of growth of the money stock, reducing the rate of inflation and encouraging economic growth. In taking up this position, which is a controversial one, they are, of course, espousing a view about the operation of the economy over time, rather than relying on balance-sheet arithmetic as outlined above. However, it is possible to sympathize with the medium-term goals of the authorities without endorsing their supply-side approach to monetary control (see section V.1 below).

As regards debt management and credit policies, or more generally interest-rate policies, the authorities have on the one hand emphasized their need to be able to vary interest rates as a means of influencing some of the credit counterparts in order to control £M$_3$, and on the other stressed their wish to give market forces greater play in the determination of interest rates. On the face of it there is some contradiction between these positions. The former is wedded to the assets supply-

---

1 See also table 2.13 below.

2 A variation of the supply-side approach to monetary control emphasizes domestic credit expansion (DCE). DCE has two main components, the domestic counterparts referred to in the text and monetary sector lending in sterling to overseas residents. The latter includes lending to both banks and non-banks. Since the abolition of exchange controls in 1979 the growth in gross movements of funds involving banks abroad has somewhat obscured the concept of DCE.

side approach to monetary control, whereas the latter would seem to lean towards a monetary base control system (see below). But perhaps it would be fairer to the authorities to interpret the difference in emphasis between the two positions as indicating an evolution in their thinking and policy.

Certainly the CCC measures of 1971, which imposed the minimum RAR of 12.5% across the banking system and extended to all banks (except the NI banks) the special deposits scheme, were designed to give the authorities leverage over the liquidity of the banks as a means of influencing interest rates and in turn affect the credit counterparts of the money stock. The theory was that open-market operations of the Bank and/or calls for special deposits could engineer a transfer of funds to the authorities and so put pressure on liquid assets. However, the theory did not work as envisaged and contributed to distortions in the interest-rate structure and, in any event, the 1½% of their ELs that the LCBs held as balances with the Bank, rather than the RAR, became the effective fulcrum for the Bank in affecting interest rates in the money market.[1] In the light of this the authorities concluded that they no longer required the RAR and, as has already been indicated, abolished it. However, they also saw the RAR as having relevance as a form of prudential liquidity requirement for the banks; this aspect of the matter is returned to below.

The distortions brought about by the RAR and by the SSD scheme referred to earlier, gave rise to an increasing concern on the part of the authorities with what is called 'disintermediation'; this arises where funds get diverted from the channels through which they would otherwise flow by virtue of the imposition of administered controls and restrictions. This response, of course, defeats the purposes of the authorities in whole or in part and may create additional problems in that once controls are introduced it may be difficult to find an opportune time for their removal. It would seem to be considerations such as these together with the commitment to monetary targets which has encouraged the authorities to explore the possibilities of monetary base control.

A monetary base system generally means one in which the banks hold, either because it is mandatory or for prudential reasons, base money which is commonly defined to include bankers' deposits with the central bank and may also include their holdings of central-bank notes and official coin as well as those held by the public. Thus in the widest sense base money constitutes deposit and note liabilities of the central bank plus official coinage. In principle this base money is under the control of the authorities, and by regulating its supply they can, on certain conditions, control or at any rate influence the volume of deposits of the banking system and more generally the supply of money.

The most widely understood monetary base system is probably the textbook mandatory one where the banks are required to hold base money in a fixed proportion to deposits. The simplest is where the proportion relates to deposits and base money on the same date — known as current accounting — but it is possible to envisage a lagged accounting system where 'current base requirements are fixed by reference to deposits in a previous period ... (or) lead accounting where the holding of base assets would put a limit on deposits for some future date'.[2] Alternatively a monetary base system might be non-mandatory or

---

1 *Monetary Control*, Cmnd. 7858, HMSO, March 1980.

2 ibid., p. 10.

voluntary, where the banking system finds it desirable to maintain a fairly systematic relationship through time between its deposit liabilities and base money.

It is apparent, however, that the authorities in their Green Paper on *Monetary Control* were not thinking in terms of a monetary base system as outlined above. For them a monetary base system 'is intended to provide a means for the markets to generate the interest rates necessary to bring the rate of growth of the money supply back towards the desired path'.[1] Thus the authorities would seem to be thinking in terms of influencing the credit counterparts to the money stock rather than in terms of a monetary base system as indicated above which, if implemented, would impinge directly on the operations of the banks. The latter would, of course, bring about changes in interest rates but these would be consequential instead of being an intermediate target and the question of how they affected the so-called credit counterparts would not be of direct concern. Friedman and other economists would argue that this approach is the more efficient way to tackle monetary control.[2] The authorities have still to be convinced and the debate is far from settled.

Closely related to the issue of monetary control is the prudential control of the monetary system. By prudential control is meant the oversight by the authorities of the banks and other financial institutions to ensure that their capital and reserve assets and their liquid assets are sufficient to enable them to meet their domestic and foreign currency liabilities. The matter of prudential control has become of increasing importance in the last ten years. During 1973-4 there occurred a so-called fringe or secondary banking crisis, when to avoid their likely default a number of financial institutions had to be extensively supported by the Bank and the London and Scottish clearing banks; the support scheme became known as the 'lifeboat' operation. This experience has prompted a more active interest in bank supervision. In addition, the Directive of the European Community on Credit Institutions requires the UK to authorize institutions taking deposits from the public; indeed, this was one reason for the introduction of the 1979 Banking Act.

The Bank, in approaching the task of more formal prudential control of the banks, has issued three papers dealing with different but related aspects of the problem: 'The Measurement of Capital', 'The Liquidity of Banks' and 'Foreign Currency Exposure'; published respectively in the *Bank of England Quarterly Bulletins* of September 1980, March 1981 and June 1981. Prudential controls, like all administered controls, impose costs on institutions and to that extent may give rise to some disintermediation. This possibility has become particularly important as banking has developed into an international industry, able to offer highly competitive services outside the jurisdiction of any single country. The authorities are undoubtedly conscious of these matters and decide their policies accordingly.

III.9   Other Financial Institutions

The United Kingdom is particularly rich in the variety and number of its financial institutions. The term 'rich' is used advisedly for financial institutions that are able to engage in maturity and risk transformation of securities or otherwise mediate

---

1   ibid., p. 8.

2   Milton Friedman, 'Memorandum on Monetary Policy', Treasury and Civil Service Committee, Session 1979-80, *Memoranda on Monetary Policy*, HC, (1979-80) 720, pp. 55-61, HMSO.

freely between borrowers and lenders, facilitate the achievement by both parties of a preferred distribution of their assets and liabilities, and help to make the allocation of scarce resources more efficient; limitations on space prevent more than a brief mention of some major financial institutions.[1]

Building societies: Building societies are mutual or non-profit-making bodies which specialize in the provision of finance for the purchase of both new and secondhand houses. There are some 270 building societies, about 12% of the number some eighty years ago. The individual societies vary greatly in size, from some very large ones with a national network of branches to those with only one office.

Over 90% of the liabilities of the building societies are shares and deposits. Both are essentially deposits, so that the term 'share' is something of a misnomer. However, the shareholder is a member of the society whereas the depositor is not, and the latter has a prior right of liquidation over the shareholder. The variety of the terms and conditions governing the payment of interest on, and the withdrawal of, shares and deposits has increased greatly in recent years as the societies have found it necessary to compete for funds, not least with the national savings movement. Shares and deposits are subject to notice of withdrawal, though in practice both are paid on demand or on very short notice, except for fixed-term deposits. The interest rates on shares and deposits are quoted *net* of income tax, which is paid by the societies at an average or composite rate and is less than the basic rate of tax. In early 1982 the interest rate recommended by the Building Societies Association on ordinary shares was 8.75%. This rate is net of tax and is equivalent to 12.5% before deduction of basic tax. The rate of growth of the shares and deposits of the building societies has been very rapid in the ten years to 1980: from £10,000m to £50,000m. This last figure is considerably in excess of the total sterling deposits of £42,000m of the London clearing banks at the end of 1980.

Mortgages usually account for about 80% of the assets of building societies and are predominantly for private house purchase. Most mortgages are for between twenty and thirty years, with continuous repayment by instalments. The average life is generally about seven years, making the assets of building societies much shorter-lived than they might appear. The recommended interest rate on new mortgages to owner-occupiers was 13.5% in early 1982. But this is the gross rate, as interest payments on a housing loan – up to £25,000 for a principal residence – are allowable against income-tax assessments: if allowance is made for income-tax relief at the basic rate, the interest rate is reduced to 9.45% net. For those who pay less than the basic rate of tax, or no tax at all, there is an option mortgage scheme, supported by the government, which reduces the cost – though this system is due to change in April 1983 when mortgage interest will thereafter be paid net of basic tax and the option mortgage scheme will disappear.

All the other assets, except such things as office premises, are classified as liquid assets by the societies. Liquid assets must be at least 7.5% of total assets, and both the type of asset and the maturity distribution are regulated by the Chief Registrar of Building Societies. At the end of 1981 the actual liquid-assets ratio was over 19% of total assets. Cash holdings and balances with banks are relatively small and vary a lot seasonally. The societies cannot for long expand the supply of finance to borrowers unless there is a corresponding net inflow of funds from new

---

1 For a more extensive treatment see Wilson Committee, op. cit.

shares and deposits; otherwise they would deplete their liquid assets and in time risk upsetting public confidence in their management. The interest rates the societies pay and the relationship they bear to the competing rates would appear to be a major determinant of the net inflow of funds to the societies.

The building societies dominate the market providing finance for home purchase and they are therefore relevant, directly and indirectly, to the activity of the house-building industry. However, they are experiencing increasing competition from the LCBs and other banks for house-mortgage lending and there is strong evidence that the rather staid world of the building societies is undergoing substantial change as it responds to new market pressures.

Insurance companies: There are some 870 insurance companies, which vary greatly in size, engaged in business in the UK, though the principal business of a considerable number is overseas. By far the greater part of UK business is carried on by the members of the British Insurance Association, which has less than three hundred members. The fundamental purpose of insurance is to facilitate the spread of risk between persons and bodies and through time.

Insurance falls into two main categories: life assurance, and a catch-all, general insurance, which includes fire, marine, motor and other accident insurance. The insurance companies also operate the pension schemes of many industrial and commercial companies. Life assurance for the most part gives rise to long-term liabilities which the companies must be in a position to meet. This gives them an interest in long-term investments and in assets that may be expected to increase in capital value over the years. General insurance, on the other hand, is carried on much more on a year-to-year basis, ideally with premiums for the year being sufficient to cover the risks underwritten and to allow for expenses and the accumulation of limited reserves. So the disposition of funds arising from general insurance is largely governed by short-term considerations; assets must be quickly realizable without undue fear of capital loss. The insurance companies as a whole, with total investments at the end of 1980 of over £65,000m, are of great importance in the UK's capital markets. They are large holders of both government and company securities. Their growth has been encouraged by tax privileges, particularly tax relief on life-insurance premiums.

The Department of Trade under the 1974 Insurance Companies Act has extensive powers of supervision over the activities of insurance companies. These powers are mainly designed to give protection to policyholders and have been influenced by membership requirements of the European Community. Insurance companies must demonstrate annually that their assets exceed their liabilities. If the Department of Trade suspects that a company might be unable to meet its liabilities it may take certain measures including the strong sanction of prohibiting the company undertaking new business. Policyholders have also the protection of the 1975 Policyholders Protection Act, 'which broadly speaking provides that where an insurance company goes into liquidation its liabilities to policyholders will be met up to 90 per cent — and in certain cases 100 per cent — by a levy on other insurance companies'.[1]

---

1   N.J. Gibson, 'The Financial System in Northern Ireland', *Northern Ireland Economic Council*, Belfast, April 1982, p. 79.

Superannuation funds: Superannuation or pension funds are financial institutions which, on the basis of contributions often by both employees and employers, undertake to provide future incomes to their members. Their size and form of organization facilitates risk-sharing and the exploiting of economies of scale. Pension funds have grown very rapidly during the past twenty-five years; their growth has been stimulated by tax incentives. Pension funds approved by the Inland Revenue (including those managed by insurance companies) are known as gross funds; such funds do not have to pay tax on their investment earnings nor tax on their capital gains.

With investment funds of some £55,000m at the end of 1980, pension funds are approaching the size of the insurance companies. Of that total figure, £25,000m was in UK company securities, almost £12,000m in UK government securities and over £4,000m in securities of overseas companies. Clearly pension funds are of major significance to the UK capital market.

Investment trusts: Investment trusts are limited companies which specialize in the investment of funds provided by their shareholders or borrowed from debenture holders or other lenders, thus enabling investment risks to be shared and economies of management to be gained. Despite the term 'trust', investment trusts do not operate, as do the unit trusts, under trust deeds which specify the terms and conditions governing the management of investment funds, but are, in fact, limited companies whose assets consist mainly of company securities and who are not allowed by their articles of association to distribute capital gains as dividends. In addition to investment trusts there are private investment companies and investment-holding companies which often perform similar functions. But these are not considered to be investment trusts in the sense used here and are not discussed in this chapter. Attention is concentrated on the group of about 200 investment trusts that are recognized as such for tax purposes by the Inland Revenue.

Investment trusts expand by raising funds from new capital issues, borrowing in the form of loan capital and by retaining some of the income and capital profits from previous investments. But once again it is the asset side of the balance sheets that is of chief interest. At the end of 1981 the total market value of investments of recognized investment trusts was almost £6,400m. Most of this was invested in company securities, practically all ordinary shares; some £2,700m was invested in the securities of overseas companies.

The size of the investment trusts makes them important operators in the ordinary share market. They also fulfil a useful function in helping to finance small companies by holding unquoted securities. Their ability to invest overseas has from time to time been seriously affected by government restrictions and tax measures, but the former are now virtually non-existent since the abolition of exchange controls in 1979.

Unit trusts: Unit trusts perform a similar function to investment trusts. But unlike the latter they do operate under trust deeds and have trustees, often a bank or insurance company. The unit trusts are authorized by the Department of Trade and are run by managers who are quite distinct from the trustees. Returns are currently collected from some 409 unit trusts; in 1960 the figure was fifty-one.

Unit trusts do not issue share capital and are not limited companies, but they issue units which give the owners the right to participate in the beneficial owner-ship of the trusts' assets. The units are highly marketable as they can always be bought from or sold to the managers at prices which reflect the market value of the underlying assets. As more units are demanded the managers provide more; for this reason they are sometimes called 'open-end' trusts, as opposed to 'closed-end' trusts such as the investment trusts which do not expand in this way.

Like the investment trusts, the assets of the unit trusts are almost entirely company securities, made up of ordinary shares. At the end of 1981 the total holdings of UK government and company securities of the unit trusts were £3,500m; they also held £1,300m of securities of overseas companies. Their rate of growth has been rapid; in 1960 their total assets were only £190m. Their growth may be an attempt by investors and others to protect themselves against inflation by participating indirectly in ordinary share investment.

The Stock Exchange: The Stock Exchange is not strictly a financial institution but an association of stockjobbers and stockbrokers which provides a market for variable-price securities, both government and company securities. Without this market where securities may readily be bought and sold, the whole business of raising funds through outside sources would tend to be more expensive and less efficient. Since March 1973 the Stock Exchange comprises the Stock Exchange of the UK and the Republic of Ireland. Before that date, though with close links, they were distinct organizations.

A feature of the Stock Exchange is the jobbing system. Jobbers are traders in securities; they act as principals, buying and selling on their own account and mak-ing their profits on the difference between their buying and selling prices, which they generally stand ready to quote for the securities in which they specialize. This function can be extremely important in giving stability to the market which might otherwise be much more volatile and possibly mislead investors.

Brokers generally act as agents for customers, buying and selling on their behalf, usually but not always through jobbers.

Speculation is a term frequently associated with the Stock Exchange and nearly always carries overtones of abuse and criticism. To some degree this may reflect ignorance of the functions of the Stock Exchange, though this is not to imply that speculation is always economically and socially beneficial. But the speculator at his best, if he is doing his job properly, will be helping to keep the price of shares in touch with economic realities, damping down the effects of irrelevant rumours and false information; he will, in fact, be improving one part of the communications network of the economic system and contributing to an 'efficient' capital market. However, the economic, social and moral implications of speculation are much wider and more far-reaching than can be dealt with here.

Traditionally the terms 'bulls' and 'bears' have been applied to particular types of speculation, though they are now used more generally to refer respectively to markets tending to rise and fall in price. But traditionally a 'bull' was someone who bought securities on a rising market hoping he would be able to sell them at a profit before he had to pay for his purchase. The 'bear' sold the shares that he had not got, on a falling market, in the hope that he would be able subsequently to buy and deliver them at a lower price.

An idea of the scale of Stock Exchange activities can be obtained from the figures on turnover; that is, sales and purchases. The total turnover during 1981 was about £191,000m. Turnover of UK government securities was some £146,000m. Clearly the Stock Exchange is of major importance to the financial activities of both the public and private sectors of the economy.

IV   TAXATION
IV.1   Introduction

Taxation and the economic role of government in society are necessarily closely linked and discussion of the one involves some consideration of the other. It is often said that taxation in a market economy has three main functions:

(1) to provide or encourage the provision of goods and services that are not easily or adequately supplied by the market if left to itself, and also to discourage the provision of those goods and services that are considered to have harmful effects on society — and perhaps the reverse for those goods and services which are considered beneficial to society;

(2) to redistribute income and wealth, and

(3) to facilitate the exercise of fiscal policy as a means of economic stabilization.

The first may be approached by making a distinction between so-called private and public goods, and noting a possible discrepancy between private and public costs and benefits — what has come to be called the externalities problem. Private goods refer to those goods where the utility a person gets from their consumption depends on how much of them he has and at the same time the more he has the less anyone else gets. Public goods on the other hand are such that, once the goods are produced, their consumption by one person does not diminish the amount available to others. Any kind of food is an example of a private good and some forms of national defence are an example of public goods. The market system can by and large handle the problem of producing and pricing private goods but not public goods, since the price system cannot operate effectively to determine an appropriate amount to produce, nor determine its distribution. It needs to be stressed immediately that pure private goods and pure public goods are extreme cases and that, in general, elements of both may be combined in the same good.

Externalities are said to arise when the costs and benefits are not internalized to the individual producer or consumer. A typical example is what has been called the 'smoke nuisance', when a producer engages in a productive activity that gives off smoke and spreads grime and dirt in the immediate neighbourhood and possibly causes chemical erosion of buildings in the surrounding area. The costs of these nuisances are generally not voluntarily paid for by the producer or reflected in the quantity produced or price of his product. This kind of example could be greatly extended, as could similar examples on the benefits side. Indeed, in so far as a so-called public good was provided privately, it would be an example of external benefits being conferred widely throughout a community. Clearly, externalities pose a fundamental problem for society, and in particular suggest that where they are present in a market-based economy, the market if left to itself will produce too much of a good which imposes external costs on the society and too little of a good which confers external benefits on it. In such circumstances there seems to be no simple answer to the question, on the one hand, of the appropriate domain of market processes and, on the other, of the role of government. These are difficult and far-reaching issues in political economy.

The second function of taxation — the redistribution of income and wealth — is closely related to the matters just discussed. Because there is no self-evident reason why a competitive market economy should lead to an optimum distribution of income and wealth — however difficult that may be to define — so governments have come to use taxation and the revenue raised thereby to bring about some redistribution. It should perhaps be said that there is also no obvious reason why government redistribution policies will be optimal, since the distribution and ability to exercise political power may itself be far from optimal; clearly these issues beg some fundamental and intractable questions.

The third function of taxation as an aspect of fiscal stabilization policy is already familiar from earlier discussion in this chapter and the preceding one.

A further feature of taxation that should be mentioned is its so-called 'supply-side' effects. Broadly speaking the argument is that taxation distorts the choice at the margin between work and leisure, investment and saving, risky versus less risky investments, and is a stimulus to the 'black economy', that is, the illegal carrying on of economic activity outside the tax net. The conclusion of those who stress the importance of supply-side effects is that, in general, taxation adversely affects output and economic growth and that on these grounds tax rates should be lower rather than higher and the role of the government in the economy smaller rather than larger. The subject is, of course, a highly controversial one but it certainly cannot be lightly dismissed by anyone who has some confidence in traditional microeconomic analysis.

IV.2   The Size of Government

It is well known that in this century governments have become, in terms of their own activities, far more important in relation to the economic life of the community. Nevertheless, it is by no means straightforward to measure the size of government economic activity relatively to the rest of the economic system. Perhaps the best that can be done is to take a number of different measures.[1]

One of these is the direct claims the general government makes through its own economic activity on the volume of goods and services available to the community. In this context 'general government' includes central and local government, but excludes such things as the nationalized industries or, more generally, public corporations. Table 2.8 shows that government expenditure claimed about 22% of the Gross National Product in the late 1960s, gradually increased to over 26% by 1975, fell to almost 22% by 1978 but increased to 24% in 1980.

TABLE 2.8

General Government: Total Expenditure on Goods and Services as a Percentage of GNP at Market Prices, 1968-80

Year	1968	1969	1970	1971	1972	1973	1974	1975
%	22.5	21.8	22.2	22.2	22.6	23.0	25.0	26.5
Year	1976	1977	1978	1979	1980			
%	25.6	23.7	22.8	22.4	23.9			

Source: NIBB, 1981 edition.

1   See A.R. Prest and N.A. Barr, *Public Finance in Theory and Practice*, 6th edition, Weidenfeld and Nicolson, 1979, chapter 8, for a discussion of the issues involved.

It is arguable that the data in table 2.8 understate the 'size' of government. They take no account of subsidies, grants and debt interest paid by the government and ignore its net lending. The reason for this is that these transactions are mainly classified as transfer payments. That is, the government raises the necessary funds by taxation and borrowing, and transfers them back to the community and overseas. Thus the government does not buy goods and services directly as far as this type of expenditure is concerned. But there is no doubt that these transfers are extremely important in relation to taxation and government borrowing, and greatly influence the economic system. When they are included in government expenditure the previous percentages are markedly increased. Table 2.9 shows that for the later part of the 1960s the percentage is over 40% of Gross National Product and that a marked jump occurred in the mid-1970s to a peak of 49% in 1975; the percentage then fell to 43% in 1977 but increased to 46% in 1980, despite the efforts to curb public expenditure. It is arguable that the figures are not completely comparable over time and, in particular, that net lending should be excluded; the correction would make little difference to the overall picture. Clearly, grants, subsidies, debt interest and net lending have been of major importance in recent years as a component of government expenditure and, as will be seen, the financing of total government expenditure has posed formidable problems for government and the monetary authorities.

TABLE 2.9

General Government: Total Government Expenditure as a Percentage of GNP at Market Prices, 1968-80

Year	1968	1969	1970	1971	1972	1973	1974	1975
%	41.8	40.3	40.4	40.6	41.2	41.1	46.4	48.9
Year	1976	1977	1978	1979	1980			
%	46.4	43.0	43.4	44.0	46.0			

Source: NIBB, 1981 edition.

IV.3   The Budget and Borrowing Requirements

The Budget is traditionally the annual financial statement which the Chancellor of the Exchequer makes in the House of Commons either in March or early April around the end of each financial year. The statement includes an account of the revenue and expenditure for the previous financial year and forecasts for the year ahead. In the ordinary way there is only one budget, but in times of crisis one or more supplementary budgets may be introduced to give the Chancellor the opportunity to modify his earlier policies by altering taxation and expenditure. Tables 2.10, 2.11 and 2.12 bring together in an aggregated form the main features of the 1982-3 Budget accounts.

The gross tax revenue of government, less repayments, plus all other public moneys payable to the Exchequer are paid into the Exchequer's Account at the Bank of England; the amount standing to the credit of this account at any point of time is known as the Consolidated Fund. Virtually all expenditure by the Government, with the major exceptions of government loans and national insurance benefits, is paid out of issues from this fund.[1] In table 2.10 is shown the Taxation and Miscellaneous Receipts of the Central Government as they appear in the *Financial Statement and Budget Report*. The receipts fall under four main headings: inland revenue, customs and excise (including EEC own resources), other duties and charges, and miscellaneous receipts. The first two refer to the great revenue-collecting departments of state, and major taxes and duties collected by these are discussed below.[2] Vehicle excise duties are collected by the Department of the Environment. Miscellaneous receipts include interest and dividends, broadcast-receiving licences and certain other receipts, of which one of the most important is oil royalties.

TABLE 2.10

Taxation and Miscellaneous Receipts of Central Government, 1982-3 (Forecast) (£m)

Inland Revenue		
Income tax	30,775	
Corporation tax	4,850	
Petroleum revenue tax	2,290	
Supplementary petroleum duty	2,040	
Capital gains tax	600	
Development land tax	40	
Estate duty	10	
Capital transfer tax	465	
Stamp duties	810	
Total Inland Revenue		41,880
Customs and Excise		
Value added tax	14,750	
Oil	5,100	
Tobacco	3,525	
Spirits, beer, wine, cider and perry	3,275	
Betting and gaming	550	
Car tax	600	
Other excise duties	20	
EEC own resources		
Customs duties, etc.	1,060	
Agricultural levies	270	
Total Customs and Excise		29,150
Vehicle excise duties		1,854
National insurance surcharge		3,443
Total Taxation		76,327
Miscellaneous receipts		6,568
Grand Total		82,895

Source: Financial Statement and Budget Report 1982-3.

1   *Financial Statistics: Explanatory Handbook*, HMSO, April 1981, p. 37.

2   EEC own resources include revenue from the Common External Tariff, agricultural levies and sugar levies that, under the EEC Treaty and subsidiary legislation, are considered as belonging to the European Community and available for its budgetary purposes. See *Official Journal of the European Communities*, 94 of 28 April 1970.

The two main categories of expenditure shown in table 2.11 are supply services and consolidated fund standing services; the first is voted annually by Parliament and the second is a standing charge against revenue; the individual programmes of expenditure and the standing services are also detailed in table 2.11.

The National Loans Fund is a cash account at the Bank of England and was set up in 1968. Most of the domestic lending of the government and all transactions relating to the National Debt, including its creation, the repayment of loans from the Fund and interest payments thereon, now appear in the National Loans Fund. Table 2.12 shows just how important the central government is as a source of capital funds for the nationalized industries, other public corporations and local authorities. The government must raise these funds either through taxation or other receipts or by borrowing. In these accounts there is a deficit of almost £8,000m forecast for the Consolidated Fund, a net borrowing of £9,600m by the National Loans Fund and a central government borrowing requirement of £9,300m, arrived at by subtracting some £300m of other funds (see below) from the net borrowing by the National Loans Fund.

The net borrowing by the National Loans Fund, the 'central government borrowing requirement' and the PSBR are closely inter-related. To get from the net borrowing by the National Loans Fund to the central government borrowing requirement it is necessary to take into account the central government's net indebtedness to various official funds, which are distinct from the Consolidated Fund, namely the National Insurance Fund, certain departmental balances and miscellaneous items, and Northern Ireland central government debt. The position for the financial year 1980-81 (the latest financial year for which complete data are available) is shown below.

		£m
	Borrowing required by National Loans Fund	13,514
plus	Deficit of National Insurance Fund	25
less	Surplus of departmental balances, etc.	−616
plus	N.I. central government debt	33
	Central government borrowing requirement	12,956

The PSBR includes the central government borrowing requirement and in addition the borrowing of local authorities and public corporations other than from within the public sector. For the financial year 1980-81 the figures were as follows:

		£m
	Central government borrowing requirement	12,956
plus	Local authorities net borrowing from other sources	951
plus	Public corporations net borrowing from other sources	−711
	PSBR	13,196

The authorities were able to finance this PSBR by borrowing £9,234m from the non-bank private sector, £3,249m from the monetary sector and by transactions with the overseas sector to the amount of £713m.[1] The financing took a number of forms such as notes and coin, national savings, Treasury bills, government

---

1 All statistics in the text are from *FS*, March 1982. For further discussion of the public sector borrowing requirement, see section V below.

TABLE 2.11

Central Government Supply Services and Consolidated Fund Standing Services, 1982-3 (Forecast) (£m)

Supply Services

I	Defence	13,945	
II	Overseas Services	1,605	
III	Agriculture, Fisheries & Forestry	664	
IV	Trade, Industry, Energy and Employment	5,424	
V	Government Investment in Nationalized Industries	572	
VI	Roads and Transport	2,019	
VII	Housing	2,318	
VIII	Other Environmental Services	568	
IX	Law, Order and Protective Services	2,475	
X	Education and Libraries, Science and Arts	2,850	
XI	Health and Personal Social Services	10,260	
XII	Social Security	11,768	
XIII	Other Public Services	1,297	
XIIIA	House of Commons Administration	16	
XIV	Common Services	2,098	
XV	Scotland	2,988	
XVI	Wales	1,168	
XVII	Northern Ireland	1,103	
XVIII	Rate Support Grant, Financial, Transactions, etc.	16,087	
	Total Supply		79,225
	Supplementary provision	109	
	Contingency reserve	2,400	
	Reduction in national insurance surcharge	−360	2,149
	Total Supply Services		81,374
	Consolidated Fund Standing Services		
	Payment to the National Loans Fund for service of the National Debt	5,175	
	Northern Ireland – share of taxes, etc.	1,493	
	Payments to the European Community, etc.	2,820	
	Other Services	29	
	Total Consolidated Fund Standing Services		9,517
	Total		90,891
	Consolidated Fund Deficit		−7,996
	Grand Total		82,895

Source: Financial Statement and Budget Report 1982-83.

securities, specialized forms of debt, and changes in the official foreign exchange reserves. A number of these require special mention.

National savings refer to a variety of savings media provided by the state and originally designed mainly to attract the small saver. The two main forms of national savings are national savings certificates, including some issues which are index-linked, that is, their repayment value is linked to the retail prices index, and is tax-free, and savings through National Savings Bank (NSB) accounts. The NSB has two types of account, the ordinary and the investment account. The ordinary account offers limited facilities for withdrawal of funds on demand and carries interest at 5%; the first £70 of interest is tax-free. The investment account requires one month's notice for the making of withdrawals and paid 13% before deduction of tax from 1 May 1982. All forms of national savings raised over £3½bn towards the financing of the PSBR in 1981-2.

As regards government securities, the 1982 budget included a notable innovation with the first issue of an index-linked government stock which may be bought by the general public; previous index-linked issues could only be held by pension funds and similar bodies. Both the principal and the interest − 2% per annum on the new issue − on such stocks are index-linked and, hence, if held to maturity are a complete protection against inflation. This development is bound to have considerable repercussions on the relative attractiveness of other forms of securities which carry no such guarantee against inflation. It should also have the effect, if inflation falls, of reducing the on-going cost of servicing the government stocks' component of the national debt.

TABLE 2.12

National Loans Fund, 1982-3 (Forecast) (£m)

(i) *Payments*		
Service of the National Debt:		
Interest		11,467
Management and expenses		133
Consolidated Fund Deficit		7,996
Loans (net)		
To nationalized industries	721	
Other public corporations	1,242	
Local authorities	−300	
Private sector	−6	
Within central government	−21	
Total		1,636
Grand Total		21,232
(ii) *Receipts*		
Interest on loans, profits of the Issue Department of the Bank of England, etc.	6,425	
Service of the National Debt − balance met from Consolidated Fund	5,175	
Total		11,600
Net borrowing by the National Loans Fund		9,632
Grand Total		21,232

Source: Financial Statement and Budget Report 1982-83.

The remaining item to be mentioned is the foreign exchange reserves; a fall in these, because of an external deficit, brings an inflow of sterling to the public sector and so helps to finance the public-sector borrowing requirement; it is in effect a selling of an asset — foreign exchange reserves — for sterling. The opposite is, of course, true for an external surplus.

From the earlier discussion of the PSBR in section III.8 it is clear that it may be related to changes in the money supply, particularly £M_3. The arithmetic analogue to the stylized presentation in section III.8 is shown in table 2.13 for the five years 1976/7 to 1980/81. Whilst causal relationships cannot be inferred from this descriptive approach the figures at least suggest that there is no simple automatic relationship between the PSBR and changes in the money stock.

TABLE 2.13

Counterparts to and Changes in the Money Stock, 1976/7 to 1980/81 (£m)

	1976/7	*1977/8*	*1978/9*	*1979/80*	*1980/81*
1. PSBR	8,518	5,591	9,199	9,897	13,254
2. Net purchases of public-sector debt by private sector	7,187	6,662	8,521	9,144	10,877
3. Sterling lending to private sector	3,391	3,743	6,296	9,330	9,248
4. External and foreign currency counter-parts	−1,034	4,007	−688	−2,435	517
5. Increase in non-deposit liabilities	859	446	991	1,207	1,466
6. Change in £M_3	2,829	6,233	5,295	6,441	10,676

Source: FS, March 1982.
Note: Relationship between rows: 6 = 1 − 2 + 3 + 4 − 5; and 1 − 2 + 3 = domestic counterparts. The PSBR for 1980/81 in the table is *not* identical with that shown in the text; certain differences in its treatment arise in relation to tables 2.6 and 7.3 of *FS*.

The annual budget as an instrument of fiscal policy has frequently been criticized because of its inflexibility. In the ordinary way the major taxes such as income tax and corporation tax cannot be varied between Finance Acts.[1] Thus though it might be thought desirable by those who favour activist fiscal policies to alter these taxes more frequently, this cannot be done without all the inconvenience of a supplementary budget. However, the authorities have more leeway over some other sources of revenue. From the point of view of flexibility one of the most important has been the power, first granted in the 1961 Finance Act, to vary by not more than 10% the rates of nearly all customs and excise duties and since the introduction of value added tax in 1973 to vary it by not more than 25%.[2] Thus there are now substantial powers to vary taxes between budgets. This, of course, leaves other crucially important problems, such as the timing and scale of tax

1   The Finance Act puts into law the budget proposals subject to the Provisional Collection of Taxes Act which allows certain tax changes to take effect immediately and in advance of the enactment of the Finance Bill; the latter is subject to any amendments made to it by the House of Commons.

2   Thus if the customs or excise rate of duty was 10% it might be varied between 9% and 11%, and as regards a VAT rate of 15% between 11¼% and 18¾%.

changes and their anticipation by the public; more generally it raises the issue of the ability of the authorities to 'fine-tune' the operation of the economy.

Alterations in government expenditure are also, in principle, a possible way of making fiscal policy more flexible. But government expenditure may be planned years in advance of its formal inclusion in the budget estimates and periodic modifications of the plans may give rise to problems, since much of the expenditure is on a continuing basis and cannot be easily varied. Furthermore, it may be extremely costly to slow down or postpone some kinds of expenditure, particularly investment expenditure. Hence frequent variation of government expenditure is not an ideal instrument of fiscal policy.

The budget accounts, as already indicated, are incomplete in a number of ways. They deal, for example, only peripherally with local government finances and the national insurance funds.[1] But if general government is considered, it is found that for 1981-2 estimated taxes on income and expenditure, plus national insurance and similar contributions and taxes on capital, totalled £102,000m or around 40% of GNP at factor cost. This is a further indication of the financial scale of government in the UK economy.

IV.4   Income Taxation

Up to April 1973 individuals were subject to income tax and surtax, with the latter chargeable in addition to income tax on incomes in excess of a certain level. From that date, the former income tax and surtax were replaced by a single graduated personal tax, known as unified tax. The main aims of unified tax were to simplify the tax structure, permit a smoother graduation in tax rates as income rises and simplify the administration of the whole system. The unified tax is constructed on the concept of earned income and so manages to dispense with the calculation of earned income relief, which was required under the previous system since it was constructed in terms of unearned or investment income. As well as earned income and investment income, a further concept requires to be mentioned, that is chargeable income. Chargeable income is the income which remains from all sources after deduction of personal, family and certain other allowances.

The main personal allowances since an amendment to the 1977 Finance Act have, with the exception of the year 1981-2, been linked to the retail price index – an example of indexation. For 1982-3 the personal allowances have been raised by some 2% more than required to take account of inflation over the past year and are as follows: for single persons £1,565 and for married couples £2,445. The age allowances for the elderly are £2,070 for a single person and £3,295 for a married couple. The allowances which had formerly existed for children resident in the UK were finally phased out under the 1979 Finance Act and have been replaced by tax-free child benefit.

Once taxable income has been determined, the various tax rates come into operation. For 1982-3 the tax bands, or ranges of earned income in relation to each tax rate, are as follows:

---

1   National insurance is discussed further in Chapter 5.

£	%
0-12,800	30
12,801-15,100	40
15,101-19,100	45
19,101-25,300	50
25,301-31,500	55
Over 31,500	60

The unified tax retains the former distinction between earned and investment income but has been modified in an important way. The first £6,250 or less of investment income is treated in exactly the same way as earned income but, above this, carries a surcharge of 15%, thus making a maximum rate of 75%.

It is evident that one of the main features of income taxation is its progressiveness. This is, of course, by design; it can be traced to notions of ability to pay. It is assumed that those with larger incomes are or should be able to pay proportionately more of them in taxation. In addition, progressive taxation lends itself to income redistribution, to the extent that government expenditure benefits the less well-off in the community; and some would argue that greater equality of income is important to the maintenance of a politically stable society. But progressive taxation also diminishes the direct reward for extra work as income increases, and may act as a disincentive to more effort.

It has also been suggested that steeply progressive taxation is a disincentive to movement from one job to another; it may be difficult to get a sufficiently large income after tax to compensate for the costs of upheaval and change. If this is correct then the tax system may misallocate resources and be a drag on economic efficiency and growth. There is also no doubt that highly progressive taxation stimulates tax avoidance – the search for loopholes in the law permitting a reduced tax bill – and indeed tax evasion which is, of course, illegal. If it is possible to spend less than a pound on advice to save a pound in tax then clearly this is a powerful incentive. The energies and resources of lawyers, accountants and tax experts generally may thus be diverted into socially costly tasks.

To the extent that some or all of these problems arise, the community may have to make difficult choices between more redistribution and a smaller total income, or somewhat less redistribution and a larger total income, with each choice being associated with varying degrees of social and political conflict. Once more there would seem to be no escape from the difficult problems which arise in sustaining the on-going life of a complex and diverse society.

It has long been a goal of taxation policy that the system of taxation should be easy to understand, equitable and cheap to administer. How far this continues to be true of the system in the UK is open to question. Concern has been expressed about the distortions and inefficiencies generated by the complex interdependencies of the whole system of taxation and the social-security system.[1] In particular, there is concern about what has come to be called the 'poverty-trap', where people who are in low-paid jobs or unemployed may find that the effective marginal tax on their additional earnings may be extremely high – in excess of 100% in some circumstances – when both taxation and loss of social-security benefits are taken into consideration. The introduction of tax-free child benefit should help to alleviate this problem.

---

1 See *The Structure and Reform of Direct Taxation*, Report of a Committee chaired by Professor J.E. Meade, Institute for Fiscal Studies, Allen and Unwin, 1978.

There are, however, various proposals for dealing more radically with these and related problems by, in effect, integrating to some degree the direct-taxation and social-security systems. One proposal is known as 'the negative income tax', which ideally is designed to permit a single assessment of income and provide either for calculating the tax due if income is above a certain level or for a transfer to be paid if it is below that level. The particular scheme that has received most official attention in the UK is known as a 'tax credit system'.[1] There seems to be little doubt that a tax-credit scheme such as that proposed could achieve some simplification and economies in present arrangements for taxation and in the administration of at least some social security benefits. However, it would be a mistake to assume that it offers a simple panacea to the problem of all those with low incomes.

IV.5   Capital Gains Taxation and Development Land Tax

Until the Finance Act of 1971 there were two capital gains taxes, the short-term and the long-term tax, but under this Act the former was abolished, leaving what is called capital gains tax. Under this tax, gains are taxable on the disposal of most assets. Important exemptions are principal private residence, private motorcars, National Savings securities, most life-assurance policies and betting winnings, gifts to charities and, if sold more than one year after purchase, British government and government-guaranteed securities. In addition, the first £5,000 of net annual gains of individuals are exempt. However, the Chancellor of the Exchequer in his 1982-3 budget announced proposals which would allow for inflation to be taken into account in the calculation of taxable capital gains. This is a major departure from past practice and should lead to the taxing of real as opposed to nominal capital gains. The rate of capital gains tax remains at 30%. Since 1971 all gains at death are exempt; and there are various special provisions for taxing gains on gifts. There are also provisions generally allowing losses to be offset against gains on those assets that are subject to tax. Gains realized by companies are ordinarily chargeable to corporation tax, which for the year 1982-3 is at 52%. However, from 1973 the effective rate of tax on company gains has been only 30% — achieved by the expedient of leaving out of account a fraction of the gain. Authorized unit trusts and approved investment trusts are exempt from capital gains tax.

The major justification put forward for the introduction of capital gains taxation is on grounds of equity. The argument, ignoring dividends, is roughly as follows. An individual may purchase £100 worth of securities in 1980 and — if he is lucky — find that in 1981 they are worth £200. If he sold the securities and if there were no capital gains tax, he could maintain his capital intact and still have £100 to spend, therefore his £100 is essentially income and should be taxed as such. But is this really equitable with progressive income-tax rates? It might be that if the £100 were spread over a number of years a lower tax charge would arise. Does this mean that gains should be averaged over a number of years, or would a compromise solution be to charge rates somewhat less than income-tax rates? The UK capital gains tax seems to favour the latter.

In discussing the £100 gain above, nothing was said about prices. But if prices have risen by 20% over the period then £120 would be required to maintain his

---

1   See *Proposals for a Tax-Credit System*, Cmnd. 5116, HMSO, 1972.

capital intact in real terms, leaving £80 in current prices as the income he might spend without eroding the former; in effect, inflation is a form of tax and indeed may be said to be levied without Parliamentary approval. The question arises — is it legitimate to tax nominal gains as opposed to real gains? The answer, at last accepted by the government, would seem to be no.

Capital gains taxation is, of course, important for other reasons besides equity. It may affect investment and saving and the functioning of the capital markets, and pose difficult problems of administration. To the extent that the return on investment takes the form of capital gains — especially the return on risky investment — taxing them may discourage such investment. This discouragement may, however, be mitigated to some extent, since the tax is postponable and payable only on realized capital gains. The allowance of losses against gains also works in the same direction. Nevertheless, the effect may well be to depress investment.

The effects on savings are perhaps even more problematical but may also be adverse, as may the effects on the operation of the capital markets. Since the tax is on realized gains this encourages the retention of the same securities as, of course, the holder has the income on the tax that would otherwise have to be paid if the securities were realized. There is therefore a discouragement to switching between securities, which reduces the flexibility of the market and perhaps makes the raising of capital more costly. A possible offset to these effects is the realization of capital losses since these are allowable for tax purposes against corresponding capital gains.

The administrative problems with the tax are particularly great where difficulties of valuation arise. This is especially true of changes in the value of assets which do not ordinarily have a market value; an example is unquoted securities. The problem of valuation may become less acute as time proceeds and the community gets accustomed to the tax.[1]

The Development Land Tax of 1976 makes development value arising from land subject to a special development tax but there is no liability to income tax, corporation tax or capital gains tax on gains subject to development land tax. The term 'development value' refers to the difference between the base value of the land and its value for development purposes. The base value 'is the highest of:
(1)   cost of acquisition plus the cost of "relevant improvements", plus any increase in current use value since the date of acquisition; or
(2)   current use value at the date of disposal, plus 15%; or
(3)   acquisition cost of the land, including all improvements, plus 15%.'[2]
The first £50,000 of realized development value in any financial year after 1 April 1980 is exempt from tax. The standard rate thereafter is 60% of realized development value.

Various people and bodies are exempt from development land tax, including the main residence of owner-occupiers for land up to one acre, and certain co-operative housing associations provided that if they dispose of dwellings or land they do so to 'a housing association registered with the Housing Corporation or to

---

1   For further discussion of all of these issues, see Prest and Barr, *Public Finance in Theory and Practice*, op. cit., pp. 333-44.

2   *The British System of Taxation*, HMSO, 1977, p. 24.

the Housing Corporation itself'.[1] Disposals to other purchasers are liable to development land tax.

No doubt the development land tax is an attempt by the state to appropriate what it considers to be inequitable capital gains from certain forms of land development. However, it is difficult to see how it can fail to raise the costs of new housing and in so doing confer actual or potential capital gains on owners of existing houses.

IV.6   Corporation Tax, Depreciation and Other Allowances, and Oil Taxation

Corporation tax draws a strong distinction between the company and the shareholder, taxing each as separate entities. A basic argument used in favour of corporation tax is the opportunity it gives the authorities to distinguish between the personal and company sectors for policy purposes. They may wish, for instance, to curtail consumption expenditure with as little adverse effect as possible on investment expenditure. An increase in income tax, leaving corporation tax unchanged, may tend to have the desired effect and may even encourage smaller dividend distributions, leaving more funds available to companies for investment purposes.

The foregoing analysis begs, however, a number of important questions. Among these are the following. Should future consumption be preferred to present consumption, in so far as larger current investment makes possible a larger future income and so consumption? Are the companies with retained profits the ones which should grow? This is not at all self-evident. It means that companies avoid the discipline of having to raise funds in the market and probably favours the larger established company at the expense of the smaller or newer company. Furthermore, greater encouragement of profit retention tends to reduce the flow of funds through the capital market to the detriment of companies dependent on it. Corporation tax also tends to distort the operation of the capital market by encouraging firms to rely more on loan or debenture capital at the expense of ordinary or other forms of share capital, since the interest on the former is allowed as a cost in the calculation of profits and hence liability for tax, whereas this is not true of the latter. It may indeed be argued that the gains from introducing corporation tax outweigh all the disadvantages. However, once a tax has been in operation for a period of years to remove it may be costly to industry and give rise to inequities. The whole matter of corporation tax is currently under official consideration, prompted, in part, by the difficulties that relatively rapid inflation has caused in the operation of the tax; there are, as yet, no indications of what, if any, changes will be made in the present system.[2]

This system, known as the *imputation system*, was introduced from April 1973. Under it, all profits, whether distributed or not, are subject to the same corporation-tax rate, but part of the tax is imputed to shareholders, and collected from the company at the time of payment of dividends. If, for instance, the corporation-tax rate is 52% and the basic income-tax rate is 30%, then a company whose activities are entirely within the UK and which had profits of 100 would have a corporation-tax liability of 52. If during a year it paid a dividend of 21 to its

---

1   Ibid. For a fuller discussion of the whole subject see A.R. Prest, *The Taxation of Urban Land*, Manchester University Press, 1981.

2   *Corporation Tax* (Green Paper), Cmnd. 8456, HMSO, January 1982.

shareholders, it would be treated as a gross dividend of 30 from which income tax of 30% had been deducted. The company would pay the 9 to the Inland Revenue and this, which is called advance payment of corporation tax (ACT), would be credited against the company's corporation-tax liability of 52. Shareholders subject to basic-rate income tax would be deemed to have discharged their tax liabilities; only in the case of those exempt or subject to higher rates would a refund or additional charge be necessary. Small companies whose annual profits do not exceed £90,000 are subject to a reduced rate of corporation tax (40% for the year to March 1982) with the scale of reduction tapering off for companies with profits up to £225,000.

The imputation form of corporation tax has certain advantages over the two-rate system when it comes to negotiating double-taxation agreements with other countries; it also facilitates the movement towards tax harmonization within the European Community, as it puts Britain broadly in line with French and German company taxation and with recent proposals by the Commission.

In assessing liability to corporation tax, allowance is made, broadly speaking, for all the costs incurred by the company, including the wear and tear of physical capital and, as mentioned above, interest on loans and debentures but not dividends paid on shares. However, depreciation is not allowed on all physical assets; there are no allowances on such things as retail shops, showrooms and offices, except in Enterprise Zones where there are 100% capital allowances for commercial and industrial buildings.

In addition to depreciation allowances for wear and tear, successive governments have attempted to stimulate investment by various kinds of incentive. Two main kinds are operative in the UK: initial allowances, and investment or cash grants. Initial allowances, introduced in 1945, are permitted in the first year in addition to the ordinary depreciation allowances and the two together are known as first-year allowances. In other words the rate at which depreciation may be written off is accelerated; the total amount of depreciation permitted remains 100%. Investment or cash grants are now largely confined to what are called the assisted areas and are known generally as regional development grants. Special investment grants are also payable to the shipbuilding and computer industries.

The position since the 1972 budget is that all capital expenditure throughout the UK on machinery and plant, excluding passenger cars, is subject to a first-year allowance of 100%, often called free depreciation; and the initial allowance on new industrial buildings is 75% plus an annual allowance of 4% on the construction cost. However, small industrial buildings of 2,500 square feet or less, subject to some restrictions as regards the time-period, qualify for 100% initial allowance. Thus as far as these allowances are concerned no distinction is made between the assisted areas and the rest of the country. However, as already indicated, the assisted areas do receive special treatment. In addition to the allowances mentioned, certain development areas receive regional development grants of 22% and 15% respectively of qualifying capital expenditure on new plant and machinery and buildings. An important feature of the system of regional development grants is that they do not affect the recipient's entitlement to the first-year or initial allowances on the *full* amount of the capital investment.

With the rapid rise in prices in the last few years many companies found themselves subject to heavy taxation on the increase in the value of their stocks. In November 1974 the government introduced measures giving special tax relief, though not explicitly related to price increases. Stock relief was subsequently changed in April 1981 so that relief is specifically given in relation to the move-ment of an 'all stocks' price index. This is an important innovation, as it is tantamount to an acceptance, at least in part, of inflation accounting.

The whole system of allowances and grants thus gives rise to many complicated issues, only a few of which can be touched on here. First, should depreciation allowances be on an original or a replacement-cost basis? This question would be of little or no significance if prices were generally stable. But in periods of rising prices it would seem that if the community is to preserve intact its physical stock of capital, it is preferable to have allowances based on a replacement-cost basis. However, if the problem is approached in a different way the argument may not be so clear-cut. Suppose a firm purchases a piece of equipment and thereafter prices rise, including the price of the equipment, then the capital value of the old equip-ment also rises, giving a capital gain to the firm. If allowances are permitted on a replacement-cost basis the firm is, in fact, receiving untaxed capital gains. Is this equitable in relation to other sections of the community or is it a useful compromise to allow only original costs in calculating depreciation, so that the apparent capital gains are subject to corporation and income tax, as was the practice in the UK until the modification relating to the increase in the value of stocks? The answer is far from obvious but clearly the issues become more acute in periods of rapid inflation.[1]

Initial allowances and investment grants should act as a stimulus to investment. The first may be regarded as reducing the amount of tax payable on a profitable investment. The second is, of course, a direct subsidy to investment and the benefits do not depend upon the availability of profits. It is not at all self-evident that the subsidy is to be preferred, as it may mean that investment takes place in forms of dubious profitability – there is therefore the likelihood of misallocation of resources, at least as determined in relation to market prices.

A major feature of investment grants and regional development grants is the extent to which they are discriminatory. They make investments in certain places more profitable than in others and some types of investment more profitable than other types. This, of course, is by design and is intended to stimulate investment in the places and in the forms the government desires. The basis for this intervention is the conviction that the market, reflecting the interacting decisions of consumers, savers and investors, if left to itself will lead to misallocation of investment and to underinvestment, and to regional imbalance in the levels of employment and economic activity. However, as far as regional employment is concerned, it is not at all obvious that this form of capital subsidization, which cheapens capital relatively to labour, with the latter generally in excess supply, is the best way to proceed.[2] But the issues that regional development grants and investment incentives generally raise are extremely complex. Some of the issues, such as the distribution of income and wealth in society and stabilization policy, were referred to in the introduction to this section but cannot be explored further here, except to say that the empirical evidence, such as it is, suggests that investment incentives have not been very effective in stimulating capital growth in the country as a whole – though they certainly seem to have stimulated growth in the assisted areas – since the overall growth rate has for many years lagged behind that of the

---

1   See Prest and Barr, *Public Finance in Theory and Practice*, Chapter 16 and the Green Paper on *Corporation Tax*, for further discussion.

2   See chapter 4, section V.3.

US and most Western European countries. Moreover, their use as stabilization instruments depends crucially on the timing and actual variation in the grants and allowances. It may be doubted that government or anyone else has the knowledge to manipulate these successfully.

Oil taxation has become increasingly important in recent years as a consequence of exploitable North Sea oil and gas discoveries, and is likely to be even more important in the next few years with government revenue estimated to reach some £4,300m in 1982-3.

The tax system has four main components. The first is a royalty of 12½% of the wellhead value, though this can be refunded in whole or in part to encourage a licensee to develop or continue production from a commercially marginal field. The second is petroleum revenue tax (PRT), which is chargeable on each field separately, currently at a rate of 70% but to be increased to 75% after 31 December 1982, on net income, defined as receipts from oil sales less royalties and operating costs (excluding interest payments) and less certain important reliefs. The third component of the tax system is corporation tax which is levied at 52% on net income after deducting royalties and PRT, and the fourth is a supplementary petroleum duty (SPD) of 20% of gross revenue less an oil allowance of half a million tonnes per 6-monthly chargeable period; the SPD was extended for a further chargeable period to 31 December 1982 but is to lapse thereafter.

IV.7   Value Added Tax

Value added tax (VAT), as its name implies, taxes value added at each stage of the productive process, with the final selling price to the consumer being made up of the cost of production plus the rate of tax. An example may help to make the matter clearer. Suppose the value added tax rate is 10% – the standard rate for 1982-3 is 15% – and that a manufacturer buys all his raw materials at a cost of 110 including tax. The 10 is known as input tax. The manufacturer processes the raw materials and sells the final product to a retailer for 220 including tax. The 20 is known as output tax, and the manufacturer pays the difference between the output tax and the input tax to Customs and Excise, namely 10. The retailer may be supposed to sell the product to the consumer for 330 including tax. Thus the output tax of the retailer is 30 and the input tax is 20, so he also pays 10 to Customs and Excise.

Thus the tax, as it were, comes to rest with the consumer, and this is why VAT is frequently described as an indirect tax on consumer expenditure. It should be stressed, however, that the foregoing is intended only as a simple arithmetical explanation of the VAT method and should not be interpreted as implying that the tax is necessarily wholly passed on to the final consumer. The problems of tax incidence are extremely complex and, in principle, require to be examined within the framework of a comprehensive model.

In substituting VAT for the previous purchase tax and selective employment tax, the government argued that the latter taxes were discriminatory in their effects on the prices of goods and services and that they should be replaced by a more broadly based indirect tax, causing less distortion of consumer choice, and so allowing a more efficient allocation of resources. It was also argued that VAT would benefit the balance of payments as it is more easily remitted on exports than purchase tax – imports are liable for VAT. Finally, VAT had either been adopted by the actual members, or was in process of being adopted by the prospective members, of the European Community — as a step towards harmonization — and so the UK had little or no alternative but to move in the same direction.[1]

There can be little doubt that the way purchase tax and selective employment tax were levied certainly distorted relative prices and that difficulties would arise in trying to levy them in a way that minimized this kind of distortion. Thus value added tax may well be superior on the basis of this criterion. However, in solving one problem another one may be created, in that it can be argued that a general tax on consumer expenditure is regressive and discriminates against those on lower incomes. Successive governments have attempted, and it would seem with some success at least as far as short-run consequences are concerned, to get round this criticism by what is called zero-rating most food, coal, gas, electricity, the construction of buildings, public transport fares, and drugs and medicines supplied on prescription. Zero-rating means that the trader does not have to charge tax on his sales and, in addition, he can claim a refund of any tax he may have paid to his suppliers because of tax paid on inputs entering into the final product.

The balance of payments argument in favour of value added tax is superficially persuasive, at least in the short term, in that imports bear the tax whereas exports are zero-rated. However, it is not at all clear what are the long-term implications for the balance of payments.

Certain other features of value added tax deserve to be mentioned. As well as a zero-rated category of goods there is also an exempted category. For exempted goods the trader does not have to charge tax on his sales but he cannot claim a refund for any tax included in the price of his purchases. Exempted goods and services include land, insurance, postal services provided by the Post Office, betting and gaming (which already carry excise duty), finance, education and health services. Small traders with a business turnover of less than £17,000 a year or £6,000 a quarter in taxable goods and services are exempt from the tax. In 1982-3 VAT is expected to raise almost £15,000m in revenue, nearly 50% of the income-tax total.

IV.8   Excise Duties and Protective Duties

Until recently the practice in the UK has been to distinguish between customs duties, which were imposed on imports, and excise duties, which were levied on home-produced goods and services. External duties had two functions; one, to raise revenue in a similar way to excise duties and two, to give protection to British-produced goods or preference to goods from specified countries. However, the accession of the UK to the European Communities obliged her to bring (by the end of the transition period, 1 January 1978) her practices into line with the rest of the Community. Thus duties for revenue purposes are now known as excise duties and are levied on both home-produced and similar imported goods. Protective duties refer to what was formerly the protective part of customs duties and these have been generally brought into line with the Common External Tariff of the European Community. This means that the UK, like other members of the Community, now operates a common tariff on imports from non-members, whilst trade between the member countries is free of customs duty. As may be seen from

---

1 See *Value-added Tax*, Cmnd. 4621, 1971; and *Value Added Tax*, Cmnd. 4929, 1972.

table 2.10, the products which are large revenue-yielders are oil, tobacco and alcohol with a total estimated yield of £11,900m in 1982-3, or almost 16% of total revenue from taxation. Moreover, this does not take account of VAT on these products.

An outstanding feature of the duties and taxes on oil, tobacco and alcohol is the large proportion that they represent of the purchase price. Ordinarily it might be expected that something which has the effect of substantially increasing the price of a product would lead to less of it, perhaps much less of it, being bought. By and large this does not seem to have happened with these three products – their demands are inelastic with respect to price. However, some doubts are beginning to be expressed about the buoyancy of the revenue from tobacco, though this may be due to other causes besides the scale of taxation. The inelasticity of demand with respect to price implies that these duties and taxes may have little direct effect on the allocation of resources. But there will be an indirect effect because the funds withdrawn by taxes from consumers will scarcely be spent by the state in the same way as if they had been in the hands of the former.

It is often argued that indirect taxes are to be preferred because they are less of a disincentive to the supply of labour than direct taxes. This is an extremely difficult issue and depends on many factors, such as the scale of duties and taxes to be substituted, say, for a reduction in direct taxes or for forgoing an increase, the type and range of the goods involved and, in particular, whether they are considered as substitutes or complements for leisure. For an individual, in choosing between additional work or leisure, may well consider not only the direct tax on extra earnings but also the type of goods and services that can be bought with additional income either now or in the future and either by himself or those who may inherit from him.[1]

It is also arguable that on equity grounds indirect taxes are regressive in that they fall more heavily on the relatively low-income groups. There would seem to be some truth in this as far as tobacco and beer are concerned, but possibly to a lesser extent for petrol, given that bus fares are largely insulated from increases in oil duties. On the other hand the relatively less well-off obtain benefits from government welfare and other services. If the community wants extensive government expenditure on welfare services and education it seems unavoidable that one way or another a large proportion of the tax revenue must be raised from the mass of taxpayers. If at the same time the latter are important beneficiaries from government expenditure then they are indirectly paying for perhaps all of or a major part of these benefits. This is in no way to deny, however, the power of taxation, or at least certain forms of it, to redistribute income and wealth.

IV.9   Capital Transfer Tax and Wealth Tax

Capital transfer tax (CTT) was introduced in 1975 at the same time as estate duty was abolished. The tax, often called a gifts tax, applies, subject to certain exemptions, to gifts made during life and to transfers on death. Transfers of what is called settled property or property held in trust are also subject to the tax. The tax is chargeable as the gifts or transfers occur and is cumulative over a maximum period of ten years. That is, in calculating the tax due on successive gifts or

---

1   See *The Structure and Reform of Direct Taxation*, op. cit.

transfers the ones made over the previous nine years are taken into account and progressively higher rates of tax apply. The rates of tax on what are known as lifetime transfers are lower than for transfers on death. The tax is in general payable by the donor but may be recovered from the beneficiary.

The main exemptions are transfers between husband and wife both in life and on death; transfers in any one year of up to £3,000 plus any unused part of the previous year's exemption; outright gifts to any one person during the tax year up to a value of £250; and transfers made out of income after tax as part of normal expenditure which leave the donor sufficient income to maintain his usual standard of living. Marriage gifts are given special treatment; transfers by a parent up to £5,000 are exempt and up to £2,500 by any other ancestor and £1,000 by anyone else. Business owners and working farmers also get special relief; for purposes of the tax, value transferred is reduced by 50% (with a smaller reduction for tenanted land). Transfers to charities up to a maximum of £250,000 are completely exempt if made more than a year before death. There are also special provisions relating to the exemption of gifts of works of art and historic buildings made during the individual's lifetime.

The first £55,000 of transfers, after taking into consideration all exemptions, is tax-free whether made during lifetime or on death. The rates for lifetime transfers then rise from 15% on the next £20,000 — for transfers on death the rate is 30% — by gradual steps to 50% on lifetime transfers and to 75% on transfers on death of over £2.5m. In future the rate bands are to be indexed for inflation. Transfers made within three years of death are subject to the rates applicable on death.

The intention behind the introduction of the CTT is to reduce the inequality of wealth distribution. It should clearly be more effective in achieving this than the estate duty which it replaced, since the latter was avoidable if gifts were made during lifetime and outside the *inter-vivos* period. However, it is arguable that an accessions tax, that is a tax on recipients rather than on donors, would have been more effective as a means of achieving greater wealth equality. For an accessions tax would encourage a spreading of gifts between recipients in a way that would reduce tax liability; this is not true of the CTT.

The precise form of the CTT and the exemptions it incorporates make it extremely important for individuals with even quite modest capital assets to plan their affairs carefully if they wish to minimize their tax liability. This too could be a source of inequity, depending on the foresight and luck of donors. Finally, like all such taxes it may encourage increased consumption expenditure and perhaps expenditure on education, travel and the like.

The then Chancellor announced in his 1974 budget that the government intended to introduce an annual wealth tax. Subsequently a Green Paper was published outlining the proposals the government had in mind.[1] In a foreword to the Green Paper the Chancellor stated that 'income by itself is not an adequate measure of taxable capacity. The ownership of wealth, whether it produces income or not, adds to the economic resources of a taxpayer so that the person who has wealth as well as income of a given size necessarily has a greater taxable capacity than one who has only income of that size.'[2] It is not clear what precise form the wealth tax might ultimately take, as it has run into much criticism both in and

---

1   *Wealth Tax*, Cmnd. 5704, 1974.

2   ibid., p. 111.

outside Parliament. A Select Committee of the House of Commons established to examine a wealth tax did not find it possible to present an agreed report and for the present, especially since the change of government in 1979, the matter would seem to be in abeyance.

IV.10   Taxation and the European Community[1]

It is evident from the preceding discussion that some of the recent tax reforms of the UK were designed to bring its taxes, or at any rate some of them, more closely into line with those of the European Community. Members are obliged under the Treaty of Rome and subsequent directives to harmonize their tax legislation as regards turnover taxes, excise duties and other forms of indirect taxation. In particular, the Community has adopted value added taxation as its main general indirect tax and this is binding on all members, though there remains considerable variety in the number and scale of rates levied. Contributions to the Community budget are in part calculated on the basis of value added tax.

The Community intends to harmonize the main excise duties on tobacco, oil and alcohol. As far as the UK is concerned this may eventually mean a reduction in the duties on tobacco and alcohol since these are much higher than in most of the countries of the present Community. Corporation-tax harmonization is still under consideration within the Community but it seems likely that the credit or imputation system will be adopted. The Community does not require harmonization of direct personal taxation.

The fundamental justification for tax harmonization within the Community stems from the very concept of the Community as, amongst other things, a common, unified competitive market. This requires, it is argued, the disappearance of all artificial barriers to trade and capital flows between the member countries, including those that might be created by different tax systems. On the basis of this approach the impetus towards uniformity or harmonization of taxation is immense. This is especially clear in the case of value added tax and excise duties and is becoming more so, as far as corporation tax is concerned, with the increasing importance of international companies and the mobility of capital, which the Community is determined to foster among its members. The need to harmonize personal direct taxation is not felt to arise as it is believed that mobility of labour is not greatly affected by differences between member countries in this type of tax.[2]

The whole process of tax harmonization carries important consequences for both the Community and its member countries. By implication it places great stress on the efficient allocation of resources as indicated by the static competitive model. By the same token it neglects, or at least puts on one side, the fundamental questions of externalities and of income and wealth distribution, except to the extent that these will or can be dealt with by harmonization of social-security arrangements and with the help of the Community budget, and by regional policy measures. Up to the present none of these areas is well developed, though some progress has been made in each of them. Finally, harmonization is relevant to the

---

1   See chapter 4, section II on the Common Agricultural Policy.

2   However, the Community intends to harmonize such matters relating to direct taxation as tax-deduction of dividends at source.

whole issue of stabilization policy. It remains to be seen to what extent it will be possible for individual members to vary indirect taxes such as value added tax as an instrument of fiscal policy. This could obviously pose serious problems for member countries and, not least, the relative fiscal power of the Community *vis-à-vis* its individual members. These matters have, as yet, had little public discussion in the UK.

V   POLICY IN RETROSPECT AND PROSPECT
V.1   The 1960s and After

In the brief review of policy below attention is concentrated on the record of the authorities in the pursuit of their major policy goals. For most of the 1960s the authorities were preoccupied with the achievement of high levels of employment, price stability, economic growth, fixed exchange rates and a 'satisfactory' balance of payments. But in the late 1960s the commitment to fixed exchange rates became less strong and was abandoned in the early 1970s; and in the last few years a reduction in the rate of inflation rather than price stability has come to dominate the other policy goals including full employment and economic growth. Indeed the authorities now see the curtailment of the pace of inflation as a necessary means to achieving more employment and faster economic growth.

During the 1960s unemployment in Great Britain averaged less than 2%, though from 1967 onwards it was in excess of this figure. But for the 1970s it averaged 4.0% with the trend ominously rising; and for 1980 the average was 6.89% and for 1981 10.5%. Thus the policy goal of high levels of employment is far from being currently achieved.

Retail prices rose over the 1960s at a compound rate of some 3.8% a year, with the rate of increase accelerating in the later years to around 5%. However, even this latter rate seems low in comparison with the rates experienced since. Over the 1970s the annual rate was over 13%, which implies that during the period prices rose by more than 300%. But even 13% is relatively mild in comparison with a rate of 24% between 1974 and 1975 and the rate of around 18% in 1980; by early 1982 the rate has fallen to 12%. Thus there has been a complete failure to achieve price stability, as measured by retail prices, and the degree of failure increased dramatically during the 1970s.

If economic growth is measured in terms of gross domestic product (GDP) then this grew at a compound rate of around 2.8% a year during the 1960s, though by no means regularly, and just about 1.5% a year in the 1970s. Between 1972 and 1973 GDP increased by over 6% but fell by about 3% between 1973 and 1975; and GDP has also fallen in 1980 and 1981. Thus whilst some economic growth has taken place it has been far from regular and has been low by international standards for developed countries.[1]

For the first half or more of the 1960s fixed exchange rates were a major goal of economic policy. But in the year or two leading up to the devaluation of sterling in November 1967 this policy came increasingly under question and by

---

1   Taking the EEC (of the nine countries) as the norm and equal to 100, GDP per head in the UK in 1962 at current official exchange rates was 109.7 and at current purchasing-power parities was 108.3. By 1977 the corresponding figures were 71.7 and 91.8. Over these 15 years the UK has fallen far behind West Germany, France, Holland and other countries in terms of GDP per capita.

1972 the Chancellor of the Exchequer was prepared to say in his budget speech that 'it is neither necessary nor desirable to distort domestic economies . . . in order to maintain unrealistic exchange rates, whether they were too high or too low'. In the light of the exchange-rate fluctuations in recent years it seems doubtful that such a cavalier statement would be made now, though this is not to say that fixed exchange rates have once more become a widely accepted policy goal in the UK. Whatever may be true of the official attitude to exchange rates and whether it be regarded as a goal or policy target, there is no doubt about the authorities' concern over the balance of payments. For most of the 1960s and in the 1970s the balance of payments has been a matter of grave concern to the authorities and from time to time they have felt constrained to take drastic action to improve the position.

Since June 1972 the exchange rate of sterling has been allowed to float, though by no means free from official intervention. During 1973 it averaged about $2.45 to the pound, falling to $1.75 in 1977. However, since the US dollar has itself experienced variations in its exchange rate during this time, a better indicator for sterling is what is called the 'sterling effective exchange rate' which is a weighted index of movements against a basket of other currencies; the base year is 1975 with the index set equal to 100. From 1973 to 1977 the rate declined from 112 to 81, a depreciation of 28%; between 1977 and 1980 the index increased from 81 to 96, a rise of over 18%.

Thus during the 1970s and into the early 1980s the UK, like much of the rest of the world, has experienced relatively variable exchange rates. This outcome must be expected when exchange rates are allowed to float, with or without official intervention (in the foreign exchange market) by monetary authorities and especially if different countries are pursuing divergent monetary policies; in November 1979 the MLR of the Bank of England was raised to 17%, an historically high level for the UK and also high relative to rates in other countries. Variability of exchange rates has important consequences for the domestic economy. In particular, a sharp appreciation in the effective exchange rate, such as occurred between 1979 and 1980, may seriously affect the competitiveness of exports and put great pressure on the profits of those companies heavily involved in export markets. This, in turn, will tend to depress domestic economic activity and increase unemployment, especially when real wages are inflexible downwards. But this is essentially the pattern of events that was taking place in the UK in 1980 and into 1981. However, there were, of course, many other influences, quite outside the control of the authorities in this period, contributing to the position of the UK economy. Nevertheless, it is arguable that an appreciating exchange rate is helpful in securing a reduction in the rate of domestic inflation, at least in the short term, through its effects on the home price of imports.

But if the economic record of the 1960s and especially the 1970s is disappointing, what were the roles of monetary policy and fiscal policy over this period? Throughout the 1960s little or no attention was given to the behaviour of the monetary aggregates. Monetary policy or more accurately credit policy was largely seen in terms of using quantitative restrictions to control particular credit magnitudes together with the manipulation of interest rates, with the latter geared to government financing requirements. Nevertheless, it is instructive to examine the growth of the monetary aggregates during part of the 1960s.

From 1963I to 1970I (where I refers to the first quarter and the data are seasonally adjusted), M_1 grew at an average rate of 3% a year and $£M_3$ at 5.4%.

The contrast with the next 3 years to 1973I is striking when M_1 and $£M_3$ grew respectively at average rates of 13% and 18.4%. It will be recalled that this period overlapped with the introduction of the CCC measures. It should also be noted that it predates the first oil crisis; the latter is important to bear in mind in assessing the 'causes' of inflation in the UK since the mid-1970s. More specifically, and notwithstanding certain problems of interpretation because of the removal of restrictions on the activities of the banks, the rapid growth in these monetary aggregates is suggestive of a boost to inflation quite distinct from the oil crisis.

From 1973I to 1979I, just before Mrs Thatcher's government took office, the respective annual rates of growth of M_1 and $£M_3$ were some 14% and 12%, again relatively high rates of growth by historical standards, though attempts were being made to slow these growth rates down from 1976 onwards.

As regards fiscal policy, difficulties arise in trying to determine whether or not a so-called 'fiscal stance' is, in some sense, expansionary, contractionary or neutral in its effects on the economy. For some years discussions of fiscal policy at the macroeconomic level have concentrated on the PSBR as an indicator of fiscal stance. Four measures of PSBR may be distinguished: (1) the nominal or actual; (2) the demand-weighted; (3) the cyclically adjusted; and (4) the inflation-adjusted or 'real'.[1]

The first is the familiar one and requires no further discussion. The second is based on the proposition that changes in different kinds of government expenditure and revenue may have different multiplier effects on output, and it attempts to weight these in relation to any actual PSBR. It is recognized that the attempt to measure such multipliers is highly precarious, thus casting doubt on the usefulness of the demand-weighted PSBR.

The cyclically adjusted PSBR is intended to compensate for the fact that even with fixed expenditure programmes, rates of tax and social-security benefits, 'fluctuations in economic activity would lead to movements in the PSBR'.[2] For example, the heavier than expected unemployment during 1981 has increased the PSBR. The cyclically adjusted PSBR tries to correct for these cyclical effects and estimate what the PSBR would be if they were removed and the economy was growing at its trend rate. In periods of recession this results in the cyclically adjusted PSBR being less than the actual PSBR. Some would wish to infer from this that the actual PSBR should be increased to keep the cyclically adjusted PSBR stable. But this suggestion raises all sorts of questions about the overall policy of government and would not necessarily be appropriate.

The fourth measure, the inflation-adjusted or real PSBR, refers to the nominal or actual PSBR corrected for the erosion through inflation of the real value of the outstanding public-sector debt. The argument is that inflation is, in effect, a form of tax on the holders of the public debt, reducing the real value of their assets, which, of course, reduces the real value of government liabilities. This latter reduction should, in principle, be offset against the nominal interest payments on the public debt, thereby reducing the nominal PSBR to arrive at the inflation-adjusted or real PSBR.

---

1 The discussion that follows relies heavily on the Treasury Economic Progress Report, *The Budget Balance: Measurement and Policy*, No. 144, April 1982.

2 ibid., p. 2.

The calculation of the real PSBR necessarily raises difficulties, especially over the appropriate price deflators to employ, but this does not in any way weaken the force of the arguments in favour of the real PSBR as an analytical concept, which has important implications for the understanding of economic behaviour and the assessment of government policy.[1] In particular, there is reason to believe that if inflation erodes the real value of the private-sector's monetary assets it will respond, in part, by attempting to restore them. This response may be of marked significance for government policy, including the terms on which it can finance its normal PSBR.

With the nominal amount of public debt recently outstanding being roughly 50% of GDP at market prices, clearly any corrections for inflation, especially if the latter is in double figures, are going to be substantial and markedly reduce the nominal PSBR. Just how significant such corrections are, may be seen in table 2.14. An average nominal PSBR of £0.9bn for the late 1960s becomes 'real' net lending by the public sector of £0.6bn. This pattern is repeated in the first half of the 1970s, though there is a distinct change between the first three years and the

TABLE 2.14

Nominal and 'Real' PSBR: 1967-80 (£bn) (borrowing = −; lending = +)

| | Annual averages | | | | | |
	1967-9	1970-72	1973-5	1976-8	1979[1]	1980[1]
Nominal	−0.9	−1.1	−7.0	−7.8	−12.6	−12.3
As % of national income at market prices[2]	−2.4	−2.0	−8.6	−6.2	−7.5	−6.2
'Real'	+0.6	+1.9	+1.3	−0.1	+1.3	−0.2
As % of 'real' national income at market prices[2]	+1.4	+3.7	+1.6	−0.1	+0.7	−0.1

Source: BEQB, vol. 21, no. 2, June 1981, p. 234.

1   Provisional estimates.

2   National income plus general government income from net indirect taxes. The 'real' estimate also includes the notional gain on net external monetary liabilities.

second three years of this period, with a fall in 'real' net lending by the public sector and particularly as a percentage of 'real' national income; in broad terms there was a shift towards an expansionary fiscal stance between the first and second three-year periods.

For the three years 1976-8 the nominal PSBR remained much the same as in the previous three years but the 'real' PSBR was negative, representing real net borrowing but on a relatively small scale, reflecting in part some decline in the pace of inflation.

---

1   To emphasize the importance of the PSBR in assessing government policy can be misleading if it distracts attention from the scale of government spending, including the real resources it represents and the effects this has on the performance of the economy.

With the advent of Mrs Thatcher's government in 1979 a new emphasis was placed on reducing the nominal PSBR and in pursuing monetary growth targets, though the medium-term financial strategy (MTFS) was not formally introduced until the 1980 budget. Central to that strategy was the announcement for a period of four years of declining target rates of growth for £M$_3$ and the structuring of fiscal policy to be consistent with those targets. The government believed that this required the PSBR to be reduced substantially as a proportion of GDP if nominal interest rates were not to be unduly high and possibly damaging to the private sector.

The initial target rates of growth for £M$_3$, which are expressed as a target range, and the projected path for the PSBR, which was not conceived of as a target, may be seen in table 2.15, together with the actual outcomes.[1]

TABLE 2.15
Growth of Money Stock (£M$_3$) and the PSBR/GDP Ratio, 1980-84

	1980-81	*1981-2*	*1982-3*	*1983-4*
Target growth range of £M$_3$ (%)	7-11	6-10	5-9	4-8
Actual rate of growth of £M$_3$ (%)	18	14½[1]	–	–
Projected PSBR as % of GDP at market prices	3¾	3	2¼	1½
Actual PSBR as % of GDP at market prices	5¾	4¼[2]	–	–

Sources: Financial Statement and Budget Report, 1980-81 and *FS,* March 1982.

1 February 1981 to February 1982, 'correcting' for new monetary sector.

2 This figure equalled the projected PSBR/GDP percentage as revised in the 1981 budget.

It would be unrealistic to have expected the authorities to have achieved some-where near the middle of the target growth range for £M$_3$ but at first sight the scale of the departures in 1980-81 and 1981-2 is surprising. However, there were major factors at work 'distorting' the growth of £M$_3$, especially the ending of the SSD scheme in June 1980, which seems to have led to a certain amount of reintermediation for the banks; other special factors have also made for unusual growth in £M$_3$ over the past two financial years. When some attempt is made to allow for these factors, and inflation, as measured by the retail price index, is taken into account at 12.7% for 1980-81 and 11% for the 12 months ending February 1982, the real growth in £M$_3$ would be small, and, indeed, negative for 1980-81. This suggests that monetary policy has been quite tight over this period and this is borne out by other factors, including the high sterling rate during 1980-81 and high nominal interest rates, with the latter in turn generating high real interest rates. Moreover, it was already indicated in table 2.14 that the 'real' PSBR was very small for the year 1980 and this was almost certainly true for 1981-2 as well; indeed net

1 The revised targets announced in the *Financial Statement and Budget Report 1982-83* are:

	1982-3	*1983-4*	*1984-5*
Target growth range of £M$_3$ (%)	8-12	7-11	6-10
Projected PSBR as % of GDP	3½	2¾	2

The revised targets for £M$_3$ were re-based on the actual growth in 1981-2.

'real' lending may have occurred. Thus, so far under the MTFS, monetary and
fiscal conditions have been broadly restrictive.

There can be little doubt that these policies have contributed to the fall in
inflation over the past couple of years. This is not to say that the monetary and
fiscal policies of the authorities are as soundly based as they might be. Their
confidence in $£M_3$ as a target variable has been shaken and their search for
alternative or supplementary monetary aggregates as targets continues. They have
shied away from a proper monetary base approach to monetary control which
really would leave the market to determine interest rates and, instead, emphasize
the so-called supply-side approach to monetary control. This in turn has
encouraged them to put great stress on the nominal PSBR which, analytically,
looks increasingly questionable and perhaps distracts their attention from the
scale of government expenditure and its effects on the functioning of the economic
system.

That the price of restrictive monetary and fiscal policies has been high in terms
of contributing to the massive and disturbing growth in unemployment and the fall
in GDP is abundantly evident. However, if it is crucially important to curb
inflation, and many would argue that it is, then a society which repudiates state
coercion may for a time have to be prepared to suffer sustained unemployment
and some loss of output — hopefully as a means to more soundly based economic
growth and a recovery in employment, perhaps encouraged by a better functioning
labour market.

V.2   Policy and the European Community

Whatever may be the merits or demerits of past monetary and fiscal policy there is
no doubt that the UK is, and has been, affected by the moves to establish economic
and monetary union amongst the members of the European Community. Some ten
years ago this was envisaged as involving absolutely fixed exchange-rate margins, or,
alternatively and preferably, a single Community currency and the establishment
of a Community system for the central banks of the member countries, possibly
along the lines of the Federal Reserve System of the United States and with
analogous powers. The harmonized management of national budgets was also
envisaged as taking place under the auspices of a Community decision-making body
which would have authority to influence member countries' levels of revenue and
expenditure, as well as the methods employed to finance deficits and the disposal
of surpluses.[1]

However, these far-reaching proposals received a cool response from member
countries and little progress was made towards implementing them. But more
recently the matter was again taken up by the Community, when Mr Roy Jenkins
was President of the Commission of the European Communities, and is reflected in
the establishment of the European Monetary System (EMS).[2]

---

1   *Report* to the Council and the Commission on the Realization by Stages of Economic and
    Monetary Union in the Community, Werner Report, Supplement to Bulletin 11 — 1970 of
    the European Communities.

2   See Roy Jenkins, 'Europe's Present Challenge and Future Opportunity', Jean Monnet
    Lecture, European Institute, Florence, 27 October 1977, and reprinted in *Lloyds Bank
    Review*, January 1978, No. 127, pp. 1-14.

The EMS came into operation on 13 March 1979, and is designed in the words of the European Council 'to establish a greater measure of monetary stability in the Community'.[1] One of the basic features of the EMS is the agreement between the fully participating members to maintain their exchange rates, except for Italy, within ± 2¼% of agreed central rates. Italy was allowed a margin of ± 6% because its currency was floating at the time. The UK decided, at least for the time being, not to participate in the exchange-rate arrangements, but is a party to other aspects of the scheme.

The participating members have found it necessary to realign their exchange rates on a number of occasions since the inauguration of the scheme, but despite these it is fairly claimed that the new arrangements have helped to stabilize exchange rates between the members during at any rate the first few years of operation of the EMS. Whether or not the members will be able to sustain this relative stability of exchange rates seems doubtful since the members are experiencing substantially divergent inflation rates.

One of the implications of a strictly fixed exchange-rate relationship between currencies, according to the monetary approach to exchange-rate behaviour, is the need to ensure that monetary policies are consistent with its maintenance. This requires, in particular, that the money supply of the subordinate or satellite currencies should be geared to this end and in effect become endogenous, and that other policies, including fiscal policies, be similarly directed. Ideally these arrangements would be carried out by careful co-ordination of policies between the members and this would certainly seem to be what the Community has in mind. For the European Council has stated that 'The European Monetary System will facilitate the convergence of economic development and give fresh impetus to the process of European Union.'[2] It still remains to be seen if the Community will be able to achieve the kind of co-ordination required and if the UK will become a full participant of the EMS.

V.3   Conclusions

The policy record of the UK for the period since the 1960s has been extremely disappointing. The simultaneous achievement of the various goals over a sustained period has continuously eluded the authorities. This failure or relative failure raises far-reaching questions about the choice of policy goals, the nature and adequacy of the policy instruments at the disposal of the authorities, and the limitations on our knowledge of the detailed and interdependent relationships between goals, instruments and targets. Moreover, these questions ultimately go far beyond the realm of economic considerations.

But the discussion in section V.1 suggests that policy errors and misjudgements have contributed significantly to the economic problems of recent years. Both monetary and fiscal policy have from time to time been used in ways which could only be expected to give rise to future economic problems; the monetary and budgetary policies of the early to mid-1970s come particularly to mind, and, to a lesser extent, the policies pursued in 1977 and 1978. However, there seems to be a greater acceptance across a range of political opinion that rapid and variable

---

1 *European Economy*, Commission of the European Communities, No. 2, March 1979, p. 7. See also chapter 3, section III.8, on this whole subject.

2 *European Economy*, ibid.

inflation imposes serious costs on the community, putting at risk both employment and living standards; and that both monetary and fiscal policy can be managed in ways that contribute to its curtailment. These developments augur well, as far as domestic measures are concerned, for the recovery of the UK economy over the next several years even though the adjustment process may be slow and costly. This is not to imply that sound monetary and fiscal policies are a sufficient condition for that recovery, but the efficiency of industry and the functioning of labour and other markets — broadly the supply side of the economy — is the primary concern of other chapters.

REFERENCES AND FURTHER READING

M.J. Artis and M.K. Lewis, *Monetary Control in the United Kingdom*, Phillip Allan, 1981.

A.D. Bain, *The Economics of the Financial System*, Martin Robertson, 1981.

Bank of England Quarterly Bulletin.

Committee to Review the Functioning of Financial Institutions (Wilson Committee), *Report: Appendices*, Cmnd. 7937, HMSO, June 1980.

Corporation Tax (Green Paper), Cmnd. 8456, HMSO, January 1982.

N.J. Gibson, *The Financial System in Northern Ireland*, Northern Ireland Economic Council, April 1982.

David Gowland, *Controlling the Money Supply*, Croom Helm, 1982.

M.A. King and J.A. Kay, *The British Tax System*, 2nd edition, Oxford University Press, 1980.

Monetary Control (Green Paper), Cmnd. 7858, HMSO, March 1980.

A.R. Prest and N.A. Barr, *Public Finance in Theory and Practice*, 6th edition, Weidenfeld and Nicolson, 1979.

The Structure and Reform of Direct Taxation, Report of a Committee chaired by Professor J.E. Meade, Allen and Unwin, 1978.

Treasury and Civil Service Committee, *Memoranda on Monetary Policy*, House of Commons, Session 1979-80, 720, July 1980; 720-II, November 1980, HMSO, 1980.

Treasury and Civil Service Committee, *Monetary Policy, Vol. I, Report, Vol. II Minutes of Evidence, Vol. III Appendices*, House of Commons, Session 1980-81, 163-I, II, III, HMSO, 1981.

D. Swann, *The Common Market*, 4th edition, Penguin Books, 1978.

3

Foreign trade and the balance of payments

J.S. Metcalfe

I THE UK BALANCE OF PAYMENTS
I.1 Introduction

The importance to the UK of foreign trade, foreign investment and the balance of international payments will be obvious to anyone who has followed the course of events since 1960. The growth of the UK economy, the level of employment, real wages and the standard of living have been, and will continue to be, greatly influenced by external economic events. It is the purpose of this chapter to outline the main features of the external relationships of the UK and to discuss economic policies adopted to manipulate these external relationships, with the primary focus of attention being on the years since 1960.[1]

To begin with, it is often said that the UK is a highly 'open' economy, and some indication of the meaning of this is given by the fact that in 1980 exports of goods and services were 32.8% of GDP and imports of goods and services were 30% of GDP, both figures being greater than the corresponding figures for the mid-1960s and substantially greater than those for 1938.[2] A high degree of openness implies that the structure of production and employment is greatly influenced by international specialization. For the UK it also means that about half the foodstuffs and the bulk of raw materials necessary to maintain inputs for industry have to be imported. In the sense defined, the UK is a more open economy than some industrial nations, for example, West Germany and France, but less open than others such as Belgium.

I.2 The Concept of the Balance of Payments

The concept of the balance of payments is central to a study of the external monetary relationships of a country but, as with any unifying concept, it is not free from ambiguities of definition and of interpretation. Such ambiguities stem from at least two sources, viz. the different uses to which the concept may be put — either as a tool for economic analysis or as a guide to the need for, and effectiveness of, external policy changes; and the different ways in which we may approach the concept — either as a system of accounts or as a measure of transactions in the foreign exchange market.

From an accounting viewpoint, we may define the balance of payments as a systematic record, over a given period of time, of all transactions between domestic residents and residents of foreign nations. In this context, residents are defined as

---

1 Earlier editions of this volume contain a discussion of external developments between 1945 and 1960. See, e.g., the 5th edition (1974).

2 In 1938 the export: GNP ratio stood at 18.9% and the import: GNP ratio stood at 20.0%.

those individuals living in the UK for one year or more, together with corporate bodies located in the UK, and UK government agencies and military forces located abroad. Ideally, the transactions involved should be recorded at the time of the change of ownership of commodities and assets, or at the time specific services are performed. In practice, trade flows are recorded on a shipments basis, at the time when the exports documents are lodged with the Customs and Excise, and at the time when imports are cleared through Customs. The problem with this method is that the time of shipment need bear no close or stable relationship to the time of payment for the goods concerned, and it is this latter which is relevant to the state of the foreign exchange market, although over a year the discrepancies between the two methods are likely to be small. All transactions are recorded as sterling money flows, and when transactions are invoiced in foreign currencies, their values are converted into sterling at the appropriate exchange rate. Because sterling is a 'key' or 'vehicle' currency, and is used as an international medium of exchange, it transpires that 76% of UK exports and roughly 38% of UK imports were invoiced directly in sterling.[1]

Like all systems of income and expenditure accounts, the balance of payments accounts are an ex-post record, constructed on the principle of double-entry bookkeeping. Thus each external transaction is effectively entered twice, once to indicate the original transaction, say the import of a given commodity, and again to indicate the manner in which that transaction was financed. The convention is that credit items, which increase net money claims on foreign residents, e.g. exports of goods and services and foreign investment in the UK, are entered with a positive sign, and that debit items, which increase net money liabilities of domestic residents, e.g. imports of goods and services and profits earned by foreign-owned firms operating in the UK, are entered with a minus sign. It follows that, in sum, the balance of payments accounts always balance and that the interpretation to be read into the accounts depends on the prior selection of a particular sub-set of transactions. It will be clear, therefore, that there can be no unique picture of a country's external relationship which may be drawn from the accounts.

When analysing the balance of payments it can be useful to make a distinction between autonomous external transactions, transactions undertaken for private gain or international political obligation, and accommodating external transactions, transactions undertaken or induced specifically to finance a gap between autonomous credits and autonomous debits. This distinction is by no means water-tight, as we shall see, but it provides a useful starting point when structuring the accounts and when trying to formulate notions of balance of payments equilibrium.

The structure of the external accounts of the UK: It is current practice to divide the external accounts of the UK into three sets of items: (i) current-account items; (ii) capital-account items; and (iii) official financing items. Current-account items and all, or part (depending on taste), of capital-account items can as a first approximation be treated as if they correspond to autonomous external transactions, while official financing items may be treated as corresponding to

---

1   Cf. the article by S. A. Page, 'The Choice of Invoicing Currency in Merchandise Trade', *NIER*, no. 98, 1981.

accommodating transactions. The structure of the external accounts and figures for the period 1977-81 are shown in table 3.1.[1]

Current-account items consist of exports and imports of commodities (visibles) and services (invisibles, e.g. insurance, shipping, tourist and banking transactions); profit and interest payments received from abroad less similar payments made abroad; certain government transactions, e.g. maintenance of armed forces overseas; and specified transfer payments, e.g. immigrants remittances; payments to and from the EEC budget; and foreign aid granted by the UK government. The rationale for collecting these items together is that the majority of them are directly related to flows of national income and expenditure, whether public or private. In particular, visible and invisible trade flows are closely related to movements in foreign and domestic incomes, the division of these incomes between expenditure and saving, and the division of expenditure between outlays on foreign goods and services and outlays on domestic goods and services. It should be remembered, however, that trade flows may change not because of changes in incomes, but because of spending out of past savings (dishoarding) or because of the need to build up inventories of means of production, changes which correspond to variations in holdings of assets. Profit and interest flows are classified in the current account because they correspond directly to international flows of income.

Capital-account items can be arranged in several ways. One may distinguish official capital flows (line 3) from private capital flows (e.g. lines 4, 5 and 6). Alternatively, one may classify by the maturity date of the assets involved and distinguish long-term capital flows (e.g. lines 3-6 inclusive) from short-term capital flows (e.g. lines 7-14 inclusive). Equally one could, in principle, distinguish capital flows according to the implicit time-horizon of the investor undertaking the appropriate decisions. The inevitable limitations of alternative classificatory schemes should not be allowed to hide one basic point, that all capital flows correspond to changes in the stocks of foreign assets and liabilities of the UK, although not necessarily to changes in the net external wealth of the UK. As such these capital flows are motivated primarily by the relative rates of return on domestic and foreign assets, after due allowance is made for the effects of risk and taxation. Flows of direct and portfolio investment in productive capital assets (lines 5 and 6) thus depend on prospective rates of profit in the UK compared to those abroad, and changes in holdings of financial assets depend on relative domestic and foreign interest-rate structures. A relative increase in UK profit and interest rates will normally stimulate a larger net capital inflow or a smaller net capital outflow, and vice versa for a relative fall in UK profit and interest rates. One important factor which should not be overlooked here is the influence of anticipated exchange-rate changes upon the capital gains and losses accruing to holdings of assets denominated in different currencies. If a sterling depreciation is anticipated, for example, this will provide a powerful incentive for wealth holders to switch any sterling denominated assets they hold into foreign currency denominated assets, in order to avoid the expected capital losses on holdings of sterling assets.[2] The 'capital value'

---

1   For further details the reader may consult the *UK Balance of Payments 1981*, HMSO, 1982. This annual publication is known as the *Pink Book*. The unavailability of trade figures for 1981 leaves this table incomplete. The estimated current-account surplus for 1981 is £8bn.

2   Subject to the possibility that forward exchange cover may have been taken (cf. section III.6 below).

TABLE 3.1

UK Summary Balance of Payments 1977-81 (£m)

		1977	1978	1979	1980	1981
Current account (credit +/debit −)						
Exports (fob) (+)		+31,728	+35,063	+40,687	+47,396	....[1]
Imports (fob) (−)		−34,012	−36,605	−44,136	−46,221	....[1]
Visible-trade balance		−2,284	−1,542	−3,449	+1,185	....[1]
Government services and transfers (net)		−1,839	−2,401	−2,855	−2,620	−2,432
Other invisibles and transfers (net)		+4,082	+4,888	+5,368	+4,493	+5,779
Invisible-trade balance		+2,243	+2,487	+2,513	+1,873	+3,347
Current balance	1	−41	+945	−936	+3,058	....[1]
Capital transfers	2	−	−	−	−	−
Investment and other capital flows						
Official long-term capital	3	−303	−336	−401	−91	−339
Overseas investment in UK public sector[2]	4	+1,432	−97	+902	+585	+237
Overseas investment in UK private sector	5	+2,967	+2,005	+3,405	+4,194	+3,431
UK private investment overseas	6	−2,334	−4,634	−6,555	−7,103	−9,470
Overseas currency borrowing (net) by UK banks	7	+364	−433	+1,623	+2,024	+1,318
Exchange reserves in sterling:						
British Government stocks	8	+5	−115	+247	+946	+258
Banking and money market liabilities	9	−24	−4	+532	+316	−145
Other external banking & money market liabilities in sterling	10	+1,481	+293	+2,580	+2,558	+2,634
External Sterling lending by UK banks	11	+58	−507	+209	−2,478	−2,968
Import credit	12	+297	+349	+72	−238	+149
Export credit	13	−635	−920	−849	−913	−1,000
Other short-term flows[3]	14	+869	+157	+405	−1,218	−378
Total investment and other capital flows	15	+4,177	−4,242	+2,170	−1,418	−6,273
Balancing item	16	+3,225	+2,171	+476	−448	....[1]
Balance for official financing	17	+7,361	−1,126	+1,710	+1,192	−845
Allocation of special drawing rights and gold subscription to IMF	18	−	−	+195	+180	+158
Total lines 17-18	19	+7,361	−1,126	+1,905	+1,372	−687
Official financing						
Net transactions with IMF	20	+1,113	−1,016	−596	−140	−145
Net transactions with overseas monetary authorities plus foreign currency borrowing by HM government[4]	21	+1,114	−187	−250	−941	−1,587
Drawings on (+)/additions to (−) official reserves	22	−9,588	+2,329	−1,059	−291	+2,419
Total official financing	23	−7,361	+1,126	−1,905	−1,372	+687

Source: *ET*, March 1982.

Notes:
1 Full trade figures for 1982 are not yet available, so it is not possible to separate the current account from the balancing item.
2 Excludes foreign currency borrowing by the public sector under the exchange cover scheme.
3 Including other external borrowing or lending.
4 Including the foreign currency borrowing by public sector under the exchange cover scheme.

effect is particularly important in inducing changes in the flow of short-term capital. It is worth commenting at this stage upon lines 8, 9 and 10, which correspond to changes in sterling balances. Sterling balances arose out of the key currency role of sterling which led to private traders and foreign banks holding working balances in sterling, and which also led governments to hold part of their official exchange reserves in sterling. This latter aspect was particularly important for the overseas sterling area countries (OSA) who traditionally maintained their domestic currencies rigidly tied to sterling, maintained the bulk of their foreign exchange reserves in sterling, and pooled any earnings of gold and non-sterling currencies in London in exchange for sterling balances. Furthermore, between 1940 and 1958, OSA countries were linked to the UK through a tightly knit system of exchange controls which discriminated against transactions with non-sterling area (NSA) countries, and especially those in the dollar area. The sterling area was effectively a currency union which allowed members to economize on their total holdings of gold and non-sterling currency reserves. One important consequence of this was that the sterling-area system created substantial holdings of UK liabilities to foreigners which had no maturity date and which could be liquidated at a moment's notice, so forming a permanent fund of contingent claims on the UK gold and foreign currency reserves. OSA countries could acquire sterling balances in the following three ways: by having a current-account surplus with the UK; as the result of a net inflow of foreign investment from the UK; and from pooling in the UK any gold and foreign currency earned from transaction with NSA countries.[1]

At the beginning of World War II, the total of sterling balances stood at approximately £500m; by the end of the war they had risen to £3.7bn, around which figure they fluctuated between 1945 and 1966. In contrast to the stability in the total quantity of sterling balances there were marked changes in the country composition; some countries, e.g. India and Pakistan, ran down their wartime accumulation of balances, while other countries, e.g. some Middle East countries, acquired new holdings of sterling balances.[2] The continued existence of the sterling-area financial arrangements depended upon two conditions being satisfied. Firstly the OSA countries had to have a high proportion of their transactions with each other and with the UK. Secondly, there had to be a continued confidence in the ability of the UK, in its role of banker to the OSA, to match short-term sterling liabilities with an equivalent volume of official reserves or other short-term assets. From 1958 onwards neither of these conditions were satisfied. The OSA countries began to transact more intensively with NSA countries and the UK moved into a position of seemingly permanent deficit on her basic balance, so increasing short-term liabilities relative to official reserves and other short-term assets, and creating

---

1 Ignoring reserve diversification activities, the flow increment of sterling balances was equal to the OSA basic-balance surplus with the UK, plus the fraction of their basic-balance surplus with NSA countries pooled in the UK. The change in UK official reserves, exclusive of any change in official foreign borrowing, less the change in sterling balances (the change in the UK's short-term liquidity position one might say) was equal to the basic balance of the UK. These relations held only as an approximations, changes in trade credit, for example, would have to be zero for them to hold exactly. The concept of the basic balance is defined below in section I.3.

2 Detailed information on this may be found in Susan Strange, *Sterling and British Policy*, Oxford, 1971, chapters 2 and 3.

the conditions for the sterling crises which became frequent in the 1960s.[1] It was not unexpected, therefore, when the sterling area effectively ceased to exist in June 1972.[2]

Recent developments with respect to sterling balances are treated in section III.6 below.

We come next to the balancing item (line 16), which is a statistical item to compensate for the total of measurement errors and omissions in the accounts, arising from, for example, the under-recording of exports and the reliance upon survey data for certain items such as foreign investment and tourist expenditure. A positive balancing item can reflect an unrecorded net export, an unrecorded net capital inflow, or some combination of the two. The major source of changes in the balancing item is likely to be unrecorded changes in net trade credit, reflecting discrepancies between the time goods are shipped and the time when the associated payments are made across the exchanges. As can be seen from table 3.1, the balancing item is very volatile and can on occasions, e.g. in 1977 and 1978, be of a magnitude far greater than the surplus or deficit on current account. The total of investment and other capital transactions together with the balancing item is known as the balance for official financing (BOF, line 17), which can, in principle, be treated as the net balance of autonomous transactions.[3] Before we come to accommodating transactions, two adjustments to the BOF have to be made in line 18, both of which relate to the UK's membership of the IMF. First, we have the allocation of special drawing rights which is treated as a credit item since it effectively adds to the official reserves of the UK (line 22). Secondly, we have the UK's reserve tranche subscription to the IMF. When the UK's IMF general quota is increased, the UK is obliged to subscribe 25% of the increase to the IMF in the form of SDRs or other convertible foreign exchange (up to April 1978 this subscription was paid in gold and the reserve tranche was known as the gold tranche), and the official reserves fall by the corresponding amount. The corresponding entry in line 18 is the requisite double entry to balance the accounts, and may be treated as the acquisition of assets at the IMF.

The total of lines 17-18, the *adjusted balance for official financing* (line 19), has to be matched by an equal amount of official financing. If, for any year, line 19 has a negative sign then the authorities must reduce the official external assets or increase the official external liabilities of the UK, undertaking the reverse operations if line 19 is positive in sign. There are three ways in which the necessary adjustments can be made. First, the UK may draw upon or add to the official gold and currency reserves (line 22). Over the period 1970-76 the average annual value of the UK's gross reserves was $5.41bn, but since then they have increased almost

---

1 If official short-term and medium-term foreign borrowing by the UK government is subtracted from the official exchange reserves, this gives a measure of 'cover' for the sterling liabilities. In 1962 the ratio of 'cover' to total sterling liabilities was 51%. By end-1967, the 'cover' had disappeared entirely, outstanding official borrowing exceeding the official reserves by £3.8bn.

2 Prior to 1972, the OSA consisted of the Commonwealth, except Canada, South Africa, Iceland, Ireland, Kuwait, Jordan and some others. Before June 1972 these countries were known as the scheduled territories but after June 1972 only Ireland and Gibraltar remain in this category. The demise of exchange control in October 1979 has formally ended the OSA/NSA distinction.

3 Prior to 1976 this measure of external transactions was known as the total currency flow.

fourfold with an average value for 1977-81 of $21.9bn. During the period since 1970 the composition of the reserves has also altered considerably, through policy decisions and changes in the market values of the various assets. At end-1970 the reserves consisted of 48% gold, 43% convertible currencies and 9% SDRs; however by December 1981 the gold portion had fallen to 31% and the convertible currency portion had risen to 56%. During 1979 the basis on which the gold and SDR portions of the reserves are to be valued was changed to a market-price-related basis. Since then the gold reserves have been revalued annually according to a formula based on the average London fixing price in the three months prior to March. The first revaluation of March 1979 increased the gold component of the reserves from 5% to 19%. Similarly, SDRs are now valued at their average dollar exchange rate in the three months to end-March 1982. Both these valuation rules are subject to annual revision. At end 1981, SDRs accounted for only 4% of UK reserves. Over the period 1975-80, the UK reserves averaged 20% of annual visible imports and 13.8% of total imports, the ratio of reserves to total imports reaching a peak of 22.1% in 1977. As a second line of defence, the UK can borrow foreign currencies from the IMF. An amount equal to 25% of the UK's quota may be borrowed automatically, the so-called reserve-tranche position which is classed as part of the official reserves.[1] The UK has further access to four credit tranches, each of which corresponds to 25% of quota,[2] but access is dependent upon the UK government adopting economic policies which meet with the approval of the IMF, this being particularly so for drawings beyond the first credit tranche. The maximum amount the UK could borrow at year-end 1981, including the reserve-tranche position, stood at SDR 8.8bn. The points to remember about IMF finance are that it is temporary (borrowings have to be repaid within 3-5 years), conditional, and cheap, relative to current commercial rates of interest. Finally, the UK has access to a considerable network of borrowing facilities built up with foreign central banks in the 1960s, primarily as a short-term defence against speculative capital flows. These have proved to be of considerable value to the UK, and have been supplemented since 1973 by direct government borrowing, mostly from the eurodollar market.

It may already be apparent that the distinction between autonomous and accommodating transactions upon which this discussion is based, is not entirely satisfactory. For example, by manipulating UK interest rates the government can create an inflow of short-term capital to accommodate a given current-account deficit, even though from the point of view of individuals or banks buying and selling the assets the transactions are autonomous. Similarly, autonomous government items such as foreign aid may be deliberately adjusted to accommodate a deficit elsewhere in the accounts. At a more general level, whenever the government adopts policies to change the balance of payments the effects of these policies will influence the totals of autonomous transactions so that they cease to be independent of the underlying state of the balance of payments. Despite these difficulties the autonomous/accommodating distinction provides a useful starting point for any arrangement of the external accounts.

---

1 Automatic borrowing can exceed the reserve-tranche position to the extent that the total IMF holding of sterling falls below 75% of the UK quota.

2 Between March 1976 and March 1978 the credit tranches were temporarily raised to 36.5% of quota, prior to the implementation of the sixth general review of quotas. See section III.9 below.

So far we have examined the external accounts in isolation, but they may equally be examined as an integral part of the national income and expenditure accounts.

From this viewpoint, the balance of payments deficit (surplus) on current account is identically equal to the excess (shortfall) of national expenditure over national income, and hence to the reduction (increase) in the net external assets owned by UK residents.[1] It follows that the UK can only add to its external net assets to the extent that it has an equivalent current-account surplus.

Finally, we should note that, although the accounts separate current-account items from capital-account items, there are several important links between the two sub-sets of transactions. We have already pointed out that a non-zero current account results in changes in the net external assets of the UK. As these assets and liabilities have profit and interest flows attached to them, any change in the total of external net assets will feed back into changes in the interest, profit and dividend flows which appear in the current account. Furthermore, because they also result in equivalent changes in national income they will affect the current account indirectly through any effects on national expenditure and the demand for imports. Similarly, within the context of a given current-account position, capital flows which change the composition of external net assets will change the average rate of return on these assets and so react back on the current account. These are perhaps the more straightforward links, but others exist, for example, between trade flows and the balance of export and import credit, and between trade and investment flows and changes in total sterling balances. As has often been said, the balance of payments is akin to a seamless web and it can be grossly misleading to treat individual items in isolation from the rest of the accounts.

I.3   Equilibrium and Disequilibrium in the Balance of Payments

It is obviously important, both for purposes of economic policy and historical analysis, to have clear notions of balance of payments equilibrium and disequilibrium. However, the formulation of such notions is not easy. As a first approximation, we could define balance of payments equilibrium as a situation in which, at the existing exchange rate, autonomous credits are equal to autonomous debits and no official financing transactions are required. This definition raises three problems. First, that of the timespan over which equilibrium is defined. Clearly, a daily or even monthly span of time would be of little value, and it is generally accepted that a sufficient span of years should be allowed so that the effects of cyclical fluctuations in income will have no appreciable net impact on external transactions. Secondly, if the exchange rate is allowed to fluctuate freely to equate the demand with the supply of foreign exchange, then equilibrium is always attained automatically, and any notion of payments disequilibrium becomes redundant. Thirdly, and in contrast, if the exchange rate is managed in some way to make it partially or completely independent of market forces, we must then accept that policies can be adopted to manipulate autonomous transactions in such a way as to make them balance. However, the problem which this raises is that the attainment of external equilibrium, at a given exchange rate, may involve unacceptable levels of employment or inflation, an interest-rate

---

1   Cf. J. Hicks, *Social Framework*, OUP, 1971, chapters 8 and 21.

structure which is counter to economic growth objectives and a trade policy inconsistent with international obligations. To take account of these issues we can formulate the following definition of equilibrium. The balance of payments is in equilibrium if, at the existing rate, autonomous credits are equal to autonomous debits over a period of good and bad years, without involving: (i) departures from full employment or price stability; (ii) departures from the desired rate of economic growth; and (iii) adoption of tariffs or subsidies inconsistent with accepted international obligations.

The question now arises of the sets of autonomous transactions to be used in this definition of equilibrium. One possibility is to consider current-account transactions alone, but equilibrium would then involve a constant level of net external wealth and there is no particular merit in this, particularly for a growing economy. As far as the UK is concerned, two sets of autonomous transactions have been used in discussions of balance of payments performance, the basic balance and the balance for official financing (BOF).

The basic balance, defined as the sum of the current account and the net flow of long-term capital, attracts attention on several grounds, not least as one indicator of secular trends in external transactions. If the basic balance is in equilibrium, any net outflow (inflow) of long-term capital results in an equivalent increase in the stock of external assets (liabilities) of the UK. Furthermore, all net flows of short-term capital must be matched by equivalent offsetting changes in official financing. Thus the basic balance puts below the line all capital flows essentially related to the role of the UK as an international banking and financing centre; capital flows which may be particularly sensitive to accommodating monetary manipulation.

Since 1969, however, the UK authorities have preferred to utilize the BOF as the appropriate indicator of external performance. In contrast to the basic balance, this places all short-term capital flows above the line, so that a zero BOF corresponds to a situation of no change in the total of officially held external net assets. There are several arguments in favour of the switch to the BOF, viz. (i) many short-term capital flows are linked to items in the trade balance, e.g. trade credit, or to the financing of long-term investment, and cannot sensibly be separated from items in the basic balance; (ii) short-term capital flows are inherently volatile, therefore they provide poor accommodation and should not be used for this purpose; and (iii) the BOF avoids the problem of separating the balancing item from the basic balance, with the attendant danger of a misleading treatment of any errors and omissions. In the short term, of course, the BOF is more volatile than the basic balance, but over the longer run the two measures should coincide, provided that short-term flows net out to zero. A further advantage of the BOF is that it shows the potential increase (decrease) in the UK money supply as a result of a surplus (deficit) in the aggregate of autonomous balance of payments transactions.

I.4 The Balance of Payments 1961-81

We shall now use our concepts of equilibrium to assess the balance of payments performance of the UK since 1961. To assist in this, table 3.2 contains average annual figures for selected items in the balance of payments in the periods 1961-4, 1965-7, 1968-71, 1972-6 and 1977-80, with 1981 entered separately because of the incomplete trade data for that year. The first sub-period covers a complete short cycle ending in a boom year, while the remaining four are somewhat arbitrary and are separated by the 1967 devaluation, the floating of sterling in June 1972, and the sharp break in the trend in the sterling exchange rate which occurred in 1976. The averages of course hide substantial annual variations but they will suffice for present purposes.

In the *Brookings Report*, R. Cooper suggested that the UK balance of payments position, at least up to 1966, could be summarized in terms of four propositions: (i) the UK is normally a net exporter of long-term capital, with a surplus on the current account; (ii) the visible trade balance is normally in deficit, but the invisible balance shows a surplus more than sufficient to offset this; (iii) the role of the UK as banker to the OSA and to the world financial community in general gives volatile short-term capital flows an important position in the balance of payments; and finally, (iv) the trading, investing and international financial activities of the UK are carried out with a very inadequate underpinning of foreign exchange reserves.[1]

Certainly the years 1956-60 discussed by Professor Cooper fit into this pattern, with an average annual long-term capital outflow of £189m offset by a current-account surplus of £149m per annum and a net short-term capital inflow of £53m per annum. After taking account of the balancing item and other factors, the UK was able to add to its reserves at an annual rate of £79m. Some of these characteristics have also continued into the period to 1981, as table 3.2 indicates. The visible balance is always in deficit and the total invisible balance in surplus, despite a growing deficit on government services and transfers. The chief source of the strength of the invisible balance has been the growing surplus on trade in services rather than a surplus on interest, profits and dividends, though this does make a positive but declining contribution to the invisible balance. From line 7 we see that the UK has maintained its position as a long-term capital exporter, while line 8 indicates the volatility and magnitude of total capital flows.

In other dimensions the traditional picture has ceased to be applicable. The first two columns of table 3.2 indicate an unmistakeable slide into fundamental dis-equilibrium in terms of the current-account deficit and the basic balance. The chief proximate source of this deterioration was the worsening balance of visible trade which occurred despite rapid growth in the volume of world trade in manufactures. A reduction in the net long-term capital outflow, relative to the late 1950s, helped cushion the basic balance, but the improvement here was more than offset by the short-term capital outflows during the sterling crises of 1961, 1964 and each of the three subsequent years. The deficit in the BOF is reflected in reserve losses, the incurring of substantial foreign debts and the liquidation (in 1967) of the govern-ment's portfolio of dollar securities.

The inevitable devaluation, which took place in November 1967, was followed by a remarkable turn-around in the external payments position, although it is not completely clear to what extent this is attributable to the devaluation alone, or to the contemporaneous acceleration in the growth of world trade or, indeed, to measures to restrict demand growth and money supply growth after 1968 (between 1969 and 1971 the average rate of growth of real GDP fell to 1.70%). During this period of severe domestic restraint, the visible deficit was almost halved, which

---

1   R. Caves (ed.), *Britain's Economic Prospects*, Allen and Unwin, 1968, chapter 3.

TABLE 3.2

Trends in the UK Balance of Payments, Annual Averages for Selected Periods (£m current prices) and Average Growth Rates for UK Real GDP and World Exports of Manufactures

	1961-4	1965-7	1968-71	1972-6	1977-80	1981
1 Visible balance	−226	−322	−191	−3,189	−1,523	··
2 Govt. services and transfers (net)	−377	−459	−485	−1,196	−2,077	··
3 Private invisibles (net) incl. interest, profits, dividends and transfers	+595	+725	+1,228	+3,104	+4,414	··
4 Invisible balance	+218	+266	+743	+1,908	+2,337	+3,347
5 Current-account balance	−8	−56	+552	−1,281	+814	··
6 Balancing item	−35	+35	+25	−74	+1,356	··
7 Balance of long-term capital	−139	−161	−223	−224	−1,591	−6,141
8 Balance of long-term and other capital flows	−183	−501	+350	−399	+172	−6,273
9 Basic balance (5+7)	−147	−217	+329	−1,505	−844	··
10 Basic balance plus balancing item (9+6)	−182	−182	+354	−1,579	+512	··
11 Balance for official financing	−226	−523	+927	−1,754	+2,342	−845
12 Gold subs., IMF and SDRs	−	−15	+65	+25	+94	+158
13 Total lines 11 and 12	−226	−538	+992	−1,729	+2,436	−687
Official financing						
14 Net foreign currency borrowing by H.M. government (inc. IMF)	+144	+420	−594	+1,356	−284	−1,732
15 Transfer $ portfolio to reserves	−	+173	−	−	−	−
16 Drawing on(+) or additions to(−) official reserves	+82	−55	−398	+373	−2,152	+2,419
17 Total official financing	+226	+538	−992	+1,729	−2,436	+687
18 Av. annual growth real GDP (1975 prices) %	3.30	1.86	2.56	2.34	1.35	−0.02 (estimate)
19 Av. annual growth vol. of world exports of manufactures %	7.95	6.77	11.45	9.50	5.00	2.00 (estimate)

Sources: ET (AS), 1982 and *ET*, March 1982. World export figures from various issues of *NIER*.

·· Not available.

when combined with the continuing increase in the invisible surplus resulted in the current account moving back into substantial surplus. Though the net outflow of long-term capital also increased during this period this was not sufficient to prevent a very strong position emerging in the basic balance, especially when account is taken of the balancing item. Furthermore, confidence in sterling returned after 1968, no doubt helped by the Basle Arrangements of that year, and short-term capital flowed back into the UK at an identified annual average rate of £573m. So strong was the improvement in the payments position, that the UK was able to repay a substantial part of the debts raised in defence of sterling in the previous two periods and, at the same time, add to the official reserves. It cannot be claimed that this period saw a return to equilibrium in the external accounts, simply because of the severe restraint on domestic growth which took place. However, it can at least be argued that the foundations were laid for a return to equilibrium once the foreign debts had been repaid.

With the benefit of hindsight it is clear that the years 1968-71 marked a watershed in the balance of payments performance of the UK. The subsequent decade is played out within an entirely different international economic environment from that which formed the postwar framework. With the adoption of a floating exchange rate in 1972 the rules of balance of payments management changed drastically, while the increase in the real price of oil after 1973 resulted in major disruption to the postwar system of international trade and investment. The resulting sharp deterioration which occurred in the UK visible balance during the years 1971-6 is clearly illustrated in table 3.2, with average deficits of quite unprecedented magnitude. Even the record invisible surpluses of this period could not prevent the average current-account deficit reaching £1.28bn. Capital outflows added to the basic-balance deficit despite the fact that the growth in private imports of long-term capital (primarily to exploit NS oil and gas resources) almost eliminated the net export of private long-term capital. To accommodate the negative balance of official financing, the governments of the period quite sensibly drew on the reserves and engaged in substantial foreign borrowing, effectively mortgaging a portion of anticipated future NS oil revenues. The current-account and basic-balance deficits were thus absorbed without an immediate cutback in output levels and the standard of living in the UK. This policy was not without its problems, as the events of 1976 and 1977 demonstrated. With overseas confidence weakened by the basic-balance position and the rapid rate of UK inflation, short-term capital flowed out of the UK on an unprecedented scale in 1976, placing substantial downward pressure on the exchange rate and resulting in heavy reserve losses. The official UK reserves fell from $7.20bn in February 1976 to $4.13bn at the end of that year, only to be replenished even more rapidly in 1977, following the successful negotiation of support from the IMF. By the end of 1977 the reserves had increased to a total of $20.5bn. The policy of official borrowing to finance the oil-related deficits resulted in total official foreign debts of $14.2bn at the end of 1976, of which $11.2bn was due for repayment by the end of 1984.[1]

By comparison, the period after 1976 indicates a remarkable turn-round in the external situation. Of course the chief contributory factor here is the growing production of NS oil, which allowed an oil products deficit of £6.5bn in 1975 to be transformed into a surplus of £1.8bn in 1981 (at 1980 prices). A further contributory factor from 1979 onwards was the decline in UK industrial output and the associated reduction in inventory levels. During this period the invisible balance continued to strengthen and so the joint outcome was for the current account to move into surplus. In the four years to 1980 the emerging petrocurrency status of the UK also attracted inflows of short-term capital which more than offset the net export of long-term capital of £1.6bn. An average annual favourable balance for official financing of £2.4bn allowed the government to increase the official reserves virtually sevenfold and to repay the major portion of the debts incurred between 1972 and 1976. Between the end of 1977 and the end of 1981 the total outstanding short-term and medium-term official debt was reduced from $18bn to $8.4bn. During 1981, however, the total capital inflow was reversed, partly under the

---

1 See *BEQB*, March 1982, Appendix table 17, and the article 'UK Official Short Term and Medium Term Borrowing from Abroad', *BEQB*, March 1976, pp. 76-81. Approximately $10.4bn represented public-sector borrowing under the exchange cover scheme introduced in 1973. The IMF standby arrangements and oil facility borrowings of early 1977 added a further $4.2bn to official debts.

influence of higher US interest rates and partly in response to the elimination of controls on capital exports in 1979. In 1981 the balance for official financing became negative, and the reserves were run down to finance this and to continue the repayment of external debt.

The period since 1971 is so atypical that it is difficult to make comparisons with the position in the 1960s. Even though the exchange rate has been free to float this has not resulted in a zero balance of official financing, indeed it is clear that sterling has been actively managed since 1972. Undoubtedly, the oil price increase and the induced exploitation of North Sea resources is the major factor dictating balance of payments performance in the 1970s and into the 1980s. Unfortunately, the size of the balancing item since 1977 and the absence to date of current-account figures for 1981 make it impossible to assess the trend in the basic balance. Even if it is favourable (as a current-account estimate for 1981 of £8bn would imply), this is in part due to the depth of the UK recession and the decline in the non-oil components of the manufacturing economy. With unemployment currently at 12.6% and with substantial spare capacity and low inventory levels it would be rash indeed to present any improvement in the current account and basic balance as a return to fundamental equilibrium. Moreover, the transitory nature of the NS oil programme raises many questions as to what will happen after the 1990s when NS oil reserves are depleted. In particular, whether the non-oil sectors of the UK economy will be sufficiently competitive internationally to prevent a return to the experiences of the 1960s.

To briefly summarize the events over the period 1961 to 1979, the one crucial factor appears to be the persistent weakness of the visible trade account, which more than offset the steady improvement in the invisible trade surplus. The advent of NS oil simply provides a medium-term respite from this trend. The resulting current-account deficits combined with the propensity to export long-term capital progressively undermined the ability of the UK to act as an international financial centre by borrowing short and lending long. The principal result of this has been the termination of the UK's role as banker to the overseas sterling area and the persistence of disruptive changes in international confidence in the external value of sterling.

I.5   North Sea Oil and Gas

Much recent economic policy discussion in the UK has been concerned with the economic effects of the exploitation of oil and gas resources in the North Sea. The production of NS oil first became substantial in 1975, and self-sufficiency was reached during 1981. It is generally argued that the effect on GDP will be relatively small, effectively offsetting the loss of real income imposed on the UK by the increase in the relative price of oil since 1973, and the direct effects on employment negligible.[1] However, the effects on the balance of payments and public-sector revenue are substantial. The major effect will therefore be to alter the environment in which economic policy is formulated and to open up prospects of substantial real growth, unimpeded by trade-balance constraints, over the next decade. Section III.5 discusses some of the policy options opened up by NS oil, and in this section

---

1   At 1978 prices, NS oil and gas contributed some 7.3% extra to GDP in 1980, perhaps rising to 9.6% GDP in 1985. *TER*, no. 112, August 1979.

we briefly outline some calculations of the likely magnitude of NS oil effects on the balance of payments and the difficulties surrounding such calculations.

The major difficulties relate to important areas of uncertainty, e.g. with respect to oil yields, trends in exploitation and development costs, the share of extractive equipment provided by UK firms and most importantly in the sterling price of oil. This last element will depend jointly on the ability of the OPEC cartel to determine the future real increase in the dollar price of oil, a decision over which the UK as a minor world producer accounting for 3% of world production will have no influence, and upon the policies which the UK government adopts with respect to the exchange rate. The more sterling appreciates relative to the dollar, the smaller will be government tax revenue from the NS. Other aspects of government policy, as yet uncertain, will be of equal importance. In particular, the production and depletion policy adopted, whether it matches production to domestic demand or allows net exports of crude oil, and the levels of royalty and petroleum revenue tax charged, which will determine the proportion of profits left to the oil producers for potential remission overseas. One further obvious difficulty is that the total benefits from NS oil to the balance of payments will not be independent of how the government feels able to exploit these benefits for domestic purposes.[1]

When calculating the direct impact of NS oil and gas on the UK balance of payments, account has to be taken of the following items. First, the net effect on the balance of trade in oil and gas, as home output is exported or substituted for imports. Second, the net trade in equipment and technical services to discover and extract the oil and gas. Third, the inflows of foreign capital to finance extraction and development, and finally, the net flows of interest, profits and dividends, remitted overseas by the foreign-owned firms operating in the North Sea. It is worth remembering that the balance of payments effects of these operations began well before the flow of NS oil began. Thus in the years 1972-6, total net imports of equipment and services to exploit NS resources amounted to £1.43bn, an amount which was more than covered by a cumulative net capital inflow of £2.38bn. During 1981 the net contribution to the balance of official financing was made up as follows: balance of trade effects +£11.9bn, net IPD due overseas −£1.9bn, and capital inflow net of imports of goods and services to exploit NS resources +£0.8bn, to give a total effect on the BOF of +£10.8bn. The most recent calculations of the effect on the BOF in 1985 suggest a net oil and gas related contribution in the range of £10.5bn to £15bn, though this figure is subject to all the previously noted uncertainties.[2]

---

1   In particular, the exchange-rate policy adopted to accommodate NS oil is an important determinant of the total economic effect on government revenue and the balance of payments. For a useful account of the effect of different exchange-rate assumptions, see S.A.B. Page, 'The Value and Distribution of the Benefits of NS Oil and Gas, 1970-1985', *NIER*, no. 82, 1977, pp. 41-58.

2   See 'NS Oil and Gas − Cost and Benefits', *BEQB*, March 1982. The figures quoted in this paragraph are at constant 1980 prices and are not directly comparable with estimates produced in Page, op. cit.

II FOREIGN TRADE OF THE UK
II.1 Structure and Trends, 1955-81

In this section we shall examine the major structural features and trends in the foreign trade of the UK between 1955 and 1981.[1] In focusing attention upon certain longer-term trends, we will find evidence of a marked decline in the international competitive performance of UK manufacturing industry; a decline which, it may reasonably be claimed, is the proximate source of the unsatisfactory behaviour of the balance of payments noted in the previous section.

Geographical and commodity trade structure: The traditional picture of UK foreign trade was one in which manufactures were exchanged for imports of food-stuffs and raw materials, with the bulk of the trade being carried out with the Commonwealth and overseas sterling area countries. That this picture is now completely out of date is shown in tables 3.3, 3.4 and 3.5, which illustrate the radical changes in trading structure which have occurred in the quarter century since 1955. To some small extent these changes reflect the relaxation of wartime import restrictions and the general postwar movement toward free-er trade that resulted from the several rounds of GATT tariff reductions. But, in general, they are the outcome of more deep-seated changes in competitive forces.

The major changes in the geographic composition of UK trade are shown in table 3.3. Several general trends are immediately apparent. Compared to 1955, the following years show an increased dependence on trade with developing countries, a trend which has been primarily at the expense of trade with the less developed members of the OSA.[2] An interesting development since 1975 is the increased importance, for obvious reasons, of the oil-exporting countries as a market for UK exports. The decline in their importance as a source of UK imports between 1975 and 1980 is the direct result of the exploitation of the UK's NS oil resources. As far as trade with the developed nations is concerned, the most striking trend is the increasing importance of trade with the EEC. In 1972, the year prior to UK entry, the current nine EEC members accounted for approximately 30% of UK exports and imports, but by 1980 the export share has risen to 43.4% and the import share to 41.3%. As table 3.3 indicates, this development has been largely to the detriment of trade with the non-advanced former members of the OSA. The growing importance of Japan as a source of UK imports may also be noted.

The switch toward a greater trade dependence on the industrialized, urbanized, high-per-capita-income countries of Western Europe, Japan and North America has been matched, not unexpectedly, by significant changes in the commodity structure of UK trade, particularly in respect of imports. The changing

---

1 Since, over the period, some 65%-70% of total exports and imports reflected commodity transactions, we here concentrate solely on commodity trade. For a treatment of invisible items in the current account see P. Phillips, 'A Forecasting Model for the United Kingdom Invisible Account', *NIER*, no. 69, 1974. Interest, profit and dividend flows are discussed in section III.7 below. For further details on invisibles, consult the COI pamphlet, *Britain's Invisible Exports*, HMSO, 1970. Delays in the publication of trade figures mean that data is only available up to 1980. The figures for 1981 are unlikely to deviate significantly from these.

2 In 1955 these countries provided 22.8% of UK imports and absorbed 21.6% of UK exports; the corresponding figures for 1977 were 6.3% and 9.4%.

TABLE 3.3

Area Composition of UK Merchandise Trade, 1955-80 (percentages)

	Imports, c.i.f.				Exports, f.o.b.			
	1955	1965	1975	1980	1955	1965	1975	1980
Western Europe	25.7	35.8	51.0	55.9	28.9	41.8	49.0	57.6
EEC[1]	12.6	23.6	36.3	41.3	15.0	26.3	32.2	43.4
North America	19.5	19.6	13.3	15.0	12.0	14.8	11.8	11.2
USA	10.9	11.7	9.6	12.1	7.1	10.6	8.9	9.6
Other developed[2]	14.2	11.9	7.9	6.8	21.1	14.8	9.4	5.6
Japan	0.6	1.4	2.8	3.4	0.6	1.1	1.6	1.3
Total developed countries	59.4	67.4	72.2	77.7	61.4	71.4	70.3	74.5
Centrally planned economies	2.7	4.4	3.0	2.1	1.7	2.9	3.3	2.8
Oil-exporting countries	9.2	9.8	13.5	8.6	5.1	5.6	11.4	10.1
Other developing countries[3]	28.7	18.4	11.3	11.4	31.8	20.1	15.0	12.4
Total	100.0	100.0	100.0	100.0	100.0	100.0	100.0	100.0

Sources: AAS various: *TI* 16 March 1972.

Notes:　1　The nine Community members as of 1980.
　　　　　2　Japan, plus Australia, New Zealand and South Africa.
　　　　　3　Small discrepancies exist between the countries listed for 1955 and those for subsequent years.

TABLE 3.4

Commodity Composition of UK Imports, Selected Years 1955-80 (percentages)

SITC group	Description	1955	1965	1975	1980
0, 1	Food, Beverages, Tobacco	36.2	29.7	17.7	12.4
3	Fuel	10.4	10.6	17.7	13.8
2, 4, 5, 6	Industrial Materials and Semi-Manufactures	47.9	43.0	34.1	35.2
7, 8	Finished Manufactures	5.2	15.3	28.3	35.6
9	Unclassified	0.3	1.4	2.2	3.0
	Total	100.0	100.0	100.0	100.0

Source: AAS, various.
Imports are measured on an overseas trade statistics basis and are valued c.i.f.

structure of UK import trade is shown in table 3.4. Most important here is the increase in the proportion of imports of finished manufactures, the share of which increased sevenfold between 1955 and 1980, and the decline in the proportion accounted for by foodstuffs, beverages and tobacco. Imports of finished and semi-manufactures now account for some 63% of total UK imports. This same trend has also been experienced by other EEC countries, although it remains the case that the UK is more dependent upon imports of non-manufactures than are, for example, France or West Germany.[1] On the export side, table 3.5 shows that changes in structure are less noticeable. While the share of exports of manufactures has increased slightly over the period, this has been matched by a virtually equivalent decline in the importance of semi-manufactures. The decline in the share of engineering products from 1975 onwards is a worrying development, to which we return below. Other major changes are the sustained decline in the share of textiles and the steady increase in the share of chemicals in total exports. Looking to the future, the possibility of substantial net exports of North Sea oil over the next ten years is likely to raise substantially the share of fuels in total exports and to diminish the share of fuels in total imports, over and above the changes that have already taken place between 1975 and 1980.

TABLE 3.5

Commodity Composition of UK Exports, Selected Years 1955-80 (percentages)

Description	1955	1965	1975	1980
Engineering Products[1]	36.5	43.5	45.3	37.5
Machinery	21.1	26.5	30.4	25.3
Road Motor Vehicles	8.9	11.6	9.5	6.7
Other Transport Equipment	5.7	3.3	3.4	3.5
Scientific Instruments	1.2	2.1	2.0	2.0
Semi-Manufactures[2]	29.7	26.8	24.0	22.7
Chemicals	7.8	9.2	10.9	11.2
Textiles	10.1	5.8	3.7	2.9
Metals	11.8	11.8	9.4	8.6
Other Semi-Manufactures and Manufactures[3]	12.6	13.2	12.6	13.4
Non-Manufactures[4]	21.2	16.4	18.1	26.4
Food, Beverages, Tobacco	6.5	6.6	7.3	6.9
Basic Materials	5.6	4.0	2.7	3.1
Fuels	4.6	2.7	4.2	13.6
Other	4.5	3.0	3.9	2.8
Total	100.0	100.0	100.0	100.0

SITC Groups: 1. 7, 86, 87
          2. 5, 65, 67-9
          3. Remainder of 6 and 8
          4. 0, 1, 2, 3, 4 and 9

Source: AAS, various.

Exports are measured on an overseas trade statistics basis and valued f.o.b.

It will be apparent from this that UK trade is increasingly dominated by an exchange of manufactures for manufactures with the advanced industrialized nations. These structural changes would imply that UK manufacturing industry has experienced and will continue to experience greater foreign competition in home and export markets. They also help to explain the disintegration in the sterling area system which occurred after 1964.

1 M. Panic, 'Why the UK's Propensity to Import is High', *LBR*, no. 115, 1975.

II.2   The Decline in Competitive Performance

The trend toward increasing visible-trade deficits, which became evident in the early 1960s, has rightly been taken as indication of a widespread lack of competitive edge in UK industry relative to foreign industry. Evidence to support this view is provided by the progressive decline of the UK's share of world exports of manufactures[1] and by evidence of the increased import penetration of the UK market by foreign competitors. The net effect of these trends is to substantially limit the scope for the UK to grow without coming up against a balance of trade constraint. Thus, for example, a well-known study by Houthakker and Magee found a UK income elasticity of demand for imports of 1.66, double the corresponding world income elasticity of demand for UK exports of 0.86. Starting from balanced trade, these figures would suggest that the UK can only grow at half the world average rate if balanced trade is to be maintained.[2] Some further indication of the problem may be gained by the fact that between 1971 and 1979, when UK manufacturing production grew at an average annual rate of 0.7%, the volume of exports of finished manufactures increased by an average of 3.36% per annum, while the volume of imports of finished manufactures increased at an average annual rate of 13.4%. A growth of imports of this magnitude, in the industries in which the UK's traditional comparative advantage is thought to lie, is obviously a serious matter. Indeed it has prompted widespread fears of the imminent de-industrialization of the UK, with the manufacturing base so eroded by foreign competition that full employment and payments equilibrium cannot be achieved without a substantial reduction in real income.[3]

The statistics of the decline in the UK share of world exports of manufactures are dramatic and indicate that the share fell from 20.4% in 1954, to 17.7% in 1959, 11.9% in 1967 and a low of 8.8% in 1974. Rough calculations for this period would suggest that a 10% increase in world exports of manufactures was associated with a 5-6% increase in UK exports of manufactures.[4] Since 1974, however, the position has changed substantially, indeed despite a 40% increase in world exports of manufactures between 1975 and 1981 the UK volume of world trade share appears to have stabilized at an average figure of 9.4%.[5]

Of itself, the decline in export share need not give rise to concern, since it may simply reflect a decline in the UK share of world manufacturing production, the

1   'World', in this context, means W. Germany, France, Italy, Netherlands, Belgium, Luxemburg, Canada, Japan, Sweden, Switzerland, USA and UK. In 1977 they accounted for 75% of manufactured exports from all industrial nations. See *TI*, 7 June 1978, p. 22.

2   H.S. Houthakker and S. P. Magee, 'Income and Price Elasticities in World Trade', *REST*, vol. 51, pp. 111-25. This study covered the period 1951-66. For a critique see A. D. Morgan, 'Income and Price Elasticities in World Trade: A Comment', *MS*, vol. 38, 1970, pp. 303-14. A more recent study for the period 1968-78 of the income elasticity of demand for non-oil imports finds a figure of 2.7 for the UK, with comparable figures for Japan and Germany of 1.9 and 1.6 respectively, cf. M. A. Akhtor, 'Income and Price Elasticities of Non-Oil Imports for Six Industrialised Countries', *MS*, vol. 49, 1981, pp. 334-47.

3   Cf. the various contributions to F. Blackaby (ed.), *De-Industrialization*, Heinemann, 1979.

4   *NIER*, no. 73, 1975, p. 12.

5   The decline in the UK manufactured exports share has also been matched by a similar fall in her share of world invisible exports, from 20.9% in 1960 to 12.5% in 1976. Unlike manufactures, however, the UK share of world invisible imports has fallen along with the share in invisible exports. Cf. J. R. Sargent, 'UK Performance in Services', in F. Blackaby (ed.), op. cit.

natural result of her early industrial start. (In 1899 the UK accounted for 32.5% of world exports of manufactures.) However, this is far too complacent a view. Once it is recognized that between 1959 and 1975 the volume of world trade in manufactures grew at historically unprecedented rates of between 7%-13% per annum, and that the UK was alone among the major industrial countries in experiencing a substantial drop in export share, there are grounds for disquiet. Furthermore, the decline in the UK's share in world manufacturing production may itself reflect the same factors which hinder UK trade performance. In this respect it is worth noting that during the long industrial boom of the 1960s and early 1970s, the UK share of OECD manufacturing output fell from 9.6% in 1960 to 5.8% in 1973.

On the import side the evidence for a loss of competitive edge is equally disturbing. Even though all the major industrialized nations have experienced a rising import share since 1955, the UK seems to be relatively more import prone than her competitors and to have a relatively high income elasticity of demand for imports.[1] Recent calculations show that over the period 1968-80 the ratio of imports of manufactures to the value of domestic consumption of manufactures increased from 17% to 25%. This trend appears widespread across manufacturing industry and is particularly significant in certain sectors, e.g. motor-vehicles, office equipment, construction equipment and miscellaneous metal goods.[2] Some care, however, is required in interpreting these figures since they reflect to some extent the increasing division of labour in the international economy which has occurred since 1958. Similar calculations on the export side indeed show a corresponding trend increase in the proportion of UK output which is exported, with the average ratio of UK manufacturing exports to manufacturing production increasing from 17.6% in 1968 to 26.1% at end 1980.[3]

To explain these developments in any precise sense is not easy, several inter-related factors are involved and the relative weight to be attached to each is difficult to establish and may vary over time. At the most general level, and since it is trade in manufactures which is crucial, there would seem to be two potential sources of the poor UK trade performance: an increasing lack of price competitiveness; and a failure to produce and market commodities of the right

---

1 A.D. Morgan, 'Imports of Manufactures into the UK and other Industrial Countries 1955-69', *NIER*, no. 56, 1971; M. Panic, op. cit.; and L.F. Cambell-Boross and A.D. Morgan, 'Net Trade: A Note on Measuring Changes in the Competitiveness of British Industry in Foreign Trade', *NIER*, no. 68, 1974, suggest that from 1963, UK manufacturing industry had never been sufficiently competitive to restore the country's trade situation to the position held in that year.

2 J.J. Hughes and A.P. Thirlwall, 'Trends and Cycles in Import Penetration in the UK', *Oxford Bulletin of Economics and Statistics*, vol. 39, 1977, pp. 301-17. See also *BB,* 19 June 1981, p. 348.

3 It may be noted that the sectors experiencing the greatest improvement in export performance, e.g. chemicals, electrical engineering, mechanical engineering and scientific instruments, are also the sectors which perform two-thirds of the non-aerospace research and development carried out in UK manufacturing industry. See 'The Home and Export Performance of UK Manufacturing Industry', *ET*, no. 286, August 1977. Import penetration ratios and export:sales ratios are now published on a monthly basis in *MDS*. A useful account of some of the pitfalls of interpreting movements in these ratios, pitfalls which arise out of the foreign trade multiplier links between exports, imports and home output, is contained in C. Kennedy and A.P. Thirlwall, 'Import Penetration, Export Performance and Harrod's Trade Multiplier', *OEP*, July 1979, pp. 303-23.

quality, in the face of rapidly changing technologies and world demand structures. Certainly in the period up to 1967 the movement of UK export prices relative to the export prices of her major trade competitors can explain some of the loss of export share. Averaged over the period 1959-67, UK dollar export prices rose at an annual average rate of 2%, compared to 1.3% for the other major industrial nations.[1] It follows that the relative price of UK manufactures rose by some 6.4% over this period and, assuming an export share elasticity of −2, this could account for 39% of the decline in UK export share between the two dates.[2] The problem with this line of argument is applying it to developments since 1967. Between then and 1974, UK relative export prices fell by 13% and yet the UK export share still declined by 26%. If we maintain an assumed export share elasticity of −2, this suggests that other factors, in the absence of any change in competitiveness, would have resulted in a decline in the UK share of world trade to 4.2% in 1974. With an elasticity of −1, the corresponding hypothetical share of the UK in world trade in 1974 is 5.4%. It would appear from this that other factors, as yet unspecified, have come to play a dominant part in determining UK export performance in the 1970s. The case for a structural break in the UK export environment is reinforced by considering the period 1974-80. During this period, the volume of world exports of manufactures increased at an annual percentage rate of 6.5%, and UK price competitiveness declined by an average of 5% points per annum. On past performance both factors should have reduced the UK share of world exports, but as we have seen, the share appears to have stabilized. This combination of circumstances lends weight to the view that non-price factors have come to play the dominant role in UK export performance.[3] On the import side there is strong evidence that the ratio of imports of manufactures to domestic demand has increased due to the decline in the competitiveness of UK manufactures. Independently of this, however, there is also a well-defined trend increase in the degree of import penetration of

1   Figures calculated from *NIER* Appendix tables, which also provide a valuable summary of international trends in labour productivity, unit costs and industrial output.

2   A share elasticity of −1 would account for 21% of the loss in export share. Batchelor and Bowe, 'Forecasting UK International Trade: A General Equilibrium Approach', *Applied Economics*, vol. 6, 1974, estimate price elasticities for UK export volume of between −1.13 and −2.80. One difficulty with any elasticity estimates is in evaluating the length of time it takes for the effects of price changes to be fully reflected in volume changes. Some estimates suggest up to five years as being the appropriate time-lag. See, e.g., H. Junz and R. Rhomberg, 'Price Competitiveness in Export Trade Among Industrial Countries', *AER*, May 1973, pp. 413-18. The export share elasticity can be taken as one plus the export volume price elasticity.

3   Other econometric research suggests that relative price movements can only account for one half at most of the UK's loss of export share between 1956 and 1976, and one fifth of the loss between 1970 and 1976. See M. Fetherstone, B. Moore and J. Rhodes, 'Manufacturing, Export Shares and Cost Competitiveness of Advanced Industrial Countries', *Economic Policy Review*, no. 3, Department of Applied Economics, Cambridge, 1977. More recent research suggests a representative price elasticity for UK manufactured exports for the period 1967 to 1975 of −1.4, while for the period 1967 to 1977 (2nd quarter), the representative elasticity is reduced to −1. Cf. C.A. Enoch, 'Measures of Competitiveness in International Trade', *BEQB*, June 1978. This article also contains a useful review of alternative measures of price competitiveness. A summary of recent estimates suggests a price elasticity for both exports and imports of UK finished manufactures of −1.25. Cf. J.R. Artus and A.K. McGuirk, 'A Revised Version of the Multilateral Exchange Rate Model', *IMF Staff Papers*, vol. 28, 1981, p. 294.

about 2% per annum,[1] which again suggests an important role for non-price factors. We have already noted the progressive shift in the pattern of UK trade toward exchanges of manufactures with the advanced industrial nations. It seems plausible to argue that the oligopolistic conditions found in such markets are bound to increase the importance of non-price factors in competitive performance and to reduce the relative influence of prices in the demand for traded goods.[2] The type and quality of manufactures produced, delivery lags and after-sales service, and the general quality of marketing effort, it is frequently claimed, play a significant part in explaining the relatively poor UK trade performance.[3]

Unfortunately, the precise role of these factors has proved impossible, as yet, to determine, although it is interesting to note that similar explanations of poor British competitive performance were employed at the end of the nineteenth century.[4] However, to the extent that non-price factors are important one would expect that an ability to innovate and market in response to rapidly changing market conditions will be an important factor in trade performance. There is evidence to show that export success in the advanced industrialized nations is positively related to the resources devoted to R and D and to measures of success in inventive activity, e.g. patenting.[5] Here it is important to remember that some 50% of UK exports in 1980 were in the R and D-intensive and high-patenting areas of engineering and chemicals. Moreover there is also evidence to suggest that the quality of UK mechanical engineering exports, as measured by the value per ton of metal processed, has been growing progressively inferior to the quality of the same exports from France and Germany, and this may be related to the stagnation in the volume of UK engineering exports since 1975. It is not difficult to link together the relative contributions of price and non-price factors, at least in theory if not in practice. The central point is that we have a sequence of interacting and mutually reinforcing, proximate sources of the trend deterioration in UK trade performance. A convenient place to begin is with the well-documented fact that since 1950 the rates of growth of output and labour productivity in the UK have been inferior to those of the other major industrial nations.[6] A relatively slow growth rate of

---

1 C.A. Enoch, op. cit., who finds an import penetration price elasticity of −0.4 for 1967 to 1977 (2nd quarter).

2 Recent evidence suggests that in 1977, three-quarters of UK exports were accounted for by 1989 enterprises and that 30% of UK exports came from foreign-owned UK firms. See, Business Statistics Office, *Business Monitor MA4: Overseas Transactions 1977*, HMSO, 1977.

3 NEDO, *Imported Manufactures*, HMSO 1965 and NEDO, *International Price Competitiveness, Non-Price Factors and Export Performance*, HMSO 1977. See also Report of the Committee of Enquiry into the Engineering Profession, *Engineering Our Future*, Cmnd. 7794, January 1980. chapter 1.

4 R. Hoffman, *Great Britain and the German Trade Rivalry 1875-1914*, Pennsylvania University Press, 1933, pp. 21-80.

5 For a review see the valuable paper by C. Freeman, 'Technical Innovation and British Trade Performance', in F. Blackaby (ed.), op. cit. See also the valuable study by K. Pavitt and L. Soete, chapter 3 of K. Pavitt (ed.), *Technological Innovation and British Export Performance*, Macmillan, 1980.

6 See, e.g., E.H. Phelps Brown, 'Labour Policies' in A. Cairncross (ed.), *Britain's Economic Prospects Reconsidered*, Allen and Unwin, 1971, and D.T. Jones, 'Output Employment and Labour Productivity in Europe since 1955', *NIER*, no. 77, 1976.

productivity implies a trend reduction in the relative level of UK industrial efficiency, which contributes to an increasing lack of price competitiveness for UK manufactures and to a relative shortage of resources for investment directed toward capacity expansion and marketing and innovate activities. A low rate of export growth, combined with rising import penetration and a low rate of industrial investment feed back to reinforce the relatively slow growth of output. In turn, a low rate of output growth reduces the scope for the UK to exploit static and dynamic economies of scale, and scarcely provides a climate conducive to risk-taking and successful innovative activity. Consequently the growth of productivity and quality change is held back, and we come full circle again to the initial source of the poor UK trade performance. A country such as the UK has no option but to maintain its technological level close to 'world best practice', if it is to maintain its historically high standards of living. As technologies mature, the centre of comparative advantage inevitably moves to low-real-wage countries, so an advanced country can only maintain its living standards by shifting its resources into new areas opened up by technological advance.[1] Like the Red Queen, the UK has to run to stand still, and if it fails it will enter the ranks of the underdeveloped nations from the wrong direction. Not only does the above account apply to the long-run trend of trade performance, it also relates to an inflexibility in the UK economic structure which makes the degree of import penetration and the volume of exports particularly sensitive to fluctuations in the pressure of aggregate demand.[2] Boom periods, it is argued, come up against constraints of available production capacity and available labour supply, diverting exports to the home market and raising the volume of imports above trend, with the possibility that a ratchet effect is involved, i.e. markets once lost to foreign goods are not readily recovered when the pressure of domestic demand slackens.

The coming on stream of NS oil raises the interesting possibility that the temporary balance of payments respite it will provide may be used to break out of the circle of cumulative competitive decline. We comment on this in section III.5 below.

Other factors: While it is the inadequate industrial growth performance which is chiefly responsible for the poor UK trade performance, several additional factors should not be ignored. On the export side, it is possible that an undue concentration on the supply of relatively slow-growing markets and on the production of commodities for which world demand was growing relatively slowly could explain the decline in export share. Appealing though this hypothesis is, evidence does not support the view that the structure of UK trade is responsible for poor export performance. A NEDO study finds no evidence in support of the view that the UK export structure is biased adversely towards the slower-growing commodities in

---

1 See the useful study on electronic calculators which focuses on the progressive diffusion of technology from innovating countries to low-wage, imitating countries: B.A. Majumdar, *Innovations, Product Developments and Technology Transfers*, University Press of America, 1982.

2 Econometric work in this field is fraught with difficulties both of formulation and execution. For evidence on the demand pressure/supply bottleneck hypothesis see, e.g., J.R. Artus, 'The Short-Run Effects of Domestic Demand Pressure on UK Export Performance', *IMF Staff Papers*, vol. 17, 1970. pp. 247-67; J.J. Hughes and A.P. Thirlwall, op. cit.; and C.A. Enoch, op. cit.

world trade.[1] Furthermore, a study by R. L. Major has shown that only 9% of the total loss in UK manufacturing exports between 1954 and 1966 can be attributed to exporting to relatively slow-growing markets.[2]

It may also have been the case that preferential trading arrangements have changed to the disadvantage of UK exporters. Isolated examples of this can be found, for example in the relaxation by certain Commonwealth countries of import quota restrictions, which led to substantial export gains for Japan and the USA at the expense of UK producers. To set against this, an EFTA study concluded that UK exports in 1965 were 2% higher than they would otherwise have been, in the absence of EFTA, although there appeared to be no noticeable effects on UK imports.[3] Of much greater importance has been the formation of the EEC. Although UK exports to the EEC have clearly benefited it also seems likely that the effects of selling to a large and rapidly expanding market have been more than offset by reductions in UK exports to non-EEC countries, possibly due to the adverse effects of discrimination against the UK. Equally, EEC entry has clearly contributed to the recent rapid growth of imports.[4]

One final factor which may be important in explaining the rising share of imports into the UK is the substantial reduction in tariff and other import restrictions which occurred after 1945. Between 1947 and 1959 the wartime restrictions on imports were virtually eliminated,[5] and from 1955 onwards the UK tariff was progressively reduced in line with agreements concluded through GATT. The UK tariff, introduced in 1932, had developed as a two-part structure with many imports from Commonwealth producers entering the UK duty-free, and imports from the rest of the world being subject to duties which, in the case of manufactures, ranged from 10% to 33%.[6] Between 1959 and 1975, the average UK tariff on semi-manufactures fell from 16.2% to 10.5% and that on finished manufactures from 21.4% to 12%. Despite the magnitude of these changes, a recent study suggests that their overall effect has proved to be relatively small, increasing

1 M. Panic and A.H. Rajan, *Product Changes in Industrial Countries Trade 1955-68*, NEDO, monograph no. 2, 1971.

2 R.L. Major, 'Note on Britain's Share in World Trade in Manufactures 1954-66', *NIER*, no. 44, 1968.

3 EFTA Secretariat, *The Effects of EFTA on the Economies of Member States*, Geneva, 1969, p. 162.

4 UK membership of the EEC is treated in section III.8 below. See also M. Fetherstone, B. Moore and J. Rhodes, 'EEC Membership and UK Trade in Manufactures', *Cambridge Journal of Economics*, December 1979, where it is suggested that the net (trade-creation minus trade-diversion) effect of EEC membership between 1973 and 1977 was to reduce average UK exports by £152m and to increase average UK imports by £994m p.a. at 1970 prices.

5 For details see M.F.W. Hemming, C.M. Miles and G.F. Ray, 'A Statistical Summary of the Extent of Import Control in the UK Since the War', *RES*, vol. 26, pp. 75-109.

6 In 1957 the average margin of preference on dutiable Commonwealth imports was 9%. See PEP, *Commonwealth Preference in the UK*, 1960. The swing in UK trade toward manufactures and the advanced industrialized nations progressively made this degree of preference less important.

the import values for semi-manufactures by 13% and that of finished manufactures by 9% relative to the values they would otherwise have had in 1971.[1]

III   ECONOMIC POLICY AND THE BALANCE OF PAYMENTS
III.1   Introduction

The coverage of this section is limited in two ways. First, pressure of space precludes more than a passing reference to events and policies prior to the floating of sterling in June 1972. Second, the concept of economic policy is limited to government intervention where the prime concern was to produce alterations in flows immediately affecting the balance of payments. It may be argued that *all* economic policy affects the balance of payments, since any non-trivial intervention in the economy is likely to produce at least minor alterations in the balance of forces affecting trade and payments flows and the exchange rate. Some policies may well have major implications for trade but, for present purposes, are not regarded as balance of payments policies. Thus, attempts to control inflation or to stimulate innovation, efficiency and growth are likely, if successful, to have substantial impacts on trade flows, but these problems are discussed elsewhere in this book and, in any case, may be judged desirable for reasons other than those concerned with the balance of payments. Equally, policies which are directed explicitly at trade flows may involve related adjustments in 'domestic' policy, as we shall see below in the discussion of exchange-rate management. Manipulation of tariff and other barriers to trade is a legitimate branch of balance of payments policy, but, in practice, government action of this nature is circumscribed by international agreements and membership of the EEC, so again pressure of space precludes more than a cursory discussion of what might be done within these constraints. Entry to the EEC is obviously a policy decision of incalculable magnitude affecting all aspects of economic behaviour but this section will confine itself to some balance of payments implications of that decision. The influence of the international monetary system upon UK policy is so important that we conclude the section by looking at recent developments in that field.

When interpreting the following discussion it is important to remember that the conduct of balance of payments policy, or for that matter of economic policy in general, is not a matter of 'fine tuning'. In part this reflects the fact that UK balance of payments performance is as much determined by the economic policies adopted in other countries as it is by policies adopted in the UK. On top of this, familiar problems of forecasting the direction and rate of change of economic variables, political and other limitations on the values of policy variables, and conflict between different policy objectives, taken together, mean that practical policy-making is more an art than a science.

---

1 A.D. Morgan and A. Martin, 'Tariff Reductions and UK Imports of Manufactures 1955-71', *NIER*, no. 72, May 1975. It is possible that this study understates the true reduction in protection afforded to UK manufacturing industry because it deals only with nominal tariff rates and not effective tariff rates — the effective rate taking into account the impact of tariff changes on the cost of imported means of production. Recent calculations for the period 1968-72 show that while the nominal rate on manufactures fell by 36%, the effective rate fell by 46%. N. Oulton, 'Tariffs, Taxes and Trade in the UK: The Effective Protection Approach', *Government Economic Service Occasional Papers*, no. 6, 1973, p. 9.

III.2 The Exchange Market Framework

It is a familiar proposition that modern industrial economies have evolved by means of a progressive division of labour and that one important pre-condition for this is the adoption of a single internal currency, to act as an intermediary in all economic transactions. The international division of labour has so far proceeded without this advantage. Since nations continue to maintain separate currencies for internal use, it follows that international transactions must proceed with the simultaneous exchange of national currencies, apart, that is, from those transactions conducted in key currencies. This exchange of currencies takes place in the foreign exchange market and it is there that the relative prices of different national currencies, exchange rates, are established.

An important policy issue which faces the government of any country is, therefore, that of the degree of restraint which it wishes to place on the exchange of its own currency with the currencies of other nations. Not only will the chosen restraints limit the type and geographical direction of transaction which domestic residents may make with foreigners, but they will also have an important bearing upon the conduct of policy to achieve internal objectives such as full employment and price stability. Successive UK governments have exercised their options in two ways: by adopting particular forms of exchange-rate policy, and by placing restrictions upon the currencies against which sterling may be exchanged for the pursuit of specified transactions, i.e. by exchange control.

Between 1945 and June 1972 the UK operated the foreign exchange market for sterling in accordance with the rules of the par-value system.[1] This required the official adoption of a par value to be expressed in terms of gold or the US dollar of 1944 fineness, which determined the central value of the spot-market rate for sterling,[2] together with the acceptance of a band of fluctuation of the spot rate around the par value.[3]

Provided the spot rate for sterling, as determined by market forces, lay within the permitted band, the UK exchange authorities did not need to take any action. Should the exchange rate be under pressure to stray outside this permitted band then the exchange authorities were obliged to intervene in the foreign exchange market, selling foreign exchange from the reserves when sterling was at its lower limit and purchasing foreign exchange to add to the reserves when sterling was at its upper limit. Thus the par-value system allowed some degree of variability in the foreign exchange rate but required that the UK keep a buffer stock of foreign exchange reserves, which it could use to keep the exchange rate within the specified bounds.

It must be noted that the par value of a currency was not fixed for all time once a country decided to abide by this system. On the contrary, a country could, when its balance of payments was in 'fundamental disequilibrium' and after consultation

---

1   This is the name given to the exchange-rate system adopted by the majority of Western nations after the Second World War. The central body of the system is the International Monetary Fund (IMF).

2   A distinction must be made between the spot-market and the forward-market exchange rates for a currency. The spot exchange rate is the price of foreign currency for immediate delivery, that is, at the time the rate for the transaction is agreed. A forward exchange rate is the price of foreign currency for delivery at a specified date in the future.

3   Until December 1971 the permitted band of fluctuation was 1% either side of par. Under the Smithsonian reforms of that time the band was widened to 2.25% either side of par.

with the IMF, change its par value. This UK governments did twice, devaluing sterling in 1949 and again in 1967.

In contrast to what is required in the market for spot exchange, IMF rules placed no formal restrictions on the movements of forward exchange rates for a currency. Nor were any necessary. In normal circumstances, the forward exchange rate will stand in a simple relationship[1] to the spot exchange rate, reflecting the role of the forward market in providing cover for the exchange risks inherent in spot-market transactions.

A major change in UK policy occurred in June 1972, when the par-value system was 'temporarily' abandoned and sterling allowed to take whatever values the balance of demand and supply for foreign exchange might dictate. However, a policy of allowing sterling to float has not meant that the exchange market ceases to be an object of policy concern. The government still has to decide to what extent sterling will float freely, without official constraint, and thus to what extent it is going to manage the exchange rate. Recent UK experience suggests a considerable degree of exchange management to iron out potentially violent fluctuations in the spot rate without, if possible, influencing its longer-term trend.

The second important aspect of UK exchange policy is that of exchange control, and here 1979 saw some important changes when, in October, the exchange-control restrictions which had been built up since 1945 were abolished. Exchange control is a complex issue with a detailed history of evolution, so that space precludes more than the most general remarks.[2] The legal basis of exchange control is contained in the Exchange Control Act of 1947, which assigns to the Treasury the authority to formulate exchange-control policy. The day-to-day responsibility for implementing the exchange-control provisions is delegated to the Bank of England, while, in turn, the daily volume of foreign currency transactions is handled by authorized exchange dealers, i.e. the commercial banks. The Exchange Equalization Account acts only as a residual purchaser or seller of foreign exchange in order to support a given exchange rate. As far as UK residents were concerned, practice after 1960 was to allow complete freedom for current transactions[3] but to restrict transactions on capital account in various ways. Exchange control in the UK was greatly complicated by the international-reserve and medium-of-exchange functions of sterling, which result in foreigners holding sterling balances. After 1958 a distinction was maintained between two such categories of sterling: external-account sterling and resident sterling. External-account sterling consisted of sterling balances held by non-sterling area residents. This was freely convertible into any currency for current and capital transactions. Resident sterling consisted of sterling balances held by residents of the UK and of the overseas sterling areas, who were treated

---

1 This is the interest parity relationship. Provided interest arbitrage funds are in perfect elastic supply then the percentage difference between spot and forward exchange rates for any pair of currencies will equal the interest differential on assets of the appropriate maturities denominated in those currencies. However, with arbitrage funds not in infinitely elastic supply, the forward rate will deviate from the interest parity value. In the limit, when the supply of speculative funds to the forward market is infinitely elastic, the forward rate will equal the value of the spot rate expected to hold at the time forward contracts mature.

2 A useful historical account of UK exchange control will be found in B. Tew, *International Monetary Co-operation 1945-1970*, Hutchinson, 1971. The interested reader may also consult the IMF *Annual Reports on Exchange Restrictions*.

3 Apart, that is, from certain restrictions on the availability of exchange for foreign travel and for the making of gifts and other transfers to non-sterling area residents.

in the same fashion as UK residents, i.e. allowed full convertibility on current account but restricted convertibility for capital transactions to non-sterling area countries.

From 1960 UK exchange-control regulations stayed broadly unchanged. However, with the float of sterling in 1972 several modifications were required, which essentially involved giving the former sterling area countries external-account status. By October 1979 the sterling area, for exchange-control purposes, consisted only of a handful of countries.[1] The major implications of the abandonment of exchange controls relate to capital-account transactions and these are discussed in more detail in sections III.6 and III.7.

III.3   External Economic Policy with a Floating Exchange Rate

In June 1972 the UK abandoned its commitment to the par-value system, and sterling began to float relative to other currencies. By the middle of 1973 sterling had been joined in this respect by all other major currencies, so that for the advanced industrial nations as a whole the par-value system had been abandoned. With sterling only one of many currencies engaged in a simultaneous float there is no simple index of movements in the international value of sterling. Sterling may appreciate in terms of some currencies while, at the same time, it depreciates in terms of others. Current practice is to rely upon the so-called 'effective exchange rate', which is a suitably weighted average of the movements of sterling compared to the currencies of those countries which are most important in UK trade.[2]

The movement in the effective exchange rate since June 1972 can be divided conveniently into three phases. The first, to November 1976, was one of almost continual depreciation, with the movement being particularly rapid after February 1976. In the last quarter of that year, the effective rate (with 1975=100) averaged 78.1, compared to an average of 94.0 in the first quarter and an average of 105.0 in 1972. Then, between the end of 1976 and the end of 1978, the effective rate was remarkably stable, rarely deviating more than 2% points either side of an average quarterly value of 81.3. The final phase, from January 1979, was one of rapid appreciation to a value of 100.6 in the last quarter of 1980, followed by a gradual depreciation to an index value varying one or two percentage points either side of 90.0 in the first quarter of 1982. The movement of sterling relative to individual currencies, in particular the dollar, has been much more volatile although the broad trends have mirrored that of the effective exchange rate. Before we analyse the causes of this sustained depreciation it will prove useful to outline some of the more important economic implications of floating exchange rates.

Floating rates and economic policy: The case for floating exchange rates rests, in large part, upon the alleged simplicity and automaticity of the free market mechanism in re-allocating resources in response to changing circumstances. In a dynamic world in which comparative advantages change rapidly and national inflation rates differ, changes in exchange rates are necessary if widespread under-utilization or misallocation of productive resources is to be avoided. The advantage of floating rates, it is argued, is that the necessary changes can occur progressively

1   See footnote 2, on page 130.
2   For details see *ET*, June 1974; *BEQB*, March 1977; *TER*, March 1977; and *BEQB*, March 1981.

at a pace dictated by the costs and profitability of resource allocation, and not, as with the par-value system, by sudden, discrete jumps dictated by speculative pressure and political expediency. The resource allocation advantages are only one aspect of the benefits derivable from the adoption of a floating exchange rate. More important for present purposes are the implications for the conduct of macro-economic policy. For it seems clear that with a more flexible exchange-rate policy the UK could have avoided most of the policy dilemmas of the period 1960-71 and that the period since 1971 would have generated impossible policy contradictions had the UK adhered to the par-value system.

There is, first, the minor point that the government no longer has to decide what constitutes an equilibrium exchange rate; to a large extent, this will be decided automatically within the foreign exchange market. One cannot go from this, however, to suggest that the conduct of domestic economic policy can proceed independently of developments in the foreign exchange market. The correct management of domestic demand is just as important with a floating exchange rate as it is with a fixed exchange rate. Balance of payments problems do not disappear with the adoption of a floating exchange rate, they are simply manifested in different forms. Developments that would lead to a loss of reserves with a fixed exchange rate, lead to a depreciation in the foreign exchange value of the currency if the exchange rate is allowed to float. In the first case, the loss of reserves will result, unless it is a once-and-for-all loss, in a policy-induced contraction in domestic income, while with a floating rate, the loss in real domestic purchasing power occurs automatically as the prices of tradeable commodities rise with the currency depreciation.

The main advantage of a floating rate is that it allows a greater independence of domestic economic policy-making. In particular, full-employment objectives may be more consistently pursued; there being some value of the exchange rate which will give exactly a zero currency flow at any, non-inflationary, level of employment. Furthermore, since a floating rate provides the minimum of linkage between the circular income of different trading nations, it follows that a floating exchange rate will isolate the level of demand for UK goods from changes in foreign incomes and preferences for UK goods. An increase in foreign demand which, under a fixed rate, would generate a multiple expansion in UK incomes, now generates an appreciation of the sterling rate of exchange, such that the final increase in the value of UK exports is exactly matched by an appreciation-induced increase in the value of UK imports, i.e. in the domestic expenditure on foreign goods. The total demand for UK goods, and therefore UK incomes, will remain unchanged.[1] The isolation of domestic incomes from external changes in demand has, of course, as counterpart the proposition that the level of domestic income is more sensitive to changes in the level of *domestic* money expenditure. In this respect, an economy with a floating exchange rate will behave in the same manner as a closed economy; the effects of changes in foreign trade upon the circular flow of income are completely negated. The policy consequence of this is that the multiplier repercussions of monetary and fiscal policy will be greater in an economy with a floating exchange rate than in the

---

1 A more detailed discussion would have to modify this argument in respect of any change in the aggregate savings ratio which followed the exchange appreciation and the possible effects on demand of any changes in international interest-rate levels.

same economy with a fixed exchange rate.[1] Correspondingly, the cost of mistakes in demand management will be increased with a floating rate, and so policy must be conducted with greater attention to underlying circumstances.

Other implications of floating rates: The relative merits of fixed and floating exchange rates are matters of considerable controversy among economists. Some of the alleged advantages of flexible exchange rates have already been mentioned. The object of the present section is to deal with two less clearcut aspects of the controversy. In particular, the view that private speculation will convert floating exchange rates into wildly fluctuating rates, and the view that a floating rate increases the uncertainty faced by international traders and investors to the detriment of the international division of labour.

The case for and against floating rates depends essentially on the view taken of the effects of speculators in the operation of free markets. If these markets are to be cleared continuously without undue fluctuations in the exchange rate, it is essential that speculators take over the role of the monetary authorities and operate in a stabilizing manner, selling sterling when the rate is temporarily 'too high' and buying sterling when the rate is temporarily 'too low'. Temporary fluctuations in the exchange rate follow, in part, because daily imbalances in the demand and supply for foreign exchange will result from random and seasonal factors, even if the balance of payments is basically in equilibrium over a longer time-span, and because short-period trading adjustments to relative price changes are likely to be inelastic. The proponents of floating exchange rates argue that speculative activity will be stabilizing and that speculators will be able to predict the trend value of the exchange rate so as to ensure minimal variations in the actual exchange rate around the trend value. Opponents fear that this will not be the case and the exchange market will be dominated by too much uncertainty for speculators to recognize the appropriate trend. Successive waves of optimism and pessimism will follow the frequent revision of expectations and generate substantial movements in exchange rates, out of all proportion to the volume of trading.

The difficulty with the above arguments is that we have little factual evidence to decide either way. Certainly the period with floating rates has witnessed some sudden, sharp movements in exchange rates out of step with underlying economic circumstances. Thus, for example, between end-September and end-October 1979 sterling depreciated by 5.5% against the dollar; it then appreciated to reverse this movement completely by end-November. On the other hand, the average quarterly movement of the sterling-effective rate over the period 1977-80 comes to 1.55 percentage points, which is not excessive and is well within the limits permissible under the par-value system. However, should private speculation prove to be less stabilizing than is thought desirable, there is no reason why the authorities should not engage in 'official' speculation, if necessary at the expense of private operators. Indeed this is precisely what the authorities have undertaken when supporting the sterling par-value against speculative pressure and when actually managing the exchange rate over various periods since June 1972. The implication is, of course,

---

1 Again this is subject to qualifications, depending upon the sensitivity of international capital movements to policy-induced changes in interest rates and the time-span considered for analysis. With floating rates, a greater degree of interest sensitivity of capital flows enhances the potency of monetary policy and limits the potency of fiscal policy for the management of aggregate demand.

that even with a floating exchange rate the authorities must maintain a stock of exchange reserves. While widespread adoption of exchange-management practices would also require the institution of international co-ordination and surveillance of exchange-rate practices, this appears neither impossible nor undesirable within the framework of an existing body such as the IMF (see section III.9 below). Finally, it must not be overlooked that destabilizing speculation can disrupt any exchange-rate framework and clearly did so with the par-value system. One of the major drawbacks of the par-value system was that it gave a one-way option to currency speculators. A currency under pressure would be pushed to one of the official intervention limits. This immediately signalled the possibility of a change in par value in a direction in which no one could have any doubt. Naturally, a large and cumulative movement of funds across the exchanges was therefore encouraged. A likely advantage of floating exchange rates is that the problem of a one-way speculative option would be much reduced.

The view taken of the effects of speculation determines the importance of the arguments on uncertainty and the inhibition of trade and investment. Provided that floating rates do not fluctuate wildly there is no reason why the bulk of trade and investment should be seriously affected. After all, exchange risks can always be covered with simultaneous deals in spot and forward markets. For sterling transactions involving the major currencies, the foreign exchange market currently provides active dealings for contracts up to one year in duration. Since some 92% of UK exports are financed on credit terms of less than six months' duration[1] with, no doubt, a similar proportion for imports, there should be no difficulty in traders covering their exchange risks. Longer-term trade contracts and international investment projects will face problems, but then in an uncertain world they always will. In addition it is argued that, should the forward premium on sterling exceed the appropriate interest differential, then traders will have to face extra costs of finance. There are two counter-arguments to this. First, the difference between forward premia and interest differentials will be smaller, the greater is the response of international capital flows to arbitrage possibilities. Particularly now that UK exchange controls have been relaxed, there is no reason to expect the costs of forward cover to be prohibitive. Secondly, suppose it could be demonstrated convincingly that additional exchange-rate uncertainty had reduced trade and investment. This could still not constitute an argument against floating rates, until the claimed costs could be shown to be greater than the employment and resource misallocation costs imposed under a par-value system.

III.4   The Exchange Rate and the Balance of Payments, 1972-81

In section I.4 we outlined the rapid changes in the UK's external position in the period since 1972, showing that from an initial surplus the current account moved into deficit during 1973-6 and then recovered from 1977 with substantial surpluses in 1980 and 1981. On the domestic front, as other chapters show, this period was also one of very rapid and variable inflation rates, high and variable interest rates and steadily increasing unemployment. The purpose of this section is to outline some of the major factors leading to the changes in the current account and the

---

1   See Business Statistics Office, *Business Monitor MA4: Overseas Transactions 1977*, HMSO, 1979.

exchange rate during the period, and their relation to domestic and international events. The first point to be reminded of when interpreting the events of the period is that the exchange rate for sterling has not been allowed to float freely, rather it has been managed quite actively, and this policy has produced economic effects which are a mixture of those occurring under the extremes of fixed and freely floating rates. We return to this point subsequently. Since the equilibrium exchange rate at any point in time reflects the balance of demand and supply of foreign exchange, it is useful to begin with an outline of the major forces affecting the volume of autonomous external transactions.

Purchasing-power parity: A convenient place to begin is the theory which relates the values taken by a currency's exchange rate to its purchasing-power parity. Broadly speaking, this means that the equilibrium exchange rate between the currencies of two countries is proportional to the ratio of the price levels in the respective countries. Moreover, providing this factor of proportionality remains constant, the proportionate rate of change of the exchange rate will be approximately equal to the difference between the inflation rates in the two countries.[1] With the exchange rate at par, the current account would then balance in the absence of net capital flows. The proximate source of the rapid depreciation of sterling between 1972 and 1976 can then be found in the excess of the UK rate of inflation over a suitably weighted average of the inflation rates in our major trading partners: it being a matter of indifference what the source of this inflation differential may be, whether it be related to excessive monetary expansion in the UK or to excessive wage-push by UK trade unions. Similarly the rise in sterling after 1978 would be related to a reduced UK inflation rate in comparison to that of our major trade partners. To investigate this further we may compare the movement in the UK's effective exchange rate, in the computation of which the OECD countries have a weight of 89%, with the movements in the consumer price indices in the UK and the combined OECD countries. The consumer price index is not perfect for this purpose but it will suffice. Between 1972 and 1976, the ratio of the OECD to the UK price levels fell by 17.8%, while the effective rate of sterling fell by 32%. Clearly sterling depreciated more quickly than purchasing-power parity would suggest, particularly during 1976 when the exchange rate was on average 15.4% points below purchasing-power parity. The effective rate remained roughly constant to the end of 1978 but it then appreciated rapidly during 1979 and 1980 despite a further 13.6% decline in purchasing-power parity. On average during 1980, sterling stood 10% points above purchasing-power parity. The decline in the effective rate after January 1981 only partially offset this movement, so that the over-appreciation of sterling still averaged 5% points during 1981. The catching-up of the exchange rate during 1979 and 1980 fits in well with many industrialists' (often vociferous) concern that an overvalued exchange rate was adversely affecting UK exports and encouraging import penetration. Of course, these calculations are rather rough and ready and depend crucially upon an assumption that sterling was at purchasing-power parity in 1972. Nevertheless they

---

[1] Probably the clearest statement of the purchasing-power parity theory is still contained in J.M. Keynes, *A Tract on Monetary Reform*, Macmillan, 1923, pp. 70-93. For a recent survey, see L.H. Officer, 'The Purchasing Power Parity Theory of Exchange Rates: A Review Article', *IMF Staff Papers*, Vol. 23, 1976. The exact formula for the percentage change in purchasing-power parity between two dates is $(P'-P)(1+P)$, where P and P' are the proportionate changes in the domestic and foreign price levels.

are sufficiently robust to serve as a basis for discussion, and indicate that purchasing-power parity is not an exact guide to movements in the effective exchange rate even though it captures the longer-term trend.[1]

How are we to explain the substantial short-run deviations from purchasing-power parity, in particular the more rapid decline of sterling between 1972 and 1976 and the subsequent perverse over-appreciation during 1979 and 1980? A vital point to remember here is that purchasing-power parity is only relevant if three stringent conditions hold true during the relevant period: the national inflation rates must be correctly anticipated by economic agents; there must be no net capital movements across the exchanges, including in this category government intervention in the foreign exchange market; and there must be no relevant changes in economic structure affecting the current account of the balance of payments. Not one of these conditions can be said to have applied over the period since 1972 and it is convenient to seek the proximate sources of deviations from purchasing-power parity in terms of capital movements and structural change. As far as capital movements are concerned, a full treatment is given in section III.6, and for the present it is sufficient to note that changes in international interest differentials and in expected international inflation differentials are a potent source of deviations from purchasing-power parity. The sustained capital outflows of 1976 were certainly influenced by anticipations of a rise in the UK inflation rate – i.e. a future decline in purchasing-power parity – and occurred despite the fact that the current-account deficit was steadily falling at the time. Similarly the substantial capital inflows of 1977 owed a great deal to the effects on confidence of an IMF-imposed anti-inflation programme, with its strict control of government spending. Recognizing the tenuous nature of expectations and market sentiment forces, one also has to recognize that the short-run relation between the exchange rate and purchasing-power parity will be difficult to predict. Short-run exchange-rate movements will tend to be volatile and to pre-date measured changes in purchasing-power parity by a time-period of indeterminable length.

On the question of economic structure, several factors are relevant. The first is the effect of UK membership of the EEC and the associated longer-term trends in UK trade patterns, referred to in sections II and III.8. *A priori* it is impossible to say how these factors have affected the purchasing-power parity of sterling. Certainly they are slow-moving, persistent forces which could reasonably be relegated to a minor role in this account. Of much greater importance have been sharp changes in the terms of trade and the progression of the UK toward self-sufficiency in oil production.

These important changes in economic structure were bound to make our simple purchasing-power parity calculation a poor guide to short-run and even long-run movements in the exchange rate. The primary element in the period to 1976 was the increase in the foreign currency prices of imported materials, foodstuffs and oil. Between 1972 and 1974 the average dollar price of primary commodities, excluding oil, increased by 96%. From this peak they subsequently fell, with the 1976 index indicating a 90% increase over 1972. By end-1979 nominal dollar commodity prices were twice as high as in 1972. Relative to the prices of world exports of

---

1   A recent study of the movements of seven other major currencies besides sterling also finds substantial short-run deviations from purchasing-power parity: G. Hacche and J. Townsend, 'A Broad Look at Exchange Rate Movements for Eight Currencies, 1972-80', *BEQB*, December 1981.

manufactures, however, primary commodity prices were only 18% greater in 1976 compared to their level in 1972 and had approximately the same relative price in 1981 as in 1972. Without question, the most significant price change was the quadrupling of the posted price of oil by the OPEC nations at the end of 1973, from $3.45 per barrel to $11.58 per barrel.[1] The implications of this development were considerable and worldwide, affecting not only individual economies but also the stability of the international monetary system. Some of the wider issues are treated in section III.9 below. Between 1975 and 1978 the price of oil remained within the range $12 to $14 per barrel, but the price rose sharply again from June 1979 with a price at the beginning of 1981 of $36 per barrel. However, the deepening world recession and the declining demand for energy gradually led to a world oil glut so that, in the first quarter of 1982, the price of oil fell by $4-$5 per barrel, the first significant reduction recorded since 1975. The effects of these price changes on the UK current account after 1974 were indeed dramatic, and are reflected in the sharp decline in the terms of trade by 23% between 1972 and 1974. It is interesting to note that relative price changes rather than quantity changes were the major influence on the current account during the period 1972-6; the exact reverse of the situation in the 1960s. Between 1972 and 1976 relative price changes worsened the non-oil balance of trade by an average of £248m p.a. and the oil balance by an average of £925m p.a., and these effects are far greater than the contemporaneous quantity effects on the trade balance.[2] It is not surprising, with the current-account deficits experienced between 1972 and 1976, that the effective exchange rate for sterling should have fallen more quickly than purchasing-power parity would indicate.

As the short-run elasticity of demand for oil and commodity imports does not differ appreciably from zero, the impact effect of the oil and other price increases was simultaneously to worsen the trade balance and to generate deflationary pressure in the UK economy. It was as if the UK government had raised indirect taxes, so cutting the demand for UK output, and had then transferred the tax proceeds to the oil-producing and primary-commodity-producing nations. In addition, the similar effects on other industrial economies produced cuts in the demand for UK exports and so provided a further deflationary stimulus: while very little help could be expected in the short run from the spending of OPEC funds on UK-produced goods.

Several options were open to the government to deal with this situation. First it could have attempted to eliminate the current-account deficits either by a severe policy-induced cut in aggregate demand, or by allowing the exchange rate to depreciate sufficiently to improve the non-oil trade balance of the UK at the expense of the other industrialized countries. Neither option proved to be feasible or otherwise desirable. The only effective policy was one of substantial foreign borrowing, combined with a broadly neutral stance toward domestic aggregate

---

1 The posted price should not be confused with the market price of oil. The posted price is the administrative price from which the OPEC countries assess the royalty payments and tax payments due from the oil-extracting companies.

2 See the article 'The Terms of Trade', *BEQB*, September 1978.

demand.[1] Over the period 1972-6 the net outcome for the UK was therefore one of rising external indebtedness, combined with falling domestic production as the deflationary effects of the change in the terms of trade worked through to expenditure and demand.

Foreign borrowing took place under three separate headings. Prior to 1972, the OPEC oil-producers traditionally received about 25% of their oil revenues in sterling and normally deposited this as sterling balances in London. With the increase in oil revenues following the Tehran agreement, the immediate response was to place much of the surplus in London. In 1974 some 37% of surplus oil funds, a total of $21bn, was placed in London. In the subsequent years the total amount of short-term finance made available in this way declined considerably, as a result of falling surplus oil revenues and an increasing unwillingness to deposit funds in a depreciating currency. In fact, between 1975-7 only $4-5bn flowed into the UK, on an annual basis, representing 12-14% of surplus oil funds. The second important source of finance was nationalized industry and local authority borrowing under the Treasury exchange cover scheme. Much of this was in the form of OPEC funds taken from the eurodollar market in the form of medium-term (3-7 year) loans. Some $3.4bn was raised in this way in the two years to the end of 1975 and a further $3.6bn to the end of 1977. Finally, the UK government has itself engaged in substantial borrowing. Most important here was the $2.5bn and $1.5bn loans raised from the eurodollar market in 1974 and 1977, the $2bn borrowed from the IMF at the end of 1975 − 60% of which represented a drawing on the specially created oil facility − and the stand-by agreement with the IMF agreed at the end of 1976 under which the UK could draw $3.9bn from its remaining credit tranches, $1.2bn being taken in January 1977.

While the policy of foreign borrowing allowed the UK to accommodate its payments deficit in anticipation of the benefits of NS oil, it also clearly prevented the exchange rate from dropping even further below purchasing-power parity than it did. As pointed out in section I.4, this increased external debt created an interest and amortization burden which implies the need for a substantial UK current-account surplus in the 1980s to service the interest and amortization payments.

Turning now to the period after 1976, the most important fact to be explained is the rapid appreciation of sterling during 1979 and 1980. The major structural factor of relevance here is the growth in production from the NS oil fields, which have made by far the major contribution to the growing current-account surpluses after 1977, as well as effectively insulating the terms of trade from the second major increase in the relative price of oil in 1979. The direct effect on the current account has been reinforced by the indirect effects on confidence and capital flows. With the UK payments position now unaffected by oil price changes, sterling is a safe haven for OPEC and other capital funds − free from the exchange risks attached to the currencies of net oil-importers such as the USA, Japan and Germany. This renewed confidence in sterling, its petrocurrency status, is adequately reflected in the average annual rate of recorded overseas investment in

---

1 Although the March 1975 budget was intended to produce substantial cuts in the government borrowing requirement, it can be argued that their net effect on aggregate demand was negligible. See *NIER*, May 1975, p. 11. A more deflationary stance was adopted in 1976 and 1977, announcing further reductions in future public expenditure. Calculations suggest, however, that over the period 1975-7 the net stance of fiscal policy had a small stimulating effect on the economy. See the article 'Why is Britain in Recession?', *BEQB*, March 1978.

the UK which amounted to £4.5bn annually during 1977-80. The comparable figure for the period 1970-76 is a mere £0.73bn. The significance of this structural change is also shown by the far greater stability of the terms of trade since 1976, the largest annual change being the 5.7% improvement between 1977 and 1978. A further structural factor which has to be taken into account is the relatively greater depth of the UK recession. While the appreciation of sterling has helped to reduce aggregate demand for UK goods, there is little doubt that the major depressing factor has been the stance of UK fiscal and monetary policy. Between 1978 and 1981, UK industrial output fell by 6.8%, while in the whole OECD area industrial output *expanded* by 6%. Naturally this relative decline, together with the associated reductions in inventory levels in the UK, has been an important factor contributing to the large current-account surpluses and thus the buoyancy of sterling. It remains an open question as to what value of sterling would currently correspond to full-employment and external equilibrium in the UK.

So far we have looked at deviations from purchasing-power parity in terms of shifts in several autonomous factors impinging upon the exchange rate. Equal weight must also be given to government intervention in the foreign exchange market. The next section deals with the theoretical pros and cons of intervention, so here we simply record that the float of sterling has been heavily managed since 1972. For example, between 1974 and 1976 annual reserve losses of $1.3bn were incurred to prevent an even more rapid slide of the exchange rate, while during 1977, by contrast, the reserves were allowed to increase by the historically unprecedented sum of $16.4bn when the effective rate was stabilized. Further reserve gains of approximately $9bn (after allowance for valuation changes) during 1979 and 1980 also prevented even greater appreciation above purchasing-power parity, while the decline in sterling during 1981 was ameliorated with a reserve loss of $0.7bn.

To sum up. Over the longer term a simple, indeed crude, measure of purchasing-power parity adequately captures the trend in the effective sterling rate. However, in any short period it is clear that the market clearing value for sterling deviated significantly from this purchasing-power-parity figure, largely as a response to structural factors and net capital flows. Moreover, it is clear that government intervention in the foreign exchange market prevented even greater deviations from purchasing-power parity than would otherwise have been imposed by a free market for sterling.

III.5   Management of the Exchange Rate

In the previous section we have indicated how the sterling exchange rate has been heavily managed during the period since 1972, the primary weapons in this management being foreign currency borrowing and changes in the stock of UK foreign exchange reserves.

There are several important reasons why a government may wish to manage the exchange rate. In the first instance it may view changes in the demand and supply of foreign exchange as temporary and so act as a speculator to prevent such transitory changes in the balance of autonomous transactions from influencing the exchange rate. This policy could be justified as one way to minimize the disruptive effects of transitory exchange-rate variations on trade and investment. As a second example, the government may take a view that the balance of autonomous transactions has shifted permanently but at the same time consider that an immediate full adjustment of the exchange rate would be too disruptive to patterns of employment and resource allocation. The exchange rate could then be actively managed toward its new long-run level at a pace which allows the pattern of resource allocation to change smoothly. The problem with this line of argument is, of course, the familiar one, how does the government know the exchange rate appropriate to different sets of internal and external circumstances? Too easily a policy of 'leaning into the wind' may become a policy of manipulation of the exchange rate to satisfy other objectives.

One very important objective in the UK context could be that of engineering a depreciation of sterling to maintain or increase the competitiveness of UK manufacturing exports and import substitutes. This policy could be justified in terms of offsetting the medium-term effects on the sterling exchange rate of NS oil which, if left unchecked, could undermine the competitiveness of UK industry and leave the country with greatly diminished foreign exchange earning power when the NS oil resources are exhausted. The appreciation of sterling during 1979 and 1980 brought this problem to the forefront of discussion with the increasing concern about de-industrialization of the non-oil sector of UK industry. The mechanism of a managed depreciation would be as follows. The impact effect would be to change relative prices. The relative prices of tradeable commodities — exports, imports and their close substitutes — will increase and, depending on the pricing policies of domestic and foreign firms,[1] the terms of trade will typically deteriorate as sterling import prices rise relative to sterling export prices. The changes in relative price then induce substitutions in patterns of production and consumption, which, though they may at first be negligible, grow in magnitude as contracts are re-negotiated and as new plant and equipment is installed to take advantage of changed profit opportunities. Available evidence would suggest that the magnitudes of these quantitative responses do produce a long-run improvement in the trade balance.[2] There may, however, be an initial deterioration as a result of the adverse terms-of-trade effect, the so-called 'J'-curve response to depreciation, as the immediate effects on relative prices precede the longer-term quantitative responses of trade flows.

Even if the elasticities of foreign and domestic demand and supply are of the right magnitude, the effects do not stop there. To the extent that the trade balance improves in terms of home currency, the aggregate demand for UK goods will be increased and this, via the multiplier effects on income, will create subsequent and partially offsetting increases in the demand for imports. Furthermore, if the economy is at or near to full employment, the devaluation-induced expansion of

---

1   On the pricing policies of UK firms following the 1967 devaluation, see P.B. Rosendale, 'The Short-Run Pricing Policies of Some British Engineering Exporters', *NIER*, no. 65, 1973, and the valuable study by D.C. Hague, E. Oakeshott and A. Strain, *Devaluation and Pricing Decisions*, Allen and Unwin, 1974. Professor Cooper has suggested that foreign suppliers cut their foreign currency prices on average by 4%. See A.K. Cairncross (ed.), *Britain's Economic Prospects Reconsidered*, Allen and Unwin, 1971, p. 181.

2   In the special case in which there is initial balanced trade and supply elasticities of traded goods are infinite, then the depreciation improves the trade balance provided that the sum of the foreign and domestic elasticities of demand for imported goods exceeds unity. For a more general statement see Kindleberger and Lindert, *International Economics*, Irwin, 1978, chapter 15 and Appendix H. Evidence suggests that this so-called 'Marshall-Lerner' condition would be satisfied for the UK.

aggregate demand will have inflationary implications which can only be prevented if domestic expenditure is reduced to make room for the improvement of the trade balance. Finally, account must be taken of the import content of domestic production, and the effect of the devaluation in raising domestic costs of production and in creating pressure for higher money wages.[1] This latter qualification is of prime importance. For unless the depreciation is associated with a reduction in real wages then the only effect of a real depreciation of sterling will be to lower the long-run profitability of UK manufacturing industry. If, in addition, domestic firms follow pricing policies to maintain rates of return then the real depreciation will be prevented, the ultimate effects of the depreciation will be purely nominal and there will not be any long-run effect on flows of exports and imports.

The conclusion to be drawn from this is that powerful forces are at work to offset the initial effects of a managed depreciation on the balance of trade. Indeed recent calculations show that the effects of a hypothetical depreciation in sterling are largely transitory with respect to the level of output and the current balance of payments, and that after six years a devaluation of 5% would produce a 4% increase in the UK's retail price index. These calculations also make clear that the effects of a devaluation depend on the fiscal policies and other policies to control money income which accompany the depreciation.[2] Certainly the depreciation of sterling. in 1976 only produced a temporary increase in the international competitiveness of UK goods which had been entirely eroded by the beginning of 1979. Discussion of the inflationary effects of an exchange depreciation raises another reason why a government may wish to actively manage the exchange rate. Some of the arguments here were stimulated by the sharp depreciation of sterling in 1976, which occurred after a period in which domestic incomes restraint had reduced the annual rate of increase of unit labour costs in UK manufacturing from 30% between 1974-5 to 11.2% in 1975-6. It has been suggested, therefore, that a managed appreciation of sterling would help to combat domestic inflation. The argument surfaced again in 1981 when the decline in sterling was alleged to threaten the then current anti-inflation policy. The main proposition here is that the rate of inflation is influenced by the pressure of demand in the labour market and by expectations of inflation, so that a currency appreciation reduces inflation on three fronts: it directly lowers domestic production costs via the cost of imported means of production, it reduces the pressure of demand for labour by its adverse effects on the demand for UK output, and by reducing inflation in this direct fashion it has the indirect effect of lowering the anticipated rate of inflation, thus moderating money wage demands and possibly increasing the viability of attempts to directly influence money wages. The effectiveness of such a policy must, however, be questioned not least because of the ambiguity over whether any persistent change in the exchange rate is a cause of, or an implication of, domestically generated inflation. Indeed, to take one extreme, if it were the case that inflation expectations

1 The average import content of UK manufacturing output is currently 21%.

2 See *TER*, March 1978, no. 96. It is particularly important that the money supply is not allowed to expand and negate the effects of depreciation in reducing real money balances and absorption. A more recent study suggests that, holding money wages constant, a 10% effective depreciation of sterling would be followed after three years by a 4% increase in wholesale prices and a 2.5% increase in consumer prices. See the article 'Sterling and Inflation', *BEQB*, September 1981.

were formed, as some economists suggest, from a knowledge of rates of growth of UK monetary aggregates, then the exchange rate will also reflect this information and its movements should not have any independent influence on the UK inflation rate. It will be clear that the competing claims of 'industrial competitiveness' and 'anti-inflation policy' upon exchange-rate policy are inconsistent, and for the present it would appear that the anti-inflation motives governing exchange-rate policy have the upper hand.

So far we have taken for granted the view that the exchange rate can be managed to achieve either balance of payments or inflation-rate effects. Such a view may prove excessively optimistic outside the short period. First, one has to recognize that in a world where all the major currencies are floating, governments may follow mutually inconsistent exchange-rate targets and find themselves in a situation of competitive exchange-rate management in which one country's policies are nullified by the action of others. Secondly, experience gained with sterling and other currencies during the 1960s and the 1970s showed that it becomes increasingly difficult for the authorities to maintain an exchange rate substantially different from its equilibrium value without inducing disruptive flows of speculative short-term capital which ultimately force a change in policy. Thirdly, and more fundamentally, there are strong arguments to suggest that any attempt to maintain an exchange rate other than that dictated by purchasing-power parity must be a failure in the long run. This argument simply takes account of the fact that any artificial, disequilibrium, exchange rate will in general be associated with a non-zero BOF and thus with changes in the stock of foreign exchange reserves and the domestic money supply.[1] One version of this proposition is as follows. If the exchange rate is notionally depreciated, the effect on the domestic price level will reduce the real value of monetary assets in general and induce a temporary trade surplus as agents attempt to restore real asset holdings to their equilibrium levels. This surplus will expand the reserves and the money supply until balance sheets are returned to equilibrium and the pre-devaluation structure of relative prices regained. The only permanent effect of the devaluation will be an equal proportionate increase in the price level and an increase in the stock of foreign exchange reserves. It must be stressed that this is a long-run argument, and that the links between changes in the reserves and the domestic money supply can be offset by domestic monetary policy. However, despite these qualifications it throws into perspective the point that management of the exchange rate is only likely to prove successful in the short run.

Unresolved issues: We have already described the direct effects on the balance of payments of the growing production of NS oil and gas since 1973, and argued that this was a key factor behind the appreciation of sterling between 1979 and 1980. In 1981 the price of oil relative to world exports of manufactures was four and a half times greater than in 1973 (this calculation leaves aside the quality premium on UK crude), and the UK has indeed been fortunate enough to capitalize on this change in world relative prices. Yet many doubt that the benefits are real, and even industrialists are sometimes prone to suggest that the UK would have been better off without the exploitation of NS resources. The key issue here is the effect of the

---

1   For useful accounts of the links between external transactions and the domestic money supply, see 'Of DCE, M_3 and Similar Mysteries', *MBR*, February 1977, and 'External and foreign currency flows and the money supply', *BEQB*, December 1978.

oil revenues on the exchange rate and whether any oil-induced appreciation of sterling above purchasing-power parity is inevitable. Two facts are key to this issue and must be borne in mind in what follows: that as much as 80% of NS revenues will accrue in taxes to the Exchequer; and that all UK production represents an equivalent gross gain to the balance of visible trade.[1] The impact effect of increased UK production is necessarily one of improving the current account and putting upward pressure on the exchange rate – an effect enhanced by the petrocurrency issues discussed in the next section. The high exchange rate crowds out the production of non-oil tradeables in the UK and, since these are labour-intensive relative to oil, has the effect of reducing the aggregate demand for labour at current levels of real wages. What is the appropriate policy response to this so-called 'Dutch-disease' phenomena?[2] Whatever policy is adopted the objective must be to generate a countervailing increase in the supply of sterling in the foreign exchange market and thus prevent any oil-induced appreciation of the spot exchange rate.

A first priority will be to expand the economy and reduce current levels of unemployment and spare capacity using tax cuts or public expenditure increases financed directly from NS tax receipts. Via the familiar multiplier mechanisms these policies will increase the demand for net imports of goods and securities, and thus help to hold down the exchange rate. Alternatively, a reduced PSBR would allow some reduction in interest rates with additional beneficial effects on capital flows and the exchange rate. Now suppose, as seems plausible, that full employment is reached before the NS resources effect on the exchange rate is eliminated. Further tax cuts will have a relatively small effect on imports of consumption goods and the best policy option would be for the government to make those socially profitable investments in infrastructure which have either a high import content, or a substantial capacity for generating employment in order to absorb resources displaced from the non-oil traded goods sector, e.g. investment in health, education, research and training. In this way the NS oil benefit could be translated into physical and human capital assets with positive effects on UK industrial competitiveness in the medium and long term when NS production begins to decline.[3] An alternative line of policy would be for the government to invest the additional tax revenues in foreign assets, either directly by exchange-market intervention and the repayment of foreign debts sensibly accumulated during the period 1974-7, or indirectly by running a lower PSBR so potentially leaving a large fraction of domestic savings free for private overseas investment. While the short-term effects of this strategy will certainly limit any appreciation of sterling, it is easy to see that in the longer-term it would only delay the oil-induced exchange-rate appreciation as the return flow of interest and profits swells current-account receipts.[4]

---

1 The tax revenue figure comes from P.J. Forsyth and J.A. Kay, 'The Economic Implications of North Sea Oil Revenues', *Fiscal Studies*, 1980, pp. 1-28.

2 On this see the interesting article by M. Ellman, *Cambridge Journal of Economics*, 1977.

3 Cf. 'The Challenge of NS Oil', Cmnd. 7143, *HMSO*, 1978.

4 If X be the annual capital outflow 'financed' out of NS revenues and r be the interest return on these investments, then after T years the return flow of interest will be rXT. The net annual gain in the supply of sterling is thus $X(1-rT)$, which is smaller the longer the policy is maintained. Thus if r is 6% the policy will become self-defeating after 16.5 years. Investment in barren assets would avoid this problem and, of course, dissipate entirely the benefits of NS oil!

It is difficult to avoid the practical conclusion, once full employment is restored, that the exploitation of the NS will leave the UK with a higher exchange rate than would otherwise prevail. Some structural change is certain to follow from this, with adverse consequences for employment in the production of manufactured trade-able goods. The pattern of comparative advantage has changed and in a way which allows a higher *average* level of UK income than would otherwise prevail. The proper response is surely not how change can be prevented but how the consequences of NS resources can be accommodated with a minimum of transitional cost and a maximum of longer-term benefit.[1]

The second related issue is that of persistent unemployment in the UK, currently well above the average levels of the 1960s, and the view that in order to eliminate this and at the same time revive UK industry, some substantial protection in the form of import restrictions will be required. The argument here is complex and hotly debated, but the broad issues are clear enough. To the extent that unemploy-ment in the UK is a reflection of the general world recession induced by the past and recent oil price increases, there is little to commend import restrictions. To adopt such a policy would be in the worst tradition of beggar-thy-neighbour diplomacy. However, to the extent that the UK's unemployment and lack of competitive edge in world markets reflect structural problems unique to UK industry, then general import restrictions, provided they are linked to a policy of investment and industrial reconstruction, merit at least a hearing if only because the alternative policy of a sterling depreciation may not prove viable for the reasons outlined above.[2] In response to the argument that foreign retaliation will be provoked, it should be remembered that any policy which improves the UK's trade balance and competitive strength, whether it be import restriction, export subsidy or devaluation, must 'harm the foreigner', so that the precise way this is achieved should be a relatively minor matter dictated by the net advantages of each policy for the UK. It should also be remembered that the purpose of such a policy is primarily to stimulate the demand for UK output so that its final effect on UK imports would be smaller than its impact effect, the difference reflecting the induced increase in imports as domestic incomes and employment increase. Indeed as the economy grows, the permitted volume of imports can also be allowed to grow in step. Practical objections to such a policy are essentially twofold. First, there are the immediate political difficulties of obtaining EEC and IMF approval, especially as any sensible policy of import restrictions would have to last for fifteen years or so, and would have to be implemented when the favourable balance of payments effects of NS oil are at their height. Second, and more fundamentally, there is no guarantee that higher levels of output and employment will lead to more productive investment, more flexible working practices and a willingness to take innovative risks. If they do not, the import restrictions could prove a recipe for stagnation rather than industrial regeneration.[3] The diagnosis then is quite simple —

---

1   On the inevitability of structural change see Forsyth and Kay, op. cit. We leave aside any discussion of a further policy option, i.e., managing the production flow from the NS to minimize the effect on the exchange rate. This involves complicated questions of inter-temporal choice beyond the bounds of realistic policy formation.

2   The most persistent advocates of this view have been the Cambridge Economic Policy Group; see, e.g., their *Economic Policy Review*, no. 4, March 1978, and the contribution by R. Neild to the book by R.L. Major cited at the end of this chapter.

3   The 7th edition of this book contains a brief account of the temporary import restrictions employed by the UK in the 1960s.

without a significant increase in the competitive ability of UK industry the long-term prospects for employment and living standards in the UK are quite grim. It is the nature of the medicine which is unknown, and while import controls may be a necessary part of any cure they will certainly not be sufficient of themselves to regenerate the UK industrial structure.

III.6 Short-Term Capital Flows and Balance of Payments Policy

In this section and the next we shall investigate the relationship between capital movements, the balance of payments and the exchange rate. As we have pointed out in section I.2, the distinction between short-term and long-term capital flows is to a considerable extent arbitrary, and the distinctions drawn here reflect matters of convenience alone. By short-term capital movements we shall mean transactions between UK and overseas residents, in currency, bank deposits and securities, transactions which are typically related to the finance of foreign trade or the optimal allocation of stocks of wealth between assets denominated in different currencies. In the next section, on long-term capital flows, we shall be concerned with the international direct investment operations of companies and public-sector bodies.

Short-term capital movements have traditionally played an important role in the overall UK balance of payments situation. Their importance is the joint result of the position of London as an international financial centre and of the historical role of sterling as an international reserve asset and medium of exchange. Thus some short-term capital movements reflect changes in the sterling balances which foreign governments and individuals have acquired as matters of commercial and financial convenience. The remainder reflect the role of London as the major centre for the eurocurrency, euroloan and other international financial markets, with banks in the UK lending and borrowing extensively in dollars and other currencies. The development of the eurocurrency and related markets since 1958 has meant the increasing integration of European and American capital and money markets.[1] The degree of integration has increased particularly quickly in the 1970s with the rapid growth of the eurocurrency market, with net deposits of $85bn in 1971 increasing to $810bn in 1980. The volume of deposits and the ease with which they may be switched between currencies has important implications for the stability of exchange rates and for the conduct of national monetary policies.

The significance of short-term capital flows for the conduct of UK policy arises from their magnitude relative to the official reserves and from their volatility. It is convenient to divide the capital flows which influence the UK balance of payments into two broad classes: speculative and non-speculative. The motive behind speculative capital flows is one of making a capital gain from anticipated movements in spot exchange rates or interest rates. A currency speculator would be indifferent between holding sterling- or dollar-denominated assets, for example, if the interest rate on sterling assets equalled the interest rate on dollar assets plus the anticipated depreciation of sterling relative to the dollar — risk premium here being ignored. If the anticipated sterling devaluation exceeds the sterling interest

---

1   Eurocurrency deposits are bank deposits in currencies other than that of the country in which the banks in question are located. For the working and development of the euro-currency markets, consult G.W. McKenzie, *The Economics of the Eurocurrency System*, Macmillan, 1976. See also, 'Eurobanks and the Inter-Bank Market', *BEQB*, September 1981.

advantage, holders of sterling assets will switch their assets into dollars while UK importers will accelerate (lead) dollar payments for imports and UK exporters will try to delay (lag) dollar payments due from foreigners. Non-speculative activities are undertaken to avoid capital gains or losses associated with exchange-rate movements, and involve simultaneous transactions in both spot and forward currency markets so that the risks associated with currency transactions may be shifted onto speculators.[1] In sum, short-term capital movements depend on a complex set of interactions between national interest rates, spot and forward exchange rates, and expectations of future changes in spot rates. Not surprisingly, short-term capital flows are highly volatile and are capable of creating substantial deviations of an exchange rate from its purchasing-power parity. The fact that the exchange market is an efficient, competitive market means that mere changes in the news may result in sudden exchange-rate movements as expectations are revised. Indeed it is quite plausible to argue that short-term exchange-rate movements will exceed those required to restore long-run exchange-market equilibrium in the face of exogenous disturbances.[2] The precarious nature of expectations in general also implies that short-term capital movements are not necessarily amenable to official attempts at their control. During periods of rapidly diverging national rates of inflation, such as experienced since 1972, money interest-rate differentials between different countries and expectations of exchange-rate changes will be greatly influenced by expectations of differences in national inflation rates. In a world of high capital mobility, the short-term capital flows induced by the expectation of divergent national inflation rates can then exert a dominant influence on the actual movements of the exchange rate, as the depreciation of sterling during 1976 illustrated so graphically.

The implications of short-term capital flows for external and internal policy closely depend upon the exchange market framework in operation. Under the par-value system the first impact of a short-term capital outflow fell upon the exchange reserves and thus on the monetary base of the banking system, this being true of both speculative and non-speculative flows. Given the poor reserve/short-term liability situation of the UK, any such loss of reserves, if heavy, almost invariably provoked a change in demand-management policy. A 'run on sterling' was normally followed by a policy to contract domestic demand and restore 'confidence', frequently in conjunction with foreign borrowing by the government. With a freely floating exchange rate however, the impact effect of a net capital flow falls not upon the reserves but upon the spot exchange rate and, in general, will not affect the money supply.[3] A capital outflow will now work to depreciate sterling and an inflow to appreciate sterling. However, any such change in the exchange rate acts upon the current account in the same way as a policy-induced parity change. Hence, a capital inflow has effects akin to those of an appreciation: discouraging exports, encouraging imports, as well as influencing the price level. It will be clear that large

1   See the 6th edition of this book for a discussion of forward market transactions. More detailed treatments will be found in Grubel, *International Economics*, Irwin, 1977, chapter 12, and Kindleberger and Lindert, op. cit., chapter 13 and Appendix G.

2   An introduction to this technical phenomena known as 'exchange-rate overshooting' may be found in R. Dornbusch, *Open Economy Macroeconomics*, Basic Books, 1980, chapter 11.

3   For a statement of the exceptions to the general rule, see the article 'External and Foreign Currency Flows and the Money Supply', *BEQB*, December 1978.

and sudden capital flows can provide difficult policy problems for economies operating with floating exchange rates.

The appreciation of sterling from the end of 1978 to the end of 1980 provides a good example of an exchange-rate movement heavily influenced by short-term flows. The inflow of funds during the two years amounted to some £13bn, and key factors in the enhanced position of sterling were changed foreign perceptions of the thrust of anti-inflation policy, in particular monetary policy, and the emerging self-sufficiency of the UK in oil, which effectively removed the risk of a sterling depreciation following upon future oil price increases. Through 1981, however, the foreign capital inflow diminished substantially, largely as a consequence of the sharp increases in US interest rates to which UK authorities were forced to respond in October 1981. By end-1981 the sterling/dollar exchange rate had fallen by 23% compared to its value at end 1980. While the appreciation of sterling provided beneficial effects on the inflation rate, it also resulted in a substantial squeeze on export profit margins and enhanced import competition in UK domestic markets, and so undoubtedly contributed to the deepening domestic recession and to the pressures to raise productivity and shed labour.

In the light of this it is relevant to enquire if the UK authorities can exert any substantial influence over short-term capital flows. In the first instance some restraint on UK residents can be obtained via exchange-control provisions, which until 1979 were a major element in UK policy. Under these provisions UK residents were denied the opportunity to purchase foreign currency except for authorized purposes, and direct limits were placed on the net foreign exchange positions which banks and other exchange dealers could undertake in the course of their business.[1] A particularly important dimension of exchange control was that limiting purchases of overseas securities by UK residents. From 1947 onwards, purchases of securities issues in non-sterling area countries could not be financed with official foreign exchange, nor could the proceeds of the liquidation of such investments be converted back into sterling at the official exchange rate. Instead, all such transactions had to pass through the investment currency market at a separate exchange rate which balanced the desire to purchase foreign currency securities with the desire to liquidate existing holdings of NSA assets. Typically the investment currency rate stood at a premium relative to the official exchange rate, the magnitude of the premium providing some indication of the degree of the restriction on potential capital outflows. Between 1950 and 1962 the premium rarely exceeded 10% and was normally less than 5%. However, from 1962 onwards the premium increased substantially, and during the years 1975-8 it varied between a high of 81% (May 1975) and a low of 24% (August 1977), with an average level of 47%.[2] In April 1965 the controls were tightened with the introduction of a 25% surrender rule, under which 25% of the foreign currency proceeds of security sales had to be converted back into sterling at the official exchange rate, a 'tax' which is estimated to have yielded £1.07bn to the reserves between 1965 and end-1977.

---

1 For details, see the article 'Limits on UK banks' foreign exchange positions', *BEQB*, December 1975. One of the last exchange-control restrictions to be introduced was that of November 1976, forbidding UK banks to finance trade between third countries in sterling. The once-for-all gain to the reserves from this order is estimated to have been £1bn.

2 The premium is the percentage difference between the investment currency rate and the spot exchange rate. See the article 'The Investment Currency Market', *BEQB*, September 1976.

Further changes occurred in June 1972 when investment in OSA countries was included in the investment currency provisions, and in March 1974 when the surrender rule became applicable to OSA investments.

Entry into the EEC, however, meant that the UK had to abide by the Community directives freeing capital movements within the Community from exchange restriction. To comply with EEC regulations the surrender rule was abolished in January 1978 though the remaining network of controls was maintained under the escape clause, Article 108 of the Treaty of Rome, of balance of payments protection. The strength of sterling during 1979 and the prospective benefits of NS oil rendered the balance of payments argument for controls nugatory, and they were partially relaxed in June 1979 and finally abolished in October 1979. From this date the capital and money markets of the UK became fully integrated with those of the rest of the world. The effects of this should not be exaggerated, since the exchange regulations applied only to UK residents and left untouched the activities of non-resident holders of sterling, who since 1958 have been free to switch between sterling and other currencies. Indeed the major impact is likely to be felt through greater competition in capital and money markets rather than in any substantial long-term change in the net flows of capital across the exchanges. To be sure, the relaxation of exchange controls has allowed a once-for-all adjustment of the asset portfolios of UK individuals and financial institutions. Recent calculations do indeed indicate an effect of this nature, with the portfolio capital outflow in the period June 1980 to June 1981 roughly four times greater than in 1979.[1] To the extent that these figures accurately reflect the abolition of exchange controls, then it is clear that this policy could be justified as one means of limiting the oil-wealth effect on the sterling exchange rate.

Exchange controls apart, two alternative means of inducing capital flows may be employed. Manipulation of domestic interest rates is a powerful weapon in current circumstances, given the increasing integration of financial markets. Its use is subject to two limiting provisos: international retaliation, and conflict with the level of interest rates needed to attain internal objectives. The remaining policy option is official manipulation of the forward exchange rate, which would allow the authorities to create for the UK a risk-free interest-rate advantage on short-term investments, as circumstances dictate. Between 1962 and 1967 the UK achieved some success with this policy, effectively counteracting pressure on the reserves on several occasions. Although such a policy may be run at a modest profit for the UK authorities, technical losses arise if the spot rate is changed while official forward contracts are outstanding. This occurred with the 1967 devaluation, when the sum of £366m had to be paid out to foreigners who at the time held forward contracts to sell sterling. Since that episode, there has been little indication of official forward activity.

The sterling balances, i.e. sterling held by non-residents of the UK, have always been of prime importance in the UK payments situation, indeed to a considerable degree changes in overseas holdings of sterling, or even the threat of changes, dominated the external economic policy of the UK between 1960 and 1976. During the period 1960-68 the reserve function of sterling placed the UK in the position of an international banker with its gold and currency reserves as backing for the short-term external liabilities. As pointed out in section I, the UK's external problems in

---

1   See the article 'The Effects of Exchange Control Abolition on Capital Flows', *BEQB*, September 1981.

the 1960s stemmed partly from a grossly inadequate ratio of official reserves to sterling liabilities. The result was a general lack of confidence in the ability of the UK to maintain its banking role, which grew particularly sharp whenever the reserves were used or threatened to be used to fulfil their function of financing a deficit. The confidence problem came to a head following the devaluation of 1967, when fears of a second devaluation resulted in many OSA governments liquidating their sterling balances in a policy of reserve diversification. For the OSA countries this simply reflected a rational response to their weakening economic links with the UK. For the UK, however, it represented the demise of a basic ground-rule of the sterling payments system, viz, that OSA countries pool their official holdings of good and foreign currency in London in exchange for sterling balances. Naturally, this development caused much official concern in the UK and inspired negotiations to obtain international support for sterling, the upshot of which were the Basle arrangements of September 1968. Under the Basle arrangements twelve central banks, together with the Bank for International Settlements, extended credit of $2bn to the UK, the facility to have a life of ten years. The finance was provided on several conditions, the most important of which was the provision by the UK of a guarantee of the dollar value of each country's official sterling reserve holding in excess of 10% of its total reserves.[1] An important outcome of these guarantee arrangements, terminated at the end of 1974, was that they increased the attractiveness of sterling as a reserve asset. Following the increases in oil and commodity prices and in the incomes of the primary producing nations in the years 1972-4, the total of official, reserve sterling balances increased to £4.1bn at end-1975 of which 70% was held by oil-exporting nations. At this time 56% of total sterling balances were held as exchange reserves, compared with a figure of 35% at end 1968. Though the 1968 Basle arrangements served to perpetuate the reserve role of sterling from a UK viewpoint, from an international perspective the reserve role of sterling declined continually during the years 1970-76. Thus in 1970 sterling holdings accounted for 8.6% of world foreign exchange reserves, while by 1980 this proportion had fallen to 2.6%, the former position of sterling being taken over by the deutschmark and the yen.

The precarious nature of the UK's position over the sterling balances became abundantly clear during 1976. In March 1976 the sterling exchange rate against the dollar began a rapid slide, from approximately $2.00 to a low of $1.59 reached at the end of October. In the absence of the guarantee arrangements on sterling balances, official holders, and in particular the oil producers, began to diversify out of sterling on a large scale, the total of official balances falling by 38% between the end of March and the end of October to a value of £2.84bn. This reduction occurred despite the fact that the Treasury Bill rate in the UK rose over the same period from 8.6% to 14.9% and at a time when non-official sterling balances actually increased. Faced with this drain upon its foreign exchange reserves the UK government was obliged to seek a new Basle facility in which eleven central banks provided a two-year standby facility of $3bn, to cover any withdrawal of official sterling balances below a value of £2.16bn, subject to the proviso that UK official reserves be not greater than $6.75bn. As part of the agreement the UK was to 'fund' a portion of the official sterling balances by offering their holders medium-term

---

1 See the 7th edition of this book for a more detailed discussion of the Basle arrangements and their subsequent re-negotiation and modification.

bonds in exchange for their sterling holdings.[1] In the event the arrangements proved to be superfluous. The prospect of a strengthening UK payments position, as NS oil began to flow and as the UK inflation rate declined, relative to the weakening US payments position, greatly increased the attractiveness of sterling relative to the dollar. The associated increase in UK reserves and the keeping of official sterling balances above the £2.16bn mark has meant that the 1976 Basle arrangements were never activated. The remarkable turnround in the attractiveness of sterling is no better illustrated than by the fact that total sterling balances had reached the figure of £17.6m at end-December 1981.

One of the most interesting developments since 1975 has been the steady growth of sterling balances held by private individuals and organizations. Between end-1975 and end-1981, privately held sterling balances increased threefold to a total of £12.9bn. This total represents 73% of total sterling balances, compared to a comparable figure for 1967 of 32%. Despite the growth in sterling balances since 1975 the UK gold and currency reserves have increased even faster, with a ratio of reserves to total sterling balances of 36% at end-1975 and 132% at end-1981. It remains to be seen whether the improvement in the reserve/sterling-balance ratio will also be associated with a reduction in the volatility of sterling balances. If not, the problems for exchange-rate management in an era free from exchange controls could be formidable.

There have been several occasions since 1975 when, in the face of substantial short-term capital movements, the UK authorities have sought to hold the exchange rate against sustained external pressures. Three notable occasions when this occurred were between February and April 1976, when the reserves fell by 31%; between June and October 1977, when the reserves increased by 75%; and between April and December 1981, when they again fell by 17%. The normal justification for intervention on this scale is to prevent a movement in the exchange rate leading to too rapid or unnecessary reallocations of resources. On each occasion, however, the authorities were ultimately forced to abandon their interventionist stance and let the exchange rate adjust. The experience of these periods seem to have heightened awareness of the potential conflicts between monetary targets and exchange-rate targets. The future of exchange-rate policy thus seems nicely poised between two possibilities. If a sustained capital inflow into the UK should re-emerge, a resort to controls on capital inflows may be forced on the authorities, as with recent experience in Germany and Switzerland. Conversely if confidence in sterling should evaporate, then the possibility of massive speculative outflows may require an early re-imposition of exchange controls both on UK residents and more generally.

III.7   Long-Term Capital Flows and Balance of Payments Policy

The purpose of this section is to discuss the balance of payments and other consequences of direct investment overseas, and to outline the various measures adopted to control overseas investment flows.

---

1   Arrangements for the sale of the bonds were completed by April 1977, with 15 countries taking up bonds to the value of £394m. A choice of bonds was offered with a denomination in terms of four 'hard' currencies with maturities between 5 and 10 years and carrying interest rates between $5\frac{7}{8}$ and $8\frac{7}{8}$%. The bonds did not carry an exchange guarantee.

Any additional flow of overseas investment by the UK will have immediate and continuing implications for the current and capital accounts of the UK balance of payments. With a fixed or managed exchange rate, the impact effect is to reduce foreign exchange reserves, as UK investors acquire the foreign exchange needed for their overseas investment. If we consider direct investment, it is likely that the construction of new capital equipment overseas will involve some increased demand for UK exports of goods and services, so that the UK current balance will improve and the charge on the official reserves is reduced accordingly. Should the new flow of foreign investment be associated with a reduction in UK home investment, there will be a fall in the level of economic activity in the UK, and activity will increase abroad if the foreign investment leads to additional investment there. There will then be further repercussions on the UK current balance which stem from the multiplier process at home and abroad, and the linkage between the capital-account and current-account transactions is likely to be such that the current account improves but not by a sufficient amount to finance the capital outflow without loss of reserves.[1] The total increase in net external assets is therefore smaller than the direct investment outflow. If the capital outflow takes the form of portfolio investment, the impact on the current account is likely to be negligible and such investment will be matched by an equivalent reduction in other net overseas assets.

In addition to the linkages between the trade balance and the flow of direct foreign investment, account must also be taken of the return flow of profit and interest income from overseas investment. In the simplest case of a steady compound growth in the stock of overseas assets in which the assets are acquired without direct resort to foreign borrowing, the return profit inflow will exceed or fall short of the capital outflow according as the rate of return on the foreign investments exceeds or falls short of the percentage rate of growth in the stock of overseas assets. It is not necessarily the case, therefore, that the investment outflow produces a deterioration in the overall balance of payments position, even when we ignore trade linkage effects.[2]

As long as the government aims to maintain a fixed exchange rate, the case for and against control of foreign investment involves balancing the short-term gain to the official reserves from limiting the capital outflow, against the cumulative loss through time of the forgone income from the foreign investment. When a floating exchange rate is adopted this particular problem ceases to be relevant. Any short-

---

1 The theoretical mechanism which underlies this argument is known as the transfer mechanism and explanations of it may be found in standard textbooks on international economics.

2 For a quantitative investigation of the balance of payments effects of UK direct investment overseas, see W.B. Reddaway and Associates, *Effects of UK Direct Investment Overseas: Interim Report*, (1967), and *Final Report*, (1968), Cambridge University Press. For every £100 of foreign assets acquired, it was found that the current account improves by £11 in the first year (extra exports) and by £4 in every subsequent year (comprising extra exports and profit receipts, net of foreign taxation and interest payments on accommodating foreign borrowing). These figures suggest that it would take roughly 22 years before a steady capital outflow of £100 per annum becomes self-financing. With 40% foreign borrowing the time-period is reduced to 12 years. These figures well illustrate the short/long-run dilemma with respect to direct investment and the desire of the UK authorities to encourage the finance of investment by foreign borrowing. The Reddaway examples were based on a constant annual foreign investment outflow, not on an outflow growing at a constant rate.

term cost to the reserves may be eliminated by an appropriate depreciation of the currency, and this will increase net exports so that the capital outflow may be transferred in real rather than in monetary terms. If full employment is to be maintained by government policy the final increase in net exports will have to be matched by a reduction in domestic investment or consumption. It is then possible to evaluate the costs and benefits of alternative levels of foreign investment by direct comparison of the estimated yields of the foreign investment flows with the forgone yields as resources are moved out of alternative home uses so as to accommodate the real transfer.

This last argument is subject to the qualification that interest and profits earned overseas generate tax revenues that accrue to overseas governments, whereas home investment generates tax revenues for the UK government.[1]

A country may wish to influence the inflow and outflow of long-term capital for a variety of reasons, not least among which relate to the resource allocation effects of foreign investment and the political and economic implications of an increase in the proportion of domestic capital controlled by foreign residents. In the UK the dominant motives for restrictions on overseas investment were protection of the exchange reserves and improvement of the balance of payments; motives which were approved under the IMF par-value rules. Policy therefore aimed at encouraging the finance of overseas investment by foreign borrowing and the plough-back of profit earned in existing foreign operations. All restrictions were abolished in July 1979.

The salient features of UK restrictions on direct investment overseas in the period 1960-79 can be quickly outlined. As far as investment in the OSA was concerned, direct investment, like portfolio investment, was free from exchange restrictions. This freedom was the *quid pro quo* for the unwritten obligation of OSA countries to pool their foreign exchange reserves in London. The balance of payments problem of the 1960s, however, resulted in the adoption of a policy of voluntary restraint on UK investment in the more advanced OSA countries. This policy lasted from April 1966 until March 1972 but the respite proved to be short-lived. The floating of sterling in June 1972 resulted in the majority of OSA countries being assigned external account status, thereby becoming subject to the same limitations as applied to investment in NSA countries. It is worth noting that this change, together with the application of the portfolio surrender rule to OSA securities meant the end of all elements of discrimination in favour of investment in the OSA, and hence the effective termination of the special economic relationship between the UK and OSA countries. From 1961 onwards, the method of restricting direct investment in the NSA took the form of treating proposed investments in terms of three categories. The least restricted category consisted of so-called 'super-criterion' projects, which were expected to bring matching returns to the balance of payments within eighteen months and which could be financed with official foreign exchange up to an effective limit of £50,000. All other projects had to be financed through the investment currency market or by overseas

---

1 A further qualification is that any depreciation designed to accommodate an additional flow of foreign investment will probably involve the UK in a worsening of its net barter terms of trade which raises the opportunity costs of that investment. Against this, however, must be set any future appreciation of the currency which follows from the return inflow of profits and interest.

borrowing.[1] Although the framework remained unchanged until 1979, the criteria were alternatively strengthened and relaxed according to the underlying state of the basic balance. The most important developments in the 1970s followed from entry into the EEC. As noted in section III.6, the UK managed to stall the relaxation of exchange controls by involving a balance of payments escape clause. In December 1977, however, restrictions on direct investment in the EEC were relaxed, with the foreign exchange limit for super-criterion projects being raised to £0.5bn and the maximum payback period increased to three years. The more important pressure for change, however, came with the strengthening of sterling in 1979 and the prospect of net exports of NS oil. Fears that this would affect the competitiveness of the rest of UK manufacturing led to the search for ways of increasing the demand for official foreign exchange by UK residents, and financing the acquisition of overseas assets through the spot exchange market was an obvious candidate. Thus in July 1979 all limitations on the financing of direct overseas investment overseas were abolished, as was the rule requiring that UK-controlled companies operating overseas remit to the UK two-thirds of post-tax earnings.

At present, the UK places no legal restrictions upon inward investment, apart from those contained in the 1947 Exchange Control Act which apply to all UK residents. However, inward direct investment is subject to Treasury approval and the criteria upon which permission is granted are aimed at maximizing the contribution which the investment inflow makes to the reserves.[2]

It is difficult to know whether restrictions have had any significant impact on the total outflow of direct investment from the UK. The most important effect of the restrictions has been to save foreign exchange. Over the period 1965-71, for example, foreign borrowing financed 56% and internally generated profits financed 47% of all UK private investment in the NSA, so leaving a small balance to be added to the exchange reserves.[3] Similarly between 1972 and 1978, 48% of UK private direct investment overseas was financed out of retained profits. Quite how the relaxation of exchange controls will effect the financing of foreign investment it is too early to say, but the indications are that the prime effect has been to reduce the importance of foreign borrowing. In 1981 the direct investment outflow from the UK (excluding oil company activities) increased by 50% over the levels attained in 1978 and 1979, and this may reflect the relaxation of capital controls.

Entry into the EEC as yet seems to have had a negligible effect on the pattern of the UK's overseas investment. During the 1970s roughly equal amounts, 30%, were directed to North America and Western Europe, with the EEC accounting for 22%. Of the total stock of UK direct investment assets in the mid-1970s, 28% were located in Western Europe and 23% in North America, compared to figures of 13% and 23% in 1962.[4] This change in the share located in Western Europe is, of course, closely related to the change in the UK trade structure noted in section II.1. At the

---

1 For further details see the COI pamphlet, *Britain's International Investment Position*, HMSO, 1971.

2 M.D. Steuer *et al.*, *The Impact of Foreign Direct Investment on the UK*, HMSO, 1973, chapter 9. Since 1972 this constraint has been waived for EEC companies and investors.

3 For further discussion, see A.K. Cairncross, *Control of International Long Term Capital Movements*, Brookings Institution, 1973, pp. 68-77.

4 For further details, see J.H. Dunning, 'The UK's International Direct Investment Position in the Mid-1970s', *LBR*, April 1979.

same time it is interesting to note that 90% of the UK's foreign direct investment liabilities are owned by firms originating in Western Europe and North America.

Associated with the stocks of foreign assets and liabilities are return flows of interest, profits and dividends (IPD) which appear in the current amount. For the UK roughly 53% of the IPD credits are related to past direct investments by UK manufacturing firms, and 7% are derived from portfolio investments. It is worth noting that, throughout the period since 1960, the outflow of foreign investment from the UK has been smaller than the return flow of IPD credits on the existing stocks of assets. While the net flow of IPD into the current account is positive, from year to year, the net receipts of foreign income are now less than 1% of GDP.

III.8   The UK and the European Economic Community

The question of UK membership of the EEC has always been controversial and the controversy has shown little tendency to abate since the UK became a full member in January 1973. The Labour government of 1974 declared its firm intention to renegotiate the original terms of entry,[1] completed the renegotiations in March 1975[2] and then settled the question in favour of membership with a referendum in July 1975. However, the case for EEC membership is still the subject of active political debate in the UK and there remains a clear possibility that the UK could terminate its EEC links in the near future. In this section we shall only comment upon the balance of payments implications of membership. Other implications are treated in Chapters 2 and 4 of this volume.

It was apparent at the time of the pre-entry negotiations that the full effects of entry into the EEC would imply a deterioration in the current account and possibly a deterioration in the long-term capital account of the balance of payments. To offset this, the UK would have to depreciate the exchange rate or employ direct policies of expenditure reduction in order to achieve the cut in real income and expenditure necessary to eliminate the adverse balance of payments effects of entry. Against this 'real resource cost' could be set the dynamic, long-run benefit of selling in a greatly enlarged market; a benefit which, it was argued, would result from greater economies of scale in production and which would be reflected in an increase in the UK growth rate.[3] Improved growth performance, it was thought, would possibly yield some offsetting dynamic gains to the basic balance, provided productivity in the UK grew faster than the Community average. Unfortunately, while it proved possible to provide plausible estimates of the balance of payments cost, measurement of the potential dynamic gains has so far eluded any precise assessment. Certainly membership of the EEC has not reversed the relative economic decline of the UK, indeed between 1972 and 1979 per capita GNP in the UK fell from 85% to 78% of the EEC average. Optimists may argue that there has been some convergence of the UK growth rate toward the EEC average[4] but to

1 *Renegotiation of the Terms of Entry into the European Economic Community*, Cmnd. 5593, April 1974.
2 *Membership of the European Community: Report on Renegotiation*, Cmnd. 6003, March 1975.
3 *Britain and the European Communities: An Economic Assessment*, Cmnd. 4289, February 1970.
4 *European Economy*, November 1981.

what extent this can be attributed to UK membership is not clear. At the time of writing any belief in the dynamic benefits of entry remains a matter of faith.

The effects on the UK current account can in principle be discussed under three headings: changes in the pattern of trade in manufactures, adoption of the common agricultural policy, and contributions to the Community budget.

The main implications for trade in manufactures follow from the customs union aspects of the Community, all tariffs on trade between the UK and other members having been reduced to zero in 1977 when the UK adopted the final stages of the common external tariff (CET) on trade with non-Community countries.[1]

It is impossible as yet to say what the final effects on the UK's pattern of trade will be. Adjustment to the tariff changes will not be immediate, and we must also take into account the discrimination which is now imposed against former Commonwealth countries (excluding signatories of the Lomé convention) and the associated loss of UK export preferences in the same countries. We have already shown, in section II.1, that the direction of UK trade in the 1950s and 1960s swung progressively toward Western Europe and away from the traditional markets in North America and the OSA. It is clear that entry into the EEC has accelerated this trend. Over the years 1963-1973 UK exports of manufactures to the EEC increased at an average annual rate of 10.7%, while imports from the EEC increased by 16.6%. However, between 1973 and 1979 these average annual growth rates of trade in manufactures increased dramatically, with exports to the EEC increasing by 20.5% and imports from the EEC increasing by 21.1%.[2] However, it remains the case that the UK trades with the EEC less intensively than do her fellow members of the Community. Thus in 1981 roughly 40% of UK exports and imports were exchanged with EEC countries, compared to an average intra-trade of the whole Community of 52%. This divergence of trading patterns is an important factor behind the adverse net budgetary position of the UK which emerged after 1979.

Assessments of the balance of payments cost of entry for the UK have tended to concentrate upon the effects of adopting the CAP system of agricultural support in place of the deficiency payments method formerly used by the UK. Under the deficiency payments method the UK imported foodstuffs at world prices, free of any import duty. Under the CAP the UK is obliged to import all foodstuffs at the common EEC prices and to impose variable import levies on imports from non-EEC sources, to bring their prices up to EEC levels. At the time of negotiation for entry it was estimated that EEC prices were between 18-26% higher than world market prices and that, given an inelastic demand for imports of foodstuffs, the UK import bill would be increased accordingly.

Finally, the UK is obliged to contribute to the budget of the Community and this involves a transfer of funds across the foreign exchanges, the gross contribution of the UK being assessed with reference to a complex formula discussed on p. 177. The net contribution is smaller than the gross contribution to the extent that the

---

1   The necessary tariff changes were to be achieved in stages; for details see *The United Kingdom and the European Communities*, Cmnd. 4715, July 1971. Following the completion of the Tokyo Round of multilateral tariff reductions in 1979, the average CET on industrial products will fall from 9.8% to 7.5% over an eight-year period.

2   For a more detailed analysis of the increasing intensity of UK-EEC trade, see A.E. Daly, 'UK Visible Trade and the Common Market', *NIER*, No. 86, November 1978. In this period to 1979 the value of intra-EEC trade increased by approximately 16% per annum.

UK receives reverse transfers from the EEC, for example, in the form of regional aid, industrial development aid and agricultural support.[1]

Estimates of the static balance of payments cost of entry produced widely varying results, although most suggested a substantial balance of payments burden[2] and thus an implicit real resource cost of UK entry to be imposed by a devaluation or other means. It was in the light of the assumed adverse balance of payments implications that the UK government renegotiated the original terms of entry. The most concrete results of the renegotiation were the creation of a mechanism for reducing the gross budgetary contribution of the UK in line with the UK's share in the total GNP of the Community, and the guarantee of continued access to the Community for Commonwealth sugar and dairy products from New Zealand.[3]

It is remarkable how inaccurate the initial estimates of the balance of payments cost have proved to be. Three factors are relevant here. First, and most important, the food-related balance of payments cost depends on the gap between EEC prices and world market prices for foodstuffs and this gap varies over time, narrowing at times of world economic expansion and widening during periods of world economic contraction. Thus the increases in world food prices between 1971 and 1974 and between 1979 and 1980 substantially reduced the import cost of the CAP system. In the intervening period world prices fell below EEC levels, and the prospects of world food prices continuing to fall in 1982 (they fell by 23% in dollar terms during 1981) must raise once again a potentially formidable burden of UK entry, as well as swelling the proportion of Community expenditure devoted to the CAP.[4]

The second difficulty arises from the complexities of the CAP pricing system. The most important issue here is that the intervention prices are not only set above world market levels but they are also set at levels which have encouraged substantial production surpluses for many commodities. Handling these surpluses either involves expenditure on storage, or subsidies to farmers to enable the surplus output to be exported to world markets. This policy is wasteful and absurd. Clearly it is in the UK's interest to press for more realistic food-pricing policies and limits on intervention buying, and to try and ensure that EEC prices fall in line with productivity gains in the more advanced farming units.[5] Formidable difficulties have also arisen because EEC food prices are set in terms of units of account and then translated into the respective member currencies at representative exchange

---

1 Cf. Cmnd. 4715, paras 91-96 and Annex A.

2 The 1970 White Paper, Cmnd. 4289, suggested a balance of payments cost ranging between £100m to £1.1bn per annum. For a comparison with other, less extreme estimates, see J. Pinder (ed.), *The Economics of Europe*, Charles Knight, 1971, chapter 6 by M. Miller. For a more optimistic assessment, see R.L. Major and S. Hays, 'Another Look at the Common Market', *NIER*, November 1970.

3 Cmnd. 6003. For additional details of the Convention which grants tariff preferences on exports to the EEC of industrial products, and some agricultural products from signatory developing countries, see P. Coffey, 'The Lomé Agreement and the EEC: Implications and Problems', *TBR*, no. 108, December 1975.

4 For further discussion, see R. Bacon *et al.*, 'The Direct Costs to Britain of Belonging to the EEC', *Economic Policy Review*, 1978, Department of Applied Economics, Cambridge.

5 An indication of Community thinking on reform of the CAP may be found in *Bulletin of European Communities*, no. 6, 1981, pp. 12-13.

rates, the so-called green currencies, fixed by administration decision. Now as long as the ratio between any two green currency rates is equal to the spot market exchange rate between the corresponding national currencies, the system works as intended, in that any agricultural commodity will sell at a common price throughout the EEC. Unfortunately, following the collapse of the Bretton Woods exchange-rate system in 1971, spot market rates for several EEC currencies have diverged substantially from the green currency rates. In particular, the steady depreciation of sterling between 1972 and 1976 drove the spot rate for sterling below the green pound rate, the percentage gap on some occasions reaching as much as 45%, despite frequent devaluations of the green pound.[1] The subsequent appreciation of sterling had by February 1981 taken the exchange rate between sterling and the european currency unit 18% above the green rate. The consequences of divergences between green and market exchange rates are extremely disruptive to agricultural trade and production in the EEC, since they undermine the principle of common prices for foodstuffs and create profitable opportunities for arbitrage between commodities and EEC currencies. To prevent this, border taxes and subsidies have to be levied on agricultural trade between EEC countries, the total amounts of subsidy involved being known as monetary compensation amounts (MCAs). As a substantial net importer of foodstuffs the UK has been a major beneficiary from the MCA system, and even though MCAs are now paid to the exporting country the amounts can still be viewed as a corresponding subsidy to UK consumers and treated as a notional net UK budgetary receipt. During 1978, for example, MCAs paid on UK food imports came to £479m, which if treated as a budget receipt reduces the UK net budgetary contribution for the year from £752m to £273m. Unfortunately for the UK, the appreciation of sterling after 1979 eliminated the need to pay MCA subsidies on UK food imports and thus any potential contribution to the net budgetary position. There can be little doubt that the MCA system is in need of reform. It began as a temporary measure to maintain a common market in food-stuffs following the currency disruptions of 1972-3, but it has subsequently developed into a permanent feature of the CAP. However, reform will require that green currencies are linked to currency exchange rates and unless market rates are stabilized this will raise formidable administrative difficulties for the CAP. It is easy to see how the establishment of a stable European currency area would provide a convenient means for shoring up the CAP and dismantling the MCA system.

The third area of difficulty when estimating the balance of payments cost of entry relates to calculation of the net budgetary contribution. This question has received a great deal of attention since 1979, because it was in 1980 that the UK shouldered for the first time the full budgetary cost of entry. The EEC budget is financed from the 'own resources' of the Community, which consist of all import duties and agricultural levies from non-EEC sources[2] plus a proportion of VAT revenue which does not exceed 1% of proceeds of a VAT levied on a uniform basis

---

1 For further discussion, consult R.W. Irving and H.A. Fern, *Green Money and the Common Agricultural Policy*, Wye College, Occasional Paper No. 2, 1975, and C. Mackel, 'Green Money and the Common Agricultural Policy', *NWBQR*, February 1978. The values for the green currencies are published monthly in *Bulletin of the European Communities*, Secretariat General, Brussels. An excellent account of the CAP and the green currency system is given in A.E. Buckwell *et al.*, *The Costs of the Common Agricultural Policy*, Croom Helm, 1982.

2 Less 10%, to cover costs of collection and administration.

in the Community. On this basis the gross UK contribution in 1982 is expected to be of the order of 20% of total own resources, even though the UK accounts for only 16% of Community GNP. The real problem for the UK, however, lies with the net contribution. After allowing for grants and loans, the UK is anticipated to receive only 10% of the Community's expenditure, leaving a net UK budgetary contribution variously estimated to lie between £0.9bn and £1.2bn during 1982. This net contribution for one year may be compared with the cumulative gross contribution of £3.19bn over the calendar years 1973 to 1978 and a cumulative net contribution over the same period of £1.34bn.[1] The estimated net contribution represents a substantial transfer across the exchanges and, not surprisingly, the UK government has sought ways of reducing this burden. Scope for action with the current EEC rules is, however, limited to two possibilities. First, a reimbursement mechanism, relating the gross contribution to the UK share of Community GNP, can be brought into operation, but the most that the UK can achieve from this is limited to a refund of 250m units of account.[2] Second, the UK net contribution is to a considerable degree dependent on structural features of the UK economy which cannot be changed quickly. The fact that the UK is still heavily dependent on imports from non-EEC sources enhances her gross contribution, whilst the small size and efficiency of her agricultural sector mean that receipts from the agricultural funds are small.[3] At the root of this budgetary problem lies the continued growth in the amount of EEC expenditure devoted to the CAP, 67% of the Community budget in 1981, which leaves relatively small amounts for the regional, social and other programmes from which the UK would be a major beneficiary. From the UK viewpoint reform will therefore involve either a trimming of the CAP system, which appears unlikely given the addition of Greece to the Community in January 1981 and with the imminent prospect of Spain and Portugal (both major producers of Mediterranean agricultural products) also becoming Community members, or a more fundamental reform of the budgetary mechanism – the more likely outcome given the fact that total Community expenditure has now effectively reached the limit set by the 'own resources' of the Community. Aware of the difficulties of reaching more fundamental reform, the UK government pressed successfully in May 1980 for a temporary reduction in its budget contribution. This provided a refund of £799m in 1980 and £813m in 1981, with the prospect of an extension of the arrangements for 1982. In April 1982 this complex issue re-emerged as a major barrier within the Community to reform of the CAP and extension of the 'own resources' basis for Community finance. At the time of writing a further solution is under negotiation but again this appears to be of a temporary nature.[4] Clearly no lasting solution is possible until the proportion of Community resources absorbed by the CAP is substantially curtailed.

---

1 At current prices. See *The Government's Expenditure Plans 1979-80 to 1982-83*, Cmnd. 7439, January 1979.

2 For details of the reimbursement mechanism, see Cmnd. 6003, paragraphs 39-42.

3 During 1982 the UK is expected to benefit from only 6% of farm price support expenditure but to contribute 27% of customs duty revenue and 19% of agricultural levy revenue in the EEC.

4 Known as the Tindemans-Thorn proposal, this would extend the UK's special budgetary status for a further three years on the basis of a formula which links the net contribution more closely to the UK share of Community GDP. See Postscript on p. 191 below.

Although the CAP and budgetary contribution questions have tended to dominate practical discussion on EEC membership, it is important to recognize that the issue of monetary unification is potentially of greater significance to the UK. In 1971, the European Commission, following guidelines laid down in the Werner Report of 1970, adopted the goal of full monetary union to be achieved by 1980. In its fullest form this would involve the irrevocable fixing of the parities of EEC countries one to another, full currency convertibility for current- and capital-account transactions, and the creation of a Community central bank with full powers to determine monetary policy in each region of the EEC. In many respects the case for monetary union is an integral part of the case for a common market in commodities. Creation of a single currency (de facto by fixing exchange rates, or by the adoption of a new currency unit) reduces transactions costs and promotes exchange and the division of labour which, it could be argued, is necessary if the dynamic gains from membership are to be maximized. Furthermore, it can be argued that once the members of the EEC develop intensive trade and investment links with one another then adoption of a fixed pattern of exchange rates is the only foreign exchange market policy consistent with price stability. Stable EEC parities are, of course, a very necessary part of the operation of CAP and other Community-wide policies. Whatever the merits of these arguments it should be realized that the costs of monetary unification are considerable.[1] As part of a monetary union the UK would abandon the right to change its parity unilaterally against other currencies, having already surrendered the ability to impose import restrictions and export subsidies for balance of payments purposes by adopting the CET. Expenditure-switching instruments are therefore eliminated from the armoury of feasible economic policies. Adjustment to payments deficits must then be by domestic deflation and the creation of unemployment, with the harmful and ultimately self-defeating implications noted in Section II.2 above. At best, a high degree of labour mobility to the other EEC countries may mitigate the effects on unemployment, while it is possible that sustained financial support from other Community members may ease, but not eliminate, the burden of adjustment. Equally, the commitment to capital-market integration would rule out restrictions on capital transactions in order to improve the basic balance.

An important step toward the objectives of monetary integration was taken in March 1979 with the formal adoption of the European Monetary System (EMS), the objective of which is the creation of a zone of monetary stability in Europe and the return of the Community to the exchange-rate certainties of its first ten years of existence. The EMS consists of two principal components, an exchange-rate structure and intervention mechanism, and a system of credits for financing payments imbalances between members. It was planned that by 1981 the credit system would have evolved into a European Monetary Fund on the lines of the IMF,

---

1 The interested reader may consult Y. Ishiyama, 'The Theory of Optimum Currency Areas: A Survey', *IMF Staff Papers*, vol. 22, 1975, pp. 344-83. For a discussion of the monetary union between the UK and Eire, see Whitaker, 'Monetary Integration: Reflections on Irish Experience', *Moorgate and Wall St.*, Autumn 1973.

but little progress has been made towards this objective.[1] The exchange-rate mechanism is a logical development of the European 'snake'. Following the collapse of the IMF adjustable-peg mechanism in 1971, the first concrete steps toward the creation of a European Monetary system were taken in April 1972 with the agreement to limit the margins of fluctuation between EEC currencies to 2.25% either side of parity rates.[2] The system proved to be ill-fated. Sterling defected in June 1972, the Lira in February 1973 and the French Franc was forced out of the snake twice, the most recent of those departures being in March 1976. Despite these setbacks the pressures toward currency stability have proved powerful and the EMS exchange-rate system is founded on a revitalized snake or currency grid. Within this grid each European currency is assigned a central rate against the other EEC countries, together with a permitted band of fluctuation of 2.25% either side of this central rate. An exception is made for countries when they join the system, who may initially adopt margins of 6% around central rates. Central banks are obliged to keep their currencies within the margins of fluctuation but, as became clear with the snake, this creates an asymmetric burden of obligation. The weak-currency country loses reserves and is always under pressure to adjust its internal policies to a greater extent than is the strong-currency country.

In the EMS an ingenious mechanism has been introduced to try and eliminate the asymmetries of adjustment and to enhance the convergence of exchange rate and economic policies. The key to this is the new European Currency Unit (ECU), which is a basket of the nine currencies, initially, but not irrevocably, of the same composition as the European unit of account. The ECU acts as numeraire for the exchange-rate mechanism and, using the currency grid rates, each currency is assigned its central value in terms of ECU together with a maximum range of divergence around this central value.[3] From this basis a divergence threshold is defined whereby a currency may not diverge from its central ECU rate by more than three-quarters of its divergence range. The point of these restrictions is that, in general, a currency will reach its divergence threshold before it reaches any of the bilateral intervention limits defined by the currency grid, and, once this occurs, there is a presumption that consultation will be initiated with *all* Community members to decide upon intervention policy, possible changes in central parities and any necessary internal policy measures. In this way it is hoped that burdens of adjustment will be more equally shared within the Community, and the

---

1 Full details of the EMS mechanisms are given in Commission of the European Communities, *European Economy*, July 1979. A brief but useful summary is given in the article, 'Britain and the European Monetary System', *MBR*, Winter 1979. The arguments for monetary integration are set out by the President of the European Commission, R. Jenkins, in 'European Monetary Union', *LBR*, no. 127, January 1978. See also, 'Intervention Arrangements in the European Monetary System', *BEQB*, June 1979; and Ch. 2, section V.2 above.

2 This scheme was known as the 'snake in the tunnel', the 'snake' representing the closely linked EEC currencies which, under the pressure of market forces, was free to move up and down relative to the dollar in the 'tunnel' defined by the Smithsonian exchange-rate limits. (See section III.9.) The 'tunnel' disappeared in March 1973 when the EEC currencies engaged in a joint float against the dollar.

3 The maximum range of divergence for each currency is less than ±2.25% and is determined by the formula ±2.25 $(1-w_i)$%, where w_i is the weight of that currency in the value of the ECU basket. The notional weight for sterling at end September 1979 was 13.6% giving a notional divergence range of ±1.94% for sterling against ECU. The divergence threshold for sterling is 75% of this, i.e. ±1.45%.

asymmetries of bilateral intervention avoided. Certainly the major realignment of EMS parities which took place in October 1981 was achieved with the full participation of member states.

Besides acting as numeraire in the EMS, the ECU has an important role as an instrument of settlement between Community central banks and ultimately as the planned reserve asset of the Community. Member countries deposit 20% of their gold and gross dollar reserves with the European Monetary Co-operation Fund on a three-month renegotiable basis, and in return have access to a variety of credit facilities, to the total value of 25bn ECU, to finance payments imbalances within the Community and to support the currency grid.[1] Of this total, 14bn ECU has been allocated to short-term monetary support and the remainder to medium-term credit facilities. Although the UK participated fully in the setting up of the EMS and contributes to the ECU credit arrangements, it has firmly declined to join the exchange-rate system, on the grounds that the disparities of economic performance within the Community make it unwise to fix parities within the narrow limits set by the currency grid and divergence indicators.[2] This position is surely sound. The EEC countries have experienced widely different inflation rates and rates of monetary expansion, the budgetary mechanisms of the Community affect their current payments accounts in different ways, and they differ considerably with respect to the effect of oil price changes upon their respective basic balances. The gyrations of the European currencies against the dollar since 1979 have amply illustrated the difficulties of attempting to fix currency values when underlying circumstances differ between countries. To fix parities is surely folly, unless a common monetary and fiscal policy can be worked out and applied for the whole Community. But such far-reaching changes are a long way off, indeed any fiscal and monetary unification proposals are likely to run foul of strong pressures to maintain national sovereignty in the formulation and implementation of economic policy. The UK government in its pronouncements clearly appreciates the force of these arguments and it is unlikely that the UK will join the EMS in the medium term or even possibly the long term.

III.9   The Reform of the International Monetary System

If the quarter century from 1945 had any one dominant characteristic in the international economic arena it was the integration of national commodity and capital markets into a unified and rapidly growing system of world trade and investment. A key role in this process was played by the international financial rules established at the Bretton Woods conference of 1944, the supervisory institution of which is the International Monetary Fund (IMF).[3] The principal features of the Bretton Woods system were, in brief, its emphasis on mutual international co-operation and its creation of a system of fixed but, in principle, adjustable exchange rates — the par-value system — together with the provision of

---

1 The gold contribution is valued at the average London fixing price during the six months prior to valuation, and the dollar portion is valued at the market rate of the two working days prior to valuation. At end-1980, ECUs contributed 18% to world foreign exchange reserves.

2 *The European Monetary System*, Cmnd. 7405, November 1978.

3 See R.N. Cooper, *The Economics of Interdependence*, McGraw Hill, 1968.

temporary and conditional balance of payments finance by the IMF to supplement reserve media in the form of gold and foreign exchange.

Throughout the 1960s it became clear that the IMF system suffered from potentially lethal inconsistencies and that, in particular, it placed the United States in an economic position which the European industrial nations became increasingly unable to accept. The first weakness was the general unwillingness of the main industrial countries to adjust par values in the face of obvious fundamental disequilibria until the force of events, aided by currency speculation, forced governments into belated action. The case of sterling in the mid-1960s and of Germany and Japan in the late 1960s are obvious examples of this failure to use the par-value adjustment mechanism in the way originally intended by the architects of Bretton Woods. Not unrelated to this was the asymmetry between deficit and surplus countries, in that the pressure of reserve losses bore far more heavily on the deficit countries than did the converse phenomena of reserve gains in the surplus countries. In practice the 'scarce currency' provisions of Article 7 of the IMF Agreement, which were meant to act as a sanction against persistent surplus countries, were never invoked.

The second weakness involved the supply of global reserve media, which under the IMF system consisted mainly of gold and foreign exchange holdings, and in particular, of US dollars. The problem was that the supply of monetary gold depended on the vagaries of mining and speculative activity, and the supply of foreign exchange depended upon the balance of payments deficits of the US, which could prove to be temporary and, more important, unrelated to global reserve needs. In the light of this there was considerable discussion in the 1960s of the alleged inadequacy of world reserves, which took as its basis the observed decline in the ratio of world reserves to world imports, from a value of 68% in 1951 to one of 30% in 1969; the latter being less than the equivalent ratio for the depressed years of the 1930s. A difficulty with this type of discussion was that it failed to make clear that the demand for foreign exchange reserves is a demand to finance balance of payments *disequilibria*, not a demand to finance the volume of trade. It failed, therefore, to recognize that the demand for reserve media will be smaller the more frequently exchange rates are adjusted in line with economic pressure, the more co-ordinated are national policies of demand management, and the greater the willingness of national governments and private capital markets to engage in mutual international borrowing and lending to finance payments imbalances. In the limit, for example, with a perfectly freely floating system of exchange rates the demand for official reserves would be zero.

Finally, there was the so-called 'confidence' problem, which followed from the increasing degree of dependence of world reserve growth on foreign exchange in the form of the dollar and to a lesser extent sterling. The problem was simply that by 1964 the total of outstanding dollar liabilities exceeded the gold reserves of the United States, and from then on this disparity between dollar liabilities and gold 'cover' increased. By December 1971 the US gold stock amounted to only 16% of the total of US short-term dollar liabilities held by overseas monetary authorities. *De facto* this meant that the dollar was no longer convertible into primary reserve assets, and so the willingness to hold dollars in official reserves decreased and the danger of a dollar crisis increased. As R. Triffin pointed out in 1960, the gold-exchange standard contained an automatic self-destruct mechanism,[1] with the

---

1 R. Triffin, *Gold and the Dollar Crisis*, Yale, 1960, and R. Triffin, 'Gold and the Dollar Crisis: Yesterday and Tomorrow', *Essays in International Finance*, No. 132, Princeton, December 1978.

potential risk of a severe liquidity crisis in which dollar and sterling reserves were liquidated and destroyed, while a given total of gold reserves was redistributed between countries. It is important, when trying to understand recent events, to realize that the Bretton Woods system had the effect of placing the United States and the dollar in a unique position in the international monetary system. Opponents of the United States have argued that the reserve currency status of the dollar enabled the United States to conduct internal policies independently of its balance of payments position and to finance an outflow of direct overseas investment on advantageous terms. In contrast, it has been argued that the USA had no choice but to adopt a passive balance of payments policy and run a payments deficit of sufficient magnitude to satisfy the global demand for dollars as an international reserve asset. Whatever the merits of these viewpoints, two aspects of the situation are clear. Firstly, because the dollar was extensively used as the intervention currency for stabilizing exchange rates, the USA had no need to concern itself with supporting the external value of the dollar. Secondly, the one option open to the USA to cure its deficit, namely a devaluation of the dollar relative to gold and therefore relative to other currencies, was steadfastly ruled out on political grounds, until the events of December 1971.

Throughout the 1960s the strains inherent to the system manifested themselves in a variety of ways. Most significant, perhaps, were the *ad hoc* measures taken by the industrial countries to supplement the existing sources of balance of payments finance. At one level were the General Arrangements to Borrow, organized in October 1962, in which the Group of Ten countries (UK, France, Germany, Belgium, Netherlands, Italy, USA, Canada, Sweden and Japan) agreed to lend their currencies to the IMF should the latter run short of one of their respective currencies. These arrangements have been renegotiated on several occasions, most recently in October 1980, and the amount of support now totals about SDR 6.5bn. Recent years have seen increasing use of the GAB, indeed 76% of the finance for the standby arrangements negotiated by the UK in 1976 came from eight of the GAB countries. In addition to this there are the currency swap arrangements between the US and the central banks of other countries, whereby each agrees to lend or acquire currency balances for an agreed time-period. Several such arrangements exist between the US and other countries and currently total $30.1bn. The UK has benefited considerably from the availability of the short-term financial aid, the UK-US swap facility being increased to $3bn by January 1982. The UK has also been able to draw upon credits provided by European central banks from 1961 onwards. A second important manifestation of strain related to the official price of gold and the clear possibility that its price might have to be increased to boost world reserves and improve the asset:liability ratio of the US. Attempts to stabilize the free market price of gold by the major central banks which had begun in 1961 had to be abandoned in March 1968 following the loss of $3bn in monetary gold stocks, sold in an attempt to hold down the free market price during the previous five months. The Washington agreement of that time created a two-tier market for gold, and effectively prevented national monetary authorities from using monetary gold stocks to finance payments disequilibria in the face of an ever-widening differential between the free market and the official price of gold. This two-tier system was abandoned in November 1973.

The final, and some would say most significant, manifestation of strain was the increasing volume of speculative capital flows which from 1967 onwards repeatedly disrupted the working of foreign exchange markets and threatened the parities of the deutschmark, the yen and the dollar. It became increasingly clear that the par-value system could not survive unless more effective methods for adjusting exchange rates in line with changing economic circumstances could be devised, and unless some means could be found for absorbing the increasing volume of short-term capital flows made possible by the growth of the eurodollar market. Not surprisingly, in the face of such obvious strains, many proposals for reforming the system were put forward during the 1960s. On the fundamental question of the adjustment mechanism, proposals ranged from the adoption of freely floating exchange rates, to mechanisms for ensuring the gradual and automatic adjustment of par values to payments disturbances, the crawling-peg proposal. However, the response of the IMF to such proposals was lukewarm. A study by the executive directors concluded by reaffirming faith in the viability of the par-value system, with the only concessions to flexibility being the suggestion of wider margins of fluctuation around par values and the temporary abrogation of par-value obligations.[1]

By far the most important development of the 1960s was international agreement on the creation of a new reserve asset, the Special Drawing Right. The outcome of several years of discussion, this scheme came into operation in 1970.

Special Drawing Rights: SDRs are book entries in the Special Drawing Account of the IMF, by means of which countries can give and receive credit on a multilateral basis to finance balance of payments deficits. At the outset, SDRs were to be held only by those national monetary authorities which participated in the IMF arrangements and which agreed to accept the provisions of the SDR scheme. The total of SDRs is agreed collectively by the members of the IMF, so that the supply of this new reserve asset is agreed by international decision; the basis for their creation being the provision of an adequate, but not inflationary, long-term rate of growth of world reserves. SDRs are thus superior to gold and foreign exchange in that their supply is not arbitrary but is, in principle, the outcome of rational discussion. The total of SDRs is revised on a five-year basis, the first allocation of $9.3bn having been made in three stages between 1970 and 1972.[2] Each country is assigned a net cumulative allocation of SDRs, in proportion to its quota in the general account of the IMF, and can treat this allocation as 'owned reserves' to finance payments imbalances. A country in deficit, for example, may use its SDR quota to purchase needed foreign exchange from other countries. One of the most ingenious features of the scheme is that utilization of a country's SDR quota is subject to the supervision of the IMF, the object being to ensure a balanced and widespread activation of the SDR facility. Use of SDRs was initially subject to three provisions: (i) they must be used for legitimate balance of payments purposes and not, for example, to diversify exchange reserve portfolios; (ii) a country need not accept SDRs in excess of twice its net cumulative allocation; and (iii) a country's average holding over a period of five years must not fall below 30% of its net cumulative allocation — essentially to prevent the persistent, as distinct from temporary, financing of a deficit with SDRs. To give effect to these provisions

---

1   *The Role of Exchange Rates in the Adjustment of International Payment: A Report by the Executive Directors*, IMF, 1970.

2   The revised Articles of Agreement to incorporate SDRs may be found in the *IMF Annual Report* for 1968, or in the book by F. Machlup. listed at the end of this chapter.

two types of transactions in SDRs are allowed, designated transactions and transactions by agreement. With designated transactions, the IMF decides the countries that will add to their SDR holdings and so provide the currencies required by the country running down its SDR holdings, the choice of countries for designation being decided on the basis of their balance of payments strength and the adequacy of their reserve holdings. In contrast, transactions by agreement involve the transfer of SDRs between countries without recourse to the IMF where the usual objective is to redeem the currency liabilities of the transferer.

The SDR was devised as a response to the experience of the 1960s. Unfortunately, it came into existence at a time when the groundrules of the Bretton Woods system were about to become void. The collapse of 1971 and the responses to it are treated further below, but here it will prove convenient to trace the evolution of the SDR in the rapidly changing world monetary environment of the 1970s.

The fundamental question surrounding the SDR has always been that of whether SDRs simply co-exist with other reserve assets or whether they are destined to replace gold and foreign exchange, or both, as the reserve base of the system.

In the initial arrangements SDRs were effectively a gold substitute, they had a gold guarantee and carried a low rate of interest on net holdings of 1.5%. On the understanding that the dollar is not devalued relative to gold then SDRs were inferior to the dollar as a reserve asset because of their lower interest yield and lesser convenience of usage. However, the dollar devaluations of 1971 and 1973 upset this situation, as did the resort to a general floating of the important currencies relative to gold during 1973. In response to these changing circumstances a series of steps have been taken since 1974 to enhance the use of the SDR as a store of wealth and as a standard of value. The first step in July 1974 was to value SDRs in terms of a basket of sixteen currencies, rather than in terms of the US dollar alone, and to set the interest rate on net SDR holdings at 60% of an average of short-term interest rates in the financial centres of the five countries with the largest SDR holdings. These rules have been progressively revised since 1974, and the latest developments in 1981 have set the SDR interest rate at 100% of the market rate and have based the valuation bracket on the currencies of the same five countries.[1] Steady progress has also been made to develop the SDR as the logical, principal reserve asset of the international monetary system. The most important changes came into effect with the adoption of the Second Amendment to the IMF Articles of Agreement in April 1978 (see below). These developments greatly extended the range of transactions for which SDRs may be employed by mutual agreement between countries without Fund authority, and reduced from 30% to 15% a country's minimum permitted holding of its SDR allocation over a five-year period. From 1 May 1981 this reconstitution requirement has been eliminated.[2]

The second development has been the further allocation of SDR holdings to

---

1 For details, see the article 'The New Method of Valuing Special Drawing Rights', *BEQB*, September 1974, and IMF, *Annual Report*, 1981. For further analysis of the issues discussed below, see F. Hirsch, 'An SDR Standard: Impetus, Elements and Impediments', *Essays in International Finance*, no. 99, Princeton 1975, and K.A. Chrystal, 'International Money and the Future of the SDR', ibid., no. 128, December 1978.

2 IMF, *Annual Report*, 1978 and 1981, chapter 3, give relevant details.

member countries, so that the third and last allocation of SDR 4bn made in January 1981 brought the cumulative SDR allocation to SDR 21.4bn.

Third, when the Seventh General Increase in Quotas came into effect in 1980, members contributed 25% of their additional quota in SDRs. Finally, a multitude of developments have taken place, extending the right to hold SDRs to non-member organizations and legalizing the use of SDRs for currency swaps and forward transactions.[1]

Despite these developments aimed at enhancing the status of SDRs, the brute fact remains that SDRs only accounted for 6% of total world reserves at end-1981 and only 3.1% when gold reserves are valued at their market price. While SDRs have been made more attractive in relation to currencies, the continued appreciation of gold between 1972 and 1980 showed that gold could be a far more effective speculative hedge against inflation than SDRs. At best, all the IMF can press for is a continued enhancing of SDRs relative to currencies. In this respect the proposed Substitution Account at the IMF, in which members would deposit currency reserves in return for SDRs, could be an important means of increasing the weight of SDRs in world reserves. Whether the proposals will come to anything during 1982 is doubtful, unless there is a sustained collapse in the dollar relative to other currencies.[2] Certainly the collapse of the gold price in 1982 makes it more propitious to press the case for the SDR as a major reserve asset.

The future of the SDR scheme is thus for the moment uncertain, not least because the tremendous growth in world reserves over the 1970s has created fears of an excess of world liquidity rather than a shortage. Even valuing gold at the old official price, world reserves increased by 193% between end-1970 and end-1974, and by a further 151% between end-1974 and end-1981. Of course, after allowing for inflation these nominal reserve gains look less impressive, as can be seen by comparing the value of world reserves relative to the value of world imports. Valuing gold at the old official price of $35 per ounce, the ratio of world reserves to world imports declined from 30% at the beginning of the 1970s to 24% in 1981, despite the spectacular growth in the value of world reserves. By contrast if gold is valued at its market price rather than the old official price the ratio becomes 32% in 1970, 47% in 1974 and 41% in 1981. Indeed, on reflection, it is plausible to argue that the downfall of the Bretton Woods system proved to be its propensity to generate world liquidity, and from this stemmed the inflation tendencies of the 1970s and the collapse of the par-value system in 1973.

1971-9: crisis and evolutionary reform: Any illusions that the creation of the SDR scheme has inaugurated a new period of stability for the par-value system were quickly shattered. Following a period of considerable uncertainty in foreign exchange markets and massive short-term capital outflows from the US, the US government announced in August 1971 that the dollar was no longer convertible into gold and that to eliminate the disequilibria in the international economic system other countries must revalue their currencies relative to gold. To add pressure toward this end, a 10% surcharge was imposed on US imports of manufactures and the US proclaimed its intention to obtain trade concessions from

---

1 IMF, *Annual Report* 1981. The total number of prescribed 'other-holders' is currently ten.

2 Cf. 'The Proposed Substitution Account in the IMF', *MBR*, Winter 1979, and P.B. Kenen, 'The Analytics of a Substitution Account', *Banca Nazionale del Lavoro*, Quarterly Review, December 1981.

Japan and the EEC. Detailed and intensive official discussions culminated in a meeting of the finance ministers of the Group of Ten countries at the Smithsonian Institute in Washington in December 1971. The main points agreed were: (i) a new set of values of exchange rates which involved a revaluation of the deutschmark and the Japanese yen; (ii) that 'pending agreement on longer-term monetary reforms', the permitted IMF margins of fluctuations around par values would be increased to ±2.25%; (iii) that the US would devalue the dollar in terms of gold by 7.89%, so creating a new official price for gold of $38 an ounce, and that this would form the the new par value of the dollar; (iv) that the 10% import surcharge would be abolished; and (v) that new discussions should be undertaken, under the auspices of the IMF, to consider the long-term reform of the international monetary system in all its major aspects.

The forum for discussion of international reform was set up in June 1972 and became known as the Committee of Twenty, holding meetings between September 1972 and June 1974 when the final report was presented. Three items dominated the deliberations of the C-20. Firstly, methods of absorbing and re-cycling short-term capital flows. Secondly, the creation of an exchange-rate system with stable but adjustable par values and with recognized and widely acceptable criteria for instigating changes in par values. Thirdly, the future reserve base of the international monetary system and in particular the role of the SDR in any reformed system. The deliberations of the C-20 could hardly be described as successful, the final report making it clear that substantial differences of view existed on fundamental issues.[1] The most concrete outcome of the C-20 activities has been its perpetuation in the form of an Interim Committee which continues to discuss proposals for reform. However, it would have indeed proved remarkable had any concrete reform proposals emerged, for the reform discussions were overtaken by two important events: the adoption of generalized floating by the major industrial countries in March 1973, and the increase in the price of oil in December 1973.

Managed floating and the oil price issue: Confidence in the Smithsonian exchange parities proved to be short-lived, and in the period to March 1973 frequent speculative crises disturbed the international monetary system, the only effective counter to which was the adoption of floating exchange rates by the major industrial nations. By April 1973, the par-value system had collapsed, perhaps the predictable outcome of the drift of the Bretton Woods system into a reluctant dollar standard.

The experiences of 1972 and 1973 have underlined a major problem faced by an exchange-rate system in current circumstances, viz. coping with the massive volume of short-term funds which can be switched very rapidly between financial centres. Short-term capital flows forced the abandonment of Smithsonian parities and have played an important part in the fluctuations experienced by floating rates (see section III.6). Various attempts have been adopted to limit such flows, for example, a two-tier foreign exchange market by Italy, direct controls on overseas borrowing by Germany and an extension of inter-central bank currency swap arrangements, but these are of a somewhat *ad hoc* and inadequate nature.

---

1   The final report of the C-20, 'Outline of Reform', was published in IMF, *Survey*, June 1974. See also, *International Monetary Reform, Documents of the Committee of Twenty*, IMF, 1974. For a valuable account of the activities of C-20 and its failings, see J. Williamson, *The Failure of World Monetary Reform, 1971-74*, Nelson, 1977.

The inception of a period of managed floating raises several difficulties for the international monetary system, in particular those of mutually inconsistent exchange-rate stabilization policies, the possibility of competitive, beggar-my-neighbour exchange-rate management, and the problem of exchange instability in the face of speculative pressure. To help avoid these problems the IMF issued guidelines for exchange-rate management in June 1974 and these were subsequently revised in April 1977 in anticipation of the pending revisions to Article 4 of the IMF agreement.[1] The revised guidelines emphasized the point that exchange-rate policy is a matter for international consultation and surveillance by the IMF, and that exchange-rate practices should be based on three principles: (i) the avoidance of exchange-rate manipulation to gain an unfair competitive advantage or to prevent effective balance of payments adjustment; (ii) the avoidance of disorderly and disproportionate short-term movements of exchange rates; and (iii) the recognition that exchange-rate management involves joint responsibilities. The experiences of the period of heavily managed intervention have been mixed. On the one hand, short-term movements in exchange rates have been more volatile than advocates of flexible rates would perhaps condone, while, on the other hand, exchange rates have been managed without any overt clashes of national interest and have changed to compensate for substantial national differences in inflation rates.[2]

More damaging to the reform movement were the increases in the price of oil after 1973, which created an unprecedented imbalance in the international economic system in the form of a massive payments surplus for the oil producers and a corresponding deficit for the oil-importing countries. The problem is simply that the ability of the oil producers to spend their oil revenues on imports of goods and services has not so far matched the increase in their revenues. Thus the major oil producers enjoyed aggregate current-account surpluses of $67.8bn in 1974 which progressively declined to give average annual surpluses of $28bn in the four years 1975 to 1978. The 40% increase in average oil prices during 1979 served to prolong the oil-related surpluses and structural imbalances in the world payments system. Indeed the oil producers' current-account deficits for the period 1980/81 averaged $87bn on an annual basis. Since, as is generally agreed, the OPEC countries have no serious alternative but to invest their surplus revenues in the advanced industrialized nations, so returning on capital account the purchasing power extracted from the current accounts of the oil-importing nations, the oil problem raises three serious issues for the stability of the international monetary system. First, there is the potential havoc which would be wrought to foreign exchange markets if surplus oil funds are invested in liquid assets and switched between currencies in search of interest return and the expected capital gain from exchange-rate alterations. The gyrations of sterling since 1976 and of the dollar since 1977 are good examples of the effects of asset switching. Clearly some means must be found of placing the funds in less liquid investments and/or creating sufficient central-bank co-operation to undertake large-scale recycling operations. Secondly, and more important, is the fact that the attractiveness of different oil-

---

1 See IMF, *Survey*, 17 June 1974, and IMF, *Annual Report*, 1977, Appendix 2.

2 IMF, *Annual Report*, 1981. On the volatility of exchange rates, see P.A. Tosini, 'Leaning Against the Wind: A Standard For Managed Floating', *Essays in International Finance*, no. 126, Princeton, 1977, and J.R. Artus and A.D. Crockett, 'Floating Exchange Rates and the Need for Surveillance', ibid., no. 127, Princeton, May 1978.

importing nations as havens for OPEC investment need bear no relation to the way in which their respective current-account balances have been affected by oil price increases. The possibility is therefore reinforced that individual countries will try to eliminate their deficits by deflation, trade restrictions or currency depreciation, the only outcome of which would be to depress world trade and output. Finally, there are the problems faced by the developing nations, which have seen the real values of aid inflows virtually eliminated by the increase in oil prices.[1]

One response to these problems involved the introduction of a variety of measures to supplement the IMF's normal resources with special borrowing facilities. One of the first developments was the creation of the Extended Facility, introduced in 1974, through which a member can borrow for balance of payments purposes for periods longer than are normally allowed under the normal credit tranche policies. Borrowings under this facility must not increase the Fund's holdings of the borrowers currency above 265% of the member's quota. As with all Fund finance, borrowing is conditional upon Fund approval of internal domestic policies to correct the payments deficit. In 1974 and 1975 the IMF created two temporary oil facilities to recycle oil-exporter funds to countries in severe payments difficulties following the increase in oil prices. The two arrangements channelled about SDR 7bn to countries in difficulty, including SDR 1bn borrowed by the UK in 1975. These temporary arrangements were replaced by the Supplementary Financing Facility, which came into effect in February 1979, with total resources of SDR 7.5bn. To further enhance access to Fund resources, the provisions of Article 5 of the IMF agreement have been relaxed pending the Eighth General Review of Quotas. From March 1981, members can borrow up to 150% of quota in a single year or up to 450% of quota over a three-year period. These enlarged facilities for assistance to countries facing large deficits relative to their quotas are underwritten by loans negotiated with the Saudi Arabian Monetary Agency, the BIS and four central banks. Despite these developments it is important to note that the recycling of oil-surplus money via the IMF has been small relative to the total amounts recycled via the international banking system and the intermediation of the eurocurrency and eurobond markets. Between 1973 and 1975, for example, the eurodollar deposits of the major oil exporters grew from SDR 4bn to SDR 21bn, the latter figure accounting for 45% of total eurocurrency deposits at the time. During 1975 and 1976 total eurobond issues amounted to SDR 21.3bn, of which, however, only 6% was lent directly to the less developed countries.[2] Lending through the euro markets has continued at a high rate since 1976 – with a total of $186bn being floated in 1981 alone[3] – and it seems clear that the IMF has probably recycled less than 5% of the oil-surplus revenues. Since 1979, however, the scope for continued private lending has come increasingly into question with the default on loans by Iran and the risks of increasing the scale of lending to debt-laden developing countries. It remains to be seen whether the euro

---

1   For discussion of the adverse effects on developing countries and possible means of easing their problems, consult C. Michalopoulos 'Financing Needs of Developing Countries: Proposals for International Action', *Essays in International Finance*, no. 110, Princeton, 1975.

2   See R.I. McKinnon, 'The Euro Currency Market', *Essays in International Finance*, no. 125, December 1977, Princeton.

3   IMF, *Survey*, 25 January 1982. Net liabilities of the international banking system amounted to $148bn in 1980.

markets can cope with the projected oil surpluses of the 1980s as well as they have with those of the 1970s. If not, the IMF, central banks and other international institutions will have to play a far greater role than in the past. Failure to recycle oil revenues would undoubtedly lead to a major world recession and default by many countries on their external debts.

The Jamaica Agreement and the Second Amendment: The final report of the C-20 advocated an evolutionary approach to the problems of world monetary reform and, despite the problems noted in the previous section, substantial progress has subsequently been made. During 1975 the Interim Committee held several meetings, and agreement on four important issues was obtained in January 1976 at a meeting held in Jamaica. From this meeting emerged the most important development in the international monetary system since 1945, the Second Amendment to the Articles of Agreement, which came into effect in April 1978.

Without doubt the most fundamental outcome of the Jamaica meeting was the agreement to amend Article 4 of the IMF agreement. The main points of the new article are as follows:[1] (i) a general return to stable but adjustable par values can take place with the support of an 85% majority in the IMF; (ii) par values may not be expressed in terms of gold or other currencies but can be expressed in terms of SDRs, the margins of fluctuation around par values remaining at ±2.25%; (iii) with the concurrence of the IMF, any country may abandon its par value and adopt a floating exchange rate; (iv) the exchange-rate management of a floating currency must be subject to IMF surveillance and must not be conducted so as to disadvantage other countries; (v) the agreed practices with respect to floating rates will operate until such time as a general return to par values is attained. In effect these changes legitimize floating exchange rates within the framework of the IMF system and without any diminution of the powers of the IMF.

The second aspect of the Second Amendment dealt with the relative positions of SDRs and gold. We have commented above on the attempts to enhance the reserve status of the SDR. The associated measures to demonetize gold were equally significant. In particular, the official price of gold was abolished and members were no longer allowed to use gold to make their general quota contributions. Furthermore, members were again allowed to trade in gold at gold market prices. At Jamaica it was also agreed that the Fund would divest itself of one-third of its stock of gold. One-sixth would be transferred to members, in four annual instalments, at the official gold price and in amounts proportional to their general quotas. The remaining one-sixth was to be sold to the world market at monthly intervals over the four year period to May 1980 and the profits on these sales, the difference between the sale price and the old official price at which the IMF had received the gold, was to be used to establish a Trust Fund, to provide balance of payments assistance on concessionary terms to those poorer countries with a per capita GNP of less than SDR 300 in 1973. In the first four years of this scheme the total profits amounted to $4.6bn, of which $3.3bn was allocated to the Trust Fund and the remainder was distributed to 104 eligible developing-country members. Trust Fund loans were for a maximum of eleven years and

---

1 The text of the proposed new Article 4 is contained in IMF, *Survey*, 19 January 1976, pp. 20-21. Full details of the revised articles of agreement may be found in *The Second Amendment to the Articles of Agreement of the International Monetary Fund*, Cmnd. 6705, HMSO, 1977.

carried interest at ½%. With the final loan disbursement made in March 1981, the machinery has now been set in motion for winding up this Fund.

The third and final outcome of the evolutionary reform process was the decision to make two general increases in quotas. The 1976 review increased quotas by 32.5% to SDR 39bn and the Seventh Annual Review, which came into effect in 1980, increased aggregate quotas to SDR 58.6bn. These changes make an important addition to Fund liquidity at a time of continued payments imbalance in the world economy. The Eighth General Review of Quotas is under active consideration at the moment.

The reforms embodied in the Second Amendment are undoubtedly important and reflect well on the IMF as an effective forum for international co-operation. However, the reforms fell short of the ideals outlined by the C-20 and their long-run effects may be in doubt.[1]

On exchange-rate adjustment, criteria for exchange-rate management and surveillance have yet to be agreed and the difficult question of whether surveillance should extend beyond exchange-rate policy has yet to be faced. On liquidity, it is plain that the SDR is currently the least significant reserve asset in the system, and that the aim of demonetizing gold is far from reached. Inflationary fears and political uncertainties in the Middle East and elsewhere have continued to make gold an attractive reserve asset. Indeed by allowing the revaluation of monetary gold in line with free market prices the reserve-asset status of this metal has been greatly enhanced. Only the US continues to value its monetary gold at the old official price and the decision by the EMS members to value the gold component of the ECU (see section III.8 above) at market-related prices puts the IMF demonetization programme out on a limb. Important questions concerning the future of US dollar liabilities, which over the 1970s have accounted for between 70% and 80% of total foreign exchange reserves, their co-existence with other reserve currencies, e.g. the German mark, and the scope for a Substitution Account, also remained unresolved.[2] Until answers to these problems are found there seems little hope of re-creating a stable international monetary system.

Postscript – EEC Budget arrangements: At the end of May 1982, agreement was reached on a UK rebate for 1982 of £476m to offset the estimated net contribution of £857m for the year. An undertaking was also reached to negotiate a longer-term solution by the end of November 1982.

REFERENCE AND FURTHER READING

Sir Alec Cairncross (ed.), *Britain's Economic Prospects Reconsidered*, George Allen and Unwin, 1971.

Sir Alec Cairncross, *Control of Long-term Capital Movements*, Brookings Institution, 1973.

---

1 For somewhat jaundiced views of the Jamaica agreement, see Bernstein *et al.*, 'Reflections on Jamaica', *Essays in International Finance*, no. 115, Princeton, 1976, and A. Kafka, 'The IMF: Reform without Reconstruction?', *Essays in International Finance*, no. 118, Princeton, 1976.

2 For a recent appraisal, see. G. Richardson, 'The Prospects for an International Monetary System', *BEQB*, September 1979.

R.E. Caves and Associates, *Britain's Economic Prospects*, Brookings Institution and George Allen and Unwin, 1968.

R.E. Caves and L.B. Krause (eds.), *Britain's Economic Performance*, Brookings Institution, 1980.

H.G. Grubel, *International Economics*, Irwin, 1977.

H.G. Johnson and J.E. Nash, *UK and Floating Exchanges*, Hobart Paper, 46, Institute of Economic Affairs, 1969.

C.P. Kindleberger and P.H. Lindert, *International Economics*, Irwin, 1978.

F. Machlup, *Remaking the International Monetary System*, Committee for Economic Development and Johns Hopkins, 1968.

R.L. Major, *Britain's Trade and Exchange Rate Policy*, Heinemann, 1979.

C. McMahon, *Sterling in the Sixties*, Oxford University Press, 1964.

J.E. Meade, *UK, Commonwealth and Common Market: A Reappraisal*, Hobart Paper, 17, Institute of Economic Affairs, 1970.

R.L. Miller and J.B. Wood, *Exchange Control for Ever*, Institute of Economic Affairs, London, 1979.

W.B. Reddaway, *Effects of UK Direct Investment Overseas: An Interim Report*, Cambridge University Press, 1967; *Final Report*, Cambridge University Press, 1968.

B. Tew, *International Monetary Cooperation, 1945-70*, Hutchinson, 1970.

B. Tew, *The Evolution of the International Monetary System, 1945-77*, Hutchinson, 1977.

S.J. Wells, *British Export Performance*, Cambridge University Press, 1964.

J. Williamson, *The Failure of World Monetary Reform, 1971-74*, Nelson, 1977.

OFFICIAL PUBLICATIONS

Bank of England Quarterly Bulletin.

British Business (weekly) (previously *Trade and Industry*), Departments of Trade and Industry.

Commission of the European Communities, *European Economy*, Brussels (quarterly).

Economic Trends (regular analyses of balance of payments in March, June, September and December issues).

IMF, *Annual Report* and IMF, *Survey* (twice monthly).

Report of Committee on the Working of the Monetary System, Radcliffe Report, Cmnd. 827, 1959.

UK Balance of Payments (*Pink Book*, annual), CSO.

4

Industry
J.R. Cable

I   UK INDUSTRIAL PERFORMANCE 1960-80

Over the last two decades as a whole the UK economy grew as rapidly as it has on average for the last century or more. Yet Britain is widely considered to have undergone a recent 'relative industrial decline' or even 'deindustrialization'.[1] To a small extent this reflects slower growth in industrial output – manufacturing, mining, construction, and electricity, gas and water – than in overall activity.[2] But the main explanation is that Britain failed to match the very rapid growth achieved by other countries.

Between 1960 and 1980 industrial output expanded at less than 2% a year on average. This was only half the American and West German rates, and less than half the rate achieved in France (table 4.1). Consequently, while industrial production more than doubled over the period in these countries, in Britain it rose by less than half. The international growth superstar was, however, Japanese industry, which grew at a quite startling rate over the same period: more than four times as fast as our own. Total production increased nearly fivefold, with car output rising at more than 20% per year and total exports at nearly 14%.

All countries achieved much faster growth before the oil crisis of 1973, when world oil prices quadrupled, than in the subsequent period to 1980. After a very severe recession in the mid-1970s, strong expansion took place from 1975 to 1979, temporarily at more than the pre-1973 rate in the case of both the US and Britain. However these two countries, and Britain especially, were most severely affected by the onset of further recession in 1980. From these comparative figures it is clearly

TABLE 4.1
Growth of Industrial Production, UK and Selected Countries, 1960-80

Country	Annual average increase in industrial production (%)				
	1960-73	1973-5	1975-9	1979-80	1960-80
UK	2.9	−3.8	3.6	−6.1	1.9
USA	4.9	−4.7	5.7	−3.1	3.8
Japan	12.6	−7.1	9.2	6.8	9.1
France	5.9	−2.4	4.2	nil	4.3
W. Germany	5.5	−3.8	4.0	nil	3.9

Source: Derived from *NIER*.

 1   See, e.g., A Singh, 'UK Industry and the World Economy: A Case of De-industrialisation?' *Cambridge Journal of Economics*, 1977, 1, pp. 113-36.
2   See table 4.3.

quite misleading to explain Britain's most recent economic problems as simply the result of a world recession, as some politicians have done.

Moreover there would have been very little recovery in Britain after 1975 had it not been for North Sea oil.[1] Production rose from 1.6 to 80.5 million tonnes in the five years to 1980, and this increase explains the threefold rise in the output index for the extractive industries over this period (table 4.2). (Production of coal, the other main activity in this sector, rose slightly from 128.7 to 130.1m tonnes.) Excluding the effect of oil and gas production, industrial output in fact increased by only 4.3% up to 1979 (just over 1% per year), before falling 7.3% in 1980, to a level only just above that first achieved in 1968 (table 4.2).

TABLE 4.2

Industrial Production by Industry, 1960, 1965 and 1970-80 (1975 = 100)[1]

	All industries	All industries excl. oil & gas extraction	Extractive industries[2]	Total manufacturing	Construction	Electricity gas, water
1960	75.9	75.9	150.0	73.6	88.7	48.6
1965	89.7	89.7	145.5	86.7	110.0	65.7
1970	99.7	99.7	118.9	98.0	111.4	84.1
1971	99.8	99.7	118.9	97.5	113.3	87.3
1972	102.0	101.8	100.1	100.0	115.4	93.6
1973	109.4	109.2	110.0	108.4	117.8	98.6
1974	105.1	105.1	89.7	106.6	105.6	98.5
1975	100.0	100.0	100.0	100.0	100.0	100.0
1976	102.0	100.7	126.1	101.4	98.6	102.3
1977	105.9	101.9	188.4	102.9	98.2	106.4
1978	109.8	104.1	233.1	103.9	104.9	109.7
1979	112.6	104.3	295.7	104.4	101.3	116.1
1980	105.3	96.7	301.3	95.3	95.9	113.0

Source: MDS.

Notes: 1 Industries are based on the Standard Industrial Classification (SIC) for the UK. This is a production-oriented classification which groups activities into Orders, with subdivides into Minimum List Headings. Thus, for example, manufacturing industry consists of 17 Orders and 122 MLHs. The 'industries' in the tables are Orders or groups of Orders.

2 Mining and Quarrying plus oil and gas extraction.

The stagnation or decline of many UK industries other than oil and gas after 1973 is highlighted by table 4.3. These trends of course reflect the response of British industry not only to the changed circumstances following the oil crisis, but also to our joining the EEC. Prior to 1973 all sectors but one had been expanding, albeit at diverse rates. Ironically the exception is mining and quarrying; throughout the 1960s the coal industry had been gradually run down in an era of plentiful and cheap imported oil, and this process continued until the 1973 oil crisis restored

---

1 For a discussion of the general impact of North Sea oil on the economy, see *NIER*, February 1978, and P.J. Forsyth and J.A. Kay, 'Oil Revenues and Manufacturing Output', *Fiscal Studies*, 2, 2 July 1981, pp. 9-17.

coal's competitive position. After the mid-1970s recession, electrical engineering, chemicals and paper printing and publishing all achieved relatively high growth up to 1979. However only electrical engineering sustained this growth into 1980, output falling by varying amounts in the two other cases. Elsewhere in the non-oil and gas sector very modest expansion took place in food, drink and tobacco, while most other sectors tended to stagnate up to 1979, with some substantial output falls in 1980. These were especially marked in metal manufacturing (28.6%) and in textiles (15.9%). Mechanical engineering on the other hand experienced a fairly steady decline over the period after 1974.

In the main those industries which did relatively well after 1975 are also those with the faster growth rates over the full period from 1960 to 1980. But apart from gas and oil, only the chemicals industry has matched the general average in other countries. And in the period from 1973 to 1980 industrial production as a whole declined in absolute terms, as well as relatively to other countries.

TABLE 4.3
Annual Growth of Industrial Production, 1960-80 (%)

Industry	1960-73	1973-80	1960-80
Mining and Quarrying	−2.4	15.4	3.5
Manufacturing:			
Food, drink and tobacco	2.8	0.5	2.0
Chemicals and oil products	5.8	0.1	3.8
Metal manufacture	0.6	−7.2	−2.2
Engineering and allied industries	3.3	−1.5	1.6
Mechanical		−1.8	
Electrical		1.7	
Vehicles	1.9	−2.9	0.2
Textiles, leather and clothing	1.9	−3.9	−0.2
Printing, paper, publishing	2.8	−1.3	1.5
Total Manufacturing	3.0	−1.9	1.4
Construction	2.2	−2.9	0.4
Electricity, gas and water	5.6	2.0	4.3
Industrial Production	2.9	−0.5	1.9
GDP[1]	2.8	0.7	2.1

Source: MDS.
Note: 1 Includes agriculture, transport and communications, distributive trades, services, public administration and defence, and ownership of dwellings.

The pattern of UK industrial growth we have been considering has resulted in changes both in the industrial structure of UK output, and in Britain's ranking among the world's richer nations. The most striking structural change is a fall in the share of manufacturing industry in national output, from 36.5% in 1960 to only 25.8% in 1980 (see table 4.4). Agricultural production and the traditional extractive industries have also declined relatively, while the rapid development of mineral-oil and gas extraction has meant that this now accounts for more than 3% of GDP. Other broad sectors of industry and commerce have maintained a roughly constant share of total output, apart from some decline in the distribution trades.

TABLE 4.4

GDP by Industrial Origin, 1960, 1973 and 1980

	1960		1973		1980	
	£000s	*(%)*	*£000s*	*(%)*	*£000s*	*(%)*
Agriculture, forestry and fishing	912	(4.0)	1,969	(3.1)	4,950	(2.6)
Mining and Quarrying	687	(3.0)	859	(1.3)	9,258	(4.8)
Petroleum and natural gas	–		43		6,302	(3.3)
Other	687	(3.0)	815	(1.3)	2,956	(1.5)
Manufacturing	8,239	(36.5)	19,837	(30.1)	49,810	(25.8)
Construction	1,363	(6.0)	5,333	(8.3)	11,661	(6.0)
Gas, Electricity and Water	617	(2.7)	1,912	(3.0)	5;565	(2.9)
Transport and Communications	1,953	(8.6)	5,403	(8.4)	16,527	(8.6)
Distributive Trades	2,756	(12.2)	7,087	(11.0)	20,211	(10.5)
GDP[1] at factor cost	22,586	(100)	64,259	(100)	193,136	(100)

Sources: NIBB; MDS.

Note: 1 Includes services, public administration and defence, and ownership of dwellings.

International comparisons of income per head must be treated with caution.[1] Official exchange rates often do not accurately reflect international purchasing power, and the standard of living in a country depends on the stock of wealth accumulated in the past as well as on the current flow of income. Subject to these caveats, the general trends in table 4.5 give an indication of the effect of Britain's poor economic performance on her international standing. French and German income per head overtook Britain's in 1961, as did the EEC average in 1967. The 1980 comparison flatters the UK somewhat, since sterling was then overvalued internationally, principally on account of oil.

Many questions have been asked in the search for explanations of Britain's economic decline.[2] Have we fallen behind because of a lack of technical progressiveness and R and D spending? Is production carried on at too small a scale to compete in world markets? Is the blame due to militant unions or inefficient managers? Has the financial system failed to steer funds to the right type of investment? Has growth of the public sector pre-empted development of our capacity to supply marketed goods? Are we still paying the price of our early

1   See I.B. Kravis *et al.*, 'Real GDP Per Capita for More than One Hundred Countries', *EJ*, June 1978, pp. 215-42.

2   See also R. Bacon and W. Eltis, *Britain's Economic Problem: Too Few Producers*, Macmillan, 1976: M. Panic (ed.), *The UK and German Manufacturing Industries*, NEDO, 1976; J.C. Carrington and G.T. Edwards, *Financing Industrial Investment*, Macmillan, 1979; and S.J. Prais, *Productivity and Industrial Structure*, Cambridge University Press, 1982.

industrial start, now reflected in our commitment to old industries and old technologies? There are no complete answers to these questions, though we consider some evidence relevant to them in later sections.

TABLE 4.5

National Income per head, UK and Selected Countries (£s per head at current prices and exchange rates)

	1960	*1973*	*1980*
USA	818	2,304	4,416
Canada	578	2,027	3,957
Japan	135	1,331	3,322
France	368	1,745	4,649
Germany	364	2,031	5,055
Italy	203	955	2,684
UK	398	1,409	3,552

Source: IFS.

II   AGRICULTURAL DEVELOPMENT AND POLICY

As in almost all other developed countries, UK agricultural production has been maintained and developed since the war at a higher level than would otherwise be the case, given the costs of domestic production and world price levels for agricultural products. Quite different methods of agricultural support were in force before and after Britain's entry into the EEC in 1973. It is primarily for this reason that table 4.6 shows agricultural developments separately for the two periods although, as we have seen, 1973 was a watershed for almost all industries. Because agricultural harvests are subject to considerable annual fluctuation, the levels of output and inputs are shown as three-year averages centred on the years 1961, 1973 and 1979.

The statistics show that production has risen somewhat faster in agriculture than in other industries over the last twenty years. They also reveal a big increase in the mechanization of production and capital intensity over the period, with total employment falling by nearly a half and the capital stock growing by more than three-quarters. The resulting increase in labour productivity is much greater than in most other industries. Just as in the rest of the economy, however, output grew more slowly after 1973, with almost exactly proportional changes in the trends in both employment and productivity. Expansion of the capital stock also slowed, but to a markedly lesser extent.

Under the pre-1973 system of agricultural support, farmers received assistance in two main ways: deficiency payments, and direct grants for capital investment and farm improvement. The deficiency payments scheme operated as follows. Agricultural products sold in the UK at world price levels, with more or less free access to the UK market for foreign producers, and some preferential treatment for Commonwealth producers. Where these prices were below the level of a guaranteed price, set by the government to encourage a certain level of home production taking production costs and farm incomes into account, the deficiency payment received by farmers was equal to the difference.

Industry

	1960-62	1972-4	1978-80	Annual average growth (%)		
				1961-73	1973-9	1961-79
Index of real output (1975 = 100)	79	110	120	2.8	1.5	2.3
Employment (000s)	666	403	350	−4.1	−2.3	−3.5
Capital stock (£bn at 1975 replacement cost)	5.8[1]	8.8	10.3	3.6[2]	2.6	3.3
Index of labour productivity (1975 = 100)	44.5	102.3	128.4	7.2	3.9	6.1

Source: AAS.

Notes: 1 Estimate obtained by extrapolating 1964-73 trend.

      2 1964-73.

Thus the UK maintained open markets to foreign producers, and consumers enjoyed the relatively low world food price levels. At the same time home production was encouraged and farm incomes were stabilized and controlled. The cost to the Exchequer varied inversely with the level of world prices. Early experience of an open-ended support scheme, with no upper limit on quantities produced at home and hence on the liability of the Exchequer, led to the introduction of 'standard quantities' for most products in the early 1960s; thereafter the guaranteed price fell on a sliding scale as these were exceeded.

The farm capital grants scheme provided assistance for investment in buildings and machinery and also projects such as land drainage, hill-land improvements and remodelling works for farm amalgamations. The rates of grant-aid tended to differ among projects, although steps were taken in 1970 towards a comprehensive scheme with a basic rate of 30%. Some subsidies were also offered for current expenditures, e.g. those associated with the use of fertilizers and lime. The guaranteed prices, grants and subsidies were reviewed annually and published in the *Annual Review and Determination of Guarantees.*[1]

Through this policy the government was able not only to maintain domestic production at a higher level than would have been achieved without official support (assuming other countries continued to support their own farmers), but also to influence the composition of agricultural output and the efficiency of the industry. Especially in the later years of the policy, guaranteed prices were manipulated to produce a *selective* rather than a general expansion. Similarly, grants and subsidies were used to bring about desired changes in the structure of the industry, and to mechanize and modernize it. The developments shown in table 4.6 were thus very much influenced by government policy.

Agricultural support has continued since 1973, but via the Common Agricultural Policy (CAP) of the EEC. The objectives are in principle very similar to those which governed previous UK policy. Thus Article 39 of the Treaty of Rome mentions securing increases in agricultural efficiency, stabilizing agricultural

---

1 Since 1977 a separate *Annual Review* has been published now that the scope for determining prices, etc. at national level is limited.

markets, guaranteeing regular supplies, and ensuring reasonable prices to consumers and fair living standards for the agricultural population. The two policies are also similar in that support to farmers comes partly in the form of price guarantees, and partly in capital and current grants or subsidies. There are two major differences, however. Under the CAP the food prices paid by consumers reflect not world prices but EEC production costs. In general these are very much higher: currently 50-60% higher in the production of pork, wheat and barley, for example; roughly twice as high in the case of beef, maize, olive oil and rape-seed; and around four times as high for butter and powdered-milk production.[1] Secondly, only a minute proportion of CAP support is devoted to improving efficiency rather than to price support: under 1% of total expenditure in 1979-81,[2] compared with about 60% going on grants and subsidies under the old UK system. This represents a failure of the EEC to implement the *Mansholt Plan* which as long ago as 1968 was designed to shift the emphasis of CAP away from price support and towards structural reform.

The CAP is administered by the European Agricultural Guidance and Guarantee Fund. Grant aid is supervised by the Guidance wing, though grants are actually paid out by each national government. Price support is managed by the Guarantee wing of the EAGGF. The aim is to bring about free intra-community trade in agricultural products, with uniform prices among the members and a common external tariff. 'Target prices' are negotiated for most products which make domestic production profitable. To maintain market prices at or close to this level there is a system of variable levies on imports from the outside world, broadly designed to equalize the supply price of foreign produce (including transport costs) and the target price. In addition, there is provision for support-buying of unsold produce when prices fall below an 'intervention-price' level. In some cases the intervention price is set close to the target price. For instance, the intervention price for grain is within 5-7% of the target price. For some products, however, such as fruit and vegetables, prices can fall significantly before support-buying occurs. The EAGGF receives its income from the exchequers of member nations, contributions being determined partly in proportion to the size of the import levies arising from each nation's external trade in agricultural products.

The costs and benefits of the CAP fall rather unequally on the EEC members. In the past Britain and Germany in particular, but Italy also, have been net contributors to the budget, while the other countries have either benefited or received roughly what they gave. In 1980 Britain's net deficit in the agricultural budget was £1.2bn but this understates the full welfare effect, which should include the loss in consumer surplus from prices being higher than their world levels. According to Kay[3] the true cost of the CAP to Britain was some £2.2bn. However the net balance for individual countries varies from year to year, depending on the outcome of annual wrangles over the level of agricultural prices, members' contributions to the fund, and the artificial exchange rates[4] used to

---

1 Source: *Eurostat*, Yearbook of Agricultural Statistics.

2 Source: ibid. Planned capital-support expenditure for the period 1980-84 is 3.6bn EU (0.76% average per year). If price support can be held at around the 12.1bn EU averaged in the first three years of the period, this would imply an increase to 6%.

3 J. Kay, *Fiscal Studies*, February 1980.

4 In the case of Britain the so-called 'green pound'.

maintain agricultural price uniformity in real terms as official exchange rates vary. The position also changes as new members join, particularly when they are countries with large agricultural sectors like, for example, Greece, which joined in 1981 and has some 30% of its workforce in farming.

Britain's agricultural sector, on the other hand, is relatively small and this has been one factor in our adverse budgetary position. The other main cause has been Britain's relatively large import trade with non-EEC countries. This had been encouraged by the pre-1973 policy, but under the CAP became liable to import levies. Since joining the Community, UK self-sufficiency in food products has increased sharply in some areas, but remains much below average for butter, fresh fruit, sugar and cheese, and to a lesser extent meat, vegetables, wheat and rye (table 4.7).

TABLE 4.7

Degree of Self-Sufficiency in Agricultural Products in the UK and EEC (value of domestic consumption as % of domestic production)

	UK		EUR-9	
	1975/6	1978/9	1975/6	1978/9
Wheat (soft)	54	76	101	118
Rye	27	73	92	114
Barley	105	110	103	113
Oats	93	95	95	100
Potatoes	83	96	98	100
Sugar	29	44	105	124
Vegetables	75	79	95	94
Fresh fruit	30	34	79	77
Skimmed milk	169	125	109	107
Cheese	61	68	101	105
Butter	20	42	107	119
Eggs	100	101	100	101
Meat	74	73	96	98

Source: Yearbook of Agricultural Statistics, 1981, Eurostat.

A second major problem for Britain in adapting to the CAP was the need to adjust consumer price levels from world to EEC levels. Food prices rose very rapidly after entry, at a rate of 19.5% per annum in the five years up to 1977, and nearly 20% more than other retail prices over the period.[1] Subsequently the index of food prices has risen less than prices in general, suggesting that the once-for-all adjustment was by then complete.

The high-consumer-prices aspect of the CAP has led it to be compared adversely with the former UK 'cheap food' policy, especially as food expenditure accounts for a higher proportion of total expenditure among poorer families. It is also questionable whether the EEC's self-sufficiency in most foods represents a desirable international division of labour, and protection against non-Community produce arguably impedes third-world development.

---

1   This should not be interpreted as the net inflationary impact of CAP. To determine this we should have to allow for the increase in food prices which would otherwise have occurred, and identify indirect effects on non-food prices, e.g. via wage increases negotiated (in part) to compensate for CAP-induced rises in the cost of living.

A third serious drawback of the CAP as a system of agricultural support lies in its tendency to generate surplus production of major products. This is because the CAP's high prices and support-buying arrangements stimulate production and remove the normal market sanction on oversupply (i.e. downward price adjustment), while simultaneously discouraging demand. In the absence of other non-market controls on supply, surpluses cannot be prevented, and at one time or another there have in fact been surpluses of butter (purchased to sustain a high target price for milk), grains, sugar, beef, fruit and wine. Thus the CAP today still suffers from the problem of open-ended financial support that was dealt with by the introduction of standard quantities some twenty years ago in Britain under the old scheme. By 1980 nearly three-quarters of the entire expenditure under all EEC policies went on farm price support, benefiting less than 8% of the total workforce. Financing the milk surplus alone took up about 35% of the budget.

In the face of the impending financial collapse of the CAP new policy guidelines were put forward in 1981 as an initial step towards its reform.[1] The two main considerations are a 'prudent price policy', and the modulation of price guarantees by means of 'multiannual production objectives' (or in plainer language, quantity controls). However, the prudent price policy has supposedly been pursued already since 1977, and the 'production objectives' are bound to give rise to problems in reaching agreement, as the CAP always has, between member states with fundamentally different agricultural situations and interests.

The other consideration which may shape future CAP development is the general aim now emerging to co-ordinate all major EEC programmes in an overall programme for economic recovery. This is particularly likely to result in pressure for better dovetailing of agricultural and regional policy.[2]

III   THE NATIONALIZED INDUSTRIES
III.1   The Scope of Public Enterprise

The nationalized industries are broadly speaking those parts of the public sector supplying marketed goods and services, rather than 'public goods' in the theoretical sense[3] or the major social services. The principal undertakings involved are the National Coal Board; British Gas; the Central Electricity Generating Board and Area Electricity Boards; the majority-owned British National Oil Corporation (since 1975); British Rail; British Airways; the National Freight Corporation and the National and Scottish Bus Groups (set up under the 1968 Transport Act); Postal Services and British Telecom; British Steel (since 1967)[4]; British Leyland (since 1975); and the bulk of the aerospace and shipbuilding industries (since 1977). Public-sector activities excluded by our definition cover public

---

1 See *Fifteenth General Report* of the European Community, 1981.

2 See also section V below.

3 A public good is one whose consumption by one person does not reduce the amount available for consumption by others (e.g. defence and broadcasting). Public goods will be undersupplied by the market and must generally be supplied and paid for out of taxation.

4 Iron and steel production had previously been nationalized from 1951 to 1953.

administration and defence, broadcasting, the health and education services, and the activities of a number of other government agencies.[1]

Altogether the nationalized industries produced an eighth (12.7%) of GDP in 1977.[2] This is a substantial part of national output, though perhaps not as large as the level of media coverage and public discussion of the industries might lead one to expect. In the same year the industries generated 9.4% of total employment and undertook 22.6% of total fixed investment (excluding housing).[3] From these varying proportions we can see that the nationalized sector is on average more capital-intensive than the rest of the economy, and in the recent past there have been major investment programmes in telecommunications and electricity, North Sea gas conversion and pipeline construction, rail electrification and in steel production.

The nationalized sector contains some of the country's most high-technology, growth industries as well as some of its oldest and most rapidly declining branches. Output trends for eleven major public enterprises over the period 1968-78 are shown in table 4.8. This should be read in the context of section I above, but since much nationalized activity centres on fuel and power production and on transport and communications, we will review developments in these areas in more detail. About sixty per cent of nationalized-industry output, employment and investment is concentrated in these sectors.

The overwhelming factor in inland passenger transport development has been the growth of private motoring (table 4.9). Between 1960 and 1980 the number of private cars currently licensed doubled from 9.4m to 19.2m, and the increase in private motoring has resulted in a rapid growth in total passenger mileage over the period, with substantial decreases in both rail and public road services. Inland air transport has expanded, but still accounts for only a minute proportion of total travel. The expansion of car ownership and private travel reflects rising real incomes, but relative price movements have at times been a reinforcing factor; before 1974 both rail and bus fares rose very much faster than did private motoring costs, at some 6.7% per annum during the 1960s compared with 4.0%, though since then they have shown a slightly lower rate of increase up to 1980, at 7.9% compared with 8.9%. In the inland freight sector, total traffic has grown in line with the economy as a whole (table 4.10). Here also there has been a major reallocation of traffic towards road services, especially private hauliers.

Total energy consumption expanded much less rapidly than GDP up to 1973, and has subsequently fallen by over 7% (table 4.11). The slow growth to 1973 may be attributed largely to technical economies in fuel use and the decline of certain fuel-intensive industries such as iron and steel and rail. Reduced demand after 1973 reflects the more general decline of the non-oil economy and more far-reaching energy savings prompted by large increases in fuel prices.

---

1   See R. Maurice (ed.), *National Income Statistics: Sources and Methods*, Central Statistical Office, HMSO, 1968, and H. Copeman, *The National Accounts: A Short Guide*, Studies in Official Statistics No. 36, HMSO, 1981.

2   R. Pryke, *The Nationalised Industries: Policies and Performance since 1968*, Martin Robertson, 1981, p. 2. See also *The Nationalised Industries*, Cmnd. 7131, HMSO, March 1978.

3   R. Pryke, op. cit.

TABLE 4.8

Growth Rates of Public Enterprises, 1968-78

	Annual average growth of output (%)		
	1968-73	*1973-8*	*1968-78*
Fuel and power			
British Gas	7.4	4.9	6.2
British Electricity Boards	3.9	0.2	2.1
NCB	–6.1	–2.8	–4.5
Transport and communications			
British Rail	–1.5	–2.5	–2.0
British Airways	12.0	5.4	8.7
National Freight Corporation	–0.6	–4.1	–2.4
National and Scottish Bus Groups	–3.1	–4.6	–3.9
Postal services	–0.6	–1.8	–1.2
Telecommunications	10.0	7.3	8.7
Manufacturing			
British Steel	0.4	–6.4	–3.0
British Leyland	1.6	–5.1	–1.8
Manufacturing[1]	3.0	–0.6	1.2

Source: Derived from R. Pryke, op. cit., table 13.1, p. 238.
Note: 1 Excludes BSC and BL (1973-8).

TABLE 4.9

GB Inland Passenger Mileage, 1960-1980[1] (000m passenger-kilometres)

Year	Air	Rail	Road		Total
			Public-service vehicles	Private transport	
1960	0.8 (0.3%)	39.7 (15.6%)	70.2 (27.7%)	143.0 (56.4%)	253.8 (100.0%)
1968	1.9 (0.5%)	33.4 (8.9%)	59.0 (15.7%)	280.0 (74.8%)	374.3 (100.0%)
1973	2.4 (0.5%)	35.1 (7.6%)	54.0 (11.8%)	364.0 (79.2%)	459.5 (100.0%)
1978	2.4 (0.5%)	35.2 (7.0%)	52.0 (10.3%)	412.0 (81.5%)	505.6 (100.0%)
1980	2.8 (0.5%)	36.0 (6.8%)	51.0 (9.7%)	433.0 (82.1%)	527.6 (100.0%)
% change 1960-80	+250%	–9.3%	–27.4%	+202.8%	+107.9% or 3.7% p.a.

Source: AAS.
Note: 1 % figures in brackets show respective contributions to the total in any one year.

The pattern of domestic energy consumption has changed dramatically since 1960 in the face of developments both within and outside the UK (table 4.11). Direct use of coal was in very sharp decline up to 1973 and has since fallen further, but at a much slower rate. (This decline is much greater than the reduction in coal output (cf. table 4.3) because coal has been retained, by a deliberate act of govern-

TABLE 4.10

GB Inland Freight Transport 1960-80[1] (000m tonne-kilometres)

Year	Road	Rail	Inland waterways	Pipelines[2]	Total
1960	49.0 (61.2%)	30.4 (38.0%)	0.3 (0.4%)	0.3 (0.4%)	80.1 (100.0%)
1968	79.0 (74.8%)	24.0 (22.7%)	0.2 (0.2%)	2.3 (2.2%)	105.6 (100.0%)
1973	90.4 (74.8%)	25.5 (21.1%)	0.1 (0.1%)	4.8 (4.0%)	120.8 (100.0%)
1978	99.1 (76.8%)	20.0 (15.5%)	0.1 (0.1%)	9.8 (7.6%)	129.0 (100.0%)
1980	93.1 (77.1%)	17.6 (14.6%)	0.1 (0.1%)	9.9 (8.2%)	120.7 (100.0%)
% change 1960-80	+90%	−42.1%	−66.7%	+3,200%	+50.7% or 2.1% p.a.

Source: AAS.

Notes: 1 % figures in brackets show respective contributions to the total in any one year.
2 Excludes the movement of gases by pipeline, and pipelines less than 16 kilometres long.

TABLE 4.11

Total UK Inland Energy Consumption by Final Users, 1960-80: Heat Supplied Basis (bn therms)

Type of fuel	1960	(%)	1968	(%)	1973	(%)	1978	(%)	1980	(%)	Total change 1960-80
Coal (direct use)	23.4	(46.4)	13.6	(24.6)	8.1	(13.3)	5.7	(9.6)	5.1	(9.0)	−78.2%
Gas	3.2	(6.3)	4.9	(8.9)	11.0	(18.0)	15.4	(26.0)	16.8	(29.7)	+425.0%
Electricity	3.4	(6.7)	5.8	(10.5)	7.5	(12.3)	7.7	(13.0)	7.7	(13.6)	+126.5%
Petroleum	12.4	(24.5)	24.1	(43.7)	29.6	(48.5)	27.1	(45.8)	24.8	(43.9)	+100.0%
Other Fuels[1]	8.2	(16.1)	6.8	(12.3)	4.8	(7.9)	3.3	(5.6)	2.1	(3.7)	−74.4%
Total	50.5	(100.0)	55.2	(100.0)	61.0	(100.0)	59.2	(100.0)	56.5	(100.0)	+11.9% or 0.6% p.a.

Source: AAS.

Note: 1 Includes coke, breeze, solid and liquid fuels derived from coal.

ment policy, as a primary energy source in electricity generation.[1]) Gas usage stagnated up to 1965, before staging a massive resurgence based initially on the replacement of town gas by cheap, imported natural gas and later, in the 1970s, by even cheaper and growing North Sea supplies. Direct use of both electricity and oil increased rapidly in the 1960s and early 1970s, but by 1980 oil consumption had dropped back to a little over its 1968 level, while electricity consumption had stabilized.

---

1 The electricity supply industry purchased 25.8% of total coal supply in 1960 and 69.1% in 1980.

III.2 Public Enterprise Abroad

The UK economy is not unusual in having a substantial sector of industry under public ownership. Moreover there are considerable similarities between countries in the pattern of public enterprise.[1] Within the EEC, for example, state ownership is the norm for postal services and telecommunications, electricity and gas distribution, the railways, parts of road transport and coalmining. All major countries have national airlines, and the steel, aerospace and shipbuilding industries are usually subject to at least a degree of state participation. Vehicle production is likewise carried on elsewhere than the UK in public or mixed enterprises (i.e. under joint public and private ownership); while Britain has BL, France has Renault and Germany has VW. The public sector is particularly large in France, and Italy has two giant state companies: IRI, a wide-ranging holding company; and ENI, an oil and chemicals firm. There are also certain state monopolies for taxation purposes; that is, the state retains a monopoly profit as part of its fiscal revenue. The match industry (in France, West Germany and Italy) and the tobacco industry (in France and Italy) are examples.

In the USA, on the other hand, public ownership is unusual. However, a significant number of industries have for many years been subject to regulation of their tariffs, profits and services, though their assets remain in private hands. The list of industries is again familiar: railroads; motor and water carriers; airlines; electric, gas, water and sanitary services; telephones, telegraph and broadcasting; plus financial institutions. The percentage of GNP taken by the regulated industries in 1965 was around 11%.[2] However the current US administration has initiated a substantial programme of 'deregulation'.

III.3 Public Enterprise Policy: Principles

If the nationalized industries are to promote the national interest they must be efficient in both a technical and an allocative sense. Technical efficiency requires simply that the maximum physical output is obtained from whatever resources are used. To achieve allocative efficiency, the nationalized industries must choose both production techniques with cost-minimizing factor combinations, and a socially efficient output level such that a correct balance of resources is maintained between each public enterprise and the rest of the economy.[3] In addition, public enterprises may be expected to take account of the social costs and benefits of their activities, e.g. the effect on road-traffic congestion of maintaining a rail service, or the loss of

---

1 See D. Swann, *The Economics of the Common Market*, 4th edition, Penguin Books, 1978, and Stuart Holland, *The Unequal Mix: European Public Enterprise*, Martin Robertson, 1978.

2 See F.M. Scherer, *Industrial Market Structure and Economic Performance*, 1st edition, Rand McNally, 1970, p. 519.

3 In the case of exhaustible resources (gas, oil and coal), additional considerations apply. In a competitive case, net price (market price less extraction costs) must grow exponentially at a rate equal to the rate of interest. In monopolistic conditions, marginal profit (marginal revenue minus marginal cost) must grow at this rate. For a non-technical treatment see R.M. Solow, 'The Economics of Resources and the Resources of Economics', *AER* (Papers and Proceedings), May 1974, pp. 1-14. At a somewhat more technical level see P.S. Dasgupta and G.M. Heal, *Economic Theory and Exhaustible Resources*, Cambridge University Press, 1979.

amenity from mining developments. In certain circumstances they may also be expected to provide uneconomic services on social grounds, e.g. supplying electricity, and transportation, postal and telephone services to remote communities.

According to orthodox theory, technical and allocative efficiency is brought about in the private sector of a market economy by the profit-maximizing behaviour of firms and by the process of competition. Thus profit-maximizing firms locate at a point of tangency between an isocost curve and a production isoquant showing the maximum outputs which can be achieved from given input combinations. Hence costs of production are minimized under all market conditions. Competition then ensures that output prices are set equal to marginal costs, and this leads to allocative efficiency (see below). Competition also prevents firms from earning more than normal profits in the long run, so that a technically inefficient firm, failing to minimize costs, will make economic losses and be eliminated. However, private-sector firms will not take account of discrepancies between private and social costs and benefits ('externalities'). In passing we may note two economic justifications for the existence of a public enterprise which are implicit in this analysis: 'natural monopoly' (where efficient production would result in a firm so large as to dominate market supply) and the existence of significant externalities.[1]

Assuming there is profit-maximizing behaviour and competition in the private sector, therefore, a first principle for public enterprise policy is marginal-cost pricing, if optimal resource allocation is to be achieved.[2] The simple rationale for marginal-cost pricing in both public and private enterprise is as follows. On the one hand the demand curve for a product tells us how much consumers will pay per unit for different quantities supplied; it represents consumers' marginal evaluation of the good or service as output is varied. On the other hand the marginal-cost curve tells us the incremental cost of producing each unit. To the extent that the money costs incurred in production reflect the true opportunity cost of diverting extra resources from alternative uses, the marginal-cost curve records consumers' evaluation of the forgone alternative product. Hence, if consumers value the good in question more than the alternative (demand price exceeds marginal cost) then welfare can be increased by diverting more resources to its production and increasing output, and vice versa. Hence, the optimal level of output is determined where price equals marginal cost.

There are difficulties in practice, however. Firstly, setting a particular price equal to marginal cost maximizes welfare only if all other prices are equal to their respective marginal costs. Otherwise the 'second best' solution will probably require divergence from marginal-cost prices all round.[3] In practice we cannot assume equality between price and marginal cost in the private sector, which is characterized by oligopoly or monopoly rather than competition.[4] In general we therefore expect private-sector prices to exceed marginal cost. This suggests a

---

1 Or if not public ownership, some form of regulation by public agencies.

2 For a more extended discussion see R. Rees, *Public Enterprise Economics*, Weidenfeld and Nicolson, 1976.

3 See R.G. Lipsey and K. Lancaster, 'On the General Theory of Second Best', *RES*, Vol. XXIV, 1956-7, pp. 11-32.

4 See section IV.3 below.

modification of the pricing rule for public enterprise whereby price is set equi-proportional to marginal cost. Thus if price is on average, say, ten per cent above marginal cost in the rest of the economy, this margin should be included in public enterprise prices in order to preserve a correct balance in resource allocation. Such a procedure will yield an optimal pattern of production of final goods, other things being equal, but it will not produce an overall optimum, since the relative prices of commodities (in general) and primary inputs such as labour will be affected. Thus, labour will be paid less than its marginal value product, and be under-supplied. In sum, optimality conditions will be fulfilled in commodity markets but not in factor markets, and the level of total economic activity will be too low.[1]

Secondly, where there are externalities price must be set equal to marginal *social* cost, rather than marginal *private* cost. Thus, a nationalized industry equating price with marginal private cost would be producing too much, from the community standpoint, if it gave rise to net external costs and too little if it conferred net external economies. From the point of view of the public enterprise, the difficulty is to assess the magnitude of external affects and adjust prices accordingly. A more general problem is that, as we have seen, private-sector prices will ignore any externalities that may be present, creating further 'second-best' problems in the system as a whole, analogous to those arising from monopoly.

Thirdly, adherence to marginal-cost prices may result in financial problems; except where there are constant returns to scale (and marginal costs equal average costs), there is no guarantee that total costs will be recovered from revenue. Under non-constant returns, marginal and average costs are equal only where the latter are at a minimum. Hence, marginal-cost pricing will equate costs and revenues only at this level of output. In practice it is expected that costs decline continuously over the relevant range of outputs in a number of nationalized industries, so that marginal cost is less than average cost and a deficit is likely to result. Since there is no agreed method of financing deficits (or distributing surpluses) in a way which will not itself affect resource allocation, there is thus a basic conflict between financial rectitude and pricing policies designed to optimize resource allocation.

Finally, even if all these difficulties are overcome, the resource allocation ensuing from marginal-cost pricing is optimal only *within* the existing distribution of income among customers. If this distribution is not accepted as being ideal, it would be perfectly justifiable for the government to modify some or all nationalized industry prices in the name of social justice. (It could be argued that this is precisely what the government does in not charging, or making only token charges, for some public-sector goods and services, e.g. health and education.)

All these considerations affect public enterprise investment decisions, as well as their pricing policies, since these require that the social costs and benefits at each point in the life of any project be correctly evaluated. In addition, it is necessary that estimates of future costs and benefits be correctly related to the present decision-making period. This requires that the returns to an investment project be

---

1 See, e.g., J.M. Henderson and R.E. Quandt, *Microeconomic Theory*, 3rd edition, McGraw-Hill, 1980.

expressed as a net discounted present value.[1] Generally speaking, the rate of time-discount used in evaluating public-sector projects should be the same as is used elsewhere (and any allowance made for uncertainty should also be the same). Otherwise the relative merits of private- and public-sector projects will be distorted. In practice, private-sector investments will almost invariably be evaluated with no regard for external effects; various ways of treating uncertainty are likely to be used; and a substantial amount of decision-making may still be undertaken by rule-of-thumb methods.[2] In so far as the government is unable to regulate all private-sector investment appraisal appropriately, the best that can be hoped for is a form of sub-optimization, the correct principles being applied at least in the public sector.

There remains the question of internal resource allocation and technical efficiency; socially-efficient pricing and investment decisions through administrative fiat will not produce an optimal outcome unless there is also pressure to minimize costs in public enterprise. As we have seen, competition and the threat of bankruptcy are believed to be the ultimate sanction on efficiency in the private sector.

Most nationalized undertakings also face a degree of competition in their respective markets. In the case of steel and cars there is competition across the full range of activities, either from other domestic producers or from imports. Similarly all the nationalized inland-transport undertakings compete both with each other and with private fleet operators, hauliers and private motoring. In international air transport British Airways competes with other national and independent airlines, though subject to IATA regulations on scheduled flights, and with charter operations. The Coal Board, on the other hand, is a near-monopoly supplier to a protected domestic market, and as we have seen coal has been sheltered from the competition of substitute fuels by government policy in commissioning new power stations. Likewise the electricity and gas industries are, by their nature, sole suppliers of their respective products. Yet taking the energy market as a whole there is keen competition between alternative fuels in some areas, especially in space heating. Of all the nationalized industries postal services and tele-communications probably face least competition, except in the delivery of parcels and, to a limited extent, from each other, though some recent steps have been taken to break the monopoly in mail-carrying and the supply of telephone equipment and services.

This all adds up to a substantial amount of competition affecting public enterprises, perhaps as much as in a good deal of private industry. But it is open to question whether it will have an efficiency-inducing effect in the absence of an ultimate threat of bankruptcy. Governments may attempt to simulate the disciplinary role of the capital market by setting suitable financial targets for the nationalized industries. However it may prove difficult or impossible to apply

---

1   Net discounted present value (R) for any product with a life of n years is given by

$$R = \sum_{t=1}^{n} \frac{B_t - C_t}{(1 + r)^t} - I$$ where B_t, C_t are benefits and costs respectively in the year

t, r is the rate of discount and I is the initial cost. The main merits of this method over its chief rival (internal rate of return or marginal efficiency of capital) are that it always gives a unique solution and always ranks projects correctly.

2   See NEDO, *Investment Appraisal*, HMSO, 1967.

adequate sanctions for their non-fulfillment. If, as may be the case, it is either politically or economically unacceptable to contemplate the closure of a nationalized undertaking (many of which supply essential services), the government may have little practical alternative to condoning financial shortfalls, allowing deficits to accumulate, and periodically writing-off debts. The awareness of this political and economic reality amongst management, workers and unions, it is argued, militates against efficiency in the public sector.

The contrast with private enterprise should not be drawn too sharply however. Profit-maximization may not be pursued in the private sector as vigorously as textbooks suggest;[1] where excess profits are available, the bankruptcy mechanism will not operate as soon as inefficiency enters (excess costs having to erode excess profits before economic losses occur); and, at least in the case of giant firms, similar considerations may apply as for public enterprise. After all, past governments have also proved unwilling to contemplate the closure of, for example, the then private Rolls-Royce and British Leyland companies.

However, this does not of itself solve the problem of public enterprise efficiency. Whatever comparison with the private sector might show, there may be a case for some additional control, e.g. in the form of efficiency audits by a parliamentary, departmental or independent body.

III.4 Public Enterprise Policy: Practice

The first phase of policy towards public enterprise was enshrined in the postwar nationalization Acts, which merely required the industries to break-even, taking one year with another. Such a requirement does little to promote technical or allocative efficiency, since it can in principle be met by setting prices equal to *average* cost, at any level. In 1961 the financial responsibilities of the industries were tightened in a number of ways, and financial targets were introduced, usually expressed as a rate of return on assets employed.[2] However policy remained open to the same criticism, since explicit pricing guidelines were lacking. Then long-run marginal-cost pricing was introduced as official policy in 1967, together with the net-present-value approach to investment decisions.[3] A test discount rate (TDR) of 8% was laid down, later raised to 10%.[4] The 1967 policy focused on the pricing of individual goods and services and on individual investment projects. Arbitrary cross-subsidization amongst different groups of consumers was to be avoided, and the need was stressed to distinguish social from purely commercial operations. The government undertook financial responsibility for non-commercial operations, e.g. by specific subsidies or grants. The existing system of financial targets was

---

1 If this is the case, however, the underlying rationale of marginal-cost pricing comes into question.

2 *The Financial and Economic Obligations of the Nationalized Industries*, Cmnd. 1337, HMSO, April 1961.

3 *Nationalised Industries: A Review of Economic and Financial Objectives*, Cmnd. 3437, HMSO, November 1967.

4 The rate chosen was expressly intended to match the return looked for by private industry on marginal, low-risk investment. Because of differences in financing methods and tax liability, the equivalent private-sector rate will be higher than any given nationalized industry rate; the original 8% was held to be equivalent to 15-16% in the private sector.

retained, as a measure of expected performance against which to compare actual achievements.

For a year or two after 1967 there was some progress towards revised pricing methods, especially in the Post Office and British Rail. However, in the early and mid 1970s macroeconomic and financial considerations became of overriding importance once more, as they had tended to be before 1967. Up to 1974 severe price restraint was applied by the government, and investment programmes were cut. This led to mounting deficits, indiscriminate subsidies to the consumer from taxpayers, and in some cases sharp reductions in investment and employment. Then followed a period of very rapid price increase, with the prime objective of first holding and then eliminating Exchequer support. Significant improvements in financial performance occurred in most cases, though with some exceptions, notably steel.

This 'interference' with the nationalized industries' price and investment policies did not contravene the 1967 White Paper's recommendations, which explicitly reserved the right of the government to intervene on national economic grounds. In the event, however, the price restraint of the early 1970s and its subsequent correction led to suspension of both the financial targets and attempts at economic pricing policies which the White Paper sought to introduce. The 1978 White Paper on nationalized industry policy,[1] whose publication followed an earlier report by the Select Committee on the Nationalized Industries[2] and an independent review by NEDO,[3] sought to reintroduce and reinforce the spirit of its predecessor, but avoid repetition of the 'mistakes' of the early 1970s.[4]

The 1978 White Paper retained the objective of optimal resource allocation and the use of marginal-cost-pricing policies and of TDR in investment decisions. It also reiterated the need to avoid cross-subsidization amongst consumers and to distinguish social from commercial services. However, the limitations of the price and investment rules in practice were recognized, and they no longer occupy the forefront of policy. The White Paper explained that in many cases prices are 'market determined' and that even where this is not so, the difficulties of practical application in marginal-cost pricing can be severe. It admitted that TDR has not lived up to expectations, and gave as explanation the fact that much investment which is undertaken forms part of an existing system, or is 'necessary for safety or security'. The main focus of current policy was therefore shifted from these matters affecting individual services and projects to the opportunity cost of capital in industry as a whole. A 'real rate of return on assets' (RRR) was defined, to be achieved by the industries on new investment. The RRR is principally related to the real rate of return in the private sector, taking into account questions of the cost of finance and of social time preference. It was set initially at 5%, and is to be reviewed every three to five years. The RRR is not the same as the financial target rate of return for each industry, which varies, and takes into account the earning power of existing assets, sectoral and social objectives, and so forth.

---

1 *The Nationalised Industries*, Cmnd. 7131, HMSO, March 1978.

2 *Ministerial Control of the Nationalised Industries*, H of C 371-I, II and III, 1968.

3 *A Study of the UK Nationalised Industries: Their Role in the Economy and Control in the Future*, NEDO, November 1976.

4 See also R. Rees, 'The Pricing Policy of the Nationalised Industries', *TBR*, June 1979.

Thus the main matters over which the government has sought to exercise control since 1978 are the RRR and the financial target together with the 'general level of prices'. Individual prices and investment priorities are left largely up to the industries themselves, subject to the vague admonition to 'pay attention to the structure of prices and its relation to the structure of costs' and to the need to consult sponsoring departments on certain major investment proposals.

The foregoing analysis shows that certain difficulties have arisen in applying socially efficient price and investment policies in public enterprise. Promoting their internal operating efficiency has been no less problematical.

Several important organizational developments have taken place over the years to this end. A number were embodied in the 1968 Transport Act which, inter alia, eliminated the regional divisions of British Rail; set up a National Freight Corporation and Freight Integration Council; created Passenger Transport Authorities for four major conurbations (now increased to five) and transferred the London Transport Board to the GLC making, effectively, a sixth; and established the National and Scottish Bus groups. In 1969 the status of the Post Office was changed from that of government department to public corporation, to be run on more commercial lines, and from 1979 it has been run as two separate corporations, one for postal services and one for telecommunications. The British Steel Corporation was reorganized into a system based on product divisions (four for steel-making, one for constructional engineering and one for chemical activities). Earlier there had been four large groups, under which system most products fell within more than one group.[1] Finally, there has been a major reorganization of the gas industry, replacing the Gas Council and the area boards by a single authority, the British Gas Corporation; and a new divisionalized internal structure has recently been proposed for British Airways. A recurring theme in all these organizational changes has been to provide for better co-ordination and planning throughout the whole of the particular industries concerned.

However there have been continuing problems over the relationship between the industries, government and Parliament, centering on the basic issue of 'public accountability'. In 1968 the Select Committee on the Nationalized Industries concluded that ministers have tended to do the opposite of what Parliament originally intended. Whereas they were supposed to lay down policies, but not intervene in management, they have in practice given very little policy guidance but been closely involved with many aspects of management.[2] As we have seen, 'interference' in the shape of efficiency audits might be desirable, but in practice has not taken this form.

As a solution to this problem, the NEDO report[3] proposed a formal, two-tiered structure, the industries to be run by Corporation Boards but under the strategic direction of Policy Councils. This was rejected in the 1978 White Paper on grounds of a likely confusion of responsibility between the Policy Councils, ministers and sponsoring departments, and a consequent slowing-down of decision-making. However the White Paper did propose that explicit ministerial directions should replace the existing system of informal persuasion, in order to clarify the extent of ministers' responsibility for the industries' performance. It was also proposed that

---

1 See *British Steel Corporation: The Road to Viability*, Cmnd. 7148, HMSO, March 1978.

2 *Ministerial Control of the Nationalised Industries*, H of C 371-I, II and III, 1968.

3 NEDO, op. cit.

a civil servant be appointed to corporation boards, to improve the understanding of industry problems on the part of sponsoring departments. Finally, as part of a general exercise aimed at making the performance of the nationalized industries more open to public scrutiny, the industries were asked to select and publish an appropriate set of other performance indicators, to supplement the financial targets which could, of course, otherwise be met in various anti-social ways, e.g. monopoly pricing. As a result the National Coal Board, for example, now publishes in its *Annual Reports* information on output per manshift, daily output per face and average costs of production.

The activities of the nationalized industries have been exposed to a limited amount of independent scrutiny since 1965, when their prices became subject to review by the National Board for Prices and Incomes. This continued during the life of the Price Commission. On its disbandment in 1980 responsibility for a vestige of price control was transferred to the offices of the Director General of Fair Trading and at the same time the nationalized industries became liable to investigation by the Monopolies Commission.[1] However the reviews made under the auspices of all three bodies relate to particular price increases or specific monopoly situations, and do not amount to a regular system of internal efficiency audits.

The idea of putting pressure on public enterprises via increased market competition has been pursued by the Conservative government elected in 1979, e.g. in making limited inroads into the Post Office's postal monopoly; introducing competition into the supply of telephone equipment; and 'deregulating' certain areas of passenger transport, bringing about greater competition between coach and rail services. This government has also gone further, to propose 'privatization' of certain areas of public enterprise, though whether this is intended primarily to promote their efficiency or to reduce the PSBR is hard to say.[2] At the time of writing several proposals have been made, but no major proposal has been implemented.[3]

The merits and disadvantages of privatization depend very much on the industry in question, how it came to be in the public sector, and what post-privatization controls on behaviour, if any, are intended. Selection on the basis of the existing profitability (and hence saleability) of the undertaking, or its potential profitability under private ownership, is not necessarily valid. In the case of a natural monopoly, for example, a return to private ownership on grounds of prospective monopoly profits would be quite inappropriate. Similarly, privatization is not to be recommended where there are significant externalities to be considered. Unless, that is, in either case suitable post-sale regulatory provisions are made to take account of these problems (which seems unlikely). On the other hand re-privatization might be appropriate in the case of an undertaking where there were no significant market power or externality problems, and where perhaps the undertaking had been taken into public ownership merely on account of financial difficulties at an earlier time.

---

1   See section IV.2 below.

2   The awful term 'privatization' is currently being used in at least three senses: the full return to private ownership of nationalized undertakings or parts thereof; charging for services previously provided free or at nominal prices; and the injection of private (usually non-voting) capital into the financial structure of existing nationalized industries, which presumably will remain subject to the general policies described. The remarks which follow concern the first of these three concepts.

3   See H.M. Treasury, *Economic Progress Report* 145, May 1982.

EEC policy towards public enterprise has so far been concerned mainly with the use of subsidies. These could be contrary to the rules and spirit of the Community, if subsidization of loss-making industries in particular countries prevented the free play of competition with the Community-wide industry. However a distinction should be drawn between subsidies granted to undertakings supplying strictly non-commercial services, and general revenue support for operating deficits. It is the latter which would be most likely to meet with disapproval, though it could be hard for the Community to apply meaningful sanctions.

The emphasis of EEC policy to date has been towards securing 'transparency' of financial arrangements for public enterprise. A directive was adopted in 1980 which would require member states to supply information on transfers of public funds to public undertakings. However, credit institutions and the energy, water and transport sectors were temporarily excluded. Moreover, France, Italy and the UK immediately applied to the European Court for an annulment.

III.5   Evaluating Public Enterprise Performance

The performance of the nationalized industries attracts a good deal of publicity. This tends to focus particularly on financial out-turns, which is understandable in view of the implications for the Exchequer and, ultimately, taxpayers. But adverse and sometimes unfair comparisons may be made or implied between the industries and the private sector.

Accurate comparison is complicated by a number of factors. Firstly, public enterprise surpluses and deficits do not correspond exactly with private profits and losses; allowance must be made for differences in funding, tax liability and accounting practice (e.g. certain items, including capital costs, being deducted as costs which would be paid out of profits in private industry). Then, in interpreting financial performance and apportioning credit or blame, account must be taken of ministerial intervention, for example, in the holding-down or raising of public-sector wages, prices and investment on national economic grounds, in enforcing 'buy British' policies, and so forth. As we saw, this was a particularly severe problem in the early and mid 1970s. Equally, allowance should be made for the nature of the activities undertaken, and for the fact that public enterprises in declining markets, such as steel, cannot, for example, diversify their interests in the way that a private company would. In this regard it may also be relevant to bear in mind the apparently general unprofitability of certain nationalized-industry activities in most of Western Europe. In the recent past these have included postal services, railways, coalmining, bus companies, airports and, latterly, steel. Telecommunications, gas and electricity, on the other hand, have been generally profitable in all countries.

There are nonetheless good grounds to suppose there is scope for improvement in the efficiency of nationalized industry. In a broad-ranging assessment of eleven nationalized undertakings, Pryke evaluates performance as ranging from 'good in parts' (telecommunications and gas) to 'almost wholly bad' (steel and postal services).[1] Detailed failings are exposed, with instances of union restrictiveness on the introduction of new technology, bad management, and a general and continuing

---

1   R. Pryke, op. cit.

problem in the poor use of capital. Adverse international comparisons are made, for example on the quality of telephone service and on labour productivity in the postal services as compared with the USA, and labour productivity, again, in West German steel and coal production.[1]

These are, however, familiar themes in British industry as a whole. As Pryke acknowledges, bad management and labour relations are not confined to public enterprise, and British Leyland's record under private ownership was disastrous; it would be interesting to see what an equally searching investigation of private firms would reveal. Some hint may be contained in table 4.12, which uses Pryke's data

TABLE 4.12
Growth of Output per Man in Public Enterprise and Private Manufacturing, 1963-78

	1963-8	*% per annum* *1968-73*	*1973-8*
Nationalized industry[1]	4.8	4.0	0.8
Private manufacturing	4.9	4.4	1.0

Source: Derived from R. Pryke, op. cit., table 13.1.

Note: 1   Weighted average of eleven major nationalized undertakings. Includes BSC from 1968 and BL from 1975.

to arrive at average trends in labour productivity in the two sectors. Despite its drawbacks, this measure is of particular interest in view of the alleged overmanning of nationalized industries. While the comparison shows a slightly slower growth of public-sector productivity in all three periods, the averages must conceal wide variations within each sector, and the overall differences would not be statistically significant. Moreover, had BL not been rescued, productivity would in fact have grown faster in the nationalized sector in the third period.

IV   COMPETITION POLICY AND CONSUMER PROTECTION
IV.1   Policy Issues

Efficient market co-ordination of economic activity depends on competition and on consumers exercising free and well-informed choices. If, on the other hand, there is market power or consumers have poor information, the 'invisible hand', which is supposed to reconcile individually self-interested behaviour with the communal good, falters or is overruled. Public policies in this area therefore seek to monitor market competitiveness and consumer interests, and apply remedies where these are infringed.

Pure monopoly is the clearest case of market power, where one firm is the sole supplier in a market. However, power is rarely absolute; the monopolist faces competition from substitute products. The intensity of this competition depends on the closeness of the substitutes, and is reflected in the position and slope of the monopolist's demand curve. The monopolist may also face dynamic competition from new products or production methods, which can erode either the demand for

---

1   Output per man-year is reported to be 135% higher in the US postal service, and output per worker twice as high in German steel production and 45% higher in coalmining.

his good or the basis of his monopoly position. Nevertheless, subject to these constraints, the monopolist is not a passive price-taker but has discretion over the price he charges, which is the essence of market power.

Where a group of firms in an industry collude to form a cartel, they can assume some or all of the market power of a monopolist. Collusive agreements have often been confined to fixing the level of price, but may also cover quantities and qualities supplied, share out markets on the basis of geographical area or type of product, or predetermine the outcome of tenders for contracts. While the rewards from collusive action can be high, in the form of monopoly profits, cartels have their problems. In particular, once a price-fixing agreement exists, participating firms have an incentive to undercut the agreed price secretly and so increase their market share. Thus tensions can arise within the group with problems in maintaining allegiance and policing the agreement. The difficulties recently encountered by OPEC countries in maintaining discipline over world oil prices during a period of over-supply vividly illustrate these problems. Because of organizational problems, cartels are most likely to succeed where the number of participants is not large. Since they must also control all or most of market supply if they are to be effective, it follows that they are most likely to be found in oligopolistic, or 'highly-concentrated' markets, where a few large firms control the bulk of production.

Even where there is no explicit agreement, the kind of rivalry which is likely to occur in oligopolistic markets will not necessarily promote social welfare. For example, there may be tacit collusion, with mutually accommodating behaviour on the part of sellers in accordance with an unspoken understanding between them. One particular form of tacit collusion is where competitive pressure is attenuated by mutual 'oligopolistic forebearance'; each firm hesitates to compete vigorously for fear of an inevitable and mutually damaging retaliation. Alternatively, competition may be intense, but take the form of product differentiation and advertising. While enlarged consumer choice and knowledgeability can increase welfare up to a point, there seems to be no natural constraint in the system to prevent this being exceeded in oligopolistic markets, and a suspicion of 'wasteful' product competition and 'excessive' advertising enters. Finally, it can be shown that where certain forms of apparently innocuous, non-cooperative oligopolistic interaction occur, the results can resemble those of pure monopoly. Thus, where firms seek to maximize their market share, and a mutually compatible equilibrium is found, it can be shown that the outcome can be identical with that of explicit collusion (joint profit-maximization), which is in turn formally equivalent to multi-plant monopoly.

Mergers between firms are a further area of concern for competition policy.[1] On the one hand it is argued that they can be desirable mechanisms for rationalizing production as circumstances change or for exploiting scale economies, and a means for good management to drive out bad, via the workings of the 'market for corporate control'.[2] Beneficial effects like these are most likely to arise from horizontal mergers, between firms competing in the same industry. However, such mergers also increase seller concentration, other things being equal, with consequential risk of reduced social welfare from the exercise of the now enlarged

1 See also K. Cowling *et al.*, *Mergers and Economic Performance*, 1980, Chapter 2.
2 See, e.g., B. Hindley, 'Capitalism and Corporation', *Economica*, November 1969.

market power in the industry. Clearly, securing market power can also have been a contributing or even the only motive for merger; mergers are after all the ultimate collusive agreement. Thus horizontal mergers pose a trade-off problem for competition policy, offering potential benefits on the one hand but also potential losses. Strictly the balance of advantages cannot be assessed *a priori* and must be determined through empirical study.

Vertical mergers between firms at different stages in the same production chain pose a similar policy dilemma. Again, they may permit efficiency gains either in production or via improved information exchange and co-ordination.[1] But they can also raise anti-trust issues, where, for instance, a manufacturer takes over the firm supplying raw material both to himself and to his competitors, and would be able to charge disadvantageous prices to them, or where a manufacturer secures control over the sales outlets for both his own and his competitors' products.

Conglomerate mergers are mergers between firms where there had previously been neither a horizontal nor a vertical link. They have been thought to raise less serious anti-competitive risks but also fewer potential efficiency gains.[2] Thus neither scale economies in production nor gains from improved production scheduling are available, and seller concentration does not increase. However firm-level scale economies may occur, e.g. in raising finance and planning investment. Moreover anti-trust concern has arisen in the USA in conglomerate merger cases in two areas. One is associated with the ability of conglomerate concerns to cross-subsidize activities, which could be used to exclude a competitor in one industry by incurring temporary losses there. The other concerns the practice of 'reciprocal buying' between divisions of a conglomerate organization, which again can be used to weaken competition.[3] Furthermore, conglomerate mergers may represent pursuit of purely managerial objectives, including growth of the firm *per se*, with few benefits to the community, while large economic power-blocs develop with potentially far-reaching socio-political as well as economic consequences.

Wherever there is market power the general concern is that this will have adverse allocative and distributional effects. Price will tend to exceed marginal cost, so distorting the allocation of resources amongst alternative competing uses and reducing consumers' surplus. In addition, supernormal profit will be earned if price also exceeds average cost, so that income is redistributed in favour of producers. It is sometimes also argued that firms with market power will tend to be technically inefficient, costs being higher than they need because the presence of excess profits blunts the desire to seek out and apply cost-minimizing techniques. However, this argument implicitly assumes pursuit of some objective other than profit (e.g. leisure or managerial objectives), maximization of which, unlike profit, does not entail cost-minimization under all market conditions. Moreover, a counter argument has been vigorously put, suggesting a beneficial effect of market power on dynamic efficiency — the rate of innovation of new products and technologies. Thus Schumpeter and Galbraith, in particular, have stressed that the profitability and relative market security under monopoly and oligopoly are important enabling

---

1 See O.E. Williamson, 'The Vertical Integration of Production', *AER*, 1971, and K.J. Arrow, 'Vertical Integration and Communication', *Bell Journal of Economics*, Spring 1975.

2 See K. Cowling *et al.*, op. cit., Chapter 2.

3 See P.O. Steiner, *Mergers: Motives, Effects, Policies*, University of Michigan Press, 1975.

conditions for firms to undertake risky and high-cost R and D expenditures.[1]
Others acknowledge the opportunity which is created but question the incentive to
exploit it, if competition is lacking.[2] Thus far there is little demonstrable proof
either way and the issue remains controversial.

Economists have recently carried out substantive research in two areas relevant
to competition policy: the magnitude of monopoly welfare losses, and the
determinants and effects of mergers. Harberger's original estimate put monopoly
welfare loss in the interwar period in the USA at less than one-tenth of one per
cent of GNP.[3] More recent estimates take into account certain technical issues and
adopt a broader view of the social costs of monopoly, including the costs of
acquiring monopoly positions, existing or potential. These suggest much larger losses:
7-13% of gross corporate product in the USA and 3.7% in Britain.[4] Work in
progress suggests that certain kinds of oligopolistic competition may be expected to
lead to losses equal to about half those under pure monopoly, though as we have
seen other behaviour patterns generate the full monopoly loss.[5] However, those
who defend monopoly on arguments relating to dynamic competition remain
unconvinced,[6] and the controversy continues.

Empirical work on mergers has not been able to identify a single, dominant
motive for merger, which is perhaps not surprising since there are so many possible
reasons why firms might wish to merge. Extensive studies of merger effects
indicate a general absence of observable, post-merger efficiency gains. Thus Meeks[7]
and Hughes and Singh[8] found little evidence of post-merger gains, but, as the latter
point out, the growth and profitability performance of merging firms at least did
not deteriorate after merger. Likewise, case-study evidence by Cowling *et al.*
suggests a post-merger efficiency increase of around three per cent a year but, as
the authors point out, this is about equal to the national average and might have
been expected in any case.[9] The results for the UK are consistent with the general
run of results for other industrialized countries.[10] Thus it appears that mergers are

1 J. Schumpeter, *Capitalism, Socialism and Democracy*, Allen and Unwin, 1943; J.K.
Galbraith, *American Capitalism*, Hamish Hamilton, 1956 (revised edition), Chapter 7. For a
selection of readings in this area see E. Mansfield, *Monopoly Power and Economic
Performance*, Norton, 1968.

2 See, e.g., J. Jewkes, D. Sawers and R. Stillerman, *The Sources of Invention*, Macmillan,
1969.

3 A. Harberger, 'Monopoly and Resource Allocation', *AER*, 1954.

4 K.G. Cowling and D.C. Mueller, 'The Social Costs of Monopoly Power', *EJ*, 1978. Gross
corporate product is the contribution to GDP originating in the firms sampled (734 in the
US case and 102 for the UK).

5 J.R. Cable, A. Carruth and A.K. Dixit, 'Conduct Structure and Relative Welfare Losses in
Quantity-Setting Duopoly', (mimeo) 1982.

6 S.C. Littlechild, 'Misleading Calculations of the Social Costs of Monopoly Power', *EJ*,
1981.

7 G. Meeks, *Disappointing Marriage: A Study of the Gains from Merger*, CUP, 1977.

8 A. Hughes and A. Singh, 'Takeovers in the United Kingdom' in D.C. Mueller (ed.),
Determinants and Effects of Mergers: An International Comparison, Oelgeschlager, Gunn
and Hain, 1980.

9 op. cit.

10 D.C. Mueller (ed.), op. cit.

not a major force making for improved industrial performance. On the other hand there is fairly widespread, though not universal, agreement that they contribute significantly to increased market power, as measured by the extent to which economic activity is concentrated in the hands of relatively few producers. Thus the general conclusion from a substantial number of studies is that at least 50%, and on some estimates a much greater percentage, of the change in concentration in recent decades can be attributed to merger.[1] Moreover, this applies both to *seller concentration* – the concentration of sales in the hands of relatively few sellers in individual industries or markets – and to *aggregate concentration* – the concentration of economic activity in the hands of giant firms in the economy as a whole. The level and recent trends in both types of concentration are discussed further in section IV.3 below.

Consumer protection is in a sense the underlying rationale of policies to control anti-competitive market structures and practices, since the exercise of market power is typically at the expense of the consumers' interests. This aspect apart, economic theory does not place much emphasis on the need for consumer protection.[2] In the textbooks consumers are assumed to have a complete ordering of their preferences for different goods and services based on full information about the characteristics of the commodities and the utility to be gained from consuming them. Consumers then attempt to maximize their utility, faced with their income and market-determined prices. Provided these prices (including the price of labour and hence income) are competitively determined, the theory implies that all is well with the consumer. In practice the consumer is not fully and costlessly informed, and may not be able to judge the utility he will derive from a certain good.[3] He may not, for example, realize that a drug may be unsafe under certain conditions or that food may be too old for use, and he may be faced by confusing packaging or subject to misleading claims by advertisers or retailers. Furthermore, he may not be able to choose how much or how little service he obtains with a good, and his right of redress against suppliers of unsatisfactory goods or services may be either unclear or impractical to exercise via the courts.

There is nothing to guarantee that it is in the manufacturers' best interests for consumers to exercise a totally free and informed choice. It is this potential divergence of interests which creates the need for policy measures.

IV.2   Policy Measures

Policies to promote competition in Britain have been developed in a series of laws begining with the 1948 *Monopolies and Restrictive Practices Act*. In 1973 the *Fair Trading Act* consolidated the existing law and codified and extended legislative safeguards for consumers. It also provided for the appointment of a Director General of Fair Trading, to centralize the application of competition and consumer law; previously this responsibility had been rather widely shared. The

---

1   See Cowling *et al.*, op. cit. Chapter 1.

2   However the economics of information and problems of market equilibrium with imperfectly informed agents are receiving growing attention. For an introductory treatment see, e.g., D. de Meza and M. Osborne, *Problems in Price Theory*, Philip Allan, 1980, and D. Swann, *Competition and Consumer Protection*, Penguin, 1979.

3   For an opposing view see Milton and Rose Friedman, *Free to Choose: A Personal Statement*, Secker and Warburg, 1980.

1973 Act is now the basis of current policy, along with the subsequent *Restrictive Practices* and *Resale Price Maintenance Acts* of 1976 and the 1980 *Competition Act*. In competition policy there are two main strands, embodying different approaches to the control of monopolies and mergers and of restrictive agreements between firms.

Monopolies and mergers which meet certain criteria may be referred for investigation by an independent administrative tribunal, the Monopolies and Mergers Commission (MC). The Commission's task is to determine whether the case in question is or is likely to be detrimental to the public interest, and make recommendations for corrective measures as appropriate. Responsibility for implementing recommendations lies with the appropriate minister; statutory orders may be made, binding the companies concerned, or a settlement reached in the form of voluntary undertakings.

Section 14 of the 1948 Act defined the public interest as 'production . . . by the most efficient and economical means . . . in such volume and at such prices as will best meet the requirements of home and overseas markets' . . .; progressive increases in efficiency and the encouragement of new enterprise; 'the fullest use and best distribution of men, materials and industrial capacity . . .'; and '. . . the development of technical improvements and the expansion of existing markets and the opening up of new markets'. No subsequent attempt has been made to improve on this comprehensive but rather vague formulation. However, it at least allowed the MC wide discretion in evolving practical criteria, as was probably intended.

Monopoly references may be made either by ministers or the Director General. The latter is expected to provide a broader-based view of the state of competition in the economy, and has a responsibility to collect data on market structure and the behaviour of firms on which the MC may draw. An economic information system has now been set up in the Office of Fair Trading for this purpose. Merger references are the prerogative of the Secretary of State, acting on advice from a Merger Panel. The panel screens merger proposals falling within the scope of the law, to determine the economic significance of each case and priorities for investigation.

From 1948 a monopoly could be referred where one firm supplied one third or more of a total market. In 1973 this was reduced to 25%, which from then on could apply to sales in a particular locality, rather than the national market. Cases of 'complex monopoly' – in effect tight oligopolies – were also brought within the scope of the legislation. Mergers which would result in a monopoly were not covered until 1965. Thereafter they became liable either via the monopoly market-share test or if the gross assets involved exceeded a certain value: £5m initially and £15m from 1980.[1] The 1980 *Competition Act* extended monopoly control to certain public-sector bodies. The Act defined these as corporate bodies supplying goods and services whose members are appointed by a minister under legislation, plus public bus services and water undertakings, certain agricultural boards and others. A principal objective was to provide a mechanism for enquiring into the efficiency of nationalized industries.[2] Previously this had been possible via the Price Commission and before that the National Board for Prices and Incomes, in the context of prices and incomes policies. The 1980 Act abolished the Price Commission, but retained a last vestige of price control, authorizing the Secretary

---

1 Special provisions apply in the case of newspaper mergers.
2 See also section III above.

of State to refer 'any price' to the Director General of Fair Trading for investigation.

Restrictive-practice agreements were originally treated in the same way as monopolies, and occupied the MC almost entirely in its first years after 1948. In 1956 a separate procedure was introduced. Agreements under which there were restrictions relating to the price of goods, conditions of supply, quantities or descriptions, processes or areas and persons supplied, were presumed illegal unless the parties could establish a case for exemption before a specially-constituted Restrictive Practices Court. A register of agreements was set up, and a Registrar was appointed to bring cases to the Court. This has the status of a High Court and consists of five judges and ten lay members.

The basic procedure still applies, though the definitive law is now the 1976 *Restrictive Practices Act*,[1] which consolidated previous legislation, and the role of the Registrar has been taken over by the Director General of Fair Trading. To be exempted, the agreement must pass through one or more of eight escape clauses or 'gateways' in section 10 of the 1976 Act.[2] Thus, paraphrasing the legislation slightly, it must be shown that the agreement is necessary:

(a)   to protect the public against injury; or

(b)   because its removal would deny to the public 'specific and substantial' benefits; or

(c)   to counteract measures taken by others to restrict competition; or

(d)   to enable the parties to negotiate 'fair terms' with others; or

(e)   because its removal would have 'serious and persistent' adverse effects on unemployment; or

(f)   because its removal would cause a 'substantial' reduction in exports; or

(g)   to maintain another agreement, accepted by the Court as not contrary to the public interest on other grounds;

or, finally, it may be shown that, while not necessary, the agreement

(h)   does not restrict or discourage competition to any material degree.

This last gateway was framed with 'information agreements' particularly in mind. Here no restrictions are accepted, but information concerning prices and so forth is exchanged. Information agreements were not covered by the legislation from the outset but were brought within its scope from 1968 onwards. Otherwise, it is gateway (b) which has been most frequently argued in cases which came to court, either alone or in conjunction with other clauses. If an agreement passes through one or more of the gateways there remains a further obstacle; the so-called 'tailpiece' requires the Court to be satisfied that, on balance, benefits to the public outweigh detriments.

Originally the restrictive-practice legislation applied only to the supply of goods, but was extended to services in 1976. There is a time limit for the registration of agreements, with penalties for non-registration, and interim orders may be made while a final decision is being made. The minister may exempt certain agreements which he deems to be in the national interest or intended to hold down prices.

---

1   A further Restrictive Practices Act was introduced in 1977 to exempt agreements involving restrictions accepted in loan-finance agreements that were caught by the extension of the legislation to cover services.

2   Section 10 refers to goods. Identical provisions are set out in section 19 for agreements relating to services.

'Resale price maintenance' is a particular type of restrictive practice which is now dealt with by the separate Resale Prices Act of 1976. Prior to 1964, when individual RPM was first controlled,[1] it was a common manufacturers' practice to specify actual prices at which their product should be retailed, with sanctions for non-compliance. Procedure for controlling resale price maintenance is very similar in form to that for restrictive practices in general, involving a general prohibition and 'escape clauses'. Although resale price maintenance remains in a few trades, for instance in the supply of books, it has in many cases been superseded by the device of 'recommended' retail prices, which are in effect maximum prices. This device has been investigated by the MC which concluded that it operated with different effects in different industries, not always contrary to the public interest.

The 1973 *Fair Trading Act* also empowers the MC to investigate uncompetitive practices in monopoly situations. The 1980 *Competition Act* added a further provision for control of anti-competitive practices. These may now be subject to a preliminary investigation by the Director General of Fair Trading, and subsequently referred to the MC if satisfactory undertakings are not forthcoming after the preliminary report.

Finally, as a member of the EEC Britain is covered by the regulations dealing with monopolies, mergers and restrictive practices in articles 85 and 86 of the Treaty of Rome.[2] The European Commission is the body responsible for applying the policies and investigating breaches in them.

The most fully developed parts of the regulations are those relating to restrictive practices. These prohibit all agreements, such as price-fixing and market-sharing, which prevent, restrict or distort competition in the EEC and extend over more than one member country. As in the UK, however, exemption may be gained via a 'gateway' if the agreement improves production or distribution or promotes progress. There is also provision for block exemptions.

EEC monopoly regulations are less clear-cut since, although any abuse of dominant position within the EEC is prohibited if it affects trade between member countries, it is not clear as yet what sort of market-share criterion constitutes dominance, or what abuses will be covered by the regulations. EEC case-law on monopoly is virtually non-existent as yet. Even less clear up to 1971 was the position of mergers. Until the case of Continental Can (an American firm) in that year, it was unsettled whether Articles 85 and 86 could be applied to merger cases. Although this particular merger was allowed on appeal to the European Court of Justice, the implicit extension of the legislation to mergers was accepted. Since then a proposed regulation concerning mergers has been approved by the European Parliament. As originally proposed, it would prohibit mergers involving firms above a specified size or market share, with provision for exemption in special circumstances, and compulsory advance clarification for very large mergers.[3]

---

1 Collective RPM (i.e. RPM maintained by the sanction of a group of firms witholding supplies) was prohibited by the 1956 Restrictive Practices Act.

2 For a useful summary of the Community's competition policy see D.W. McKenzie, 'Fair Competition in the EEC', *TI*, 13 December 1973. See also D. Swann, op. cit., pp. 55-68 and 159-75, and K.D. George and C. Joll, 'EEC Competition Policy', *TBR*, March 1978.

3 For a discussion of the regulation see Kurt Markert, 'EEC Competition Policy in Relation to Mergers', *Antitrust Bulletin*, Vol. XX, No. 1, Spring 1975.

However there was very slow progress towards its implementation and late in 1981 the European Commission submitted an amendment to its original, 1973 proposal with a view to reopening discussions. The amended proposal restricts control more closely to mergers with a Community dimension and involves member states more closely in the decision-making process.

The concept of overall government responsibility for consumer protection (as opposed to piecemeal responsibility) is relatively recent. Under the 1973 Act the Director General of Fair Trading was again assigned a key position. He has a duty to collect and assess information about commercial activities, in order to seek out trading practices which may affect consumers' economic interests. If he finds areas in which there is cause for concern, he then has two options. The Director General may either make recommendations to the relevant minister as to action which might be useful in altering the malpractice, whether it concerns consumers' economic interest or their health, safety and so on. Or, presumably where more severe action is demanded, he may set in motion a procedure which could lead to the banning of a particular trade practice. To do this he makes a 'reference' along with proposals for action to the Consumer Protection Advisory Committee (CPAC), which considers whether his proposals are justified and whether the practice is covered by the legislation. After taking evidence from interested parties, this body reports to the relevant minister, who may then make an Order, subject to the agreement of Parliament.

Another of the Director General's main functions in the area of consumer protection is to make sure that those who are persistently careless of their existing legal obligations to consumers mend their ways, either by his seeking a written assurance or, failing this, in the courts. Lastly, the Director General has obligations to pursue an informal dialogue with industry; to publish information and advice for consumers; and to encourage trade associations to use voluntary codes of practice to protect consumers.

IV.3   Policy Appraisal

Competition policy in Britain has now undergone over thirty years of development, with modifications to remedy shortcomings and fill in gaps in earlier Acts. In the last ten years it has been considerably extended in scope, with accompanying administrative reforms. In principle a comprehensive battery of investigative powers now exists. The underlying principle is one of case-by-case review, judging each case on its effects on the public interest. This has the advantage of flexibility and being able to take account of any positive effects there might be from restrictions on competition. But the procedure can be cumbersome, slow and costly; for example each MC investigation takes months and some have taken years. Thus it is difficult to process large numbers of cases unless large-scale resources are committed, which they are not. Thus if the number of potential cases is large, policy can have relatively little quantitative impact, unless each decided case has big deterrent effects.

The alternative would be to proscribe certain situations and behaviour – e.g. 'monopoly' and 'monopolization' – *per se*, without reference to their effects in individual cases. This approach, which is adopted in the USA, rides roughshod over arguments in defence of monopoly. On the other hand it is more straightforward and 'justiciable'. That is, it requires courts to do what they are best suited for: to find on the question of fact whether an infringement has occurred and if so apply the penalties as laid down by law. It also results in policy being relatively removed from the political arena. By contrast in Britain, since responsibility for implementing recommendations lies with the minister (except in individual restrictive practice cases), policy is subject to influence by the government of the day.

By the end of 1980 the MC had reported on nearly forty monopoly supply situations,[1] covering such diverse products as beer, breakfast cereals, fertilizers, cigarettes, colour film, soap and detergents, contraceptives, wallpaper, building bricks and tampons, and a wide range of services, including those supplied by architects, barristers and solicitors, veterinary surgeons, stockbrokers, surveyors, the cross channel ferries and credit-card companies. Recent reports involving public-sector undertakings include those on commuter services in London and the South East (British Rail), domestic gas appliances (British Gas), the Central Electricity Generating Board and the Severn–Trent Water Authority.

The number of monopoly reports is small, though the rate of referral and reporting did increase in the 1970s; two-thirds of all the reports were made in the period from 1973. In the past there have been reservations about both the quality of the MC's analysis and the government's unaggressive approach in applying remedial measures, relying very heavily on informal undertakings.[2] Again, there has more recently been some sign of stronger action, e.g. in the case of the drug manufacturers Hoffman–La Roche, which ultimately went on appeal to the House of Lords.[3] Nevertheless, it is questionable how far this strand of policy has yet had far-reaching effects on the firms actually investigated or any strong deterrent effect on behaviour elsewhere.

Effective merger control may be the best safeguard against monopoly, insofar as it is easier to stop monopoly situations in the making than to break them up or control their behaviour once established. The indictment of UK policy here is that no merger controls at all existed until 1965, seventeen years after the first legislation, during which time seller-concentration increased substantially, as we shall see in a moment. Since 1965 a great many proposed mergers have been screened, but only a small proportion have been referred to the MC. Thus between November 1973 (when the Fair Trading Act came into force) and the end of 1980 over 1,300 merger cases were screened, of which only 33 were referred. Of these, very few proposals were stopped but several more allowed to proceed only after certain assurances had been given. Again, in purely numerical terms the impact of policy can hardly be said to have been widespread. When a government review body was set up in 1977 to consider the effectiveness of competition policy, it was widely anticipated that the onus of proof would be shifted in merger cases, forcing the companies to demonstrate positive benefits. In the event this did not happen.[4] Had it occurred, there is little doubt merger activity would have been greatly reduced.

1 The authoritative sources on all aspects of competition policy and consumer protection activity are the *Annual Reports of the Director General of Fair Trading*, HMSO.

2 See C.K. Rowley, *The British Monopolies Commission*, Allen and Unwin, 1966 and A. Sutherland, *The Monopolies Commission in Action*, CUP, 1970.

3 Monopolies Commission, *Chlordiazepoxide and Diazepam*, HC 197, 1973.

4 See the Green Papers, *A Review of Monopolies and Mergers Policy*, Cmnd. 7198, May 1978, and *A Review of Restrictive Trade Practices Policy*, Cmnd. 7512, March 1979. The 1980 Competition Act implemented other recommendations of the review body.

Table 4.13 records the actual merger rate in the 1970s,[1] giving an indication both of the general level of activity (the Business Monitor M7 series) and of the incidence of mergers within the scope of the Act. On average these accounted for just under 20% of the total (considering industrial and commercial mergers only), but as the table shows the new £15m criterion would have more than halved the number of mergers falling within the scope of the legislation between 1978 and 1980. The general level of merger activity is subject to considerable fluctuation, with the last major merger boom in 1972-3. In the period since 1965 there has been little sign of secular decrease in merger activity that might be attributed to policy. The proportion of conglomerate mergers has increased markedly in recent years (table 4.14) but this is as likely to reflect reduced opportunities for horizontal mergers (so many firms having been taken over already) as any influence of policy.

TABLE 4.13

Merger Activity, 1970-80

| | Proposals covered by Fair Trading Act | | | Business Monitor M7 |
| | All cases | | Industrial and commercial | Industrial & commercial |
	Number	£m assets acquired	Number	Number
1970	80	2,597	72	793
1971	110	1,687	95	884
1972	114	3,588	95	1,210
1973	134	4,878	114	1,205
1974	141	7,621	85	504
1975	160	5,786	116	315
1976	163	4,123	133	353
1977	194	4,675	155	481
1978	299 (103)	11,999 (10,973)	202 (89)	567
1979	257 (131)	13,140 (12,091)	220 (106)	534
1980	182 (140)	22,289 (21,964)	141 (107)	468

Figures in brackets show the outcome if a £15m assets criterion had been in operation throughout 1978, 1979 and 1980.

Source: Office of Fair Trading and Department of Industry's Business Monitor M7.

Whatever impact monopoly and merger policy may have had in individual cases, it has not prevented a strong trend towards increased seller concentration both in individual markets and at the aggregate level (though it is true that this trend has decelerated since about 1968). Concentration can be measured in several ways, of which the simplest and most commonly used is the 'concentration ratio': the combined market share of, e.g., the top five firms (CR_5).[2] Trends in the growth

---

1 See also K. Cowling *et al.*, op. cit.; A. Hughes and A. Singh, op. cit.; and G. Meeks, op. cit.

2 The measurement issue is somewhat controversial. See L. Hannah and J. Kay, *Concentration in Modern Industry*, London, 1977, Chapter 4 and P.E. Hart and R. Clarke, *Concentration in British Industry 1935-75*, CUP for NIESR, 1980, Appendix 1A.

TABLE 4.14

Percentage of Proposed Mergers by Number and Value of Assets Acquired, Classified by Type of Integration, 1965-80

	Horizontal		Vertical		Diversified	
	By no.	*By assets*	*By no.*	*By assets*	*By no.*	*By assets*
1965-9	82	89	6	5	12	7
1970-74	73	65	5	4	23	27
1975	71	77	5	4	24	19
1976	70	66	8	7	22	27
1977	64	57	11	11	25	32
1978	53 (58)	67 (69)	13 (12)	10 (9)	34 (30)	23 (21)
1979	51 (54)	68 (70)	7 (8)	4 (4)	42 (38)	28 (27)
1980	65 (66)	68 (68)	4 (4)	1 (1)	31 (30)	31 (31)

Figures in brackets show the outcome if a £15m assets criterion had been in operation throughout 1978, 1979 and 1980.

Source: Office of Fair Trading.

of concentration are clearly very relevant in appraising competition policy and have been widely studied.

Two recent studies analyse developments since the interwar period.[1] Hannah and Kay focus on the period 1919-76.[2] Changes in concentration were divided into two component parts: due to merger between firms, and due to internal growth within firms. Two merger booms were identified, one in the 1920s and one in the 1960s. The former, reinforced by internal growth as firms benefited from increasing returns to scale at the plant level, produced a 'spectacularly large' increase in concentration 'broadly equivalent in its effect on market structure to that of two thirds of all firms being eliminated from the manufacturing sector'. It was during this period that some of today's giant firms, such as ICI and Unilever, were born. Mergers continued to occur over the next three decades but were offset by the internal growth of small and medium-sized firms, so that concentration actually fell during this time. Large firms, on the whole, failed to maintain their high rates of internal growth, probably reflecting the fact that the minimum point on their long-run average-cost curves had been reached. This continued offsetting influence also meant that the net impact of the merger boom in the late 1960s was not as great as the earlier boom.

Hart and Clarke report a slow rise in concentration from 1935 to 1958 followed by a considerable acceleration in the next ten years, after which there was little further increase up to the early 1970s.[3] Thus the three-firm concentration ratio at MLH level rose from 26% in 1935 to 32% in 1958 and 41% in 1968, but then increased by only about one percentage point up to 1973. Within this overall

1 Other studies include R. Evely and I.M.D. Little, *Concentration in British Industry*, CUP, 1960; W.G. Shepherd, 'Changes in British Industrial Concentration 1951-8', *OEP*, 1966; K.D. George, 'Changes in British Industrial Concentration 1957-58', *JIE*, July 1967; P.E. Hart, M.A. Utton and G. Walshe, *Mergers and Concentration in British Industry*, CUP for the NIESR, 1973; and G. Walshe, *Recent Trends in Monopoly in Great Britain*, CUP, 1974.

2 L. Hannah and J. Kay, op. cit.

3 P.E. Hart and R. Clarke, op. cit.

average there were considerable differences between industries, and moreover individual industries tended not to show rapid increases over the whole period. More disaggregated data, at product group level (closer to the economist's notion of a market than the broader MLH industries), confirm the rapid increase in the 1960s and subsequent slowing down. Thus the average CR_5 rose from 55.4% in 1958 to 63.4% in 1968, but then only 65.1% in 1975.

There is no doubt that concentration has risen markedly in the UK and now stands at a high level. The latest published statistics at both MLH and product group level are for 1977. Table 4.15 gives a frequency distribution by class of concentration for 162 MLH industries and 817 product groups respectively. Amongst other things this underlines how the broader MLH data understate the true level of seller concentration at market level; thus in over half the product groups CR_5 exceeded 70%, compared with just under 30% of MLH industries. Note that in nearly one in six product groups, five firms controlled 90% of the market or more. Overall, the statistics strongly suggest that oligopoly is the prevailing market structure.

TABLE 4.15

Seller Concentration, Selected UK Markets, 1977

| Concentration class (range of five-firm concentration ratio, %) | Number of markets in class | | | |
| | Product group basis[2] | | MLH basis | |
	No.[1]	%	No.	%
0-9	0	0.0	0	0.0
10-19	6	0.7	6	3.7
20-29	25	3.0	15	9.3
30-39	37	4.5	21	13.0
40-49	102	12.5	34	21.0
50-59	101	12.4	22	13.6
60-69	124	15.2	16	9.9
70-79	145	17.7	15	9.3
80-89	140	17.1	18	11.1
90-100	137	16.8	15	9.3
Total	817	100.0	162	100.0

Source: Business Monitor (PO 1006). Statistics of Product Concentration of UK Manufacturing.

Notes: 1 The meaning of this column is that there is no product group in which the largest five firms account for less than 10% of total sales, six in which they account for 10-19%, and so on.

2 The markets included are sub-Minimum List Heading product groups in mining and manufacturing, for which five-firm concentration ratios are available.

Earlier (1963) data suggested the UK level of market concentration is much higher than in France and Italy, and much the same as in Belgium and the Netherlands.[1] Strictly comparable data for West Germany is not available, but the

---

1 See M.C. Sawyer, 'Concentration in British Manufacturing Industry' *OEP*, November 1971, and Louis Phlips, *Effects of Industrial Concentration, A Cross Section Analysis for the Common Market*, North Holland, 1971.

data which does exist suggests a pattern similar to that in the UK (cf. the last two columns of tables 4.16 and 4.15).

Alongside the trend towards a higher degree of seller concentration in individual markets there has been a similar, accelerating increase in overall concentration, as measured by the share in net output of the 100 largest firms in the economy. Before World War I this was less than 20%, rising to 33% in 1958. Over the next twelve years the rate of increase roughly trebled, and in 1970 the largest 100 firms accounted for nearly 50% of net output.[1] The precise connection between overall concentration and seller concentration in individual markets is not well documented. But of the largest 100 manufacturing companies between 1968 and 1974 approximately half were known to have two or more 'monopolies' (25% shares in particular markets) and, of these, twenty companies had five or more monopolies.[2] Of course, the emergence of giant corporations in the economy may be seen to have broad socio-political implications, over and above any monopolistic tendencies in individual markets.[3]

TABLE 4.16

Seller Concentration in West Germany, 1977

Concentration class (range of concentration ratio, %)	Three-firm CR		Six-firm CR	
	No. of industries	%	No. of industries	%
0-9	13	8.2	5	3.8
10-29	58	36.9	29	22.1
30-59	57	36.3	55	42.0
60-100	29	18.5	42	32.1
Total	157	100.0	131	100.0

Source: Monopolkommission, Hauptgutachten III, 1978/79 *Fusionskontrolle bleibt vorrangig*, Nomos Verlagsgesellschaft, Baden-Baden, 1980.

Superficially, restrictive-practice control appears more successful. By the end of 1980 there were 4,468 registered agreements (including 495 relating to services) of which 3,295 had been abandoned (84 relating to services). Not all these cases were heard by the Court; since 1956 only 658 goods agreements have been referred. Most abandoned agreements were either terminated voluntarily after the results of key cases became known, or simply left to expire. Undoubtedly, a great mass of overt price-fixing that had existed before 1956 no longer exists, and by the mid-1970s the DGFT was able to say that no more significant known cases remained to be dealt with (though this was before the extension of the legislation to cover service agreements).

However this is not necessarily conclusive evidence of success. Firstly, both the escape clauses in the 1956 Act and the quality of the Court's reasoning and

---

1 S.J. Prais, *The Evolution of Giant Firms in Great Britain: A Study of Concentration in Manufacturing Industry in Britain 1909-70*, CUP, 1976.

2 J.D. Gribbin, 'The Conglomerate Merger', *Applied Economics*, 1976, 8, pp. 19-35.

3 See Cowling *et al.*, op. cit., Chapter 2.

decisions have been adversely criticized. Indeed, doubts have been expressed over the suitability of judicial practices for resolving complex economic issues.[1] Secondly, it is questionable how far the abandonment of restrictive practices has actually affected behaviour in the markets concerned. As we have seen, cartel arrangements are most likely in fairly concentrated, oligopolistic markets, where they may merely formalize the mutually accommodating behaviour which would in any case occur. Removal of an agreement in these circumstances would not touch the underlying, structural cause of this behaviour. Moreover where restrictive agreements have been abandoned, firms may have been able to substitute alternative arrangements. The extension of the law to embrace information agreements in 1968 was in response to such a development. It is also possible that the introduction of restrictive-practice control in 1956 may have intensified merger activity. Very few studies have been undertaken into the consequences of restrictive-practice abandonment[2]; it would be a useful extension of present policy to require the MC to undertake such follow-up studies.

On the consumer protection side, a number of references have been made to the CPAC. By the end of 1980 eighteen voluntary codes of practice had been introduced covering, amongst others, package holidays, new and used car sales, shoe sales and repairs, funeral services, mail-order trading, laundering and dry-cleaning. Various other practices have been investigated, including advertising, bargain-offer claims, party-plan and door-to-door selling, as has the conduct of a large number of individual firms. The 1968 Trades Description Act has been reviewed, and the 1974 Consumer Credit Act implemented (under which the OFT is responsible for licensing traders). A working party on advertising reported in 1980, and a wide range of leaflets has been published containing various kinds of consumer information.

The variety and detail of the consumer protection activities undertaken since 1973 is in some ways impressive. As expected, the overwhelming emphasis has been on voluntary solutions: negotiated codes, assurances and the like. The advantages of this approach, its flexibility, cost-effectiveness and constructiveness, are heavily stressed by the Director General of Fair Trading in his *Annual Reports*. Its main drawback is perhaps that voluntary co-operation is most likely to be forthcoming and effective where it is least needed.

V   REGIONAL POLICY
V.1   Rationale

Regional policies seek to reduce or eliminate disparities between different geographical areas in incomes, industrial growth, migration and, above all, unemployment. If markets operated in a smooth frictionless fashion, it might be argued that there is no need for such policies, since the disparities would be self-eliminating. Thus the argument would be, for example, that regional unemployment indicates a labour-market disequilibrium with excess supply of labour at the ruling wage levels, to which the ultimate corrective mechanism is lower real wages and product prices. In practice, however, there are market frictions and such disequilibria have certainly proved themselves non-self-curing in the past. This no

---

1 See, e.g., R.B. Stevens and B.S. Yamey, *The Restrictive Practices Court*, Weidenfeld and Nicholson, 1965, and D. Swann *et al.*, *Restrictive Practice Legislation in Theory and Practice*, Allen and Unwin, 1974.

2 For an early example see J.B. Heath, 'Restrictive Practices and After', *MS*, 1961.

doubt reflects both downward rigidities in nationally determined wages and prices, as well as the immobility of capital and especially of labour, the latter on account of such factors as rehousing problems, imperfect knowledge of job opportunities elsewhere, and social ties.

Moreover, even with frictionless markets, government intervention would be justified if private and social costs and benefits diverge. Thus a firm might choose a location in the south-east of England on the basis of the costs actually entering its accounts. But the socially optimal location could be elsewhere, e.g. in Wales, Scotland or the North, when account is taken of social costs such as traffic congestion, the availability of social overheads like schools, hospitals etc, as well as less tangible benefits such as the preservation of existing community life in areas which might otherwise become depopulated.

If the firm's production costs are higher at the socially optimal location there is a real resource cost in diverting it there and a subsidy may be required. However, welfare is raised and policy intervention remains justified as long as the benefits exceed the costs. In practice, UK policy has been based on a premise that location does not significantly affect costs, at least for much of manufacturing, and there is some evidence to support this. Thus, one study estimated that some 70% of manufacturing is 'footloose', i.e. not critically affected by costs at different locations.[1] Another writer suggested that some two-thirds of manufacturing is probably footloose with respect to transport costs, which are obviously an important consideration in this context and have always received much attention in location theory.[2] A third, very comprehensive study found little evidence of continuing excess costs in plants which had moved in relation to the levels in parent or original plants, although it could take five years for initial excess costs to disappear.[3] Thus it appears that a serious efficiency loss would not be inevitable if at least a good deal of manufacturing industry were relocated, though there could obviously be specific exceptions.

The regional imbalances which policy seeks to redress originate from complex geographical, technological and historical causes. In the UK case, a major influence on the character of the regional problem since the mid-1950s has been falling employment in agriculture and the decline of the former staple industries, especially coal, cotton-textiles, steel and shipbuilding. In the earlier phases of industrialization in Britain these had located close to sources of power and raw materials in the North, Scotland and Wales. More modern industries, particularly those using electrical power, have developed elsewhere. Thus structural developments in the economy create tendencies for centres of economic activity to shift, while demographic developments remain largely shaped by the past. It is against these tendencies that regional policies must pull. For example, it has been estimated that there has been a cumulative shortfall of one million jobs over the last fifteen years in Northern Ireland, Scotland, the north-west and the north of England, relative to developments in the UK as a whole, despite the 350,000 jobs shifted to these areas via regional policies.[4] However, the UK regions[5] are nearly

---

1   R.J. Nicholson, 'The Regional Location of Industry', *EJ*, 1956. But see A.J. Brown, *The Framework of Regional Economics in the UK*, CUP, 1972, on the reliability of this result.

2   L. Needleman, 'What Are We To Do About The Regional Problem?', *LBR*, January 1965.

3   W.F. Luttrell, *Factory Location and Industrial Movement*, NIESR, London, 1952.

4   See *Cambridge Economic Policy Review*, Vol. 6, No. 2, July 1980, p. 36.

5   The standard regions of the UK are: Northern; Yorkshire and Humberside; E. Midlands; E. Anglia; S. East; S. West; Wales; W. Midlands; N. West; Scotland; and N. Ireland.

all mixed urban-rural areas with a fair spread of activities, and the imbalance between them is not as severe as in some other countries, e.g. Italy.

Until recently UK regional policy has not sought to address the problem of declining employment and population in inner cities. Indeed the exodus to the suburbs and new towns has been encouraged by both central and local government, in the course of policies designed to relieve congestion and assist urban renewal in large conurbations.[1] However, the existence of serious problems in inner cities is now recognized and this is reflected in recent regional policy developments, especially concerning the creation of 'Enterprise Zones'.

Like Britain, the EEC also has a number of regional problems in older industrial areas developed around iron-ore and coal. These include the Ruhr, Saar and Lorraine. However a further, serious EEC regional problem stems from the existence of low-income agricultural areas to which industrialization has never come. Originally these were mainly in parts of France and, especially, the south of Italy (where gross value added was under half the national average in 1978 and little more than a quarter of that in Hamburg, the richest part of the EEC).[2] With the expansion of the Community this aspect of the EEC regional problem has been intensified by the addition of the Irish Republic and Greece. The flourishing industrial centres of the EEC outside Britain, on the other hand, lie mainly along the Rhine-Rhône valleys, from the Netherlands to northern Italy. These are estimated to have accounted for some 60% of the Gross Product of the EEC before its enlargement in 1973. Some commentators now speak of a 'golden triangle' in Europe, lying roughly between Hamburg, London and Milan.

V.2   Policy Measures

The strategy underlying UK regional policy has been to identify specific areas requiring assistance, primarily on the basis of above-average unemployment rates. Firms located in or moving to these areas have then been offered various financial incentives, while administrative controls have been placed on industrial expansion elsewhere. Both the qualifying areas and the type and value of financial incentives have been changed frequently in the last twenty years, and the degree of control on industrial development outside the assisted areas has also fluctuated. Policy measures were first introduced in the prewar Special Areas Act of 1934. Postwar policy has been implemented through the Distribution of Industry Acts since 1945, the Local Employment Acts from 1960, the 1972 Industry Act, and various Finance Acts.

Regional policies now distinguish four main types of area for special treatment. First there are the rather broad *Development Areas*, each covering the whole or most of one of the standard regions of the UK. These have existed in their present

---

1 For example, under the 1946 New Towns Act and the 1952 Town Development Act more than twenty New Towns have been established and rather more enlarged. This policy may have conflicted with regional policies, since the New Towns have by no means all been in Development Areas, and may have been a counter-attraction to firms which otherwise might have responded to regional incentives.

2 *Regional Trends*, 1982.

form since 1966 (though with some boundary changes)[1]. *Special Development Areas* are smaller districts within Development Areas. They were first created in 1967 to deal with problems caused by colliery closures, but the concept was later broadened to include other areas. *Intermediate Areas* date from 1969, and are the so-called 'grey areas' lying outside Development Areas, but suffering problems similar in kind if not in acuteness, and likely to decline relative to areas which either had natural advantages or were already receiving assistance. *Enterprise Zones* were introduced in 1980. These are very small districts (averaging only around 500 acres) intended to help solve problems of economic and physical decay, primarily in older urban areas.[2]

The geographical boundaries of the 'areas for expansion' at the time of writing are as follows.[3] There are ten Special Development Areas in Great Britain. The largest is in Scotland, centred on Glasgow and taking in Dunbarton, Renfrewshire and parts of Ayrshire and Lanarkshire. Two other Scottish SDAs lie to the north and south of the Firth of Tay. England has three SDAs: the industrial area of the North East from Newcastle down to Hartlepool; Greater Merseyside; and the Falmouth-Camborne area of Cornwall. The four Welsh SDAs are Anglesey; East Flintshire (adjoining the Merseyside SDA); and two areas of South Wales in the mining valleys to the north and west of Cardiff. The Glenrothes, Livingston and Skelmersdale New Towns also offer SDA benefits. Development and Intermediate Areas mostly adjoin SDAs, generally forming large blocs. Together they cover the whole of N.W. Central and S.W. Scotland; the N.E. coast of England and its hinterland; the coastal part of Lancashire and all of N. Wales; S. Wales apart from the Carmarthen area; all of Cornwall and much of Devon. Development or Intermediate Areas are also found around Corby; in E. Lincolnshire; on Humberside; in parts of East and West Yorkshire; and West Cumberland. Northern Ireland is treated as an additional, special case. Finally, a total of eleven enterprise zones are now operating in Belfast, Clydebank, Corby, Dudley, Hartlepool, the Isle of Dogs (London), the Lower Swansea Valley, Newcastle/Gateshead, Salford/Trafford, Speke and Wakefield.

The regional aid presently on offer takes the form of Regional Development Grants (RDGs) and Regional Selective Assistance (RSA). RDGs cover 22% of the cost of new buildings, works, plant and machinery in SDAs and 15% in DAs. RSA is usually in the form of a further, discretionary grant towards capital and training costs for projects meeting job-creating criteria. Also available are exchange-loss guarantees for certain EEC loans and rent subsidies on government-provided workshops and advance factories. Higher levels of support are given in Northern Ireland, including Industrial Development Grants of 30-50% of fixed investment costs, rent-free factories, 40-50% R and D grants and other forms of assistance.

---

1 Development Areas were first created in 1945. From 1960 to 1966 policy had been geared to a larger number of smaller Development Districts, based on employment exchange boundaries.

2 A fifth type of area, the North Midlands 'Derelict Land Clearance Area', received certain subsidies to encourage the modernization and construction of industrial buildings from 1972 to 1974.

3 Regional aid provisions are prone to frequent change. The details given describe the system taking effect from August 1982, after implementation of the policy changes announced in 1979. See Department of Industry, *Incentives for Industry in the Areas for Expansion*, November 1981, and *Guide to Regional Industry Policy Changes*, July 1979-August 1982.

Administrative control over industrial expansion outside the assisted areas has been exercised mainly via *Industrial Development Certificates* (IDCs) relating to new factory buildings or extensions. Up to 1972 they were required in *all* areas for projects above a certain minimum size, and after 1966 their issue was strictly controlled in the Midlands and South East. From 1972 IDCs have not been required in Development Areas, and since 1974 a three-tier system has applied to the rest of the country although, in the recession which followed, IDC control has apparently not been applied strictly. Office development has been subject to a similar control. This began in London in 1964, and was later extended to certain other areas, although it subsequently lapsed in some. However, the control of office development has never been regarded as a major policy instrument for dispersing jobs to the regions, and has tended to operate more with regard to intra-regional considerations.

Special provisions apply to new and existing firms within Enterprise Zones. These reflect the (Conservative) philosophy underlying their creation: the belief that private initiatives can be stifled by excessive public-authority involvement and government rules and regulations.[1] Therefore in addition to financial benefits (100% capital allowances and exemption from both general rates on industrial and commercial property and development land tax), firms are intended to benefit from simplified government procedures and speedier administration of controls over development. In particular, firms are promised simpler planning proposals (subject to the adequate protection of health, safety and the control of pollution); exclusion from the scope of Industrial Training Boards; speedier processing of requests for customs, warehousing, etc; minimal requests to supply statistics to government, and abolition of any remaining requirements for IDCs.

Regional policy is currently being pursued much less vigorously than at certain periods in the recent past. This is partly due to the fact that, in a general recession, IDC controls are not being strictly enforced. However, it also reflects deliberate government policy, announced in 1979, to reduce both the value of regional incentives and their availability by raising the qualifying minimum-expenditure levels and reducing the qualifying areas. The plans put forward were intended to cut total regional expenditure from £609m in 1979 to £376m in 1983, and the fraction of the workforce in the qualifying areas from over 40% to 25%.[2] Even before this reduction was announced, the intensity of regional policy had declined from the much higher levels registered from the mid-1960s to the mid-1970s. Table 4.17 illustrates the varying force of regional policy over the last two decades.

Since 1973 Britain has also been covered by EEC regional measures. Up to 1969 there had been little cohesive action on regional problems within the Community, and even some competition among member states to attract foreign investment to their own problem areas. Then a memorandum of that year from the European Commission led, after much debate and postponement, to the setting up of a Regional Development Fund in 1975. This operates on a quota basis, and up to 1981 Britain had received 1.3bn ECU, some 23.8% of the total 5.3bn ECU disbursed, a share second in size only to Italy's 2.1bn ECU (40.0%).[3] However,

---

1 See the Budget speech of the Chancellor of the Exchequer, *Hansard*, 26 March 1980.
2 See the announcement by the Secretary of State for Industry, *Hansard*, 17 July 1979.
3 ECU (European Currency Units) have replaced European Units of Accounts in EEC publications since the European Monetary System was introduced. In 1980 £1 = 1.67 ECU.

TABLE 4.17

Regional Expenditure and IDC Refusals, 1960-80

Financial year	Total government spending on regional policy in real terms (£m, 1975/6 prices)	IDC refusals[1] (%)
1960/61	34	17
1964/5	75	26
1969/70	612	16
1972/3	493	10
1975/6	611	12
1979/80	322	2

Source: Cambridge Economic Policy Review, Vol. 6, No. 2, July 1980, p. 1.

Note: 1 Refusals of permission for industrial developments in the Midlands and South.

this has not resulted in assistance to firms over and above that previously discussed, since receipts from the Fund go to the government rather than to the promoters of individual projects. In principle the EEC funds are intended to be additional to government spending in the regions, but in 1980 there was some dispute between Britain and the European Commission as to whether this had actually been the case.

Latest developments in EEC regional policy shift the emphasis somewhat away from the quota system and the Regional Development Fund, and incidentally make it more difficult for national governments merely to substitute European for domestic finance of existing regional programmes.[1] The moves reflect concern that regional disparities within the Community have widened over the last ten years, and seek to focus policy more sharply on the most serious problems. The current policy guidelines also emphasize the need to knit regional policy and other Community programmes more closely together. This applies particularly to loans for the rationalization of coal and steel production under article 56 of the European Coal and Steel Community Treaty (from which Britain has benefited most)[2] and agricultural support under the CAP. As we have seen, the regional problems within the Community centre on these industries, which makes the policies potentially powerful instruments to correct regional imbalances. However, this has not always happened in the past, and indeed it has been found, for example, that farmers in the more prosperous areas have benefited most from the CAP.

Under the remodelled policy, studies are to be carried out into the regional impact of all major Community programmes. The intention is to make regional considerations figure more prominently in their design; thus, for example, we may expect pressure in the future for the CAP to give more help to the Mediterranean regions. Secondly, a 'non-quota' section of Community regional policy was set up in 1979, within the quota-based regional fund. The non-quota section will provide finance for specific measures proposed by member governments to deal with particular problems, and negotiated with the Commission. This will give added flexibility in directing funds towards the most pressing problems though, for the time being at least, the non-quota section will account for only 5% of total

1 See the 13th, 14th and 15th *General Reports* of the European Community.

2 Though a member of the EEC since only 1973, Britain has received some 40.7% of the 1.521m ECU in loans under article 56 between 1961 and 1981.

Community regional expenditure.[1] A side-effect will be to give the Commission
more influence over the type of regional measures employed, which hitherto have
been a matter of fairly wide discretion for national governments. It is too early to
say how Britain will be affected by the new system in the longer term. The first
five non-quota section schemes were approved in 1981, and included a joint
proposal by Ireland and the UK for development in the border areas of Ireland and
Northern Ireland. However this involved expenditure of only 3.69m ECU out of a
total 40.59m ECU.

V.3   Effectiveness of Regional Policy

Moore and Rhodes[2] estimate that policy has succeeded in raising employment in
the depressed areas by some 325,000-350,000 jobs in manufacturing over the past
two decades, the rate of job-creation reaching a peak of about 25,000 a year in the
late 1960s. These numbers may not seem high, for example in relation to the
present unemployment level, but it must be remembered that this itself is
abnormally high; in fact the cumulative number of jobs added by regional policy is
roughly equal to average unemployment in the whole of the UK at any time in the
postwar period up to 1966. Other studies confirm a positive effect of regional
policy on investment in plant and machinery[3] and on firms' relocation decisions.[4]

Since the objective of policy is to mitigate regional disparities, its impact should
ultimately register on regional indicators of industrial output, incomes and above
all unemployment. Table 4.18 shows the latest regional unemployment data
available at the time of writing and comparative figures for 1960, 1966 and 1975
(when major phases of regional policy began). While unemployment has increased
dramatically in all regions over the period, the indexes showing unemployment in
each region *relative to the UK average* have in general declined.

In interpreting these trends it must be recalled that there are two forces at work:
structural factors and policy. Recent research[5] suggests that up to 1966 structural
factors were operating very strongly against the most depressed regions (Northern
Ireland, Scotland, the North and the North West). However, policy exerted a
beneficial effect in each case. In the period 1966-75 the adverse structural effects
were less severe (and in fact became positive in the case of the Northern region)
while policy, as we have seen, was at its height. In general, we may conclude that
policy contributed substantially to the narrowing of differentials up to 1975,
especially after 1966.

A similar breakdown of employment changes into structural and policy effects
for the period since 1975 is not available. The continuing narrowing of regional
unemployment differentials in this period in table 4.18 is surprising for two reasons.

---

1   The Regional Fund was fixed at 1,540m ECU for 1981 (compared with 1,165m ECU in
    1980), of which 77m ECU was reserved for the non-quota section.

2   B. Moore and J. Rhodes, *Methods of Evaluating the Effects of Regional Policy*, OECD,
    Paris, 1977.

3   See, e.g., A. Beacham and T.W. Buck, 'Regional Investment for Manufacturing Industries',
    Yorkshire Bulletin of Economic and Social Research, May 1970; and C. Blake, 'The
    Effectiveness of Investment Grants as a Regional Subsidy', *SJPE*, February 1972. See also
    S. Fothergill and G. Gudgin, *Unequal Growth: Urban and Regional Employment Change in
    the UK*, Heinemann, 1982.

4   R.S. Howard, 'The Movement of Manufacturing Industry in the UK 1945-65', *Board of
    Trade Journal*, 1968.

5   See *Cambridge Economic Policy Review*, Vol. 6, No. 2, July 1980, Chapter 1.

TABLE 4.18

Regional Unemployment Rates, 1960, 1966, 1975 and 1981

	1960		1966		1975		1981	
	%	*Index (UK=100)*	%	*Index (UK=100)*	%	*Index (UK=100)*	%	*Index (UK=100)*
N. Ireland	5.0	385	5.3	379	7.9	193	18.3	162
Scotland	3.4	263	2.7	193	5.2	127	13.6	120
North	2.8	215	2.5	179	5.9	144	15.0	133
North West	1.9	146	1.4	100	5.3	129	13.7	121
Wales	2.6	200	2.8	200	5.6	137	14.5	128
W. Midlands	0.8	62	0.8	57	4.1	100	13.5	119
Yorks. & Humb.	–	–	1.1	79	4.0	98	12.1	107
East Anglia	–	–	1.4	100	3.4	83	9.1	81
South West	1.6	123	1.7	121	4.7	115	9.9	88
E. Midlands	–	–	1.0	71	3.6	88	10.1	89
South East	–	–	0.9	64	2.8	68	8.0	71
UK	1.3	100	1.4	100	4.1	100	11.3	100

Source: DEG; AAS.

First, as we have seen, the strength of regional policy has been very much reduced over this period. Secondly, regional differentials have in the past tended to widen in times of recession. What the latest statistics most probably show is the spread of the current, very deep recession to previously more prosperous industries and regions.

This is undoubtedly true in the case of the West Midlands, which has been transformed from the region of lowest unemployment in the whole country in 1966 to a position comparable with Scotland and the North West, with unemployment nearly 20% above the national average. The principal factor in this transformation has been the decline of car production and associated engineering trades. By contrast East Anglia, within the European 'golden triangle', has been the most dynamic of the regions, with a 15% growth in employment relative to the national average.

In assessing the effectiveness of regional policies, questions may be asked not only about their impact on regional imbalances but also about the nature of the policy instruments used and their cost-effectiveness. So many different measures have been employed at one time or another in the last twenty years that it is not possible to evaluate each in detail. Statistical analysis indicates that all three major types of policy instrument – IDCs, capital subsidies of one kind or another, and contributions towards operating costs (like the former Regional Employment Premium) – have exerted a separate, significant influence.[1] Nevertheless, there have been a number of debates over the merits of alternative measures in the past. Where, for example, the majority of financial incentives have related to capital expenditures, policy has been criticized for its capital bias. This, it was argued,

1 See B. Moore and J. Rhodes, 'Evaluating the Effects of British Regional Policy, *EJ*, Vol. 83, 1973, pp. 87-110; and 'Regional Economic Policy and the Movement of Manufacturing Firms to Development Areas', *EC*, 43, pp. 17-31, February 1976. The Regional Employment Premium (REP) was paid, in addition to capital subsidies, to firms in Development Areas from 1967 to 1976.

makes policy especially attractive to capital-intensive industries, which is clearly not conducive to creating more jobs. Indeed, by lowering the relative price of capital inputs, policy could result in unduly high capital/labour ratios in production. Secondly it has been argued that the use of *automatic* financial incentives (like cash grants, tax allowances and REP), as opposed to *discretionary* regional grants tied to specific programmes of job-creation, has reduced the cost-effectiveness of regional support, since more aid is given to firms already in Development Areas, as opposed to those moving in. Similarly, the system of cash grants for investment in plant and machinery which was in force for a time,[1] as opposed to incentives in the form of reduced tax liability, was criticized on grounds that it did not differentiate between efficient and inefficient firms (i.e. those making profits and others). Finally, it is a widely held view that the very frequent changes which occurred in the type and value of regional incentives, and the areas in which they applied, were inimical to the long-run success of the policy. With regional policy in its present state of abeyance these issues do not have the urgency they once did; they will no doubt re-emerge as and when regional policy itself revives.

VI   INDUSTRIAL POLICY
VI.1   The Nature of Industrial Policy

Defining the boundaries of industrial policy is difficult because most government policy decisions touch on industrial production in some way. Fiscal and monetary policies are obvious examples. Pay and price controls likewise can have an impact on industry quite incidental to their main, anti-inflationary purpose, as can the regional and competition policies discussed earlier. Even defence and social policies like housing can be included, if for no other reason than their effect on the composition of final demand and hence relative industry outputs.

However, the principal objectives of all these policies are either macroeconomic or are concerned with raising welfare where there is market failure of some sort. Their effects on industry are mostly incidental, often unintended and sometimes conflicting. These effects complicate the formulation of what we may call 'deliberative' industrial policy: policies which explicitly seek either the achievement of particular production targets or individual structures, or to promote growth, investment and technical progress in individual firms and industries.

Several strands of industrial policy in this narrower sense have developed in a rather piecemeal fashion over the last twenty years or more. The government has supported R and D and innovation both by contributing to its cost and via the National Research and Development Corporation (NRDC) and other means. Recently it has taken measures to promote new enterprises, mainly in the form of assistance to small new firms setting up. Large sums have been spent on structural reorganization, particularly in declining industries where the government has come to the aid of ailing firms either through specific industry schemes (as in cotton textiles, aircraft and shipbuilding) or more generally via the former Industrial Reorganization Corporation (IRC) and National Enterprise Board (NEB). Tax incentives for investment have been in force throughout the period, although as we

---

1 Between 1966 and 1970 capital incentives for investment in plant and machinery took the form of cash grants at the time of the expenditure, as opposed to tax remissions on the profits subsequently generated.

have seen these have often operated with regional considerations in mind, and public money has also been made available to firms for general investment. Finally, a branch of industrial policy has made some attempt at strategic planning. This began with the establishment of the National Economic Development Council (NEDC) in 1962, culminated in the National Plan of 1965 and continued, in a much watered-down form, through the Industrial Strategy of 1975 to the work of the individual Economic Development Councils (EDCs) and Sector Working Parties (SWPs) at industry level.[1]

Together with agricultural support and policies towards the nationalized industries, which we have already considered, these have been the main dimensions of the deliberative part of recent UK industrial policy. The system of investment incentives is discussed in chapter 2, section IV.6. We review each of the others in more detail in the following paragraphs, and conclude by considering the argument for a more coherent policy, perhaps drawing on experience from other countries.

VI.2   Innovation Policy

Government support of R and D spending and industrial innovation is widespread amongst industrialized countries. In the USA, Britain, France and to a lesser extent West Germany it is heavily connected with defence programmes, but civil projects are also promoted. The basic rationale for the latter is that the social rate of return from innovation far exceeds the private benefits. The difference arises because the innovator will not be able to appropriate all the returns from his innovation, even when he has the protection of patents; others will eventually benefit in ways that are not reflected in his returns. Thus if R and D and other innovative effort is left entirely to market forces, too little will be undertaken.

Case studies of US innovations in the early 1970s by Mansfield put the median social rate of return at 56% compared with a private return of only 25%.[2] In estimating the social returns Mansfield took account of both resource savings and the added consumers' surplus, and applied conservative measures. His analysis also highlighted the large variations in private returns and showed that in nearly one-third of cases it would not have been rational for firms to invest in the projects if the returns had been known in advance with certainty. Yet in nearly all these cases the social return was positive. Similarly large gaps between social and private returns have been found in subsequent studies, and influence current thinking on innovation policy.[3]

The latest available statistics show that in Britain the government met 47% of the total cost of R and D in 1978.[4] This is comparable with the position in the US

---

1   See A. Silberston, 'Industrial Policies in Britain 1960-80' in C.F. Carter (ed.), *Industrial Policy and Innovation*, Heinemann, 1981.

2   See E. Mansfield, 'Measuring the Social and Private Rates of Return on Innovation' in *Economic Effects of Space and Other Advanced Technologies*, Strasbourg, Council of Europe, 1980.

3   See A. Shonfield, 'Innovation: Does Government have a Role?' in C. Carter (ed.), *Industrial Policy and Innovation*, Heinemann, 1981.

4   *AAS*. See also *ET*, August 1981.

and the EEC and higher than in Japan, where the government contributes 40%. The total expenditure of £3.5bn represented 2.4% of GDP, which at first sight again compares favourably with the US (2.3%), Japan (2.0%) and the EEC (1.9%).[1] However more than half UK government R and D is on defence, compared with only a quarter in the EEC as a whole, and none in Japan. Hence the comparison based on civil projects is less favourable. On this basis the UK expenditure is some 1.8% of GDP, slightly more than the US and EEC (1.7%) but less than in Japan, Germany and France. Moreover we must remember when interpreting these figures that GDP per head is relatively low in the UK.

One of the criticisms of UK R and D effort has been its heavy concentration in certain narrow fields, notably aerospace and the nuclear programme. The social value of highly expensive programmes like Concorde has been much debated, while much of the value of past research on the British gas-cooled nuclear reactor may now become wasted if future nuclear power stations are equipped with the American pressurized-water system. However the latest statistics show a substantial fall in the proportion of industrial R and D in aerospace, from 21.6% in 1975 to 18.2% in 1978, while there has been rapid growth in electronic components (16.9 to 22.4%) and also computers (3.8 to 5.3%). Even so, R and D spending remains much less evenly spread than in most other countries, including Japan.

Institutional measures to encourage technical progress in Britain began with the establishment of the NRDC in 1948, to finance the development of inventions made in universities, government laboratories and by private individuals, where this was in the public interest. The total resources at its disposal were however not large, some £15m a year towards the end of its existence, when it also undertook some manufacturing. In 1982 the NRDC was merged with what remained of the NEB, to form the British Technology Group.[2]

The government also sponsors work on behalf of industry in its own research establishments, funds research in universities and through various Research Councils, and supports co-operative research associations in a number of industries. It has also supported the computer manufacturer ICL, in order to preserve an independent British mainframe computer industry, and in 1979 some existing schemes to support microelectronics and its applications were extended to form a co-ordinated strategy for the industry. £70m of government money was made available to supplement private investment in production of microelectronic chips. In addition the NEB committed £50m to a new UK microelectronics firm, INMOS, and received £25m from the government for its first production plant to be built in South Wales. A microprocessor application project (MAP) was also launched, to be administered by the Department of Industry. This provides programmes to increase awareness and training at senior levels in industry, the trade unions and public-sector bodies, as well as financial contributions towards firms' costs in commissioning consultants and developing specific microprocessor applications. These increased activities will doubtless lead to further growth of total R and D expenditure in this area, beyond that recorded up to 1978.

---

1   Eurostat, *Government Financing of Research and Development*, 1981.
2   See also section VI.3.

VI.3 Structural Reorganization

Under this heading we are concerned with government assistance to declining industries and failing firms, and with intervention to promote growth, exploit scale economies and encourage the birth and development of small new enterprises. It may be asked whether government action of this type is either necessary or appropriate; in textbook models these adjustments come about naturally via the long-run competitive process of entry and exit, merger and internal growth. However, only for analytical convenience can it be assumed that there are no costs and frictions in the adjustment process which government intervention can ease. In practice, capital market sanctions can be slow to operate, with persistence of profits both above and below the norm.[1] Financial institutions may not be responsive to the needs of companies at all stages of their growth and development.[2] And it is reasonable to suppose that the private and social costs of redeploying inputs (e.g. due to the duration of unemployment) may in certain cases be greater through widespread bankruptcy and subsequent market responses than under a more gradual, administered process. Where the government acts merely as a catalyst, aiding adjustment that would ultimately occur through the operation of market forces, its actions may be considered uncontroversial. If however the end-result were to maintain industries permanently at an artificial level of production, other considerations of resource allocation would arise.

The government has of course been directly involved with the major contraction or expansion of several industries in the public sector, especially coal, rail, steel, telecommunications and gas. Action in the private sector was initially undertaken by means of schemes for specific industries facing changed trading conditions, intensive foreign competition and decline.

The 1959 *Cotton Industry Act* provided for government contributions to encourage contraction and rationalization of the industry, hit by competition from the Far East. A drastic reduction in spinning and weaving capacity was brought about, though a second policy phase which sought to encourage modernization (mainly by offering 25% grants for approved investments in plant and machinery) did not live up to expectations. In the case of the *aircraft industry*, the government in the early 1960s used its position as the industry's dominant consumer to force a reorganization of nineteen companies into five groups (two producing airframes, two aero-engines and one helicopters). Assistance to the *shipbuilding industry* began in the shape of cheap credit schemes for at first home and later foreign shipowners who placed orders in UK yards. This was in the period 1963-6. In 1967 the Shipbuilding Industry Board was set up to administer a £68m reorganization of 27 major yards into four or five large regional units over a three-year period. In both the aircraft and shipbuilding cases, government Committees of Inquiry[3] had concluded there was no case for maintaining production at artificially high levels, for reasons concerning the balance of payments, unemployment or defence. Both industries ultimately passed into public ownership in 1977.

---

1 See D.C. Mueller, 'The Persistence of Profits', *EC*, 44, 1977, 369-80.

2 See *The Functioning of Financial Institutions*, Cmnd. 7937, HMSO, 1980.

3 See *Shipbuilding Industry Committee, 1965-66 Report*, Cmnd. 2937, HMSO, 1966 and *Report of the Committee of Enquiry into the Aircraft Industry*, Cmnd. 2853, HMSO, 1965.

Government intervention across private industry as a whole was facilitated by the establishment of the Industrial Reorganization Corporation (IRC) in 1966[1] and by the 1968 Industrial Expansion Act. The IRC had an initial, revolving capital of £150m and was intended to seek out opportunities for rationalization in private industry, especially where there was a prospect of export stimulation or technical advance, and in these cases initiate and finance mergers which might not otherwise occur. During its existence the IRC was associated with some spectacular mergers (including Leyland–BMC and GEC–AEI–English Electric). With hindsight not all would be judged successful, and the broader success of the IRC is hard to judge. At times its activities clashed with competition policy, and it was quickly abolished by the Conservative government in 1971. The Industrial Expansion Act permitted government support for schemes to improve efficiency, e.g. via expanding capacity and introducing technical improvements, which would benefit the economy but required financial backing. There was some scope for helping rationalization, but the aim was to extend and amplify the work of the IRC, rather than overlap with it.

Under the 1970-74 Conservative government the emphasis swung away from 'structural' solutions and towards greater reliance on the pressure of competition as a stimulus to reorganization and greater efficiency. The first expression of this was a declared intention to allow market forces to put down 'lame duck' firms, but this was soon modified when concern about the social and national implications of the failure of Rolls-Royce and Upper Clyde Shipbuilders led the government to intervene in early 1971.

Measures to help small firms, implementing the recommendations of the Bolton Committee,[2] were also presented as a means of fostering new competition. The small-firms policy began with the establishment of a small-firms division within the (then) Department of Trade and Industry, to safeguard their interests, and local advisory centres were subsequently set up and various financial reliefs given. However, less pro-competitive and more in the spirit of the earlier Industrial Expansion Act were the powers to grant selective financial assistance to industry contained in the 1972 Industry Act.[3] This act also provided for special grants to the hard-pressed shipbuilders, until a longer-term solution for the industry had been worked out. A further provision was that grants might be given only in exchange for state shareholdings in the companies concerned. This was not used by the Conservative government, but was subsequently implemented by its Labour successor, in particular during its rescue of British Leyland in 1975.

The emphasis on extending state ownership in the provision of assistance to industry appeared to have been greatly extended by the Labour government when it set up the National Enterprise Board (NEB), also in 1975. In some ways a successor to the IRC, the NEB had an initial finance of £1,000m to assist firms and promote industrial reorganization. At the time there were some expectations that the NEB would lead to a major extension of public ownership, to include at first

---

1 See *Industrial Reorganisation Corporation*, Cmnd. 2889, HMSO, 1966.

2 *Report of the Committee of Inquiry on Small Firms*, Cmnd. 4811, HMSO, 1971.

3 See also Chapter 2, section IV.6.

100 and then 25 of the largest UK companies. But this did not materialize, and in practice the NEB was mostly occupied in dealing with the securities and other property in public ownership which had been transferred to it, including Alfred Herbert, Ferranti, Rolls-Royce and BL. The return of a Conservative government in 1979 heralded the end of the NEB in its original form. The 1980 Industry Act ended its function to extend public ownership, promote industrial reorganization and encourage industrial democracy, and the Secretary of State for Industry subsequently took over its responsibility for first Rolls-Royce (after the resignation of the entire NEB) and later BL. What remained of the NEB was ultimately merged with the NRDC to form the British Technology Group, its focus thus shifting to new ventures, including the previously mentioned Inmos project.

The present Conservative government has predictably returned to the policy of encouraging enterprise and small firms. 'Enterprise packages' have featured in three successive budgets, including the most recent one in 1982. The latest package illustrates the kind of measure involved. Many involve some form of tax relief. Companies under certain sizes pay preferential 'small companies' rates of corporation tax, and new companies can claim tax relief for pre-trading expenditure and for certain investments qualifying under a 'Business Start-Up Scheme'. There are also special tax arrangements concerning the purchase of own shares by unquoted trading companies and money borrowed to invest in close companies; these are designed to assist investment in small and family companies. Other kinds of measures include arrangements to encourage profit-sharing and employee share-option schemes, which are seen as valuable incentives to the encouragement of 'enterprise', and a 'Loan Guarantee Scheme' under which some £300m of public money has been made available up to 1983.

The effects of all these policies for structural reorganization on the size structures of industries, plants and firms is hard to assess, because there are so many other factors at work. On the other hand it is important to see the various measures, particularly those seeking to promote exploitation of scale economies and those seeking to promote small firms, in the context of the existing distributions of firm and plant size. These are highly skewed; the grant majority of plants and firms are small, but output is heavily concentrated in a comparatively tiny number of very large units (table 4.19). Thus in 1978 90% of manufacturing plants employed less than 100 employees (of which over 60% in fact had no more than ten workers), but contributed only 17.7% of total net output. At the other end of the scale less than six hundred plants with over 1,500 employees, only 0.5% of the total, were responsible for no less than 35.9% of net output. A similar pattern can be seen in the case of firms. The average number of plants per firm is only 1.2. Again this reflects the fact that the vast majority of firms are small, single-plant enterprises, but a few very large firms have many plants.[1]

Over time, there has been a long-term trend towards large-scale production. Plants with over 1,500 workers accounted for 15.2% of total employment in private-sector manufacturing industry in 1935, and for 33.6% in 1978; those with under 100 employees accounted for 25.6% in 1935 and for 20.2% in 1978. During the 1970s, however, there has also been a very large increase in the total number of

---

1 For an analysis of multiplant economies of scale, see F.M. Scherer, *The Economics of Multi-Plant Operation*, Harvard University Press, 1975. On the more general issue of scale economies and their extent, see C.F. Pratten, *Economies of Scale in Manufacturing Industry*, Cambridge University Press, 1971, and Z.A. Silberston, *EJ*, March 1972.

firms and plants; after remaining static in the 1960s, the number of manufacturing establishments rose from around 70,000 in 1968 to 75,000 in 1972 and then to the figure shown in table 4.19. All of this increase occurred in the smaller-size categories, the number of plants with more than a hundred workers actually falling over the period. Despite this, the change in the shares in total output of the different size categories has not changed dramatically. Thus while it may be that there are ICIs and Unilevers of the future among the small firms of today, it should be borne in mind that the present policies encouraging small enterprises affect only a small proportion of existing production activity.

TABLE 4.19
Distribution of Manufacturing Plants and Firms by Employment Size, 1978

Employment size-category	No. of Units	(%)	Total employment 000s	(%)	Total net output £m	(%)
(a) Establishments[1]						
1-99	97,223	(90.0)	1,435	(20.2)	10,083	(17.7)
100-499	8,431	(7.8)	1,800	(25.3)	13,997	(24.6)
500-1,499	1,800	(1.7)	1,482	(20.9)	12,369	(21.8)
1,500 and over	594	(0.5)	2,389	(33.6)	20,385	(35.9)
Total	108,048	(100.0)	7,106	(100.0)	56,834	(100.0)
(b) Enterprises[2]						
1-99	84,518	(93.8)	1,151	(17.3)	7,786	(14.4)
100-499	4,228	(4.7)	849	(12.8)	6,308	(11.7)
500-1,499	842	(0.9)	704	(10.6)	5,689	(10.5)
1,500 and over	546	(0.6)	3,937	(59.3)	34,192	(63.3)
Total	90,134	(100.0)	6,642	(100.0)	53,975	(100.0)

Source: Census of Production, 1978 (Business Monitor PA 1002).

Notes: 1   Manufacturing and construction industries. An establishment of the smallest unit capable of supplying census information, usually a factory or plant at a single site or address.
        2   Manufacturing only. An enterprise means one or more establishments under common ownership or control.

VI.4   Industrial Strategy

British industrial policy has never gone so far in peace-time as to adopt a full-blown industrial strategy, with binding sectoral output targets or even a coherent list of priority industries towards which the government would assist the mobilization of resources. The nearest approach to such a strategy was the National Plan of 1965.[1]

The Plan was the culmination of a strand of development based on the belief that there might be some advantage in the contemporary French system of 'indicative planning' to help co-ordinate economic growth. This had seen earlier

1   Department of Economic Affairs, *The National Plan*, Cmnd. 2764, HMSO, 1965.

expression in the establishment of the NEDC ('Neddy') in 1962. This remains in being and is a tripartite body representing employers, trade unions and government at a very senior level, supported by a permanent staff. Some twenty-one 'Little Neddies' (EDCs) were also set up on a similar basis for individual industries. The general hope was for a consensus approach in analysing and helping overcome impediments to faster growth, at both the national and the industry level.

The National Plan itself was not a plan in any *dirigiste* sense, but more a set of industry-by-industry projections of the implications for them of an assumed growth of the economy at 4% a year from 1964 to 1970. Though it followed a NEDC report on the obstacles to faster growth,[1] the Plan was the work of the newly created Department of Economic Affairs, set up in an aura of enthusiasm for the age of the 'white-hot technological revolution' following the election of a Labour government in 1964.

In the event, the planning exercise was short-lived, brought to an end by the national economic crisis measures of 1966. The Plan's 1969 successor, *The Task Ahead*,[2] which was originally to have been the Second Plan, turned out to be a much less detailed and ambitious document, merely discussing the possible use of resources under alternative growth rates. However, the institutional structure of the NEDC and EDCs survived, and during the Conservative government of 1970-74 the focus shifted towards more low-key activity concerning problems of growth and efficiency at industry level. A wide range of analyses was carried out. The results were disseminated within industries via newsletters and reports, with some inter-industry exchanges.

The industrial strategy concept was revived in 1975,[3] with Labour once again in power. This time the strategy was launched by NEDC. The basic objective was for Britain to become 'a high-output, high-wage economy ... by improving our industrial performance and raising the growth of productive potential': very much the same sentiments as those of a decade earlier. Once again the first stage was to analyse the short-term difficulties facing individual sectors and recommend ways of overcoming them. The emphasis then was to turn to analysing performance and agreeing on medium-term programmes of action to improve competitive performance. A further set of tripartite bodies was set up for this purpose, the Sector Working Parties (SWPs). In selecting the sectors the governing idea was 'picking winners', i.e. industries which were 'intrinsically likely to be successful' or potential growth centres. By 1970 40 SWPs had been created, covering about 40% of manufacturing output.[4]

The work of the SWPs has, like that of the EDCs, been very varied, involving studies and recommendations on things like investment and productivity, man-power and training, product design, development and standardization, the identification of markets, marketing techniques and export finance. Management and union representatives are intended to see that the programmes are practically viable, and government representatives to see that the programmes are harmonized nationally. Under the Industrial Strategy the government is also committed to take

---

1 NEDC, *Conditions Favourable to Faster Growth*, HMSO, 1963.

2 Department of Economic Affairs, *The Task Ahead: Economic Assessment to 1972*, HMSO, 1969.

3 See *The Regeneration of British Industry*, Cmnd. 5710, HMSO, 1974, and *An Approach to Industrial Strategy*, Cmnd. 6315, HMSO, 1975.

4 Included in the total are 11 remaining EDCs which have taken over the role of SWPs.

steps in support of the sector programmes, such as providing extra financial assistance for investment (as in the case of microelectronics), for entry into export markets and for industry training schemes. The government also undertook to 'identify the industrial implications of the whole range of government policies' and give more weight to the needs of industry in shaping them.

The current (Conservative) government's approach to industrial policy is one of deep scepticism towards the value of planning and government interference, and of greater confidence in market forces to reveal growth potential and solve co-ordination problems. Nevertheless NEDC, the EDCs and SWPs remain in existence, though to what extent they may have lost effectiveness and the ear of government is difficult to judge.

VI.5   Conclusions

'Deliberative' policy towards private manufacturing industry in the UK has been limited in extent. The individual strands of policy are not without merit, but their success has been mixed.

On the available evidence government support of R and D and innovation is justified in welfare terms. Even were this not so, it would be highly risky for one country to withold support when others give it. Total R and D spending in the UK compares quite favourably on an international basis. But both the expenditure figures and the comparative performance of UK industry suggest there is a case for greater non-defence spending. Moreover the returns might be higher if rather more industries were to benefit than the very few in which effort is heavily concentrated at present.

This is all the more so since policies for structural reorganization have focused on the problems of contracting industries and some large, failing firms, rather than on promoting new industries. The recent policy emphasis on small firms is the present government's corrective. While this could pay dividends in the extremely long term − if the foundations are laid for some industrial success stories of the twenty-first century − the administrative costs are high because there are many small firms, yet in the foreseeable future only a minor proportion of total activity is affected.

The value of the work undertaken by the SWPs and EDCs and co-ordinated under NEDC is hard to judge. Jointly they provide a forum for dialogue between government and industry, and this could result in the government discovering more about the micro implications of its macro policies, so avoiding some of the adverse effects which were listed in *An Approach to Industrial Strategy*[1] arising from unduly sharp and frequent changes in economic regulations, pre-emption of resources for the public sector and personal consumption, and intervention in the nationalized industries. But opportunities for dialogue are at best a necessary rather than a sufficient condition for a lasting improvement. At the level of individual industries, many topics have been discussed and many reports issued dealing with specific problems affecting performance. There is, however, a doubt about the effectiveness of the tripartite, consensus line of attack in the UK. This, some feel, may be quite good at diagnosing the causes of poor performance, but much less able to agree on remedies and go on to implement them.[2]

1   Cmnd. 6315, HMSO, 1975.

2   A. Silberston, op. cit., 1981.

The overall effectiveness of industrial policy may have been reduced by frequent changes of government and the lack of a broad political consensus on the need for a policy and its general shape. As we have seen, Conservative strategy relies heavily on market co-ordination, and seeks to encourage the independence of firms and to create a favourable environment for private initiatives. When Labour has been in office the emphasis has tended more towards large-scale organization and supplementing market processes with some form of information exchange or planning. While it is possible to dispute which is the superior approach, there may be an argument that either would be better than a policy which vacillates between them, as governments change. Certainly it must be bewildering to industry to see both 'bigness' and 'smallness' in fashion at different times, institutions like IRC and NEB come and go, and the frequent changes that have occurred in the value and types of financial assistance on offer. Greater continuity of policy, of whatever kind, would at least provide a more stable context for the planning of investment and longer-term development.

It is sometimes suggested that the UK could learn from the experience of other countries' industrial policies and in particular from France and Japan.[1] The French reputation is for 'indicative planning', wherein much of the value it is believed lay in the consultation process leading to sectoral projections, rather than in the execution of plans as such. But as we have seen this has already been tried in the UK; the National Plan of 1965 was an attempt to import this system, and the consultative machinery still remains. The discredit into which planning somewhat undeservedly fell in the UK after the crisis measures of 1966 has tended to impede further attempts. In any case, planning has been much less effective in France itself since the late 1960s, when politically stronger governments have placed more emphasis on macroeconomic and social policy. The Japanese strategy has been to identify a number of priority industries and concentrate effort and resources in these. This has been achieved without central direction, within a market economy, but utilizing certain institutional features not present in the UK: strong government influence (via the banks) over the supply of corporate investment funds; control over access to foreign exchange in an economic system which has until recently been highly protected; and a commitment to the 'consensus approach' to decision-making which is part of Japanese culture.

While there are few readily importable features of French and Japanese experience at the level of practical policy, there are perhaps two more general lessons. The first is the importance of clearly articulated goals, and the second is the need to take the long-run view.[3] Both have been conspicuously absent in the UK.

---

1 For an extended discussion, see C.J.F. Brown, 'Industrial Policy and Economic Planning in Japan and France', *NIER*, August 1980.

2 ibid. It has also been achieved largely at the expense of competition policies and the provision of social services, which raises questions about the kind of society being aimed at.

3 Brown, op. cit., points out that Japan's selection in the early 1950s of strategic industries such as steel, oil-refining, petrochemicals, automobiles and electronics, with high technology and good long-term growth prospects, may have seemed least rational in the short run at the time.

REFERENCES AND FURTHER READING

D.A. Hay and D.J. Morris, *Industrial Economics, Theory and Evidence*, OUP, 1979.

F.M. Scherer, *Industrial Market Structure and Economic Performance*, 2nd edition, Rand McNally, 1980.

B.S. Yamey (ed.), *Economics of Industrial Structure*, Penguin, 1973.

S.J. Prais, *Productivity and Industrial Structure*, CUP, 1982.

R. Rees, *Public Enterprise Economics*, Weidenfeld and Nicolson, 1976.

R. Pryke, *The Nationalised Industries: Policies and Performance since 1968*, Martin Robertson, 1981.

D. Swann, *The Economics of the Common Market*, 4th Edition, Penguin, 1978.

E. Mansfield, *Monopoly Power and Economic Performance*, Norton, 1968.

K.G. Cowling *et al.*, *Mergers and Economic Performance*, CUP, 1980.

G. Meekes, *Disappointing Marriage: A Study of the Gains from Merger*, CUP, 1977.

D.C. Mueller (ed.), *Determinants and Effects of Mergers: An International Comparison*, Oelgeschlager Gunn and Hain, 1980.

L. Hannah and J. Kay, *Concentration in Modern Industry*, London, 1977.

P.E. Hart and R. Clarke, *Concentration in British Industry 1935-75*, CUP, 1980.

S.J. Prais, *The Evolution of Giant Firms in Great Britain*, CUP, 1976.

B. Moore and J. Rhodes, *Methods of Evaluating the Effects of Regional Policy*, OECD, Paris, 1977.

C.F. Carter (ed.), *Industrial Policy and Innovation*, Heinemann, 1981.

F.M. Scherer, *The Economics of Multi-Plant Operation*, Harvard University Press, 1975.

C.F. Pratten, *Economies of Scale in Manufacturing Industry*, CUP, 1971.

A. Whiting (ed.), *The Economics of Industrial Subsidies*, HMSO, 1976.

For information on current developments see also:

National Institute Economic Review (especially February issues each year, and the regular statistical section and calendar of economic events) and

Economic Progress Reports (published monthly by the Information Division of the Treasury).

5

Labour
David Metcalf and Ray Richardson

I EMPLOYMENT
I.1 The Working Population

In September 1981 the working population (or labourforce) in the UK was officially estimated at 26.3m persons. The total was composed of 21.1m employees in employment, 1.9m employers and self-employed, 335,000 HM Forces and 3.0m registered unemployed.[1]

The working population has recently started to decline. By September 1981 it was down by nearly 400,000 from its peak in March 1979 (using the seasonally adjusted figures)[2]. This is in contrast to the normal tendency, which is for the officially estimated working population to increase. Between 1950 and 1966 it fell only in 1958. Admittedly, there was a sustained fall of roughly 800,000 between 1966 and 1971, but whether this fall was genuine or a reflection of quirks in the methods of data collection and estimation is not entirely clear. In 1971 the authorities introduced a new method of estimating the number of employees in employment, and from then until 1979 there was a continual rise in the mid-year estimates of the working population, totalling about 1.25m workers. The decline since 1979 is unlikely to be artificial and is probably a result of the very deep recession which the economy has experienced.[3]

In seeking to understand what determines the size of and changes in the labourforce, it is first necessary to consider the size and demographic composition of the population. For example, younger and older males are always less likely to be in the labourforce than males aged between twenty-five and fifty-five. It is convenient to discuss these issues in terms of activity rates (sometimes called labourforce participation rates), which express, for any age and sex group, the proportion of working to total population. Further, changes in activity rates for the two sexes are best analysed separately, because male activity rates have tended to fall, while female activity rates have tended to rise.

Economic growth tends to reduce male activity rates. In particular, younger males stay in the educational system longer and older males retire earlier, especially when growth is accompanied by improved retirement pensions. Between 1961 and 1979 the proportion of boys who stayed on in school rose from 23% to 50% for 16-year-olds and from 13% to 21% for 17-year-olds.[4] In addition, the number of males attending universities approximately doubled over the same period. For older men, the reported activity rates have fallen in each successive Census of Population; for example, the activity rate of 65-69-year-olds fell from

---

1 *DEG*, February 1982, p. 56.
2 ibid.
3 *BLS*, p. 220; *DEG*, March 1977, pp. 250-2; and *DEG*, February 1982, p. 56.
4 *AAS*, 1971, p. 106 and *AAS*, 1982, p. 126.

48% to 31% over the period 1951 to 1971.[1] For all males over 65 years of age the estimated activity rate has fallen from 25% in 1961 to 19% in 1971 and to 10% in 1979.[2] In part, these long-run changes reflect the fruits of economic growth, both directly through increased incomes and indirectly through greater government support to education and retirement pensions.

Superimposed on the inverse relation between long-run growth and male activity rates is a complex, and not necessarily stable, reaction to fluctuations in growth. The dominant postwar reaction of the male labourforce to fluctuations in growth has been positive; the male labourforce has tended to contract (or grow less rapidly) during economic recessions and to grow (or contract less rapidly) during periods of economic expansion. There are exceptions to this general pattern, most notably in the recession which began in 1974. Between 1974 and 1977 the number of male employees (either in employment or unemployed) *rose* by more than 300,000; in contrast, during the recessionary period of 1969-72 the number of male employees *fell* by 340,000. The different experience in the two recessions is worth exploring more fully. In both periods, male unemployment rose; in the earlier period it increased from 440,000 to about 680,000; in the later period it increased from 460,000 to 1,050,000. Male employment fell in both periods; by 580,000 in the earlier recession and by 280,000 in the later one. It will be seen that by one measure, the loss of jobs, the second recession was much less severe; but by the other measure, the increase in registered unemployment, it was much more severe. No fully convincing reasons for these changes in labour-market behaviour have so far appeared.

After 1979 the traditional relationship was re-established. Between September 1979 and September 1981, male unemployment rose by 1,170,000, while male employment fell by 1,240,000; on balance, therefore, there was a small fall in the total number of male employees.

It was suggested above that the typical response to long-run growth is that the male labourforce contracts, while the typical response to short-run growth is that the male labourforce expands. These two responses, the negative and the positive, are not contradictory, as they might seem at first sight. The first concerns people's response to a permanent increase in wealth levels; the second concerns their response to what is presumed to be a temporary rise in employment prospects. This is an application of the fundamental notions in economics of income and substitution effects. If a worker is not planning to supply the maximum amount of labour at all times, he can choose the most advantageous periods when the supply is to be offered. On many calculations the most advantageous periods occur when wages are high and jobs are easy to find; that is, in expansionary conditions. Consequently, a recession is a period during which there is less point in offering one's services. This view therefore predicts that over the business cycle the size of the labourforce will be positively related to the state of the economy. It is usually termed the 'discouraged worker effect', meaning that as the economy contracts, the number of people in employment falls by more than the increase in the number counted as unemployed.

There is an alternative and opposite view to the one just described, labelled the 'added worker effect'. It suggests that as 'primary' (i.e. permanent) members of the labourforce are made unemployed in recessions, 'secondary' (i.e. temporary)

---

1   *ST*, 1975, p. 84.

2   *ST*, 1982, p. 63.

workers are drawn into the workforce so as to provide an additional source of income for the family; the result is that the number of unemployed rises more than the number disemployed. This view obviously has some validity but it is basically a qualification to the 'discouraged worker' hypothesis. It stresses that many households plan imprecisely, that unpredicted events are important and force changes even in carefully laid plans, and that savings, credit and social welfare payments may be inadequate to maintain family living standards for more than a relatively short period. These and other factors are all of obvious practical importance, but they should not be taken to imply that the 'discouraged worker' hypothesis, with its emphasis on rational calculation, is thereby unrealistic and likely to be misleading.

Whereas male activity rates have declined over the long run, female activity rates have increased very sharply. Ignoring the self-employed and HM Forces, females accounted for nearly 41% of the labourforce in 1981, as compared with just over 30% in 1950. In discussing long-run changes, however, a distinction should be made between married and non-married females. The activity rates for young non-married females has fallen, while those for older non-married females have risen; for example, between 1951 and 1979 they are estimated to have fallen for 20-24-year-olds from 91% to 78%, and to have risen for 45-59-year-olds from 61% to 71%.[1]

The reasons for the distinctive pattern for young non-marrieds are not clear, but they are probably connected with (a) the rise in the extent of girls and young women staying on at school and attending universities, and (b) the rise in the number of one-parent families financially supported either by the state or by alimony or other family resources.

For married women the picture is unambiguously one of increased activity rates, albeit at different rates for the different age-groups. Table 5.1 shows the striking changes that are officially estimated to have taken place.

TABLE 5.1
Wives' Activity Rates (%) by Age, Great Britain, 1951, 1976 and 1979

Age-group	1951	1976	1979
16-19	38	52	41
20-24	37	55	58
25-44	25	56	58
45-59	22	61	61
60+	5	14	10
All ages	22	49	50

Source: ST, 1979, p. 84 and *ST*, 1982, p. 63.

The importance of these changes can hardly be overstated, and their implications extend far beyond the labour market. What is of immediate importance here is to consider the reasons for the rise. One possibility is that there has been a widespread reduction in the extent of sex discrimination in the labour market. For this to have happened, however, there would have been either a consistent rise in the wages of females relative to those of males or a significant shift in the employment structure, with large numbers of females joining the better-paid and more attractive

1 *ST*, 1979, p. 84 and *ST*, 1982, p. 63.

occupations. Neither of these developments seems to have taken place, certainly not on a major scale, in the first 25 years after the Second World War. Whether or not sex discrimination, usefully defined, has been extensive, there have been no conclusive studies demonstrating changes in its extent.[1]

Turning to influences primarily affecting married women, we can point first to the fact that the average number of children per family has fallen over time. Whether this is a cause or effect of higher participation is not known. What is known is that activity rates have risen for younger wives as well as for older wives, and that, in at least some countries, activity rates have also risen for married women with young children. This suggests that declining family size is, at most, a partial explanation of rising activity rates.

A second possibility is that, due to the introduction of new products, there has been a rise in the productivity of the housewife, effectively allowing her to produce the same amount of services as before but in less time. By itself this improved productivity does not necessarily make for greater participation by the wife in the labourforce because, at the same time, everyone's income has risen. With the rise in income one might expect both the family's demand for housewifely services and the housewife's demand for personal leisure to increase, thereby decreasing the incentive to join the labour market. Only if the domestic-productivity effect is strong will the net effect be to release housewives for market work.

A third possible explanation of the rise in activity rates for married women is that social attitudes have become increasingly tolerant of wives, and even of mothers, working. This explanation is probably the most popular of all and there is certainly no doubt that attitudes have changed. Again, however, there is the difficulty of deciding the extent to which changes in attitudes were an independent cause or were themselves a response to changes in practice. It does seem plausible that the two world wars were very influential in this matter. They were, as far as the labour market was concerned, exogenous events inducing many women to join the market for the first time. This process surely changed social attitudes, encouraging working wives. It is also notable that over the last twenty years the largest increases in activity rates for married women are associated with older women, who experienced to the full the turmoil of wartime. However, one note of caution is worth sounding about the impact of wartime exigencies. The available data are very sketchy, but they suggest that the increase in the proportion of wives who work in the market is very much an international phenomenon, extending even to countries where the direct impact of the war was quite modest.

The above explanations all run in terms of supply influences, implying that progressively more married women are willing to work in the market. Demand influences may also have been important. One possibility is that the growing similarity of regional employment structures, in part perhaps a result of the attempts made by successive governments to induce greater regional evenness of employment, have been successful in bringing work to women who previously had very limited job opportunities.

It is certainly the case that female activity rates have tended to rise more rapidly in those regions where they were historically low. It is officially estimated that in

---

1 For an analysis that suggests that there have only been small changes in the extent of occupational segregation by sex, see C. Hakim, 'Sexual divisions within the labour force', *DEG*, November 1978, pp. 1,264-8, and C. Hakim, 'Job segregation: trends in the 1970s', *DEG*, December 1981, pp. 521-9.

1979 female activity rates by region had a range of only seven percentage points, from a low of 42% for Wales to a high of 49% for Scotland and the West Midlands.[1]

In fact, there has not been merely a geographical redistribution of jobs. Since the end of the 1930s the UK economy has generally been run at unprecedented and persistent tightness. It seems most plausible to us, in the absence of hard statistical confirmation, that it is this influence rather than deliberate geographical dispersion that explains a major part of the rise of women in the labourforce.

A second, structural, argument relating to demand influences could be made. It might be suggested that female activity rates have risen because expansion has been particularly marked in industries employing a high proportion of female to male workers. It is shown below, in section I.4, that these female-intensive industries have indeed enjoyed a relative expansion, certainly since the Second World War. However, most of these sectors are not inherently female-intensive and we would again put principal stress on the general expansion of the economy when considering demand influences which account for the rise of female participation in the labour market. Essentially, what has been happening here has been the tapping of a labour reserve.

It has not been easy for economists to do very convincing empirical work on the patterns of wives' activity rates over time, because suitable data are not readily available. There has, however, been a certain amount of work seeking to explain cross-sectional patterns, i.e. patterns at a point in time, which can be translated into explanations of the time-series developments. One study investigated the variation in married females' activity rates between towns and cities in Great Britain.[2] It was shown that wives' activity rates were greater, the higher were female wage rates and the lower were male wage rates; wives' activity rates were also higher for the foreign-born, for those who lived in the larger cities and for those who lived in towns with low male unemployment rates.

More recently, some of these results were confirmed in a study using survey data on nearly 4,000 wives. It was shown that wives were more likely to be in the labourforce if their own potential wage was high, if their husband's wage was low, if they did not have young children, if they were West Indian or Irish born and if their husband was in employment.[3]

As with males, there have been considerable fluctuations in the female labourforce superimposed on the longer-run trends. Again, the tendency has been for the female labourforce to expand most rapidly when the economy is growing fast and to expand slowly or even to contract when the economy moves into recession. In the two years after September 1979, for example, the female labourforce fell by 216,000; there was a rise in female unemployment of 436,000 and a fall of those in work of 652,000. It should be noted that a fall of this size in the female labourforce is much larger than has been usual in postwar recessions.

---

1   *Regional Statistics*, 1981, p. 93.
2   C. Greenhalgh, 'Labour Supply Functions for Married Women in GB', *EC*, August 1977. Somewhat similar, but not identical, results can be found in R. McNabb, 'The Labour Force Participation of Married Women', *MS*, September 1977.
3   R. Layard *et al.*, 'Married Women's Participation and Hours', *EC*, February 1980.

I.2   Aggregate Employment Patterns

Between 1950 and 1965 the number of male employees in employment in the UK
followed an upward trend, from 13.6m to 14.9m. Since 1965 there has been a
trend in the reverse direction, so that by June 1981 the number was down to only
12.3m. Within the latter period, the rate of decline has varied substantially. It was
fairly rapid up to 1972, much slower between 1973 and 1978, and exceedingly
fast thereafter. In the period from December 1978 to September 1981, the number
of male employees in employment fell by no less than 1.3m, or nearly 120,000 per
quarter. Such a sustained and substantial fall is without precedent in the postwar
period.[1]

In contrast to the pattern for males, female employment continued to rise until
1979. Between 1959 and 1979 there was a 25% increase in the number of females
in work and only three years during which female employment fell. From
September 1979, however, the latter has fallen in each quarter, from a total of
9.5m to one of 8.9m, i.e. by an average of just over 80,000 per quarter.[2]

One of the important differences between the male and female labourforces is
the degree to which they work on a part-time basis. As at June 1978, the latest
period for which reliable data are available, fully 40% of the female labourforce
worked only part-time (i.e. normally worked for less than 30 hours per week), as
against only 5% of men. Part-time work has also been on the increase. Between
1971 and 1978 the number of females working full-time was virtually static at just
under 5½m; the number working part-time, however, increased in each year, by an
average of over 131,000. The great majority of these part-time workers are wives.[3]

I.3   Spatial Employment Patterns

The spatial pattern of jobs and workers in Great Britain is changing rapidly both
within and between regions.

For example, the resident labourforce in the seven British conurbations fell by
more than 650,000 between 1961 and 1971.[4] During the same period, Greater
London lost more than 25% of its jobs in manufacturing, many of them to other
parts of the country, particularly to the rest of the South East region. This
reduction in workplace and labourforce densities, together with shifts between
the standard regions, has sometimes been a response to natural market forces and
sometimes a result of deliberate planning policy. Thus, in the period since the
Second World War there has been a great planned expansion of New Towns that
ring many of our major cities. Often, firms have wished to expand their operations
around their existing inner-city sites but have been denied planning permission.
They have therefore been obliged to move either to a nearby New Town or to a
more distant depressed region. Of course, many firms have moved for reasons
other than planning difficulties, for example because suitable nearby land was not
physically available, because labour was increasingly scarce locally, because local
transportation facilities were deteriorating, or because government subsidies made
such moves profitable.

---

1 *BLS*, p. 221; *DEG*, October 1975, p. 1,030; and *DEG*, February 1982, p. S6.

2 *DEG*, October 1975, p. 1,030; and *DEG*, February 1982, p. S6.

3 *DEG*, February 1981, p. 61.

4 J. Corkindale, 'The Decline of Employment in Metropolitan Areas', *DEG*, November 1977.

The loss of workplaces in many of the major cities may or may not imply higher urban unemployment. For example, in London there has been no substantial change in unemployment, relative to other areas, during the period of major job-loss. This implies either that the population is leaving London at the same rate as jobs, or that commuting patterns are changing. Clearly some cities are suffering from the loss of jobs (Glasgow is often said to be in this category), while others benefit from the reduction of congestion that decline implies.

Until recently, when specific urban problems became more acutely perceived, the most noticed spatial aspect of employment was the inter-regional one. In the latter context the pattern of unemployment across regions was of most concern but attention was also paid to variations in activity rates by region.

A recent article in the *Department of Employment Gazette* gave estimates of regional activity rates in the past and some projections for the future. Table 5.2 reproduces some of the data, and it can be seen that there has been a substantial narrowing of the differences between the activity rates over time.

TABLE 5.2
Actual and Projected Regional Activity Rates (%) for the Civilian Labourforce, 1961 and 1986

	Males		Females	
	1961	*1986*	*1961*	*1986*
North	86	76	31	46
Yorkshire & Humberside	86	76	37	48
East Anglia	79	78	30	46
West Midlands	88	77	41	49
North West	87	75	42	49
East Midlands	86	77	37	47
South East	85	77	39	47
South West	79	72	30	45
Wales	84	73	28	44
Scotland	87	77	35	50
Great Britain	85	76	37	47

Source: DEG, November 1981, p. 474.

I.4 Employment by Industry and Occupation

In September 1981 the manufacturing sector of the British economy employed less than 29% of all employees at work.[1] Adding the number of employees in agriculture, mining, construction and gas, electricity and water, we still get less than 39% of all employees, implying that the service sector now accounts for well over half of the employment in the country. The recent tendency for the service-sector labourforce to grow relative to the whole labourforce began in the mid-1950s, when the manufacturing and service sectors each employed about 42.5% of the total number of employees. The marked absolute decline in manufacturing employment began in 1966. In that year, manufacturing employment stood at 8.4m; subsequently it has fallen in nearly every year (1969, 1973, 1974 and 1977 are the exceptions) and in nearly every individual manufacturing grouping, so that in

1 *DEG*, February 1982, pp. S7-8. See also Chapter 4, section I.

December 1981 there were only 5.8m workers employed in manufacturing.

Within the service sector the main growth areas have been professional and scientific services, particularly in education and medical and dental services. In the twelve years to June 1981, the numbers employed in professional and scientific services rose by nearly three-quarters of a million. Some service sectors have become smaller over this period, for example transport and communications (due mainly to the rapid decline in railway employment), but the general long-run tendency has been one of growth.

The principal reasons for these employment shifts are the differences between the sectors in their rates of growth (a) of final, including foreign, demands and (b) of labour productivity. There are changes in the final demand for an industry's products as a result of movements in the wealth of the economy as a whole, the structure of prices and the appearance of substitute products, particularly of rival products produced abroad. Thus, in conditions of generalized recession and an unusually high exchange rate, employment in manufacturing has recently fallen with unprecedented rapidity. Between December 1979 and December 1981 it fell by 17%, or nearly 1,200,000 workers.

In addition to changes in final demand, changes in labour productivity can also affect the structure of employment. Over the long run it is clear that labour productivity has grown faster in manufacturing than in most of the service trades and that this has resulted in a contraction in the relative demand for labour in manufacturing. It also seems to be the case that labour productivity has very recently been increasing at an unusually rapid rate in British manufacturing. What is said to be happening is that, in order to survive extreme recessionary pressures, many employers are able to or are being forced to reorganize work practices and introduce new standards of efficiency. Whatever the reason, there does seem to have been a sharp increase in labour productivity relative to trend.[1] Whether this relative productivity gain will survive a return to more prosperous and easygoing conditions is not clear.

Another way of examining the composition of the labourforce is to examine the division between the private and the public sectors. Over the period 1961 to 1980 there was an increase in the proportion of the employed labourforce working in the public sector, from 24% to nearly 30%. The rate of increase was most rapid in the years 1966-7, 1969-70 and 1974-5, when the level of private employment fell sharply and public employment was fairly stable.

Within the public sector, total employment in the public corporations (i.e. roughly the nationalized industries) has been fairly constant in spite of the growth in the number of nationalized industries. Local authority employment has risen sharply, by 61% between 1961 and 1980, mainly because of a growth in the education sector. Over the same period, central government employment grew by 30% mainly because of the growth in the National Health Service.[2]

These structural changes are also reflected in the relative growth of female employment, referred to above, because much of the service sector has made

---

1 M. Small, 'Labour Productivity Output per Person in Manufacturing, *ET*, January 1982, pp. 127-9.

2 The most detailed discussion of public-sector employment trends is to be found in M. Semple, 'Employment in the Public and Private Sectors, 1961-78', *ET*, November 1979, pp. 99-108. More recent figures are to be found in S. Briscoe, 'Employment in the Public and Private Sectors, 1975-1981', *ET*, December 1981, pp. 94-102.

intensive use of female labour. Thus, approximately 68% of the employees in professional and scientific services are female, as against 24% in agriculture, only 4% in mining and 7% in shipbuilding. It is true that the textile and clothing industries are also female-intensive, but their decline has not been great in comparison to the expansion of the service sector. It is also worth emphasizing again that a significant number of females, particularly in the rapidly expanding service sectors, work only part-time. Thus, in June 1978 55% of the 1.25m females working in education and 41% of the nearly 1m in medical and dental services were part-time workers.[1] This compares with only 23% for manufacturing, and it may suggest that some of the sectoral shifts that have occurred are not a purposeful move away from manufacturing but the use of a previously unused labour reserve that would not be available for full-time work, or perhaps even for part-time work in other sectors.

I.5   Hours Worked

To clarify discussions of work one should distinguish between normal basic hours, normal hours and actual hours of work. The first term relates to the number of hours a person is expected to work at basic rates of pay; the second includes any guaranteed overtime paid at premium rates; the third, and for most purposes much the most interesting notion, includes all overtime, guaranteed or not. Actual hours are typically in excess of normal hours, but by including absenteeism and sick days in the picture the situation may be reversed.

As with activity rates, two lines of enquiry can be distinguished for hours worked by the labourforce as a whole. First, one wants to explain the trend; second, one wants to explain temporary variations around it. Further, it is revealing to examine the structure of hours worked, e.g. by occupation or wage level.

Over a long period, average actual hours of work have fallen, from around sixty hours per week in the early part of the century to just over forty hours by 1981. Initially, the fall was in hours per day; subsequent reductions have been first in days worked per week and second in weeks per year. There is therefore a clear tendency for extra leisure to be bunched, there being 'economies of scale' in leisure activities.

For many years, normal hours fell more rapidly than actual hours, implying an increase in the number of overtime hours. Thus, between 1948 and 1968 normal weekly hours of male manual workers fell from 44.5 to 40.1.[2] Actual hours in the same period tended to rise until the mid-1950s and fall thereafter. Since the late 1960s, however, normal hours have been relatively constant but actual hours have tended to fall.

Hours of work fluctuate a good deal from year to year. The changing tempo of the economy is the principal explanation of these variations, with the length of work-weeks falling in recessions and rising in expansions. Thus, the average hours worked by manual male workers fell from 46.2 per week in 1979 to 44.2 per week in 1981. Over the same period, the percentage of operatives in manufacturing industries who worked any overtime fell from 34.2% to 26.7%, a postwar record low.[3]

---

1 *DEG*, February 1981, p. 66.
2 *BLS*, p. 160.
3 *DEG*, February 1982, p. S50 and p. S14.

There are wide variations between industries in actual hours worked. In 1978 the average annual hours worked per manual employee in Great Britain was 2,144 in construction, as against 1,655 in mining and quarrying. Within manufacturing the range was from 1,992 in the timber and furniture sector, to 1,694 in clothing and footwear.[1]

Some of the variation observed in such a cross-section is due to different industries being at different stages in their own business cycle. Additionally, some industries have relatively old labourforces whose work-weeks are naturally shorter. Nevertheless, there are persistent real variations across industries and occupations in hours worked, and these certainly affect the attractiveness of the different jobs. Some research work has shown for a sample of ninety-six industries in Britain that the number of hours offered by the average manual male worker was positively affected by the hourly wage rate and low skill levels, and negatively affected by the number of fellow workers employed in the factory, residence in the South East and Midlands, and residence in conurbations. Further, the number of work hours demanded from the male worker was greater when the worker was more skilled, aged between 25 and 54, and working in industries that were fast-growing or highly concentrated; fewer hours were demanded from young males and from those who tended to work alongside females.[2]

Manual workers have longer work-weeks than do non-manuals. For men in 1981 the reported difference averaged 5.8 hours per week; for women, the corresponding figure was only 2.9 hours. Also, males, particularly in the manual occupations, tend to work longer hours than females.[3]

I.6   The Quality of the Labourforce

As time goes on, the average skill level of members of the labourforce rises. This is one component of the increased quality of the working population, implying that, from a given number of workers and a given quantity of supporting factors of production, potential output grows over time. Other important sources of higher quality are better health levels, an improved spatial distribution of employment and, up to a point, shorter working weeks. In quantitative terms the increase in skill levels has had much the largest impact on productivity of any of these sources.

There is no precise, independent measure of the increase in average skill level in the UK over any period and no comprehensive indication of the allocative efficiency of labour between various skill levels. In recent years, however, a number of studies have been made, mainly of the educational system. The formal education sector is not the only source of skill augmentation but the model testing its efficiency has general applicability. The problem at issue may be described as follows. If the sector is organized efficiently, the net social value of a pound of expenditure will be the same at the margin for all types and levels of education. What we must do, therefore, is to equalize the social profit on all educational activities.

The terminology employed here may be disagreeable to some people. However,

---

1   *DEG*, September 1980, p. 972.

2   D. Metcalf, S. Nickell and R. Richardson, 'The Structure of Hours and Earnings in British Manufacturing Industry', *OEP*, July 1976.

3   *DEG*, February 1982, p. S50.

as long as account is taken of all sources of cost and benefit, whether they be material or psychic, there can be no real objection. It is true that some sources may not be measurable in practice and that others may be measured only imperfectly. These defects do not suggest that no measurement should take place, merely that decisions and judgements should not be based solely on what is measurable.

In fact the measurement of the profitability of education and training programmes is decidedly imperfect. The usual measure of benefits is some estimate of the expected increase in monetary earnings enjoyed by the trainee, i.e. his expected full earnings minus the earnings he would otherwise expect were he not to undertake the training under consideration. To take a concrete example, in estimating the profitability of a university degree a comparison is made between the observed earnings of people already graduated and those of people who stopped just short of going to university. This provides an earnings differential for each age-group, which stands for the earnings increase expected by the current trainee at each stage of his working life.

This estimate is extremely crude, and a number of adjustments can be made to improve on it. For example, not all of the crude differential can be attributed to education because ability and motivation levels differ between the two groups from which data are drawn. Consequently, an effort should be made to estimate the independent effect of ability differences.

Once the estimate of benefits has been obtained it is necessary to estimate the costs of the training. The principal cost is the output that could have been produced by the trainee had he been in full-time work. Its value is usually measured by the monetary earnings he forgoes while being trained or educated. Added to the forgone earnings are the direct costs of instruction, represented by salaries of teachers, cost of buildings, etc.

Two early research efforts for the UK were by Blaug[1] and Morris and Ziderman,[2] and both contain a clear account of the procedures and difficulties involved. The latter was more comprehensive and among its conclusions were (1) that postgraduate qualifications were not very profitable for society, and (2) that higher national certificates were very profitable indeed. If these calculations were correct they suggest that the UK educational system was inefficiently structured and was turning out the wrong mix of graduates.[3]

Many workers receive considerable amounts of training after they leave school, and successive governments, particularly during the last twenty years, have attempted to influence the provision of such training. Prior to 1964, the great bulk of industrial training was provided on the initiative of individual employers, often within a context of industry-wide understandings between trade unions and employers' organizations. This voluntary system was widely believed to be defective. In particular, it was said to lead to inadequate provision of training, especially for certain highly skilled manual trades. The principal argument here was that many firms who would otherwise be willing to provide training did not do

---

1 M. Blaug, 'The Rate of Return on Investment in Education in Great Britain', *MS*, September 1965.

2 V. Morris and A. Ziderman, 'The Economic Return on Investment in Higher Education in England and Wales', *ET*, May 1971.

3 For a useful, though complex, survey of the relevant work on Britain, see G. Psacharopoulos and R. Layard, 'Human Capital and Earnings', *RES*, July 1979. See also the interesting article by A. Dolphin, 'The Demand for Higher Education', *DEG*, July 1981.

so on a sufficient scale because they could not be sure of retaining the skilled labour after training had finished. This argument carries with it some implicit assumptions concerning who pays for the training (as opposed to who provides it or makes it available) but it was nevertheless influential in leading to the 1964 Industrial Training Act.

The 1964 Act created a system of Industrial Training Boards (ITBs). By 1969 there were 27 ITBs, of widely differing size, which together covered about 65% of the working population. The principal function of the Boards was to improve the quantity and quality of training provided in industry, and their principal mechanism was a system of levies and grants. Each Board imposed a levy, essentially a payroll tax, on all but the smallest firms in their industry. The revenue raised was then returned to those firms in the industry which ran approved training schemes. The intention was to make all potential users of the skilled labour contribute to the costs of training.[1]

Certain adjustments were made to this system under the 1973 Employment and Training Act, but more radical changes were introduced with the 1981 Employment and Training Act. Using the powers given to him under this Act, the Secretary of State for Employment announced in November 1981 that he had decided to abolish all but seven of the ITBs. Elsewhere, he indicated that he was satisfied that 'the training requirements of the sector concerned can be effectively met on a voluntary basis with less cost and bureaucracy'.[2]

At the same time, the government has published a White Paper which sketches what the Employment Secretary claimed to be 'the most far reaching and ambitious set of proposals for industrial training ever put before Parliament'.[3] The proposed scheme is complex and might be amended subsequently, but it includes (1) a youth training scheme,[4] which is expected to provide places for 300,000 young people at any one time, at a cost of £1bn per annum, (2) a system of grants to employers to provide the Unified Vocational Preparation Scheme, (3) a reform of the existing arrangements for training in craft, technician and professional skills, and (4) a greater emphasis on adult training and retraining.

II   UNEMPLOYMENT
II.1   Composition of the Unemployed[5]

Stocks, flows and durations: In 1981 the number of people unemployed in the United Kingdom averaged 2.7m, equivalent to 11.3% of the labourforce.[6] Males

---

1 For a good discussion of the issues involved in training see A. Ziderman, *Manpower Training: Theory and Policy*, Macmillan, 1978; see also B. Showler, *The Public Employment Service*, Longman, 1976, especially chapter 5.

2 *DEG*, November 1981, p. 463.

3 The White Paper, *A New Training Initiative: A Programme for Action*, is discussed in *DEG*, December 1981, p. 501 and pp. 508-9.

4 See section II.3 below.

5 See S. Nickell, 'A Picture of Male Unemployment in Britain', *EJ*, December 1980, K. Hawkins, *Unemployment*, Penguin, 1979, and the whole issue of *Political Quarterly*, Jan.-March 1981.

6 Official figures refer to people registered as unemployed. Some people register but are not available for work, e.g. occupational pensioners. However, on balance, official figures understate true unemployment because many people do not register as unemployed. The main such group is married women who traditionally have not usually been eligible for benefits, though recent social-security changes will moderate this non-registration.

account for a little over two-thirds of this total. In 1979 there were some 4.2m unemployment registrations and 3.5m cases of people leaving the register. These registrations and deregistrations do not all refer to separate people: some individuals have more than one spell of unemployment. The average duration of each completed spell of unemployment was approximately two-thirds of a year (2.7m/4.2m) or 33 weeks.

This average-spell duration is an important statistic because the main reason the stock of unemployed people rises is that the average duration of unemployment rises and not that more people become unemployed. For example in 1955 when unemployment was at an all-time (peacetime) low of 1.1%, the average duration of each spell of unemployment was only 3½ weeks. Since 1966 flows into unemployment have been remarkably stable at around 4m per year, so the higher unemployment rates primarily reflect longer-spell durations.

The incidence of unemployment among people is very unequal. With 4m registrations a year and a labourforce of 24m, in 6 years the number of registrations equals the size of the labourforce. Therefore if a person is in the labourforce for 48 years he would, if unemployment were distributed equally, expect to have 8 spells of unemployment during his lifetime. Yet we know many people never suffer a single spell of unemployment. Indeed, in any year some 3% of the labourforce account for 70% of the total weeks of unemployment.[1] Clearly a fraction of our labourforce must be constantly at risk of long-term unemployment and/or recurrent spells of unemployment. Unfortunately the group who bear the burden of unemployment are concurrently towards the bottom of the pay distribution, work in the most risky occupations, and are those who also suffer a higher incidence of ill-health — labour-market disadvantage is cumulative.[2]

Demographic characteristics: In October 1981 there was the following pattern of unemployment rates by age in Britain.[3]

	under 25	25-54	55+
Males	24%	11%	16%
Females	23%	6%	5%

Young workers have high rates of unemployment because on average they have a very high propensity to become unemployed and many have recurrent spells of unemployment, while some older workers have both a higher likelihood of entering unemployment than the 25-54 group, and once unemployed, remain so for a relatively long time.[4]

There is no doubt that youth unemployment has worsened since the post-1974 recession. In 1973 males under 20 had an identical unemployment rate to all males (3.5%). But now their unemployment rate is double the all-male rate. Why is

---

1 R. Disney, 'Recurrent spells and the concentration of unemployment in Great Britain', *EJ*, March 1979. S. Owen, 'Do the faces in the Dole Queue change: the Distribution of unemployment amongst individuals 1970-4', MSc. dissertation, University College Cardiff, 1978.

2 See R. Layard, D. Piachaud and M. Stewart, *The Causes of Poverty*, Royal Commission on the Distribution of Income and Wealth, Background Paper No. 5, HMSO, 1978.

3 *DEG*, January 1982, table 2.15.

4 *DEG*, August 1979, pp. 789-90.

this?[1] At least three explanations have been suggested. First, young workers are harder hit in a recession than adult workers and, conversely, their employment prospects pick up faster when the economy improves. Firms economize on labour in a recession and they reduce recruitment. This hits young workers because of their high turnover rates and lack of labour-market experience. This is the dominant factor in the rise in youth unemployment. Second, the relative pay of youths has risen. Finally, if industries which employ youngsters suffer most in recessions then this would compound employment problems of young people. This last argument has not operated recently. It is manufacturing which has experienced the largest employment fall during the current recession. But youngsters are disproportionately employed in the non-manufacturing sectors like distribution, construction and insurance, banking and finance.

The higher unemployment experienced by older workers partly reflects the fact that the structure of jobs and wages within the firm makes it difficult to allow for the waning productivity of older workers, who are therefore specially prone to redundancy. And once older workers become unemployed they suffer long spells because firms tend to prefer younger workers. A quarter of all vacancies and a third of labouring vacancies have an explicit upper age limit of 50.[2] The higher unemployment of older workers also reflects their higher incidence of illness and disability.

Unmarried men experience unemployment rates half as large again as married men of the same age and socio-economic group. It is not clear whether this reflects the institution of marriage — single men have less pressure to take up another job — or whether married men are simply of higher quality than single men and so are desired both by women and by employers. The fact that unmarried men are more likely to suffer from mental instability and alcoholism than their married counterparts hints that the labour-quality point is important.

Once men are married their incidence of unemployment increases dramatically with the number of their dependent children. In 1972 the following male unemployment rates were extracted from the General Household Survey (GHS) for married men:

Number of dependent children	0	1	2	3	4	5+
Unemployment rate (%)	3.2	2.8	3.9	4.5	10.3	12.3

There are many reasons for this. First, the level of family support for those in work is substantially below that for those out of work. In 1982 a working head of household with a 3-child family received £17.55 a week child benefit but (if we assume the children to be aged 9, 11 and 13) got twice that amount if on Supplementary Benefit. Second, families with a large number of dependent children are less mobile. Third, lower-skilled groups — those most at risk of unemployment — have slightly larger families, but the positive relation between family size and unemployment also holds for particular skill groups. Fourth, the sociological literature suggests that groups who are alienated from society and who suffer a feeling of powerlessness are prone to both higher fertility and higher unemployment.

---

1 *DEG*, August 1978, pp. 908-16, and P. Makeham, *Youth Unemployment*, Research Paper 10, DE, March 1980.

2 *DEG*, February 1978, pp. 166-72.

Socio-economic (SEG) Group: There are marked disparities in the incidence of unemployment by occupation. The 1972 General Household Survey indicates the following male unemployment rates:

SEG	Unemployment rate (%)
Senior and intermediate non-manual (e.g. managerial, professional)	1.2
Junior non-manual (e.g. clerical)	3.3
Foreman and skilled manual	4.0
Semi-skilled manual	6.7
Personal service (e.g. waiters, barmen)	19.3
Unskilled manual	14.2

Further, people classified by the Employment Service as general labourers account for around a third of the unemployed. Their lack of training causes unskilled workers to bear the brunt of macroeconomic fluctuations and firms' expansions and contractions. The persistently low level of vacancy to unemployment ratios also reflects the lack of demand for these workers which prolongs their unemployment spells. For example in March 1982 the registered vacancy to unemployment ratio for general labourers was 0.03. Our economic system puts the least skilled at the most risk of unemployment.

Geographical structure: During the forty years 1930-70 the main geographical focus was 'the regional problem'. Although this had a number of dimensions, it was encapsulated in the variation in unemployment rates by region. For much of the postwar period Scotland, Wales and Northern England had unemployment rates some three times as large as those in the Midlands and the South East. As the amount of structural and frictional unemployment appeared to be rather similar in every region, commentators were led to suggest that differences in demand pressure across the regions were the key to the regional problem.[1] But the policy implications of such a finding are unclear. It is very difficult to boost demand in one region without the main impact of the extra spending leaking out into other regions.

In the 1970s regional differences in unemployment relativities have become much less severe. The coefficient of variation (i.e. standard deviation/mean) of unemployment rates across the 10 British regions fell from .42 in 1966 to .20 in February 1982.

Perhaps because the regional structure of unemployment is now so much less unequal, the focus of attention has recently shifted to local labour markets and the decaying cores of our inner cities. Local labour markets which have a disproportionate number of people at risk of unemployment – the young, the old, the single and large families – have relatively high unemployment rates. These demographic factors account for the bulk of the variation in the 1971 male unemployment rate across 32 London boroughs.[2]

Unemployment in the central areas of our great conurbations is now seen to be the major spatial labour-market problem. The Department of the Environment

---

1 R.J. Dixon and A. Thirlwall, *Regional Growth and Unemployment in the United Kingdom*, Macmillan, 1975; P. Cheshire, *Regional Unemployment Differences in GB*, NIESR Regional Papers II, CUP, 1973.

2 D. Metcalf and R. Richardson, 'Unemployment in London', in D. Worswick (ed.), *The Concept and Measurement of Involuntary Unemployment*, Allen and Unwin, 1976.

recently sponsored a number of Inner Area Studies. A typical conclusion from these studies was that the unskilled are 'trapped' in the inner city, and they suggested subsidized migration as a way of reducing the unemployment problem in the central cores. But, as the likelihood of unemployment for a person with given characteristics – a single, older, general labourer for example – is only modestly higher if he lives in the inner city than if he lives in the suburbs, it is not really clear how such subsidized migration would help.[1]

II.2   Why has Unemployment Risen?[2]

Recorded unemployment is now eight times as large as it was in the 1950s:

Male unemployment, %, UK	
1951-5	1.3
1956-60	1.8
1961-5	2.1
1965-70	2.9
1970-75	4.4
1976-80	7.3
1981	13.7

Two sets of factors have been advanced to account for the higher unemployment. First, the 'full-employment' or equilibrium rate of unemployment has risen. Second, fear of inflation and/or balance of payments problems has inhibited successive governments from using fiscal and monetary policy to reduce deficient-demand unemployment.

The 'full-employment' rate of unemployment: If we take the 1965-70 period as one of equilibrium or full employment, there are grounds for thinking that at the same pressure of demand – measured for example by vacancies or capacity utilization – male unemployment would now be above the 1965-70 figure of 3%.

Let us initially dismiss three reasons sometimes advanced to account for the upward creep in the full-employment unemployment rate. First, it is not due to the changed composition of the working population. Young plus old workers, who have relatively high unemployment rates, now account for a smaller fraction of the labourforce than they did 10 years ago.[3] And women, who have lower-than-average unemployment rates, comprise a growing fraction of the labourforce. Second, the geographical and occupational mismatch between unemployment and vacancies has

---

1   A useful discussion of this problem is P. Cheshire, 'Inner Areas as Spatial Labour Markets: a Critique of the Inner Area Studies', *Urban Studies*, 1979, pp. 29-43.

2   See S. Nickell, 'The Determinants of Equilibrium Unemployment in Britain', *EJ*, forthcoming 1982, and 'Wages and Unemployment', *EJ*, forthcoming 1982. Official statistics do not measure female unemployment accurately. Therefore in this section we concentrate on male unemployment.

3   In 1972 those aged under 24 plus those aged over 60 accounted for 30% of the labourforce. By 1982 this proportion had fallen to 28%. Although younger workers are an increasing proportion of the labourforce, this is more than offset by the declining share accounted for by older people; see *DEG*, April 1981, pp. 167-73.

not worsened.[1] For example the coefficient of variation (standard deviation/mean) of unemployment across 172 local labour markets fell from .67 in 1966 to .53 in 1973.

Third, the most controversial of the factors advanced concerns benefits. It is widely believed that when the replacement ratio, defined as unemployment benefit and/or supplementary benefit relative to earnings, rises, this causes working people to become unemployed or to prolong unemployment. The most careful statistical analysis indicates that the elasticity of unemployment duration with respect to the replacement ratio is +0.6.[2] To see how much extra unemployment this can account for, we can take boom years to standardize for any business-cycle influence:

	Replacement ratio (= benefit paid per recipient/post-tax male manual earnings, full-time workers aged over 21)	Unemployment
1964-5	.33	330,000
1973	.37	580,000

The replacement ratio rose by 12.1% between these two years. So the extra unemployment generated is

$$12.1\% \times 0.6 \times 330,000 = 24,000$$

This is around one-tenth of the increase in unemployment of 250,000 between 1964-5 and 1973. Assuming such estimates are reliable, it is clear that the disincentive effects associated with more generous unemployment benefits account for only a modest fraction of the rise in unemployment.

In any event, since 1973 the world has changed. At a time of high overall unemployment the job opportunities not taken by those deterred by benefits may well be taken by other unemployed men. Further, the replacement ratio has fallen, not risen, over the last decade, so changes in benefit levels have reduced rather than increased unemployment.

Two interrelated factors which influence the demand for labour have had an impact on the equilibrium rate of unemployment. First, employment in Mining, Manufacturing, Construction and Utilities has fallen by 4m since 1966. This big change in the structure of employment will tend to raise unemployment because a smooth transition from production industries to service industries is difficult.

Second, there has been a striking rise in real wages in manufacturing relative to increases in labour productivity. The share of labour in value added rose (1970 = 100) from 95 in the 1960s to 105 in the 1970s, and simultaneously employment in manufacturing fell by 3m between 1966 and 1981.

There are a number of reasons for this rise in real wages relative to the value of the output produced by labour. It is normal for the share of wages in value added

---

1   See R. Turvey, 'Structural Change and Structural Unemployment', *International Labour Review*, September/October 1977; N. Bosanquet, 'Structuralism and Structural Unemployment', *BJIR*, November 1979.

2   S. Nickell, 'The Effect of Unemployment and Related Benefits on the Duration of Unemployment', *EJ*, March 1979.

to rise in a recession even though employment is falling. And the 1970s and 1980s had more recession years than the 1960s. Further, a higher fraction of the labour-force is now unionized and the premium in pay for people covered by union collective agreements over non-union individuals doubled between 1968 and 1972.[1] Finally, the rise in oil and other input prices in 1974 and 1979 worsened the terms of trade faced by the British economy but real wages did not fully adjust downwards in either instance. In consequence profits have been squeezed. The share of real profits in net domestic income fell from 13% in the 1960s to 8% in the 1970s.[2] The profit squeeze was probably compounded by the lack of inflation accounting in manufacturing, price controls and international competition.

Scott has argued that the profits squeeze has, in turn, been associated with a reduction in investment and, in particular, in labour-using investment, and that this has been associated with a substantial fall in employment in manufacturing and a rise in aggregate unemployment.[3]

Nickell calculates that the decline in employment in the Production Industries sector coupled with the rise in labour's share in value added raised the equilibrium unemployment rate by around 2% in the 1970s. He suggests that in 1979 the equilibrium or full-employment rate of male unemployment was 6%:

	%
1965-70 rate	3
plus increase associated with decline in production industry employment and rise in labour's share in value added	2
plus increase associated with other factors	1
	6

But this is less than half the 1982 level of unemployment, so cyclical — deficient-demand — factors are the dominant cause of current unemployment.

Deficient demand: Successive governments have been reluctant to use fiscal and monetary policy to get rid of this deficient-demand unemployment — equivalent to 1.5m people. Yet there is strong evidence that unemployment can be reduced by expansionary fiscal and monetary policy. In wartime, for example, unemployment falls to near zero. In the 1950s in the US unemployment approached 10%. It was widely believed that this was due to technological factors. Yet the expansionary macroeconomic policy — tax cuts and the extra spending associated with the Vietnam War — soon halved the level of unemployment.

So if stimulating demand could do the trick, what stops us? There are three main constraints, dealt with in more detail in chapter 1. First, government revenue as usually measured tends to fall short of public spending, and there is a public-sector borrowing requirement. Second, the expansionary fiscal and monetary policy will probably result in higher wage settlements. Third, in an open economy like Britain the balance of payments worsens when macroeconomic policy is expansionary.

---

1   R. Layard, D. Metcalf and S. Nickell, 'The Effect of Collective Bargaining on Absolute and Relative Wages', *BJIR*, November 1978.
2   *BEQB*, June 1979, p. 183. Real profits allow for the distortions arising from inflation.
3   M. Scott, *Can We Get Back To Full Employment?*, Macmillan, 1978, chapter 5.

II.3   Moderating Unemployment

If unemployment is to be cut to 2m – itself high by postwar standards – by 1986, the economy needs to generate around 1,200 jobs every day in the four years 1982-6. Unemployment is currently 3m. In addition the DE calculate that the labourforce will rise by around 0.75m in this period. Therefore 1.75m extra jobs are needed to reduce unemployment to 2m. This is a depressing prospect because during the previous most rapid growth of employment (1960-65) employment only rose by around 600 jobs a day.

Reductions in income tax or in the national insurance surcharge are a very expensive way of generating employment, with each extra job having a gross annual cost of between £20,000 and £40,000. Even British Leyland has only cost the taxpayer £25,000 per job supported, spread over the seven years since 1975. So reflation via tax cuts would certainly not boost employment sufficiently, and anyway is ruled out because of the inflationary consequences. This is why successive governments have turned to special employment measures in an attempt to buy more employment per £. In this section we first examine these special employment measures. Then we turn to see how the incidence of unemployment might be made more equal and the incomes of unemployed people improved.

Special employment measures: In January 1982 558,000 people were covered by the various special measures, reducing the unemployment figure by 325,000. In 1982/3 spending on these schemes will top £1bn. As they have evolved since the mid-1970s we can classify three types of scheme[1]:

Measures to raise labour demand, e.g. wage subsidies and job creation.
Measures to reduce labour supply, e.g. by reducing participation rates of
    older men or sharing available work in firms suffering from the
    recession.
Measures to keep youths off the unemployment register.

In deciding whether to establish, expand or contract a particular measure Whitehall compares it with what would happen if the same money were used for income-tax cuts. The criteria on which such comparisons are based include the impact of the measure on employment and unemployment, the balance of payments, the inflation rate, and the level and distribution of output.

Between 1975 and 1979 the largest measure was the Temporary Employment Subsidy (TES) under which the employer was paid £20 a week for each job he preserved when, without the subsidy, he otherwise would have made the employees redundant. This was so successful at exporting unemployment in textiles, clothing and footwear from Britain to the EEC that the EEC caused us to withdraw it. The TES also scored better than income-tax cuts on nearly all the evaluation criteria. Indeed the DE calculate that the net cost to the Exchequer of TES was zero, because the flowback of money to the Treasury in the form of fewer unemployment benefits paid out and more tax revenue gathered in exceeded the subsidy payments made to firms.

TES was a subsidy *preserving* marginal employment. An alternative possibility is a subsidy to firms who *create* extra employment. It has been calculated that if

---

1   For a full discussion see D. Metcalf, *Alternatives to Unemployment*, Policy Studies Institute, forthcoming 1983, and R. Layard, 'The Costs and Benefits of Selective Employment Policies: The British Case', *BJIR*, July 1979.

firms were paid £70 a week for up to a year for each extra employee they took on over and above a previous benchmark employment level, some 250,000 jobs could be created at an annual exchequer cost of £0.5bn or £2,000 per job per year. The reason that the cost per job is so low is that the subsidy is concentrated on the *extra* employees being hired. By contrast cuts in the payroll tax are spread very thinly right across the board, giving firms little incentive to hire extra people.[1]

Job-creation schemes can be thought of as 100% wage subsidies to selective public employment. These schemes have a number of advantages over general public spending if the aim is to reduce unemployment as much as possible per unit of expenditure. In particular such schemes can be targetted on unemployment-prone low-wage groups, and they use labour-intensive techniques so that little of the public spending leaks out into higher-wage jobs elsewhere in the economy or into imports. The Community Enterprise Programme (CEP) only has 30,000 places. It is targetted towards providing public employment for the long-term unemployed. As there are a million individuals who have been unemployed over a year, it is not surprising that in the 1982 budget the government announced a new scheme of Community Work which might have up to 100,000 places. But to keep the cost of the scheme down, individuals will only be paid their unemployment benefit plus an allowance of around £15 a week, whereas CEP pays the 'rate for the job'. In any event this is not going to make much of a dent in the problem of long-term unemployment.

The second set of special measures concentrate on reducing the labour supply. This can be achieved either by reducing labourforce participation rates, e.g. encouraging longer education or early retirement, or by worksharing. Early retirement and worksharing have been extensively subsidized in the EEC. We also have schemes in Britain. The Job Release Scheme pays men aged 62 or over and women aged 59 a tax-free allowance (£50.50 in March 1982 for a married man) if they retire early, providing their employer agrees to replace him or her from the unemployment register. Under the Temporary Short Time Working Compensation Scheme firms are encouraged to adopt short-time working instead of redundancies. Firms are eligible for support for nine months at the subsidy rate of half of normal earnings for workless days. In early 1981 almost a million individuals ('sharers') were covered by this scheme, equivalent to nearly a quarter of a million jobs supported. A year later, as output recovered, only 168,000 sharers were covered. The government should be cautious about expanding measures to reduce the labour supply much further. We have as many as 3m unemployed because the government is worried about inflation and believes that inflation would be higher if unemployment fell. This inflation effect occurs whether unemployment is reduced by cutting labour supply via schemes like early retirement or via expanding labour demand by wage subsidies. But when labour supply is cut we get more leisure — voluntary and involuntary — while when labour demand is raised we get valuable output.

---

1 For details of TES see *DEG*, July 1977, pp. 692-6; May 1978, pp. 544-6 and November 1979, pp. 1122-3. See also B. Deakin and C. Pratten, *The Effects of the Temporary Employment Subsidy*, Occasional Paper No. 53, DAE, Cambridge UP, 1981. For a formal treatment of the incremental employment subsidy, see R. Layard and S. Nickell, 'The Case for Subsidising Extra Jobs', *EJ*, March 1980. For a less formal discussion, see R. Layard, 'Unemployment in Britain: Causes and Cures', Centre for Labour Economics, LSE, Discussion Paper 87, May 1981. A small version of the incremental employment subsidy — the Small Firms Employment Subsidy — existed in the late 1980s, see *DEG*, May 1978, pp. 549-54 and November 1979, p. 1124.

Rising unemployment among teenagers resulted in a number of special employment measures for youths. The Youth Opportunities Programme (YOP) caters for some 550,000 entrants – or 1 in every 2 school-leavers – at a gross cost in 1982/3 of £735m. The bulk of YOP entrants are placed in a firm to gain work experience. They receive an allowance and cost the firm nothing. YOP ran into a number of criticisms. Many unions argued that employers substituted youths for adult workers and that YOP did not provide 'proper jobs', though these criticisms seem contradictory. Also worrying is that in 1980 only a third of YOP entrants were in employment when their YOP place terminated – though this probably reflects the recession rather than inadequacies of YOP. In response to this criticism the government has proposed the Youth Training Scheme (YTS), a more training-intensive version of YOP. When it is fully operational it will provide 300,000 places at any one time at an annual cost of £1bn. In effect this represents a 'pre-vocational' training year for many unemployed school-leavers. The big worry about YTS is whether it will kill off the regular youth labour market for 16- and 17-year-olds. If employers are getting such labour at little wage cost, they may have little incentive to hire teenagers through the normal channels. In this case 300,000 would be a minimum estimate of the number of places required. It may well prove necessary to subsidize the regular employment of youngsters to encourage employers not to rely solely on YTS as the source of teenage recruitment.

Distributional issues: The national insurance system as originally conceived has completely broken down in the face of higher unemployment (see section III for a description of the national insurance system). In 1982 under half the unemployed people were receiving unemployment benefit. This poor coverage occurs because unemployment benefit is exhausted after 12 months, and for other reasons. Imagine the public outcry and legal shambles if half those involved in car crashes were not covered by insurance. Yet that is exactly the coverage that our so-called 'national insurance' provides for the unemployed. The remainder are forced to rely on means-tested relief and, as successive reports of the Supplementary Benefit Commission (SBC) have shown, they are among the poorest of the British poor.[1]

Lengthening unemployment spells have caused many more people to be unemployed for over 52 weeks. In mid-1982 over 1m people had been out of work over a year – contrast this with the corresponding figure of 21,000 in 1956. Employment quotas and subsidies have been suggested as methods of reducing this long-term unemployment.[2] If such measures are thought to have too large efficiency costs, benefits could be raised.

The Manpower Service Commission is in a dilemma over the long-term unemployed. It has a whole series of managerial objectives like increasing its share

---

1 See for example SBC, *Annual Report 1978*, Cmnd. 7725, HMSO, October 1979, paras. 3.20, 13.18. Supplementary benefit has short-term rates and (higher) long-term rates for those who have been on SB for more than one year. But the unemployed *never* qualify for the long-term rate. In 1982 this denial imposed a financial penalty of £10.60 on an unemployed married man. See R. Disney, 'Theorising the Welfare State: the Case of Unemployment Insurance in Britain', *Journal of Social Policy*, January 1982, for a fuller discussion of the failure of national insurance in the face of high unemployment.

2 See S. Nickell, 'A Picture of Male Unemployment in Britain', *EJ*, December 1980, for a fuller discussion of quotas and subsidies, and *DEG*, January 1980, pp. 9-12 for a discussion of long-term unemployment.

of hirings (what it calls 'placing penetration'). Thus in 1978-9 2.7m vacancies were notified to the Employment Service, of which they filled 1.8m, and those placements accounted for 20% of all engagements by firms.[1] If the MSC starts to submit 'difficult to place' individuals, employers may cease notifying their vacancies to the MSC. Consequently many individuals seldom get submitted for a job by the MSC. The number of submissions is inversely related to unemployment duration. While the MSC's managerial objectives are understandable, it does not seem right that the people who need the most help from the Employment Service in fact seem to get the least. One way round this problem, recognized by the MSC, would be for the Job Centre to try to match a man or woman to a job only after (say) one month of unemployment instead of, as now, on the day the person joins the unemployment register. Many people would have left the unemployment register during the 4-week period, so more MSC resources would then be concentrated on those facing poorer employment prospects.

A shorter work-week — negotiated through collective bargaining rather than introduced by the DE as a special employment measure — has been suggested as a method of sharing unemployment. If for example the work-week fell from 40 hours to 38, and no extra overtime hours were worked, average hours worked would have fallen by 2/40 or 5%. Would extra men and women be hired to fill the gap? If the hourly wage remains constant then the firm's labour costs will also have fallen by 5% and so it has an incentive to hire the extra labour. But there may be difficulties — reorganization of shift lengths, extra hiring costs and the fact that the unemployed are mainly unskilled when the firm may require skilled workers. If, as trade unions demand, hours are reduced while weekly pay remains constant then the unit labour costs will be increased by 5% and, especially where the firm faces international competition, the incentive to hire extra labour is attenuated. It is often claimed that unit labour costs will not rise because labour productivity will rise. But presumably if it is possible to raise productivity this would already have been done. Anyway, if productivity goes up this vitiates the need for any extra employment, so defeating the original reason for the shorter work-week. The Department of Employment have calculated that if the potential output lost by a reduction in the work-week from 40 to 38 hours was made up as follows:

	%
increased employment	35
higher output per man	20
more overtime	35
lower output	10

then unemployment would fall by 210,000, net government spending would be lowered by £500m (lower unemployment benefit, and more tax and national insurance revenue) but labour costs would rise by 4.4%. The inflationary effect of the increase in labour costs would in turn weaken our competitive position and damage our longer-term employment prospects. In late 1979 and early 1980 over one million manual workers in engineering, plumbing, printing, retail food and the exhibition industry negotiated a cut in their standard work-week to below 40 hours. It is interesting that employment does not seem to have risen in these trades relative to employment elsewhere.

---

1   See MSC, *The Employment Service in the 1980s*, London, 1979, and *DEG*, June 1979, pp. 558-63.

Summary and prospects: In 1982 unemployment is 3m, 1m people have been out of work for over a year and the population of working age is growing. A decade ago unemployment was around a third of its current level. Many factors have been advanced to account for the growth in unemployment over the last ten years. For example it is frequently held that the following have contributed to higher levels of unemployment: changing composition of the workforce; housing policy, causing labour immobility; higher social-security benefits; employment protection legislation; and health and safety legislation. In fact there is no evidence that these factors are responsible. Two factors which have contributed to higher unemployment are the rising share of labour in value added and the mismatch caused by the decline of the production industries. Neither of these two factors are likely to be reversed much in the short run, and anyway they have only added around two or three percentage points to the unemployment total.

Clearly the main cause of current high levels of unemployment is insufficient demand. Demand could be stimulated by tax cuts or by government spending. But tax cuts will not generate sufficient employment to make a big dent in unemployment. Government spending is more employment-intensive: capital spending boosts employment in construction while extra current spending implies more policemen, teachers, social workers and nurses. Both the TUC and the Labour Party have advocated large increases in public spending. For example the Labour Party suggested raising public spending in 1982/3 from £115bn to £124bn. Unfortunately the TUC and Labour Party are both silent on how any inflationary pressure generated by this extra spending might be contained. The trade-off between extra jobs and higher inflation is discussed in chapter 1 and we consider below (section V) whether incomes policy can make that trade-off more palatable.

III   WEALTH, INCOME AND PAY

The distribution of wealth, income and earnings are topics which excite great controversy. In this section we describe these distributions, and discuss some of the theories advanced to account for them. Our analysis of labour earnings looks at the pay structure by industry, occupation and sex. We then turn to problems of poverty and low pay.

III.1   Distribution of Wealth[1]

The measurement of personal wealth, and its distribution, is notoriously difficult. There are three main methods by which the distribution of personal wealth can be estimated. First, a sample survey could be undertaken of individuals' assets and liabilities to determine net wealth (sometimes referred to as net worth). Such a survey is desirable in principle but would be difficult to execute because of such problems as a low response rate and the difficulty of determining the composition

---

1   For a full discussion see Royal Commission on the Distribution of Income and Wealth (Diamond Commission), Report No. 7, Cmnd. 7595, HMSO, July 1979. This Royal Commission was set up in 1974 and, alas, closed down in 1979. It did sterling work on improving available information on wealth and income distributions. Its findings have been brought together in an excellent brief non-technical publication, *An A to Z of Income and Wealth*, HMSO, January 1980.

and valuation of items to be included in wealth. Second, the investment income method works backwards from statistics on investment income to determine the distribution of capital from which this investment income is derived. Third, under the present British tax system the only time an individual's wealth becomes known is at death when a return is filed for capital transfer tax (CTT). These estate returns to the Inland Revenue form the basis of most of our knowledge on the distribution of wealth. The calculations assume that the wealth of the individuals who die comprises a sample of the assets of the living. They are then adjusted for elements of wealth not accounted for in CTT data such as the wealth of those excluded from CTT statistics because they have relatively small wealth holdings.

The data in table 5.3 show that in 1979 the wealthiest 1% of the adult population held a quarter of all the marketable wealth (e.g. dwellings, land, shares, Building Society deposits) in the UK. This is more than the amount held by the whole of the bottom 75%. In 1976 more than half the adult population had net wealth of less than £1,000, while 4 in 1,000 had wealth in excess of £100,000. These very wealthy 146,000 individuals each had an average wealth over £300,000. Even if they received no real return on it, this amount is greater than the typical person would earn in a lifetime of work.

The total value of personal wealth was £488bn in 1979. Physical assets — dwellings, land, vehicles and consumer durables — and financial assets each account for around half of this total. Less wealthy individuals hold the bulk of their wealth in the form of houses and life-insurance policies, while shares and land are proportionately much more important for richer people.

Wealth can be accumulated by savings out of inheritance, earnings, entrepreneurial fortunes, capital gains and financial windfalls. Overall some 60% of wealth represents savings out of earnings — thus older individuals have more wealth than new labourforce entrants — but those in the top 5% of the wealth distribution are much more likely to have accumulated their wealth via inheritance or entrepreneurial fortunes. It is clear that rich people inherit a disproportionate amount of their wealth.

So far we have only considered marketable wealth. If we allow for the imputed value of the stream of future pension benefits which are locked away and not marketable, the share of wealth held by the bottom 75% of the distribution doubles to 40%. This is because virtually all members of the adult population have accrued rights to state pensions and the number of people in occupational pension schemes is growing.

The distribution of wealth has certainly become much less unequal over this century. The share of the top 1% fell from 61% to 24% between 1923 and 1979. This mainly reflects the higher rates of estate duty (now capital transfer tax) and the spread of owner-occupation from 10% of dwellings in 1900 to over 50% in 1980. Price changes are also important. Less wealthy people hold more of their wealth in the form of housing while the rich hold more shares. So if house prices rise relative to share prices, the distribution of wealth becomes more equal.

III.2   Distribution of Income

The distribution of total income from all sources (i.e. from employment, pensions, dividends, etc.) is less concentrated than the distribution of wealth. This is because earnings from employment are the main source of total personal income and these

TABLE 5.3

Distribution of Personal Wealth held by Adult Population UK, 1979

Percentage of wealth owned by	1979 Marketable wealth	1979 Marketable wealth plus rights to occupational and state pensions
Most wealthy 1% of population	24%	13%
2%	32%	18%
5%	45%	27%
10%	59%	37%
25%	82%	60%
50%	95%	81%
Total	£488bn	–

Source: ST, 1982, No. 12, table 5.26.

earnings are more equally distributed than the investment income provided by personal wealth.

The *composition* of total personal income in the UK may be seen from table 5.4. Some two-thirds of personal income comes from employment. Social-security benefits and other cash grants have doubled in importance since 1950. This reflects higher real pensions and the growing number of pensioners and unemployed.

The *distribution* of personal income in 1976-7 is shown in table 5.5. The data are derived from the Inland Revenue, supplemented by information from the Family Expenditure Survey on incomes which are not taxable or are below the tax threshold. The data refer to tax units, i.e. generally treat a married couple as one unit. The distribution of income is less concentrated than the distribution of wealth. The top 1% (10%) of each distribution only account for 5% (26%) of income but they hold 24% (59%) of the wealth.

TABLE 5.4

Composition of Personal Income, UK, 1980

Source	%
Wages and salaries	65
Income from self-employment	8
Rent, dividends and interest	8
Private pensions, annuities, etc.	6
Social-security benefits and other current transfers	13
Total: £183bn	100

Source: ST, 1982, No. 12, table 5.1.

Half the units had annual incomes under £3,000 and less than one-tenth had incomes above £10,000. The fact that there are relatively few people with high incomes makes the redistribution of income, and greater provision of desirable health and education services, difficult. While it may be possible to squeeze many thousands of pounds of tax out of a rich individual, there are not many of them, so that the extra revenue raised by squeezing them harder is quite small. Nevertheless, the share of the top 20% of the income distribution, with 43% of income, is seven times the share of the bottom 20% who account for only 6% of the total. Likewise, the top half of the income distribution has three times the share of the bottom half. It should be borne in mind that these figures refer to the distribution at one specific point in time; many of those in the bottom half of the distribution in 1978-9 (e.g. some pensioners and students) will be in the top half at other points in their life. The inequality in lifetime incomes is less than the inequality of the income distribution observed at any particular point in time.

Some of the inequality is redressed via taxes on incomes and benefits in the form of cash and services like education and health. Income tax makes the distribution a little more equal (see table 5.5). After tax the share of the top 10% falls from 26% to 23%, while the share of the bottom 40% rises from 16% to 19%. Likewise social-security benefits and spending on education and health boost the incomes of the poor *proportionately* more than those of the rich. But poorer families receive *absolutely* less from state spending on education, health and transport subsidies.[1]

TABLE 5.5

Distribution of Personal Income before and after Income Tax, UK, 1978-9

Quantile groups	Income before tax		Average income before tax	Income after tax		Average income after tax	Av. income after tax as % of income before tax
	(£m)	*(%)*	*(£)*	*(£m)*	*(%)*	*(£)*	
Top 1%	6,344	5.3	21,819	3,830	3.9	13,172	60.4
2-5%	12,807	10.7	11,012	9,793	9.8	8,420	76.5
6-10%	12,054	10.1	8,292	9,682	9.7	6,660	80.3
Top 10%	31,206	26.1	10,733	23,305	23.4	8,015	74.7
11-20%	19,677	16.5	6,768	16,162	16.3	5,559	82.1
21-30%	16,103	13.5	5,538	13,381	13.5	4,602	83.1
31-40%	13,391	11.2	4,605	11,279	11.3	3,879	84.2
41-50%	10,972	9.2	3,774	9,266	9.3	3,187	84.4
51-60%	8,767	7.3	3,015	7,643	7.7	2,629	87.2
61-70%	6,971	5.8	2,398	6,349	6.4	2,184	91.1
71-80%	5,440	4.5	1,871	5,095	5.1	1,752	93.6
81-90%	4,178	3.5	1,437	4,061	4.1	1,397	97.2
Bottom 10%	2,904	2.4	999	2,882	2.9	991	99.2

Source: ST, 1982, No. 12, table 5.23.

Note: Based on tax units. The total number of tax units is 29.1 million.

The income figures presented and discussed in table 5.5 should be treated cautiously for the following reasons: (i) the data ignore income in the form of imputed rent from owner-occupied houses, fringe benefits, home production and capital gains; (ii) the data are uncorrected for tax evasion and misreporting; (iii) the data refer to money but not real incomes and this is important because inflation affects people differently according to the basket of goods they consume; (iv) income alone does not capture other aspects of welfare such as leisure, security

---

1   J. Le Grand, *The Strategy of Equality*, Allen and Unwin, 1982.

and job satisfaction; (v) family composition has changed over time such that there are now more old and young people living alone; this will tend to increase the dispersion in income observed over time; (vi) the data refer to current and not lifetime income distributions.

III.3 Distribution of Earnings

The distribution of earnings, like the distribution of income, is positively skewed (median earnings are less than mean earnings). However, the earnings distribution is more equal than the distribution of income because the latter includes a return on wealth which, as we have seen (section III.1), is very concentrated.

The dispersion of earnings in April 1981 (full-time workers, men aged twenty-one and over, women aged eighteen and over, whose pay for the survey week was not affected by absence) was as follows.[1]

		As a % of median			
	Median earnings per week (£)	*Lowest decile*	*Lower quartile*	*Upper quartile*	*Highest decile*
Men	126.5	66	80	130	167
Women	82.2	68	81	130	173

Both men and women at the lowest 10% point earned around two-thirds of median pay, while the best-paid 10% earned over two-thirds more than the corresponding median.

There are two particularly important and interesting facts concerning the distribution of gross weekly earnings of male *manual* workers. First, the dispersion of the distribution has been quite stable for almost a century:[2]

Distribution of weekly earnings, manual men (% of median)		
	1886	*1981*
Lowest decile	68.6	69.7
Lower quartile	82.8	82.8
Median	100.0	100.0
Upper quartile	121.7	122.5
Highest decile	143.1	150.6

---

1   DE, *New Earnings Survey*, 1981, Part A, table 1. The data in this section refer to individuals, not families or Inland Revenue income units. Many people only work part-time or part of the year and therefore the distribution of annual earnings of those who worked at any time during the year is different from the distribution above, because the annual earnings distribution has a concentration of people in the lower tail.

2   A full discussion of the evidence on the distribution of earnings and evaluation of theories seeking to explain this distribution is contained in A.R.Thatcher, 'The New Earnings Survey and the Distribution of Earnings', in A. Atkinson (ed.), *The Personal Distribution of Incomes*, Allen and Unwin, 1975. E.H. Phelps Brown, *The Inequality of Pay*, OUP, 1977, contains much evidence on this topic.

This stability suggests that we might seek to explain the distribution of earnings by factors such as differences in ability, motivation and luck, which might be expected to remain fairly stable from one generation to the next, rather than by appeal to institutional factors such as the growth of unions, or social forces such as the extension of public intervention, which have changed dramatically in the last century.

Second, the position an individual occupies in the distribution changes from year to year. Evidence on the gross weekly earnings of all full-time adults who were in the New Earnings Surveys in 1970 to 1974 (*DEG*, January 1977) indicates that the lowest-paid workers received by far the largest percentage increase in earnings between one survey and the next, while the higher-paid workers tended to experience much smaller percentage increases. Such movements are known as 'regression towards the mean'. Between 1970 and 1974 21% of male manual workers were in the lowest-paid tenth in at least one of the five surveys, but only 3% were in this tenth in all of the surveys. These movements refer to weekly earnings of full-time workers and therefore reflect the variable nature of many components of manual workers' earnings (e.g. overtime, short-time, bonuses, piecework), the effects of job changes and the incidence of wage settlements. Movements in individuals' hourly earnings, which may more nearly reflect skill and motivation, or in annual earnings, which may reflect the incidence of unemployment, could be more or less dramatic than the fluctuations in weekly earnings.

One important explanation of the positive skew in the earnings distribution relates to the coupling of natural ability and training. In a smoothly functioning, competitive labour market, earnings will reflect productivity at the margin. Among all the determinants of marginal productivity we may concentrate here on a worker's 'natural ability' and training. If, for a given level of formal training, a man comes to the labour market with relatively great motivation, ability and drive he will tend to earn more than the average worker. Further, it is established that on average the more naturally gifted man tends to undertake more than average amounts of training. An unskewed distribution of ability combined with a skewed distribution of training produces a skewed distribution of productivity. The last, in an approximately competitive market, produces a skewed earnings distribution.

This simple picture is only a partial explanation of the actual earnings distribution. First, not everyone has equal access to the educational and training sectors, even where natural ability is the same for all. One implication is that relatively bright working-class children have difficulty in getting sufficient secondary and advanced education. This means that ability is not properly harnessed with education, thereby reducing the degree of earnings inequality.

Second, in some activities, including many of the professions, free entry of labour is restricted and earnings are pushed above the competitive level by union activity. The impact of such behaviour on the distribution of pay depends on (i) the numbers affected, and (ii) the size of the union mark-up. Union activity among male manual workers probably reduces inequality because although a similar proportion of skilled and unskilled workers are covered by union agreements, the pay premium associated with union coverage is higher for unskilled workers than for the skilled.

Third, luck plays a significant part in determining earnings, particularly in any one year. The last qualification is important because a more valid measure of material well-being than current earnings is the discounted sum of lifetime earnings.

If a man is lucky one year but unlucky the next we would have a misleading view of his well-being by looking at either year in isolation. Similarly, if a man is receiving a low wage currently because he is training, but expected to do well when he is trained, it would be mistaken to view him as a poverty case. The same may apply to people approaching retirement.

The General Household Survey (GHS) provides each year information on individual earnings and related individual characteristics such as age, schooling, work experience, race and family background. The 1975 GHS has been extensively analysed.[1] Let us consider the factors which generated the distribution of pay among the 5,000 or so full-time male employees in the sample.

Consider first the distribution of hourly earnings. Years of full-time education have a substantial effect on hourly earnings. Holding constant father's occupation, work experience, ethnic background, health and marital status, each additional year of education raises pay by between 5% and 10%. Does this mean education is a good weapon against poverty? The trouble with ordinary education is that while a person is being educated you do not know whether or not he is going to end up poor. In any case there is such a spread of earnings for people with a given level of education that even if all education disparities were eliminated the remaining inequality would be still over 93% of what it is now.

Of course one could go further than eliminating educational disparity. Positive discrimination could be practised whereby those who had low earnings potential would be given *more* education than others. But this implies the ability to spot low earners while they are still being educated and it is doubtful whether this is practicable. It could, however, be done for adult training – by then people have shown what they can and cannot earn – and there is strong evidence that short periods of vocational training are able to improve a person's position in the occupational hierarchy.[2]

Family background, measured by father's occupation, influences hourly earnings directly and indirectly via education levels. An individual with a non-manual father had, *ceteris paribus*, hourly earnings 12% higher than those with unskilled fathers.

Marriage is also associated with higher pay. After controlling for other factors, married men had hourly pay 14% greater than single men. This may be because marriage puts pressure on individuals to work harder or may simply reflect the fact that better-quality men are more likely to get married.

Pay is influenced by work experience. On average an individual with between 30-40 years of work experience earns, *ceteris paribus*, twice as much as a person with 5-10 years experience. But the individual who gets stuck in a particular manual job has little prospect of a real wage increase (other than from general economic growth) after the first 10 years.

One particularly important finding concerns the influence of colour and country of birth on pay. Other things being equal (i.e. holding constant age, experience, weeks worked, years of schooling, marital status, etc.), West Indian-born workers receive hourly earnings 14% lower than whites. Other non-whites receive, on

1 R. Layard, D. Piachaud, M. Stewart, *The Causes of Poverty*, Royal Commission on Distribution of Income and Wealth (Diamond Commission), *Background Paper*, No. 5 (to *Report* No. 6, *Lower Incomes*), HMSO, 1978, especially chapter 4. This is by far the best discussion on the factors generating the distribution of pay in Britain. The remainder of this section draws freely on this source.

2 D. Metcalf and S. Nickell, 'Occupational Mobility in Great Britain', *Research in Labor Economics*, vol. 5, 1982.

average, some 22% less than whites. These differentials occur because black and brown workers tend (like women) to be crowded into low-paying occupations and industries. Thus while 58% of Pakistani males and 32% of West Indian males working in Britain are unskilled or semi-skilled, the corresponding figure for whites is 18%. Further, virtually no whites with degree-level qualifications do manual work but around one-fifth of such men from minorities do manual work, and minority men with high qualifications are much less likely than whites to be in professional and management occupations.[1]

This occupational structure discourages them from undertaking extra schooling or training because the pay-off to such investment is lower than it is for whites. Further, their occupational status may lead potential employers to conclude that non-whites are feckless when in fact their higher average turnover rate or higher average absenteeism rate are characteristics of their occupations and industries, and not inherent racial characteristics. For example, a study of labour turnover at London Transport[2] showed that, other things being equal, blacks had a longer duration of employment than whites. The occupational composition of black and brown workers, as compared to white workers, has (quite rightly) become a pressing policy issue. The problem is in many ways analogous to that facing women (see section III.6).

The factors above account for around a third of the variance of *annual* earnings. Another third is explained by differences in the number of weeks worked in the year by each individual. This is itself influenced by human capital factors. Individuals with relatively high hourly earnings work more weeks — it is the unskilled who bear the burden of unemployment and, to a lesser extent, sickness.

We now turn to examine some more narrowly defined aspects of the distribution of earnings. The next three sections analyse the pay structure by occupation, industry and sex. The lower tail of the income distribution is studied in the final sections on poverty and low pay.

III.4   Wage Structure by Occupation[3]

The foundations of wage theory are contained in two famous principles. First, Adam Smith's principle of net advantage states that when competition exists in the labour market the 'whole of the advantages and disadvantages' of different occupations will continually tend towards equality. Note that this principle does not imply that wages will tend towards equality, but that (suitably discounted) lifetime returns to one occupation will tend to equal those in another occupation. The returns that make an occupation attractive or unattractive are both pecuniary and non-pecuniary. Second, we have the principle of non-competing groups, which evolved from the work of John Stuart Mill and Cairnes; this states (broadly) that certain non-competitive factors may inhibit the tendency towards equality in net advantages.

---

1 D. Smith, *Racial Disadvantage in Britain*, Pelican, 1977. See also DE (Unit for Manpower Studies), *The Role of Immigrants in the Labour Market*, 1976, for a comprehensive discussion.

2 J. Smith, *Labour Supply and Employment Duration in London Transport*, Greater London Paper No. 15, 1976.

3 The forces generating the occupational pay structure excite considerable controversy. For a full discussion see G. Routh, *Occupation and Pay in Great Britain 1906-79*, Macmillan, 1980.

Linked to these two principles are two sets of reasons for the existence of occupational wage differentials: compensatory wage differentials and non-compensatory wage differentials.

Compensatory wage differentials are those differentials which are consistent with competition in the labour market. If individuals were not compensated for the factors listed below (in the form of higher wages when at work), then the supply of labour to those occupations would tend to be deficient. All other things being equal, individuals will tend, for example, to be compensated in the form of higher wages for entering occupations that (1) require long periods of education and/or training, (2) are dangerous or dirty, (3) are subject to lay-offs or have a relatively short working life. (4) Also if they are risk-averters, they will desire to be compensated in terms of the mean earnings of the occupation if the dispersion of the earnings around the mean is very large. (5) Differentials will also accrue to wholly exceptional workers, such as professional sportsmen and entertainers, this being an example of economic rent applied to the labour market.

Non-compensating occupational wage differentials are different. They occur where economic or institutional reasons inhibit competition in the labour market. For example, closed shop agreements inhibit union members from non-union competition. Legal restrictions boost solicitors' pay for conveyancing work. And minimum-wage legislation might raise the pay of those at the bottom of the earnings distribution above the competitive level.

Earnings by broad occupational groups are presented in table 5.6. It will be seen that earnings of non-manual workers are greater than those of manual workers. This reflects in some large part the relative education/training intensities of the two groups. There is also evidence of other compensating differentials. Bricklayers (group 16) earn 270p per hour, while general labourers (group 18) earn 229p: the bricklayers are being compensated for their relatively low earnings while apprenticed. Within group 7, firemen earn 314p per hour while security guards earn 255p. The firemen are being compensated because their job is more dangerous.

There is also evidence of individuals being compensated for being more able, or having more alternative job opportunities, or undertaking a more skilled task, even though the length of education and training is similar to that of their less-skilled colleagues. In group 3, for example, teachers in further education earn £208 per week, which is £35 more than secondary-school teachers earn. Within group 17, the earnings of a lorry driver are positively related to the size of vehicle: drivers of heavy-goods vehicles (over 3 tons) earn 29p per hour more than other goods drivers.

Trade unions are able to influence the occupational earnings structure if the demand for labour is inelastic and/or if they can control the labour supply. For example, miners (group 16) earn 414p per hour, which is 62% more than postmen (group 7) earn. This reflects, in part, the strength of the National Union of Miners, conferred by the inelastic demand for domestic coal which results from the currently used methods of electricity generation, together with limitations on coal imports. In contrast the lengthy postmen's strike of 1971 certainly did not bring the country to a halt, partly because telephonists and other postal workers continued working and tolerable substitutes were therefore available for the postal workers' services.

TABLE 5.6

Earnings by Occupation: Full-Time Adult Men, April 1981

	Average gross weekly earnings (£)	*Average gross hourly earnings (p)*
Non-manual		
1 General management	–	–
2 Professional and related management and administration	189	–
3 Professional and related in education, welfare and health	180	–
4 Literacy, artistic, sports	171	–
5 Professional and related in science, engineering and technology	169	–
6 Managerial	163	–
7 Clerical and related	119	297
8 Selling	125	306
9 Security and protective service	153	347
Manual		
10 Catering, cleaning, hairdressing	103	223
11 Farming, fishing and related	94	208
12 Materials processing (excluding metal)	124	270
13 Making and repairing (excluding metal and electrical)	122	282
14 Processing, making, repairing (metal and electrical)	130	293
15 Painting, repetitive assembling, product inspection	117	270
16 Construction, mining	127	280
17 Transport operating	120	251
18 Miscellaneous	118	261
Total: Manual	122	269
Total: Non-manual	163	420
Total: All occupations	140	331

Source: DE, *New Earnings Survey*, 1981, Part D, table 86.

Note: Both sets of figures exclude those whose pay was affected by absence. The gross hourly earnings figure excludes the effect of overtime.

III.5 Wage Structure by Industry[1]

There are a number of reasons for studying the industrial wage structure. First, it is important to know whether labour can be allocated among industries independently of wages or whether expanding (contracting) industries must pay higher (lower) wages to get the labour they require. Such information is useful in designing a pay policy. Second, how are the gains in labour productivity distributed? They can go to labour in the form of higher wages, or firms in the form of higher profits or consumers in the form of lower prices. Analysis of the industrial wage structure provides evidence on the topic. Third, it is important to know whether, independent of the characteristics of the individuals working in the industry, highly concentrated industries or industries with large plants pay higher wages; such data would be useful in, for example, designing our monopoly legislation.

---

1 The most substantial recent work on this issue is R. Wragg and J. Robertson, *Post-War Trends in Employment, Output, Labour Costs and Prices by Industry in the UK*, Research Paper No. 3, DE, June 1978.

Wage changes and employment changes: Price theory implies that in the long run, given competitive conditions, each industry will, *ceteris paribus*, pay for a given grade of labour a wage identical to that paid by other industries. The *ceteris paribus* assumption implies that there are no differences in the non-pecuniary attractions of different industries or location or in the cost of living by location. In the long run, therefore, the growth in industry wage levels should not be correlated with the growth in the amount of labour employed. In the short run an industry which expands its demands for labour will tend to have to raise the wages it pays because of short-run inelasticities in labour supply. Therefore the theory predicts a positive association in the short run between changes in employment by industry and changes in wages by industry.

It is clear that in the long run there is no relationship between changes in pay and changes in employment. Wragg and Robertson studied 82 manufacturing industries over the period 1954-73. The pay changes in each industry were very similar but employment experience was very different. Indeed, the weaving industry suffered a loss of employment of 6.2% p.a. yet had a higher than average increase in earnings. They went on to study 22 sectors of retail distribution over 1950-71, with similar results. Annual employment growth varied enormously (the coefficient of variation (standard deviation/mean) was 7.64), while pay increases among the 22 sectors were very similar (coefficient of variation of 0.13). In the long run, therefore, expanding industries do not have to increase their pay at a rate above the average to meet their labour requirements, and industries where employment is contracting still give around average pay rises. This reflects the continual churning which goes on in the labour market − 10m job changes a year, and around 0.75m new entrants to the labourforce and individuals retiring from it − which allows the labourforce to adjust steadily to the changing requirements imposed by the economy.

But what of the short run? It appears that there is a positive association between earnings changes and employment changes. This upward-sloping short-run market-labour supply curve implies that to avoid labour shortages developing a pay policy might need to permit such shortage sectors to pay above the norm.

Wage changes and productivity changes: An industry may react to an increase in physical productivity by lowering its relative product price or raising the relative wages it pays. If wage changes among industries are significantly (positively) related to movements in value productivity (i.e. variations in physical productivity and product prices taken together), this implies that non-competitive forces, such as ability to pay, determine the wage structure. In contrast, if the differential wage changes are unrelated to change in value productivity by industry, this implies that competitive forces dominate in the explanation of wages. We anticipate such forces will be important because there is no reason, on equity or efficiency grounds, to expect that sectors with high labour productivity or growth in labour productivity will, *ceteris paribus*, pay high wages; working with bigger machines, if the intensity of work is unchanged, is no reason for higher pay.

The statistical associations found for 1954-73 for 82 manufacturing industries by Wragg and Robertson among the growth rates of output per head (i.e. labour productivity), earnings, unit labour costs and prices, are clear and unambiguous. Earnings changes are very similar across the 82 industries while labour productivity changes differ markedly. In turn, there is a negative association between labour productivity changes and movements in unit labour costs and, finally, a negative relation between labour productivity changes and price rises. Likewise another study[1] found no association between industrial capital: labour ratios and earnings. Individuals who work with a lot of capital do not receive higher pay, *ceteris paribus*, than individuals working with little capital. These suggest that workers who cannot increase their productivity easily (such as musicians or nurses) do not find their relative position in the pay structure worsening persistently. Further, they also indicate that, after allowing for general inflation, the gains from increased labour productivity flow mainly to consumers.

Industry characteristics and wage levels: There has been considerable interest recently in the idea that the labour market is segmented into two (or more) sectors, one of which is high-paying, with well-developed internal labour markets allowing for promotion within the firm, employing high-quality labour with low quit propensities, and the other with opposite characteristics. Some recent studies on the structure of earnings in British manufacturing industry throw some light on this idea.[2]

Industries which are highly concentrated or where large plants predominate pay more than atomistic small-plant sectors. Concentrated industries have relatively high average pay largely because they employ superior-quality labour, and because they are highly unionized. But even after controlling for labour characteristics and unionization, concentrated industries pay a little more than unconcentrated industries. This may reflect a sharing of monopoly profits with their employees in an attempt to buy good industrial relations or it might be an attempt by existing firms to forestall entry by new firms (though both reasons seem *a priori* unlikely).

Industries with small plants − Agriculture, Distribution and Miscellaneous Services (e.g. catering) − have lower pay than industries with large plants even when labour quality is held constant.[3] This reflects the disutility of working in large plants and the low incidence of shift work and payments-by-results in such small-plant sectors.

This evidence provides modest support for the notion of a segmented labour market. Big firms in monopolistic industries (the so-called primary sector) pay high wages relative to small firms in unconcentrated industries (the secondary sector). This wage differential is attributable, apparently, to higher labour quality, the disutility of working in large plants, the higher profits of concentrated industries and the higher density of union membership in the primary sector. However, the policy implications of such findings are far from clear. Should we, for example, encourage unionization in the secondary sector or discourage it in the primary

---

1 W. Hood and R.D. Rees, 'Inter Industry Wage Levels in the UK Manufacturing Industry', *MS*, 1974.

2 D. Metcalf, S. Nickell and R. Richardson, 'The Structure of Hours and Earnings in British Manufacturing industry', *OEP*, July 1976; M. Sawyer, 'The Earnings of Manual Workers: A Cross Section Analysis', *SJPE*, Vol. XX, No. 2, June 1973; A. Tylecote, 'Determinants of Changes in the Wage Hierarchy in UK Manufacturing Industry: 1954-70', *BJIR*, Vol. XIII, No. 1, March 1975; K. George, R. McNabb and J. Shorey, 'The Size of the Work Unit and Labour Market Behaviour', *BJIR*, July 1977.

3 See R. Layard *et al.*, *The Causes of Poverty*, Background Paper No. 6, Royal Commission on Distribution of Income and Wealth, HMSO, 1978, Appendix table 18. It should be noted that once the industry-concentration ratio and unionization have been controlled for, plant size has no *independent* impact on pay; see R. Layard, D. Metcalf and S. Nickell, 'The Effect of Collective Bargaining on Relative and Absolute Wages', *BJIR*, November 1978.

sector? Should we encourage small plants to merge? Further, to the extent that labour quality is important, the evidence does not tell us which firms will choose a low-wage, low-labour-quality, low-productivity strategy as against a high-wage, high-quality, high-productivity strategy.

III.6   Wage Structure by Sex[1]

Evidence: Females account for 42% of employment in Britain, yet among full-time workers in 1981 men were 8 times more likely than women to be earning over £200 a week and 25 times more likely to be earning over £300 a week. Females earn less than males in each broad occupational and industrial group: the data in table 5.7 show that the hourly earnings of full-time female adult workers were, on average, 73% of male hourly earnings and that the percentage differential between male and female pay is higher for non-manual workers than for manual workers.

There are two broad reasons why average male pay exceeds average female pay. First, and most important, women are crowded into the low-paying occupations and industries. Second, within occupational groups women tend to be paid less than men. In education, for example, women are disproportionately represented in the relatively low-paying primary segment, and within primary-school teaching women earn 13% less than men. It must be noted, however, that even within primary teaching the main reason for the differential is not that women are paid less than men for doing the same job but rather that women are under-represented in the higher-paying headship and deputy headship jobs. This example could be repeated for other occupations and industries.

Reasons why women earn less than men: A major reason why women earn less than men is that their attachment to the labourforce is weaker than that of men. This relatively weak attachment is in large part because it is widely believed that it is the role of women rather than men to drop out of the labourforce to care for young children: the lower lifetime commitment of women to the labourforce is a response to centuries of social conditioning rather than an inherent trait. Attitudes on the roles of the two sexes can certainly be influenced by economic factors; for example the two world wars, which caused the demand for female labour to rise substantially, were particularly important in raising the labourforce status of women. This suggests that the respective roles of men and women are thus amenable to change via economic and other influences. The observed weaker labourforce attachment causes females to be crowded into the lower-paying segments of the labourforce and, in some cases, to be paid less than men in a given task. Some manifestations of the relative labourforce attachments of men and women, which partially determine their occupational composition, include the following.

---

1   A useful summary of the existing literature is B. Chiplin and P. Sloan, *Sex Discrimination in the Labour Market*, Macmillan, 1976. A readable, thorough, statistical analysis is S. Nickell, 'Trade Unions and the Position of Women in the Industrial Wage Structure', *BJIR*, July 1977. For details of the equal pay and equal opportunity legislation, see DE, *A guide to the Equal Pay Act 1970*, HMSO, 1975; Home Office, *A Guide to the Sex Discrimination Act*, 1975. For an excellent progress report on the legislation see *DEG*, September 1979, pp. 863-6. Restrictions on hours women may work are discussed in *DEG*, April 1979, pp. 331-2.

TABLE 5.7

Male-Female Hourly Earnings, Full-Time Workers, April 1981

	Female (p)	Male (p)	Female/Male (%)
Total manual	188	269	70
Total non-manual	259	420	56
Total	241	331	73
All Wage Boards and Wage Councils			
Manual	163	209	78
Non-manual	183	282	65
Occupations: manual			
Catering, cleaning, hairdressing	181	223	81
Materials processing (excluding metals)	185	270	69
Making and repairing (excluding metal and electrical)	184	282	65
Processing, making, repairing (metal and electrical)	203	293	69
Repetitive assembling, etc.	195	270	72
Transport, etc.	205	251	82
Occupations: non-manual			
Clerical	229	297	77
Selling	174	306	57
Security	308	349	88

Source: DE, *New Earnings Survey*, 1981, Part D, tables 86, 87.

Note: Data refer to adult workers whose pay in the survey week was not affected by absence and excludes the effect of overtime.

Labour turnover is a little higher for women than for men. Such turnover imposes costs on the employer; at a minimum these costs will be the hiring costs incurred when replacing employees. For example, in 1979 11% of male employees had changed jobs in the last twelve months but 13% of women employees had done so. And in manufacturing the separation rate of women is two-thirds higher than the male rate.[1] It is often argued that these figures reflect a composition effect, i.e. that females are disproportionately represented in industries and occupations which themselves have high turnover. This appears not to be true: in every industry and every occupation except one, female turnover is greater than male turnover. An alternative possibility, however, concerns the age composition of the labourforce. Young workers have dramatically higher turnover rates than prime-age and older workers. Therefore some of the observed higher female labour turn-over may occur because younger workers account for a higher fraction of the female labourforce than the male labourforce.

Females are also somewhat more prone to absenteeism. In a particular week in 1979 9% of women and 8% of men worked fewer days than usual (excluding absences caused by holidays).[2] Absenteeism also causes costs to employers, for example, by disrupting production schedules.

1   *ST*, No. 11, 1981, table 5.12; *DEG*, February 1982, table 1.6.
2   *ST*, 12, 1982, table 3.24.

Because women have higher turnover rates than men, employers have less incentive to pay for female training. A profit-maximizing employer will be willing to pay for his employees' training if he can get a return on his investment by paying the trainee less than the value of his services when the training is completed. Given that women are more likely to quit or to be absent from a firm than men, employers will prefer to train men. This is compounded by hours legislation prohibiting women from working over a certain number of hours per week or at certain times.

Similarly, girls have less incentive to finance their own education and training. Staying on at school or university or taking a computer programming course entails costs, for example tuition costs or forgone earnings (i.e. earnings that could have been received if working). If a woman has children this will involve a period out of the labourforce; further, women retire at a younger age than men. Thus the time over which she will receive benefits (in the form of higher earnings) from the training is less than for a man. Thus, of those young persons entering employment in 1978, 37% of the boys entered apprenticeships to skilled occupations or employment leading to recognized professional qualifications, while only 8% of girls followed this route. In contrast one third of the girls are immediately segmented into clerical employment. The contrast is even clearer if we consider highly qualified people (i.e. those holding an academic or professional qualification of degree standard). In 1980 8% of men held such qualifications but only 3% of women in the working population did.[1]

If females go out of the labourforce for a period in their twenties or thirties they will accumulate less experience and seniority (on-the-job training, learning by doing) than males. On all these grounds, females will tend to be less productive than males. They will therefore earn less within a given occupation and will be less likely to progress up the occupational hierarchy.

Females will also tend to be paid less than men if the firm draws them from a limited geographical area: they will incur lower transport costs on average than men. Also, women may tend to work in more pleasant conditions.

The structure of the industries in which females work is a further element in the explanation of the sex differential. Females are disproportionately represented in small plants and atomistic industries, which tend to pay less and offer poorer career prospects than larger plants and concentrated industries; also a relatively low proportion of the female labourforce is unionized, which reflects in part the higher costs of organizing in industries consisting of small plants.

Discrimination: It is frequently alleged that the main cause of pay differentials is that discrimination exists against women. Studies suggest that in 1975 the hourly pay of men was between 8% to 29% higher than that of women with similar education, experience and father's occupation.[2] More narrowly, employer

---

1 *ST*, 12, 1982, table 3.24.

2 See R. Layard *et al.*, *The Causes of Poverty*, Background Paper No. 5, Royal Commission on the Distribution of Income and Wealth, HMSO, 1978, pp. 52-6, and Christine Greenhalgh, 'Male-Female Wage Differentials in Great Britain', *EJ*, December 1980. Broadly, these estimates are derived by computing separate earnings-functions for men and women. Then an estimated female wage is calculated by assuming that a female of particular characteristics is paid according to the male wage structure. The difference between the estimated female wage and the actual female wage is termed 'discrimination'. Such calculations are, as the authors recognize, very difficult to undertake accurately.

discrimination means that if the net value of the woman's service is identical to that of the man the latter receives a higher wage. The only way that the woman can offset the employer's discrimination is to accept a lower wage. If *all other things are equal* yet firms pay, because of discrimination against women, higher wages to men than to women, then higher profits will accrue to the firm that replaces men with women. Male sales assistants are paid 230p per hour whilst females are paid 162p per hour. It is unlikely that if both males and females were equally productive, firms would not substitute female labour for male labour.

It should be noted that none of the above discussion implies that women are not discriminated against in society at large – they obviously are. The crucial question is how that discrimination can be ended, and the problem here concerns the causal relationship. We believe that if females could be given greater incentives than they have at present to remain in the labourforce, accumulate experience, undertake training, travel longer distances, etc., then this will cause the distinction between the traditional roles of men and women to be eroded fairly speedily.

The equal pay and equal opportunity legislation which effectively came fully into force in 1976 should provide some incentive to stronger female labourforce attachment. However, should this legislation prove too frail other policies exist to improve the lot of women in the labour market and these will be considered below.

The purpose of the Equal Pay Act is to eliminate discrimination against women in connection with wages and fringe benefits. A woman is to receive equal treatment when she is employed (a) on work of the same or broadly similar nature to that of men; (b) in a job which, though different from those of men, has been given an equal value to men's jobs under a job-evaluation exercise. Thus the Act was designed to ensure that if the net value of a woman's services is identical to that of a man both will receive identical wages and conditions.

The intentions of the Act can be overcome in a number of ways. Men and women can be segregated by job. This has already happened. The standard occupational classification lists 396 occupations but the 1979 New Earnings Survey reports only 35 occupations with sufficient men and women to provide comparisons of their earnings. It seems possible that this Act will therefore compound rather than reduce occupational segregation. If women believe that they are nevertheless doing work of equal value, the jobs can be subjected to a job-evaluation scheme. But the employer can give a relatively high weight in such a scheme to attributes such as physical strength where men have a relative advantage, and a low weight to manual dexterity where women have the advantage (although there is a right of appeal on the 'fairness' of the job-evaluation scheme). Legislation precludes women from night work and limits the number of overtime hours women may work; an employer may therefore pay large shift-work or overtime supplements.

Despite these qualifications and reservations it is clear that implementation of the Equal Pay Act was associated with a narrowing of the sex differential. Average hourly female earnings rose from 65% of male earnings in 1974 to 74% in 1977. This is a very large compression in such a short space of time. It is probably mainly due to the requirement in the Equal Pay Act that in collective agreements female hourly earnings must not be set below the lowest male hourly earnings. But the changing occupational composition of the female labourforce, such that females are increasingly represented in the higher-paying occupations, and flat-rate elements (e.g. a cash increase of £6 a week rather than percentage increases) in the 1975-7 pay policy, probably also played a part in narrowing the sex differential.

Although the narrowing of the pay differential is to be welcomed it is not without offsetting disadvantages. It is noticeable that between 1976 and 1978, the first three years of the full operation of the Act, female unemployment rose around 50% while male unemployment fell. The disproportionate rise in female labour costs surely contributed to this relative rise in female unemployment. Nevertheless female *employment* continued to rise during this period.

The Sex Discrimination Act was potentially important in overcoming the current under-representation of women in high-paying sectors. It covered education and the supply of goods and services as well as employment. The Act said that women must be given equal treatment in the arrangements for selecting a candidate for a job, in the terms on which a job is offered, on access to promotion, transfer and training or any other aspects of the job and on dismissal. The Act established the Equal Opportunities Commission with fairly wide powers: it can help individuals to bring cases if it considers them of wider interest; it can conduct formal investigations compelling people to give evidence; it can serve non-discrimination notices and seek injunctions against persistent discriminators. Unfortunately the EOC has so far done little to raise the status of women. Indeed, since this hapless organization was established male-female pay differentials have widened!

The Employment Protection Act (1976) should also favourably influence women's labourforce commitment. It provides for six weeks' paid maternity leave and twenty-nine weeks' unpaid leave with no loss of seniority or status. This legislation is of particular significance for women in highly skilled sectors.

The government could consider a number of alternative strategies to improve the labourforce status of women. First, it might encourage them to join unions: the male-female wage differential is, *ceteris paribus*, smaller in those industries which are highly unionized. Second, more girls could be encouraged to take apprenticeship or college training by providing them with differentially large training grants. Third, female quotas, especially in the higher occupational grades, could be enforced. Finally, women's pay could be forced up relative to men's pay by subsidizing women's employment.

III.7 Poverty[1]

One aspect of income distribution which causes widespread concern is the problem of poverty. Low earnings from work are only one part of the poverty problem, which also encompasses hardship faced by, for example, old people, sick or disabled people, families with large numbers of children, fatherless families, and the unemployed.

In this section we discuss measurement problems, the characteristics of low-income families, and the role of the social-security system. Low pay is discussed more fully in the next section.

Measurement

Poverty can be defined as an absolute or relative standard. Absolute standards are based on consumption of necessities. The quantity of necessities consumed is

---

1 For a full discussion see Royal Commission on the Distribution of Income and Wealth, *Lower Incomes*, Report No. 6, Cmnd. 7175, HMSO, 1975; R. Layard, D. Piachaud and M. Stewart, *The Causes of Poverty*, Background Paper to Cmnd. 7175; and P. Townsend, *Poverty in the United Kingdom*, Pelican, 1979.

valued at current prices to obtain a monetary poverty standard. Relative standards are normally related to some measure of income in the general population. So, broadly, absolute standards attempt to estimate subsistence needs which do not vary with social progress, while relative standards relate poverty to rising living standards.

If poverty is defined on the basis of the *absolute* living standard in 1971, numbers in poverty declined from about a fifth of the population in 1953 to about a fortieth in 1973. In twenty years, on this absolute standard, the numbers in poverty declined dramatically — by a factor of eight. But in *relative* terms there was little change. The net income of the poorest 5th percentile was about the same proportion of median income in both years.[1]

Recent practice in Britain has been to base poverty standards on the current values of the supplementary benefit scale rates. This defines poverty in the *relative* sense because the scale rates are set in such a way that they increase broadly in step with general standards of living.

At the end of 1977 the number of families and people with incomes normally below their supplementary benefit (SB) level were:[2]

	Families	People
before supplementary benefit added to income	4.0m	6.2m
after supplementary benefit added to income	1.3m	2.0m

Nearly two-thirds of the 4.0m figure are pensioners. The remainder consist of sick and disabled people, the unemployed and the low-paid. Naturally, once social-security benefits are taken into account the number of families with incomes below SB levels falls, but it is still very worrying that over a million families have incomes below SB. This occurs mainly because some people who are eligible for SB do not claim it.[3]

A number of problems exist in measuring living standards. Should the income unit, for example, be the individual, the family or the household? How are we to control for household size and composition? Presumably larger households need more income than smaller households to get a similar standard of living. Likewise older children cost more to maintain than younger children. Therefore to measure comparative living standards sensibly, normal net household income must be adjusted for these size and composition effects. The adjustment factors are known as *equivalence scales*. The effects of adjusting the distribution of normal net household income for household size and composition are substantial. The

---

1 G. Feighan, P. Lansley and A. Smith, *Poverty and Progress in Britain 1953-73*, CUP, 1977.

2 DHSS, *Social Security Statistics*, 1981, table 47.07.

3 There are other ways of measuring poverty than merely counting heads. One way is to calculate a 'poverty gap' in money terms. The poverty gap is simply the amount by which income falls short of the official poverty line. In 1975 before social-security benefits (i.e. national insurance benefits plus supplementary benefits) were paid the poverty gap was £5.86bn or 5.8% of GDP. But after social-security benefits were paid the gap was only £0.25bn or 0.25% of GDP. When put like this the performance of the British social-security system is not unimpressive, though this is not to deny that families who are still falling below the poverty line face real hardship. Also the official poverty line itself is held by many people to be inadequate. For an excellent exposition and application of this method of analysing poverty, see W. Beckerman, 'The Impact of Income Maintenance Payments on Poverty in Britain 1975', *EJ*, June 1979.

equivalent income distribution is considerably more equal: fewer households have low or high incomes and more have intermediate levels of income.[1]

Role of Social Security

The current position: Poor people are aided by the state in three main ways: (i) National Insurance benefits, e.g. retirement pensions, sickness and unemployment benefit, are paid to those satisfying the statutory conditions; (ii) benefits for children (child benefit) and disabled people (e.g. mobility allowance) are paid without a means test but also without National Insurance conditions; (iii) supplementary benefit is paid to non-working persons aged 16 and over who involuntarily fall below a prescribed level of income laid down by Parliament, below which it is felt to be wrong that any family's income should be allowed to fall. Family Income Supplement, an income-related addition to pay, is used to boost the net incomes of low-paid working family men. In addition there is an array of means-tested benefits both in kind (e.g. school meals and dental treatment) and in money (e.g. rent and rate rebates). In 1982/3 social-security spending totalled £30bn, a quarter of all public spending.

It was originally hoped that the National Insurance system as proposed by Beveridge in 1942 would provide a level of benefits equal at least to the official poverty line, and that supplementary benefit would wither away except as a last resort for the few people who fell through the National Insurance net. This hope has not been realized. Over 10% of the population live in families which rely on SB to bring them up to poverty-level incomes.

Criticisms: The current system has been criticized on a number of grounds, although some of the criticisms are contradictory. First, the growth in the numbers receiving SB shows that some groups are not adequately catered for by the other anti-poverty measures. Important groups here include retirement pensioners, unemployed people and fatherless families. Aggregate unemployment rises not because more people become unemployed but because on average each person is unemployed longer. More people become unemployed for over 1 year (1 million in 1982) and so exhaust entirely their National Insurance unemployment benefit. Lone parents are another group who have grown rapidly in recent years (750,000 in 1980) and many have no income source other than SB.

The second criticism of the current arrangements is that, despite a battery of measures to alleviate poverty, a substantial number of people still exist below the poverty line defined by the supplementary benefit level. Some 1m families or 2m people lived below the official poverty line in November 1977. There are two main reasons for this. First, many people, especially pensioners, while eligible for supplementary benefit, do not claim it. Second, many individuals are poor despite working: their weekly earnings are below the official poverty line. The Family Income Supplement was introduced in 1971 to mitigate poverty associated with low earnings.

The third criticism concerns the income-related nature of many benefits. The core of the problem is whether benefits should be related to income or whether the National Insurance system should be designed to ensure that everyone has a tolerable minimum income, with the tax system taking back some benefits from

---

1 R. Van Slooten and A. Coverdale, 'The characteristics of low income households', *ST*, No. 8, 1977.

those who do not need them. The criticism has two main strands. (i) Benefits which are related to means are traditionally unpopular and discourage a full take-up. Many of those eligible for supplementary benefit do not claim; the take-up rate of rent and rate rebates appears only to be around 50% of those eligible. (ii) It may result in absurd marginal tax rates for those with low incomes. This is known as the poverty trap: as the earned income of the family rises it loses not only monetary supplementation such as FIS but also benefits in kind such as free school meals or prescriptions. DHSS estimates that at the end of 1977 50,000 families with children might have been liable to receive no increase in net income from a £1 rise in earnings and a further 60,000 might have received less than 25p.[1] Given the government's belief that high marginal tax rates discourage proper work effort, this is clearly anomalous.

Fourth, it is widely held that many people have little incentive to work because payments when out of work are greater than or approximately equal to payments in work. This problem is real but exaggerated. It occurs primarily in the case of individuals with large families who receive tax rebates (which last for only a limited period) on becoming unemployed; see section II.2 for a fuller discussion.

The final criticism concerns the benefits in kind. These distort the price system, the consumer paying less than the cost of providing the service (e.g. 'free' school meals or milk). Critics argue that individuals should be assured of some minimum money income and then left to spend it as they wish, with the purchases priced according to cost. This raises much wider issues than poverty relief and will not be pursued here.

Reform of social security: A number of important changes took place recently in the social-security system. These affect the National Insurance system, family support, supplementary benefit and new benefits for the disabled.

National Insurance contributions are earnings-related. Employees in the full state pension scheme pay 8.75% of their pay as National Insurance contributions (up to a ceiling, equal to £220 in April 1982) and employers pay 10.2%. These contributions include components to help finance the National Health Service, Redundancy Fund, and Unemployment and Sickness Insurance as well as Old Age Pensions.

The benefit side is changing too. The New Pension Scheme introduced in April 1978 consists of two components. The *basic* flat-rate pension is uprated annually in line with the prices index. The *additional* pension is earnings-related. The employee will get one-eightieth of his earnings (between a specified floor and ceiling) for each contribution year after 1978, subject to a maximum of twenty eightieths. The average married couple will, when the scheme is fully mature in 1999, receive a total pension equal to at least two-thirds of the man's real take-home pay. So this scheme will help to eliminate poverty in old age. If an employer runs an occupational scheme which is at least as good as the state scheme he can opt out of the additional segment of the state scheme and he and his employees pay correspondingly lower contributions.

Unemployment benefit is to be taxable from 1982. This is correct in principle but poses practical difficulties. And from 1983 the burden of paying and administering sickness benefit for the first 8 weeks of sickness is to be moved from

---

1 *ST*, No. 12, 1982, p. 90.

the state to the employer.[1] The earnings-related supplement to these benefits was axed in 1982. These changes raise a number of thorny issues of principle. First, they reverse efforts of successive governments to reduce the numbers on SB – cuts in insurance benefits will, as the government recognize, cause more families to rely on SB. Second, individuals who are sick or unemployed and find they no longer receive earnings-related benefits might wonder why they have to pay earnings-related contributions in the same way as before. Third, the idea that the employers administer sick pay represents a retreat from the principles of the Beveridge Report.

The system of family support has been reconstituted. Child benefit, a universal tax-free weekly amount per child, has replaced the old system of child tax allowances (CTAs) and family allowances. The new system has three important advantages. First, individuals who had low incomes and paid no tax gained no advantage from CTAs, but they do get child benefit. Second, child benefit is paid for all children whereas family allowances were paid only for second and subsequent children. Third, child benefit is paid to the mother whereas the benefit of CTAs went to the father.

It should be noticed that child benefits – £5.85 per week per child from November 1982 – are primarily designed to achieve horizontal equity rather than vertical equity. They help ensure that, at given income levels, families with children do not have wildly different living standards from families without children. While they may incidentally help low-income families, this is a secondary consideration. If relief of poverty were the main reason for child benefits, there would be little point in paying a tax-free universal benefit which costs over £600m per year extra public expenditure for each £1 per week per child increase. It is an open question whether or not family support should be more concerned with relief of poverty and less with horizontal equity. The government will also have to decide in time whether to stick with a flat amount per child or to vary the amount by age of child, family size or some other factor.

The system of supplementary benefits has also been changed with a view to simplification. The discretionary nature of the system makes it inevitable that it becomes complicated and, possibly, anomalous over the years. Special needs payments, heating addition, rent allowances, children's rates varying by age, etc., all make the system difficult to understand. It is hoped that reduced discretion will produce a simpler system.

A number of new benefits were introduced for disabled people in the 1970s. These include attendance allowance for people who need looking after constantly or nearly constantly; mobility allowance to help disabled people offset the costs of getting around (previously only those with invalid trikes received such help); non-contributory invalidity pension (NCIP) to provide a weekly income as a right to disabled people of working age, including a special NCIP for housewives. The Pearson Report[2] has also recommended a new benefit for disabled children. It seems probable that this patchwork of benefits will shortly be ripe for review to see whether they could be integrated into a unified benefit for the disabled which would vary according to degree of disability.

---

1 See *Income During Initial Sickness: A New Strategy*, Cmnd. 7864, HMSO, April 1980. Such employer's sick pay will be taxable.

2 Pearson Report, *Report of Royal Commission on Civil Liability and Compensation for Personal Injury*, Cmnd. 7054, HMSO, March 1978.

Alternative Reforms

Despite the changes taking place, many other proposals for reforming social security are put forward. This is not surprising. It is right that a programme which accounts for one quarter of public spending should be under constant scrutiny.

There have been three main sets of suggestions concerning the direction of reform.[1] They have a superficial similarity, in that under each scheme individuals will be guaranteed a minimum income at around supplementary benefit level and the need for supplementary benefits will be substantially reduced. In fact, however, the schemes are very different.

The first suggestion is for a 'new Beveridge Plan'. Under the original Beveridge proposals it was proposed that social *insurance* should guarantee everyone a minimum standard of living. This subsistence income was to be provided as a right, without a means test; the part played by SB was to be virtually phased out. In the postwar period, however, National Insurance benefits have usually been below the prescribed minima laid down by supplementary benefits. The suggestion is therefore to implement fully the original Beveridge proposals. One of the aims of the new pension scheme (discussed above) is to ensure pension benefits of sufficient size virtually to eliminate the need for pensioners to turn to supplementary benefits to augment their income. Higher child benefits are also held to be important. Advocates of this universalistic approach to curing poverty generally qualify it by suggesting that the benefits from raising social-security payments could be taxed and thereby directed towards those with lower incomes.

This policy would obviously be successful in raising the incomes of non-employed disadvantaged individuals. It does not involve high marginal tax rates and is therefore less likely to have disincentive effects on working harder. Further it would not involve any major administrative problems. It does have two disadvantages. First, it would be costly. The Meade Report calculated it would cost an additional 4-7p on the basic rate of income tax. However, this is merely another way of stating the seriousness of the poverty problem. Second, the problem of the employed with low incomes remains. This problem would be moderated if income-tax thresholds were raised. But minimum-wage legislation — the policy most frequently advocated to raise earnings by the back-to-Beveridge protagonists — may result in unemployment among the very groups it is designed to help.

The second scheme for reform, the Social Dividend, is the boldest. Under this scheme a non-taxable flat-rate sum would be paid weekly to every individual irrespective of income. This would be accompanied by a proportional personal income tax. All other elements of the social-security system (insurance contributions and benefits, supplementary benefits and family allowances) would be abolished. This system has the advantage that the benefit paid is insensitive to income. Work incentives may nevertheless be impaired because it is generally agreed that the proportional tax rate would have to be over 50%. The scheme also has the administrative drawback of extending income tax to everyone, however small his income.

The third alternative, which has many variants, is the Negative Income Tax. This scheme involves a minimum-income guarantee and a break-even income. If an

---

1 See Meade Report, *The Structure and Reform of Direct Taxation*, IFS, 1978, chapter 13 for a clear exposition of the Social Dividend and New Beveridge Schemes. For a concise description of the difficulties involved in reforming social security, see A. Prest, 'The Structure and Reform of Direct Taxation', *EJ*, June 1979.

individual is employed and earns between the minimum and the break-even income, his earnings are supplemented (by the negative income tax); beyond the break-even income he pays positive income tax. The FIS is thus a prototype NIT. This scheme could be all-embracing, covering the whole range of government welfare programmes, or could be oriented towards particular problems such as poverty caused by large families. The essential problem with this scheme is that a choice must be made between high marginal rates of negative income tax and low minimum levels of payments. For example, from 1982 the point at which a single individual starts paying income tax is £1,565 p.a. If the NIT is operated with a rate of 50% this means that 50p is payable to an individual for every £1 by which his income is less than £1,565. Thus the basic minimum payment is only £783. If this basic minimum is too low the tax rate could be raised to 75% giving a minimum of £1,174. Such a high marginal tax rate is likely to have disincentive effects on labour supply. Further problems with the NIT, which could be overcome with time and ingenuity, are (i) that the unit to which it applies, the individual, the family or the household, must be determined; (ii) that the NIT must be on a weekly basis, but (positive) income tax has always been assessed yearly; (iii) that people not in employment have to claim the NIT; (iv) that assets may be difficult to incorporate into the NIT scheme.

III.8 Low Pay[1]

Low pay is one part of the poverty problem. Industries which are at the bottom of the earnings structure tend to be characterized by high proportions of small plants, of women workers, of unskilled workers and of falling demand for labour. It is also clear that low-paid workers are disproportionately represented in the service sector.

Low pay is also related to age and skill. Teenagers, workers in their early twenties and workers over fifty are disproportionately represented. Older and unskilled workers not only tend to have relatively low earnings, but also to suffer higher rates of unemployment. Unemployment rates referring specifically to unskilled workers are at least three times the national average unemployment rate. The annual earnings differential between them and other workers is therefore greater than apparent from a comparison of the earnings of those in work.

Two important features of the structure of the low-pay problem are worth noting. First, if the low paid are described as those in the lowest tenth of the distribution of manual earnings, we observe considerable movement across the boundary of this lowest tenth. 21.4% of manual men were in the lowest-paid tenth at least once in the five years 1970 to 1974, but only 2.9% were in this tenth in each of the years.[2] Second, low pay must be seen as part of a general problem of labour-market disadvantages in that it is associated with a high incidence of job instability, ill-health and lack of fringe benefits. The low-paid worker is more vulnerable to the interruption of earnings power, cannot save for old age or emergencies, and can only borrow at very high interest rates such as through HP. Thus low pay is an important element in the cycle of poverty.

---

1 For a comprehensive survey of the low-pay problem see Chris Pond, 'Low Pay', in N. Bosanquet and P. Townsend (eds.), *Labour and Equality*, Heinemann, 1980. See also, D. Metcalf, *Low Pay, Occupational Mobility and Minimum Wage Policy in Britain*, American Enterprise Institute, 1981.

2 *DEG*, January 1977.

In Britain we approach the problem of low pay in two main ways. First, the FIS is a form of negative income tax. Second, the wages councils provide a form of minimum-wage legislation.

FIS was introduced in August 1971 to help mitigate poverty caused by low pay. When family income falls short of a prescribed level (from November 1982 £82.50 per week for a one-child family plus £9.00 for each additional child), the family is paid a benefit equal to one half of the difference between its total gross income and the prescribed level (with a maximum supplement of £21 for a one-child family and £2 for each additional child). This is a potentially powerful policy to raise the welfare of the low-paid but unfortunately only half those who would benefit take up FIS. Families who receive FIS are also automatically entitled to certain other benefits, including free school meals, free milk and vitamins for expectant mothers and children under school age, and exemption from NHS charges for prescriptions, glasses and dental treatment. FIS has the considerable merit of attacking *family* poverty. This is important because the bulk of low-paid people are young workers and married women, and most such workers do not live in the poorest families. So raising low pay via a national minimum wage would leave much family poverty untouched.

Elements of a minimum-wage policy exist via the wages councils which set minimum rates in certain industries. Direct state intervention in fixing minimum wages first occurred in 1909 with the Trade Boards Act. In 1945 trade boards were renamed wages councils. There are forty wages councils. They are generally believed to be ineffective in helping low-paid workers and are thought to inhibit the development of voluntary collective bargaining arrangements.

A national minimum wage (assuming it is set above the existing wage for low-paid workers) will raise the money earnings of those who remain employed, but will cause some unemployment. Recall that the old and unskilled, the people the minimum wage is designed to help most, already have the highest unemployment rates. It may also give only a temporary boost to the low-paid. Overseas evidence suggests that the original wage differentials are quickly restored. Proponents of minimum-wage legislation also argue that it raises the productivity of labour. So it will if capital is substituted for labour, but this is an inefficient substitution and unemployment will also result. It is sometimes said, however, that the minimum-wage legislation will have a 'shock effect' and thereby raise productivity without any loss in employment. This is unlikely to be widespread in that it implies that firms currently have a careless attitude towards profits. Further, many of the low-paying industries are competitive and are therefore unlikely to need a national minimum wage as a spur to efficiency.

This suggests that provision of more training facilities, better information about wages and opportunities both locally and nationally, inducements to labour mobility, wage subsidies, and running the economy with lower, more evenly distributed unemployment levels, are likely to be more effective solutions to the problem of low pay than is a national minimum wage.

IV   TRADE UNIONS AND INDUSTRIAL RELATIONS
IV.1   Trade Unions

At the end of 1980 there were estimated to be 12.9m trade-union members in the UK.[1] This implies that 54% of the nation's employees (in employment plus unemployed) were trade-union members, a significant expansion from the corresponding figure of 42% for 1964. During the 1970s, the growth in trade-union membership was very fast by historical standards. From the end of 1969 to the end of 1979, the growth rate was no less than 28%, more than three times greater than the corresponding figure for the 1960s. It may very well be the case, however, that 1979 will represent a high-water mark of union membership for many years. Although the official estimates are not yet available, it is widely suspected that in the years 1980, 1981 and 1982 the number of people belonging to trade unions fell by a total of between 1 and 1½ million.

The principal explanation of the recent membership decline is almost certainly the fall in the number of people in work, particularly in manufacturing. Over a longer period, the change in membership from year to year seems to be statistically associated with the rate of price inflation, the rate of change in average money wages, the size of the potentially unionizable labourforce (all positively) and the level of unemployment (negatively). Although these empirical associations are reasonably well established, we do not have a convincing theoretical explanation for them;[2] other factors, for example changes in the structure of the labourforce by sex, occupational status and industry, are also likely to have been important. During the seventies, for example, the growth in trade-union membership was much faster among women (at 56%) than among men (20%); the absolute membership rate for women, however, is still below that for men.

The number of unions is still tending to fall, down from 630 in 1965 to 438 in 1980, in spite of small increases in 1973 (probably the result of the 1971 Industrial Relations Act) and 1977. Nevertheless in 1980 there were still 69 trade unions with less than 100 members each.[3]

In addition to those in formal trade unions, many workers belong to other associations that engage in collective negotiations and bargaining; for example, many individual business concerns have what are sometimes called 'company unions'. Other workers are in industries that have wages councils, public bodies that are designed to reproduce many of the features of collective bargaining where trade-union growth is inherently difficult.

In 1973 and 1977 the *New Earnings Survey* gave disaggregated estimates of the number of workers covered by various types of collective agreement. It was suggested that 17% of full-time male workers and 28% of full-time female workers were not party to a collective agreement. For both sexes the service sectors, particularly the distributive trades and personal services, were heavily characterized by individual negotiation; in the manufacturing sector, clothing and footwear had relatively little collective bargaining.

Formal unionization is particularly extensive among male workers, manual workers, semi-skilled workers and workers in the manufacturing and public sectors.

---

1   *DEG*, February 1982, p. 54.
2   G. Bain and F. Elsheikh, *Union Growth and the Business Cycle*, Basil Blackwell, 1976. See also the review by R. Richardson in *BJIR*, July 1977.
3   *DEG*, February 1982, p. 54.

There are no absolutely reliable figures, but the most authoritative study estimated that in 1974 union density ranged from only 12% in distribution to between 95-100% in coalmining, tobacco, cotton textiles, electricity, water, sea transport, entertainment and national government.[1]

Unionization is more limited in newer industries and in the expanding white-collar trades. Where unions have been involved in the latter sectors they have traditionally differed from those in the blue-collar sectors in their aims, attitudes and militancy. Recently, however, the extent of white-collar organization has been growing, and with it has come more aggressive union behaviour; for example, 1981 saw the first extensive and sustained outbreak of industrial conflict in the civil service.

The past few years have seen the publication of some statistical analysis attempting to explain the variation in union density across industries. One factor that certainly seems to be influential is the average plant size by industry, with larger plants being much more likely to be unionized. The willingness of employers to recognize unions is also of considerable importance.[2]

There has been some work on the closed shop, i.e. on the arrangements that make union membership a condition of employment; there are both pre-entry shops, where membership is required before a worker can be hired, and post-entry shops, where a worker must join on being hired. Post-entry closed shops are the much more common form. The incidence of closed shops in Great Britain has grown strongly in the last 15 years. One estimate is that they now cover at least 5.2m workers, nearly 25% of all employees. They are estimated to be particularly common in mining, in gas, electricity and water, in printing, in transport and communications, and in shipbuilding. They are rare in agriculture, in professional and scientific services, and in insurance, banking and business finance.[3] Although closed shops quite properly arouse strong emotions, it should be recalled that in most cases their existence has been preceded by very high levels of union densities. A closed shop, or union membership agreement, is nearly always a formal recognition of extensive unionization. On many occasions, managements appear to have seen them not so much as leading to a significant increase in union power but as a potential force for making industrial relations more orderly. Whether they were correct in taking this position remains an open question, but there can be little doubt that some of the surge in the extent of the closed shop during the 1970s was due to at least tacit management approval.

IV.2 Economic Analysis of Unions

The existence and activities of trade unions raise very large questions in the fields of politics, sociology and law. On a somewhat narrower and more practical front, trade unions have had a considerable influence on the operation of work rules, consultation procedures and worker representation. Economists, however, have tended to concentrate on the impact of trade unions on wages and resource allocation. We shall do the same here.

---

1 G.S. Bain and R. Price, *Profiles of Union Growth*, Basil Blackwell, 1980, pp. 13-78.
2 G.S. Bain and F. Elsheikh, 'Unionisation in Britain', *BJIR*, July 1980.
3 J. Gennard, S. Dunn and M. Wright, 'The Extent of Closed Shop Arrangements in British Industry', *DEG*, January 1980, pp. 16-22.

The theoretical analysis of union behaviour by economists is not very satisfactory. At its simplest, the union is implicitly assumed to have organized all the relevant workers and to be facing a set of unorganized employers. In many respects, the analysis is analogous to the standard treatment of monopolies in product markets. In this context, the decision that the union has to make is to trade off jobs for higher wages.

The union is seen to face a given demand curve for its members' services. Higher wages mean fewer jobs (a) because they tend to raise product prices and reduce consumer demand, and (b) because they are liable to raise the price of the labour relative to other factors of production and encourage factor substitution. In this model, therefore, it is the prospect of reduced employment possibilities that disciplines the union wage claims. In order to predict what a union will decide to press for, it is necessary to know both the elasticity of the demand curve facing it and the relative value placed by the union on job opportunities and wages. In order to know the second of these it is necessary, in the spirit of this model, to know something about how decisions are arrived at within the union.

Economists frequently ignore some of these qualifications and simply predict that unions will secure a greater wage where they face a relatively inelastic demand curve. As a corollary of this prediction, it is also suggested that in situations where demand elasticities are high a union may have nothing to offer its potential members and may therefore not exist. If we add to this some consideration of the costs of successful organization, we have at least an embryo theory of union density patterns. It is usually said that such costs are low when the workforce in question is (a) stable and so not subject to high rates of quits or lay-offs, (b) concentrated among relatively few employers, (c) concentrated geographically, and (d) possessed of certain attitudes, sometimes labelled 'class consciousness'.

The simple theory of union behaviour sketched above is greatly weakened by the assumption that employers are not organized but act atomistically. When they too are organized, as they usually are in the UK, we enter the world of bargaining and bilateral monopoly. The theories relating to such a world are often elegant and are sometimes entertaining but they are rarely fruitful. Certainly they have not yet produced operational models that have been widely accepted by those who wish to understand the real world. This failure is not confined to the analysis of union behaviour but appears throughout economics whenever strategic, or 'game', situations are central. We therefore have in this area a very fragile theoretical platform from which to survey and analyse the real world.

So much for a sketch of the principles of effective unionization. A number of recent studies have attempted to measure the impact of collective bargaining on the structure of relative wages.[1] From these it would appear that unions have a large impact. A typical estimate would be that average hourly pay in an industry whose labourforce is completely covered by a collective agreement is at least 20% greater than the average wage in a completely uncovered industry. Some recent work, however, has used a more satisfactory body of data and has concluded that a more realistic estimate would be 8%.[2] This is, no doubt, a more plausible estimate.

---

1 See J. Pencavel, 'Relative Wages and Trade Unions in the UK', *EC*, May 1974; C. Mulvey, 'Collective Agreements and Relative Earnings in UK Manufacturing in 1973', *EC*, November 1976; articles by J. Pencavel, D. Metcalf, A. Thompson *et al.*, and S. Nickell in *BJIR*, July 1977.

2 M. Stewart, 'Relative Earnings and Individual Union Membership in the UK', LSE Centre for Labour Economics, Discussion Paper No. 110, September 1981.

In the 1960s many industrial-relations specialists became concerned at the apparently haphazard nature of local bargaining, which was often superimposed on official bargaining and which, it was claimed, contributed to strike activity and inflation. For example, the Donovan Report[1] suggested that many sectors of British industry had two systems of collective bargaining, with informal workplace bargaining between shop stewards and plant management existing simultaneously with formal company or industry-wide bargaining; the Report expressed its distaste for the informal element. It is interesting, therefore, to examine how the wage premium associated with union coverage varies by type of agreement. It appears that in manufacturing industry the wage premium associated with a national agreement is, at best, small, while those covered by district, local and company agreements have a large wage advantage. However, many such supplementary agreements also have a national flavour. The industrial-relations literature is rich in descriptions of institutional mechanisms whereby local bargains struck in one plant are transmitted to plants of the same firm in other areas or to plants of different firms. Thus even supplementary district, local or company agreements may have national dimensions.

It is not clear at whose expense unions extract this wage premium. For much of this century the share of wages in national income was broadly constant,[2] which would imply that union members gain at the expense of non-union members. Such unorganized workers tend either to be relatively low paid or relatively high paid. It is not known which of these two sets of workers might lose from unionization, but a recent, rather technical, work suggests that in the United States the principal losers would be the unorganized low paid and the unemployed.[3]

In the last decade or so, labour's share in national income appears to have risen.[4] Indeed, between 1968 and 1970 union membership and the share of wages in manufacturing national income both rose by 10%. In this case, unions may have secured their wage gains at the expense of profits rather than at the expense of their fellow, non-union, workers. This may, in turn, result in lower investment and a slower growth in real wages in the future.

IV.3   Strikes and Industrial Relations

Strikes: The significance of strikes can be measured by the number of stoppages that occur, by the number of workers involved in the stoppages or by the number of worker days lost through stoppages. Of these, the last has been by far the most volatile in the UK during the last 20 years. 1981 was a year of relatively few strikes, and only 4m worker days were lost; in contrast, more than 29m worker days were lost in 1979 and nearly 12m in 1980. The 1981 figure represents less than 2 hours per year per employee in the labourforce.[5]

---

1   *Report of the Royal Commission on Trade Unions and Employers' Associations 1965-1968* (Donovan Report), Cmnd. 3623, HMSO, 1968.
2   E.H. Phelps Brown, *Pay and Profits*, Manchester UP, 1968.
3   J. Pettengill, *Labour Unions and the Inequality of Earned Income*, North-Holland, 1980.
4   A. Glyn and R. Sutcliffe, *British Capitalism, Workers and the Profits Squeeze*, Penguin, 1972; M. King, 'The UK Profits Crisis: Myth or Reality', *EJ*, March 1975.
5   *DEG*, February 1982, p. S44.

Although the UK has a rather poor international reputation for strikes, its performance, as measured by working days lost per thousand employees, is not unusual for a developed economy. During the last decade the UK has usually lost many fewer days than Spain, Italy or Eire, and significantly fewer than Canada, Finland and Australia; however, the record is much poorer when compared with Holland, Japan, Western Germany and France.[1]

The incidence of strikes is very unevenly distributed across workers, firms, industries and occupations. During the period 1977-80, and after standardizing for differences in the size of the labourforce, the industries that consistently lost most days through strikes were drink, iron and steel, metal manufacture, many of the engineering industries, including motor-vehicles, and printing. In contrast, agriculture, textiles, clothing, the public utilities and most of the service trades lost very few days.[2]

Another feature of strike behaviour is the strong inverse relation between plant size and days lost through strikes. For manufacturing plants employing more than 1,000 workers, days lost averaged 2,050 per 1,000 workers over 1971-3; this may be compared with only 15 days per 1,000 workers in plants employing between 11 and 24 workers.

It is important to note that the vast majority of plants are not affected by stoppages. For example, between 1971 and 1973 95% of plants in manufacturing industry were free of stoppages. Thus, only 5% of manufacturing plants had at least one stoppage in these three years. Of these, two-thirds had only one stoppage but a small minority had a large number. Britain apparently suffers from a concentration of stoppages in the docks, in coalmining and in a small proportion (between 2 and 5%) of plants in manufacturing industry, especially motor-vehicles and shipbuilding.[3]

More generally, strikes seem more likely when inflation is rising and when unemployment is low, and less likely when recent wage changes are high. Comparing different industries, strikes are more likely in those industries with relatively few female workers, extensive payments-by-results systems, rapid technical change and slowly growing wages.

There has been much comment in recent years on payment of supplementary benefit to strikers' families. It is certainly true that state support to strikers' families increased in the 1970s compared with the earlier postwar period. This increase was associated, in part, with a change in the pattern of strikes, in particular with an increase in the number of longer, official strikes, particularly in the public sector (e.g. postmen 1971, miners 1974, firemen 1977, and steelworkers 1980). But the proportion of those eligible who actually received supplementary benefit was, at most, around one-third. Further, SB seems to have played only a minor role in the budgets of those on strike. Only 15% of the postmen's income while on strike came from the state. Strikers and their families rely far more on running down their savings, deferring HP, rent and mortgage payments, living off wives' pay and back-pay, and tax rebates. Gennard provided persuasive evidence that state income support did not cause or prolong strikes; he also suggested that

---

1 *DEG*, February 1982, p. 69.

2 *DEG*, July 1981, p. 295.

3 *DEG*, November 1976, pp. 1,219-24.

modifications in the availability of SB to strikers' families would, in some cases, cause hardship and would possibly sour industrial relations.[1] In spite of this, the present government decided to change the rules governing transfer payments to the families of strikers. It reduced the weekly supplementary benefit paid to strikers' families by £12, eliminated the rule by which the family's first £4 of tax refunds would be disregarded when deciding benefit entitlement and made supplementary benefit payments subject to income tax. It might be claimed that these changes have made a significant contribution to the fall in the number of strikes, but there is, as yet, no direct evidence to support this claim.

Industrial relations: Strike activity is the most heavily publicized aspect of industrial relations but is by no means the most important one. It arouses considerable public comment and often provides dramatic situations with great political significance but, in so doing, it tends to obscure other aspects of the relationships between employer and employee which make up industrial relations. The British 'system' of industrial relations has been the subject of much analysis and debate, particularly since the mid-1960s. There are a number of reasons for this.

Most generally, there has been a growing unease over the power that trade unions are thought to be acquiring. Whether they have grown in power and in what respects this might have happened, and in what ways any such changes might affect behaviour or events, are all questions whose answers are by no means easy to establish. But if opinion polls are to be believed, there is a considerable body of opinion in the country which holds that in a variety of ways unions are too powerful.

There is certainly a strong feeling that unions cause or exacerbate inflation. There is also a debate as to the tactics that are proper in the pursuit of wage claims. There is finally a debate on the question of the closed shop, the circumstances in which it should be allowed, and the rights and position of individual workers who do not wish to be union members.

Among professionals in the field of industrial relations, there has been a narrower, more technical debate. For at least the last 10 to 15 years there has been much concern over the British 'system' of industrial relations, sparked off by two principal worries.

In many sectors the traditional industry-wide collective bargaining had become less important. Sustained full employment in the postwar period made the role of shop stewards and local negotiations much more important; in many manufacturing industries, local agreements were mounted on the back of industrial agreements, causing substantial 'wage drift'. Also, the majority of strikes were unofficial.

These concerns, coupled with certain legal judgments particularly affecting the position of individuals, led to the establishment of a Royal Commission[2] to investigate the industrial-relations system.

The Commission thought that the principal problem in industrial relations was that two systems — the formal and the informal — existed. It further believed that

---

1   J. Gennard, *Financing Strikers*, Macmillan, 1977, and J. Gennard, 'The Effects of Strike Activity on Households', *BJIR*, November 1981.

2   *Report of the Royal Commission on Trade Unions and Employers' Associations*, (Donovan Report), Cmnd. 3623, HMSO, 1968.

certain industries where the conflict between the two systems was very apparent, e.g. engineering, were industries whose bargains set a pattern for others. It saw the remedy in integrating the informal systems and stressed the desirability of both plant bargaining and full employer recognition of unions. However, it strongly believed that the reform should be voluntary rather than imposed by law. It recommended the establishment of a Commission on Industrial Relations, a form of investigatory tribunal, to facilitate this voluntary reform. It believed implicitly that if reform could be achieved in a few key sectors this would percolate through the rest of the system. The Report was not well received by independent observers, who felt that it merely pushed people in the direction they were already going anyway, and that it did little to change the ground-rules of the industrial-relations system or to get at the problem of excessive wage inflation.

Legislation: The Report resulted in actions by both Labour and Conservative governments. Labour established a Commission on Industrial Relations whose functions the Conservatives subsequently altered; on returning to power in 1974, the Labour government abolished the CIR. In 1969-70 the Labour government proposed additional reforms but withdrew them in the face of strong union and backbench opposition. It was left to the Conservatives to legislate substantial reform but their Industrial Relations Act (1971) had a stormy history, arousing bitter hostility in the trade-union leadership, before it was repealed in an early action by the Labour government of 1974. That action, the Trade Union and Labour Relations Act, together with the associated Trade Union and Labour Relations (Amendment) Act (1976), in many ways restored the pre-1971 situation, but in some respects the position of trade unions was further strengthened. For example, under its controversial closed shop provisions, it was no longer unfair for an employer to dismiss employees for refusing to join a union in those situations where employers and unions had agreed to a 100% union-membership provision.

Additional industrial-relations legislation was also introduced. The Employment Protection Act (1975) encouraged constructive union activity. Employers were required to disclose certain information judged to be relevant to collective bargaining, consult with unions on the handling of redundancies, and face more pressure to recognize independent trade unions when their employees wished to be represented. The legislation also gave powers to the Advisory, Conciliation and Arbitration Service and extended the legal rights of individual employees, e.g. in maternity pay and leave provision. The position of unions was also strengthened by the passing of the Health and Safety at Work Act (1975) and the Industry Act (1975). The latter gave worker participation in an embryonic form by encouraging Planning Agreements, i.e. agreements between individual employers, union and the government relating to the operations of firms.

Worker participation in its fullest form was considered by the Bullock Committee.[1] The majority of the Committee recommended that when employees numbered 2,000 or more in a firm they should have the same number of board seats as shareholder representatives. Together, these two groups would co-opt a (smaller) third group of independent directors. Worker directors could continue to act as shop stewards and would not be excluded from any boardroom discussion when, for example, the subject was wages. These proposals would have affected

---

1 *Report of the Committee of Inquiry on Industrial Democracy*, Cmnd. 6706, HMSO, 1977.

about 1,800 private companies grouped into 738 enterprises, employing around 7m people. Reaction to these proposals was mixed, and the Labour government was unable to present agreed legislation to Parliament. Under the Conservative government it does not seem that worker participation will be encouraged by legislation, but the main opposition parties all seem to regard it with more favour.

Since its return to power in 1979, the Conservative government has announced a series of measures designed, in the words of the Chancellor of the Exchequer, 'to create a more reasonable balance of bargaining power between the partners in industry'. The first set of measures formed the 1980 Employment Act which proposed, first, that closed shop agreements should become more difficult to enter into, and that individuals who suffer damage from the operations of a closed shop agreement should have some additional legal redress. Second, the Act made provision for public money to encourage the taking of secret ballots on certain questions such as union elections and strike calls. Third, it redefined the limits of lawful picketing so as to seek to influence who may picket and where picketing may take place. The Act also amended certain parts of the Employment Protection Act relating, for example, to trade-union recognition, unfair-dismissal provisions and maternity provisions. Finally, it changed the immunity which the law provided for so-called 'secondary' industrial action, such as blacking and strikes.[1]

The second set of measures were initially proposed in November 1981 and at the time of writing (April 1982) are still being considered by Parliament and may well be amended before becoming law. As originally formulated, the proposals *inter alia* (i) give substantially greater compensation for those unfairly dismissed when a closed shop agreement is enforced, (ii) make it more likely that the trade union involved will make a contribution to such enhanced compensation, (iii) make provision for periodic review of existing shops, (iv) make unlawful certain practices which require, or put pressure on, contractors to use only union labour, (v) make trade unions liable to be sued in certain circumstances, i.e. modify the existing legal immunities that trade unions enjoy, and (vi) restrict the definition of what constitutes a trade dispute, implying in turn a restriction of the legal immunities of those who organize industrial action.[2]

The intent of these proposals is fairly clear, but so too was that of the 1971 Act, which turned out largely to be a failure. Whether these proposals will share the same fate is likely to depend more than anything else on the economic climate in which they are used and the result of the next general election.

V   WAGE INFLATION AND PUBLIC POLICY

Of all the areas of controversy and disagreement in economics, the one that is most confused and least resolved is probably that of inflation, particularly its causes and cures. It is widely agreed that the most important immediate determinant of price inflation is changes in money wages. This is because wages are the major component of production costs and, as a matter of fact, the prices of finished

---

1 A recent but rather partisan attempt to place this legislation in context is given by R. Lewis and B. Simpson, *Striking a Balance?*, Martin Robertson, 1981.
2 A full description of the proposals can be found in *DEG*, December 1981, pp. 510-14, and *DEG*, February 1982, pp. 61-3.

goods usually change only after costs have changed. There are, of course, other components of costs, and changes in these may also affect prices. Thus, the rate of price inflation is additionally affected by changes in (a) non-wage labour costs, e.g. training costs or National Insurance costs, (b) productivity, (c) taxes or subsidies on goods and services, (d) the foreign currency price of imported goods, (e) the exchange rate and (f) profit margins. In the recent past, each of these has had an influence on the price level for a time but changes in wages have been even more important.

The determinants of at least some of these non-wage cost components are not a matter of very great controversy, though they are often very difficult to forecast at any given time. However, there is very little agreement as to what determines the course of wage costs, and correspondingly little agreement on how that course might be changed by policy. As a consequence, we are now unable to forecast changes in average wages in the UK with any accuracy. As wage changes are so central to many economic events, this inability is one reason why macroeconomic forecasting is extremely hazardous and conjectural. In recent years it has often been necessary for forecasters to take a range of possible wage changes and to make separate calculations for each. With such large unknowns, traditional economic policy formation becomes very difficult.

V.1   Explanations of Wage Inflation

A traditional view is that average wage changes are largely the result of changes in the aggregate demand for labour relative to its supply. This may be true in two senses. One is that as demand increases relative to supply, people in work tend to work more overtime and hence have increased total earnings. The other, and this is what is being considered here, is that as demand increases relative to supply, earnings increase for a given number of hours and amount of effort – this may be called wage inflation. Many different types of economists believe that wage inflation is caused by tight labour markets, i.e. where the demand for labour is high relative to its supply.

At least until the mid-1960s many economists, following the work of Phillips,[1] believed that there was a stable relationship between wage inflation and the state of aggregate demand as measured either by unemployment, or vacancies or an index of unused industrial capacity. It was not, however, thought that aggregate demand was the sole determinant of wage inflation. Phillips noted that wages also seemed to respond to a very rapid rise in import prices, and other economists felt that recent price changes, whatever their source, might influence current wage inflation.

They also added further variables to the Phillips framework, for example, the level of industrial profits or the degree of industrial concentration. In addition to these influences it was felt that the position and shape of the Phillips Curve was the result of the institutional arrangements in the economy, for example, the collective-bargaining structure. Thus, a change in these institutions might affect unemployment and inflation simultaneously. All these additional arguments having been made, it was nevertheless widely felt that changes in the rate of wage inflation from year to year were mainly the result of changes in the level of

---

1   A.W. Phillips, 'The Relation between Unemployment and the Rate of Change of Money Wage Rates in the United Kingdom, 1861-1957', *EC*, November 1958, pp. 283-99.

aggregate demand relative to supply. It was also felt that the principal way the government could influence the level of aggregate demand was by varying its fiscal policy, which meant a change in taxes or government expenditure that produced a change in the public-sector financial deficit or surplus.

Since the mid-1960s faith in the Phillips' framework has been progressively reduced in the UK. In other countries, for example the United States, many economists have continued to see value in it, although there too it is being increasingly questioned. The main reason for the change in view is that wage inflation and unemployment have often moved in the same direction rather than inversely. At the same time there has been a revival of interest in monetary analysis, which tends to restore to a position of importance the rate of increase in the supply of money as an explanation of the rate of inflation.

In some respects, the followers of Phillips and the monetarists agree with one another. Both believe that a policy of reducing the level of aggregate demand relative to supply will reduce wage inflation. One group would say that this would result in permanently higher unemployment, the other would deny this and claim that the rise in unemployment was temporary; they might therefore disagree as to whether the policy is desirable.

Further, both groups contain economists who believe that policy changes other than those of a fiscal or monetary nature can influence wage inflation. Many of those who worked within the Phillips framework saw in incomes policy a chance to shift the whole Phillips Curve, producing less unemployment and lower inflation. Monetarists have tended to be sceptical of incomes policies, partly because the latter have often been accompanied by monetary expansion. However, a monetarist certainly could argue that an incomes policy might reduce inflationary expectations and thus make a tight money policy work more quickly and smoothly. It would, however, be difficult for a monetarist to argue that monetary control and incomes policies were alternatives. In addition, both groups could agree that a whole range of microeconomic institutional changes might affect either the position of the Phillips Curve or the 'natural' rate of unemployment.

There are, however, many observers who believe that wage inflation is the result of the configuration of unions or of collective-bargaining structures. The latter group also tends to believe that the course of wage inflation is largely uninfluenced by variations in such indicators as the unemployment rate, except for relatively brief periods.

A relatively early expression of this diverse group is to be found in the work of Hines, who attributed wage inflation to trade-union pushfulness.[1] Hines set out an index of trade-union pushfulness $\Delta T = T_t - T_{t-1}$ (where T_t denotes the proportion of the labourforce unionized, or union density, in year t). His thesis was that ΔT is a measure of union activity which manifests itself simultaneously both in increased union membership and density and in pressure on money wage rates. He tested this hypothesis with aggregate data from 1893-1961 and found, broadly, that through time excess demand for labour had become less important as a cause of inflation and that in the postwar period wage-pushfulness was a key factor in the explanation of inflation.

Given the controversial nature of this topic and the originality of Hines' contribution, it is not surprising that the latter has been subjected to careful

---

1   A. Hines, 'Trade Union and Wage Inflation in the UK 1893-1961', *RES*, 1964, and
    A. Hines, 'Wage Inflation in the UK 1948-62: A Disaggregated Study', *EJ*, 1969, pp. 66-89.

scrutiny. The most wide-ranging critique is that of Purdy and Zis,[1] who examine Hines' theory, data, estimation technique and interpretation, and re-estimate his model to take account of their various criticisms. When this was done, the impact of ΔT on wage changes, although still positive, was much reduced. This is confirmed by Wilkinson and Burkitt,[2] who used carefully constructed data on unionization by industry and found that ΔT is significantly associated with changes in only one industry, textiles, out of the eleven they studied.

The statistical studies discussed above have neither confirmed nor rejected the central place of unions in the inflationary process and, in consequence, the debate concerning the underlying causes of inflation continues unabated. It is generally agreed that a correlation exists between the growth in the money supply and the rate of inflation, and that this correlation is stronger in the long run than in the short run. What is in dispute is whether inflation is caused by excessive growth in the money supply or whether union power or some other social force causes money wages to rise which in turn induces the authorities to expand the money supply in order that unemployment does not result.

V.2   Incomes Policy

History: Since the mid-1960s different governments in the UK have used incomes and prices policies for a number of purposes.[3] The principal aim of these policies has been to reduce the rate of inflation, but important subsidiary aims have, from time to time, been to reduce the extent of restrictive labour-market practices, to increase labour productivity generally, to encourage a shift in the structure of earnings and to improve the competitive environment in industry. Here we shall concentrate on the anti-inflationary aim.

There has been a wide variety of forms in the policies. For example, they have differed as to whether they were voluntary or compulsory, as to whether they had a flat-rate norm (i.e. so many pounds per week) or a percentage norm, and as to whether they permitted exceptions or not.

From April 1965 to June 1966 the incomes policy was voluntary, i.e. there were no sanctions on those who chose to disregard its guidelines. From mid-1966 to mid-1967 the policy became both compulsory and more severely anti-inflationary in intent. After July 1967 there was a more ambiguous period where compliance with a somewhat more relaxed policy was 'essentially voluntary'. Shortly after coming into power in June 1970, the Conservative government discontinued the incomes policy, but by mid-1971 they felt obliged to resume some direct action, with particular emphasis on achieving a gradual decline in the level of settlements in the public sector. By the autumn of 1972 they were trying to get TUC and CBI agreement on a more comprehensive but still voluntary policy; when this was not forthcoming, they announced a compulsory and initially severe incomes and prices policy in November of that year. This had three phases and lasted until a Labour government was elected in March 1974. After that time the statutory rules were ignored and a number of 'special cases' were recognized.

---

1   D. Purdy and G. Zis, 'Trade Unions and Wage Inflation in the UK', in D. Laidler and
    D. Purdy (eds.), *Inflation and Labour Markets*, Manchester UP, 1974.

2   R. Wilkinson and B. Burkitt, 'Wage Determination and Trade Unions', *SJPE*, June 1973.

3   For a discussion of earlier policies see A. Fels, *The British Prices and Incomes Board*,
    Cambridge UP, 1972, particularly chapter 1.

While in opposition between 1970 and 1974, the Labour Party had become officially hostile to incomes policies, particularly to those having statutory provisions. This was partly because there was scepticism of the economic advantages of such policies but much more because of political imperatives. In 1969 relations between the trade-union movement and the Labour government had become extremely strained following the publication of a White Paper on industrial relations (*In Place of Strife*). During the subsequent period of opposition there were moves to restore friendly relations, and a particular expression of the rapprochement was the so-called Social Contract. Under this, a future Labour government would enjoy generalized and specific support from the trade-union movement in return for legislation and policies designed to strengthen the position of the trade unions and their members. Among the matters on which the trade-union leaders felt strongly was the undesirability of statutory incomes policies. They felt that such policies, by undermining the role of free collective bargaining, struck at the very core of the justification for trade unions, at least as they are organized in the UK.

As a result, and in spite of quite exceptionally high wage inflation, the Labour government did virtually nothing directly to affect wage inflation between spring 1974 and summer 1975. However, a continuation of such a posture was widely thought to be impossible. It was not widely believed that in the absence of direct action wage inflation would quickly fall below 25-30% p.a. and it was recognized that such inflation as had already been experienced was going to be difficult to digest. On the other hand, there was great scepticism that a purely voluntary incomes policy, even if negotiated, would work.

In the event a very simple voluntary policy, albeit one with explicit sanctions held in reserve, was agreed between the government and the TUC and was adhered to very widely. This was followed, in the summer of 1976 and the summer of 1977, by two more stages, both fairly simple and neither backed with explicit sanctions, although during the third stage the government did take various disciplinary actions against firms that paid more than the suggested guidelines. In the summer and autumn of 1978 the Labour government tried to secure trade-union adherence to a fourth successive year of the largely voluntary policy but the trade-union movement was unwilling to comply.

The Conservative government, which came to power in May 1979, has been uninterested, indeed hostile, to incomes policies, voluntary or statutory, even when wage inflation went back up to 20% in early 1980. The most that can be claimed is that the present government has an incomes policy for the public sector. Whether it is a useful use of words to call this an incomes policy is a matter for debate, but even in the public sector the government has not seriously sought to impose a rigid norm.

As with the choice between voluntary and statutory there have been changes in the type of norm used. Most of the early policies had percentage norms, but the Conservative government's Phase II, from April 1973 to September 1973, had a flat-rate component (the exact formula was a permitted £1 + 4%). In July 1975 the Labour government announced a norm of £6 per week for everyone except those earning more than £8,500 per year, who were not allowed any increase at all. This was followed in the next year by a more complex formula of a minimum of £2.50 per week and a maximum of £4.00 per week, or, within those limits, 5%.

The effect of these flat-rate guidelines, of course, is to reduce the relative earnings differentials between pay groups. This erosion of differentials certainly created political and industrial-relations problems and probably began to affect adversely the allocation of labour. As a result, in Stage 3 of the Labour government's policy there was a reversion to a percentage norm (10% of earnings) plus some allowance for genuine productivity deals.

Three other aspects of the norms are worth mentioning. First, in November 1973 the Conservative government permitted a form of indexation, whereby workers could make agreements under which they would receive wage increases if the price level rose above a certain threshold. The intention here was that prices would not so rise and that the indexation clause would not in fact be triggered. This was an interesting idea and reflected the belief that wage settlements incorporate an allowance for expected future inflation. If most settlements include such a hedge against the future they will, in aggregate, raise costs and produce the very price rise they are seeking to protect against. If, therefore, the inflation hedge can every-where be eliminated, the rise in costs, and hence in prices, might be avoided. The indexation scheme was an attempt to eliminate the inflation hedge by making the compensation for price increases conditional on their arrival rather than their prospect. Unfortunately the policy was a failure. The price index chosen was one that reflected the prices of imported goods, and many of these rose dramatically in 1973 as the major economies of the world boomed together. Once the threshold clauses were triggered a wage/price/wage spiral was set off because the wage compensation for price inflation was virtually 100%. Had a different index been used, or had commodity prices not exploded, or had the compensation not been roughly one-for-one, the policy might, in retrospect, have been judged more favourably.

The second point about norms is that there is no longer an attempt to relate them seriously to productivity increases. In the 1960s the ostensible purpose of the policy was to limit average wage increases to average productivity increases, thus securing constant unit labour costs for any given level of output. More recently, with inflation generally so much higher, the goal of constant unit labour costs is seen to be far too ambitious and has been replaced by the more modest aim of reducing the increase in unit labour costs over what it would otherwise have been.

The third point about norms is that some incomes policies have been combined with tax policies, in that the Chancellor of the Exchequer has announced income-tax reductions that are conditional on incomes-policy success. For example, in March 1977 Mr Healey announced a 2p cut in the standard rate of income tax contingent upon the successful negotiation with the trade-union movement of Stage 3 of the incomes policy. The theory behind this is that disposable incomes can rise (via the tax cuts) even if wage rates, and hence unit labour costs, do not. It also means that the wage rate or earnings norm is somewhat misleading because to it must be added the tax cuts, and these differ in value to different taxpayers.

The 1965-70 incomes policies permitted wage increases greater than the norm on four grounds: where there was a serious labour shortage in a particular industry, occupation or region; where the wages of a particular group of workers were 'seriously out of line' with their traditional place in the wage structure; for low-paid workers; and for productivity deals. More recent policies have also allowed exceptions for 'unsocial hours', and to allow the phased equalization of wage rates between the sexes to take place. The problem with most of the permitted exceptions is that they can often be used by powerful groups to circumvent the spirit of the policy. This is felt to be particularly true for productivity deals, which are often seen to be phoney.

Effectiveness of incomes policy: An incomes policy is likely to lead to some loss of allocative efficiency in the economy, by inhibiting changes in relative wages. Does it provide some compensating benefits by slowing down the rate of wage and price inflation below what they would otherwise have been?

The accumulated evidence on the effect on wage inflation of incomes policies as they have been applied in the UK suggests very strongly that they have generally been ineffective. Earnings increases are usually reduced below what they would otherwise have been in the early stages of the policy; but increasingly, and most notably when a government is compelled to dismantle the policy, earnings rise again to reach a level very close to that which they would have reached had no such policy ever existed.

For example a Department of Employment Working Party[1] estimated that over the years 1965, 1966 and 1967 earnings rose about 4% less than they otherwise would have done without a policy, whilst in 1968 and 1969 earnings rose 4% more than they would have done had there never been a policy. The total impact of the policy was nil. This raises the question, why are incomes policies taken off? Presumably the answer is that, at least as they have been applied in the UK, they become politically or economically unsustainable after a while.

This is also the conclusion reached by two extremely thorough studies of the effect of incomes policies over the whole postwar period. In one study the authors summarize all the recent literature and conclude 'incomes policy apparently has little effect either on the wage determination process or on the average rate of wage inflation'.[2]

In the other study, a careful and subtle statistical analysis, the conclusion was that wage increases in the period immediately following the ending of the various policy experiments matched any reductions gained during their operation.[3]

One reason for these findings is that incomes policies have often been introduced while the economy was being expanded. This was notably the case with the policies of the Conservative government in 1972 and 1973. It is precisely in such circumstances that one might expect least success because tight labour markets lead both workers and employers to try to circumvent the policy, the former because they want higher wages and the latter because they want more labour. Arguably one of the few incomes policy successes was with Stage 1 of the Labour government's policy in 1975. At the time, unemployment was rising rapidly and output was stagnant or falling, so that macroeconomic policy and the incomes policy were working in harmony against inflation. It could be argued that in these circumstances the incomes policy contributed nothing, that the success in reducing inflation should be ascribed to macroeconomic or monetary policy alone. However, most observers agree that the incomes policy at least caused the reduction in wage inflation to come earlier than it would otherwise have done.

Another strand of thinking on incomes policies is that in some circumstances they might raise the rate of wage inflation. This view is based on the proposition that the policy norm might become a floor rather than a ceiling – the norm might be seen as a minimum entitlement. This view probably influenced the Labour

1 DE, *Prices and Earnings in 1951-69*, HMSO, 1971, para. 57.
2 M. Parkin *et al.*, 'The Impact of Incomes Policy on the Rate of Wage Change', in M. Parkin and M. Sumner (eds.), *Incomes Policy and Inflation*, Manchester UP, 1972.
3 S. Henry and P. Ormerod, 'Incomes Policy and Wage Inflation', *NIER*, August 1978, pp. 31-9.

government in 1978 when it pitched the norm quite low, at 5%, and hoped that any excess, or drift, would still keep wage inflation in bounds. In the event, the tactic was transparent and the experiment backfired. 5% was judged to be far too low in comparison with most workers' expectations and any small chance that the continuation of the policy might secure official union support disappeared.

Incomes policies in the future: In spite of the fact that they are widely judged to have had only a temporary success in reducing the rate of wage inflation, while at the same time frequently giving rise to political embarrassments, incomes policies have always retained their advocates. The latter usually become more numerous with the passage of time after any previous incomes policy experiment has been scrapped, because the costs of alternative policies then become more clearly revealed. The principal anti-inflation alternative to incomes policy has been economic contraction, either passively tolerated or actively engineered. The deeper that alternative has bitten and the higher the unemployment rate has climbed, the more people have tended to turn back to incomes policies in the hope that they might offer a more sensible and rational way of conducting our economic affairs. In such a context, the failures of previous incomes policies are attributed to errors in their form or design rather than to generic defects.

The most recent revival of interest in incomes policies appeared after about 2½ years of seeking to manage the economy without one. During that time, unemployment soared to another postwar record but wage inflation came down only to around 10%. Their advocates are now tending to stress the possibility that incomes policies can increase employment without raising inflation. It is admitted that all incomes policies are likely to generate economic costs; for example, they might make the structure of wages more rigid than it would otherwise be, thereby adversely affecting the efficiency with which labour and other resources are allocated. It is claimed, however, that the size of any such costs is likely to be greatly exceeded by the benefits of a successful incomes policy, in particular, by the increase in employment which it would bring about. If this is true, the only problem is to design a successful policy. In attempting to do this, some economists have begun to advocate a form of incomes policy that was originally designed some years ago but never put into practice. Its principal mechanism is a tax levied on employers who grant wage increases in excess of the government's norm.[1]

The main reason for reviving this particular incomes policy variant is the belief that previous policies in the UK have not provided sufficient incentives for wage bargainers to comply with their terms. Even when incomes policies have been statutory in form, their penalties for non-compliance have not usually been clear or believable, particularly to those engaged in wage negotiations. A tax on excess settlements, however, is likely to be clear to everyone, even if some of its implications are in doubt.[2]

---

1 The idea seems originally to have been proposed by H. Wallich and S. Weintraub, 'A tax-based incomes policy', *Journal of Economic Issues*, June 1971. It has been revived more recently by R. Jackman and R. Layard; see, for example, R. Layard, 'Is Incomes Policy the Answer to Unemployment?', *EC*, August 1982.

2 It should be stressed that different writers favour different taxes, even when they are all sympathetic to the same broad ideas; thus, for example, some would advocate seeking to tax all excess settlements while others, for reasons of administration, would confine the tax to large employers. A complete discussion of the available permutations would take many pages and would be out of place here.

Whatever its particular form, the tax is held to give an important additional incentive to employers to resist above-norm settlements; further, the tax would increase total costs of production and thereby threaten employment, so that it might also give trade unions an additional reason not to push as hard for 'excessive' wage increases. Both sides of the labour market, therefore, are said to be given a clear reason to moderate their wage settlements.

The discussion surrounding this device is necessarily speculative, because it has not so far been tried in practice. However, many observers doubt that it would work effectively for more than a relatively brief period. They look at what has happened in labour markets since 1970 and note that many firms have been under immense and sustained economic pressures. During that time, wage settlements have always greatly outstripped productivity increases, even when firms generally have been facing profits difficulties, liquidity crises, loss of markets and problems of mass redundancies. The picture has been similar on the workers' side. The rapid rise in unemployment has certainly attenuated wage inflation, but even in early 1982, with 3m people out of work, the annualized rate of increase in money earnings was nearly into double figures.

In such a context many believe that it is easy to exaggerate the long-term impact of an excess settlements tax. Certainly, employers and workers have not been short of incentives to moderate wage increases during the last decade. Whether a new tax would provide a peculiarly effective incentive is not clear but the potential effectiveness of such a policy will, no doubt, be a matter of searching debate over the next few years.[1] Already at least one political grouping, the Liberal–Social Democratic Party Alliance, is thought to be likely to adopt it as official policy.

REFERENCES AND FURTHER READING

A.B. Atkinson, *Economics of Inequality*, Clarendon Press, 1975.
British Journal of Industrial Relations, July 1977. Symposium of Labour Economics and Industrial Relations.
Department of Employment, *British Labour Statistics: Historical Abstract 1886-1968*, HMSO, 1971.
E. Hobsbawm, *Labouring Men*, Weidenfeld and Nicolson, 1968.
W.J. McCarthy (ed.), *Trade Unions*, Penguin, 1972.
E.H. Phelps Brown, *The Inequality of Pay*, Oxford UP, 1977.
Royal Commission on the Distribution of Income and Wealth, *An A to Z of Income and Wealth*, HMSO, 1980.

---

1   As an example see the article 'An Inflation Tax' by R. Jackman and R. Layard, and the comment by R.C.O. Matthews in *Fiscal Studies*, vol. 3, No. 1, March 1982.

Statistical Appendix

TABLE A-1

UK Gross Domestic Product, Expenditure (at 1975 prices), 1969-81 (£m)

Year	Consumers' Expenditure		General Government Final Consumption	Gross Domestic Capital Formation		Value of Physical Increase in Stocks and Work in Progress	Exports of Goods and Services	Total Final Expenditure at Market Prices	Imports of Goods and Services	Adjustment to Factor Cost[1]	Gross Domestic Product at Factor Cost[2]
	Durable Goods	Non-Durable Goods and Services		Excluding Dwellings	Dwellings						
1969	3,675	52,638	18,829	14,767	4,187	1,019	20,457	115,452	-22,728	-8,826	83,829
1970	3,987	53,827	19,103	15,610	3,850	802	21,576	118,668	-23,938	-9,167	85,484
1971	4,750	54,974	19,673	15,652	4,091	278	23,048	122,427	-25,187	-9,514	87,654
1972	5,770	57,500	20,484	15,514	4,309	-19	23,318	126,923	-27,694	-10,243	88,815
1973	6,064	60,268	21,453	17,043	4,152	2,483	26,031	137,494	-30,941	-10,918	95,635
1974	5,302	59,811	21,774	16,741	3,826	1,386	27,884	136,724	-31,243	-10,576	94,905
1975	5,367	59,382	23,039	16,267	4,149	-1,483	27,197	133,918	-29,011	-10,432	94,475
1976	5,641	59,174	23,213	16,384	4,265	624	29,665	138,966	-30,232	-10,786	97,948
1977	5,224	59,359	22,948	16,253	3,908	1,387	31,594	140,673	-30,559	-10,874	99,240
1978	5,932	62,290	23,435	16,769	4,067	833	32,193	145,519	-31,757	-11,895	101,867
1979	6,595	64,890	23,834	17,334	3,623	1,404	32,957	150,637	-35,338	-12,398	102,901
1980[3]	6,280	65,197	24,216	17,591	3,129	-2,232	33,067	147,248	-34,108	-12,411	100,729
1981[3]	6,373	65,094	24,290	16,792	2,363	-2,062	n.a.	n.a.	n.a.	-12,164	n.a.

Sources: *NIBB*, 1981; *ET(AS)*, 1982; *ET*, April 1982.

Notes: 1 Adjustment to Factor Cost represents taxes on expenditure less subsidies valued at constant rates.
2 For the years before 1973 the value of GDP as shown in the last column differs from the sum of its components. This is because the various items have been separately linked to the later series based on 1975 prices. See *NIBB*, 1981, p. 109.
3 Certain figures not available due to industrial action.

TABLE A-2

UK Prices, Wages, Earnings, Productivity, 1969-81: Index Numbers (1975 = 100)

Year	Retail Prices (All Items)	Weekly Wage Rates	Hourly Earnings (manu-facturing)	Average Weekly Earnings (GB)	Average Earnings Non-Manual Employees (GB)	Output per Person Employed (GDP)	Output per Man-hour Worked (manufacturing)
	1	2	3	4	5	6	7
1969	51.0	40.5	38.0	42.3	46.0	92.4	83.0
1970	54.2	44.5	43.8	47.1	49.3	94.3	85.6
1971	59.3	50.3	49.3	52.4	55.1	97.3	89.0
1972	63.6	57.2	55.8	58.9	61.4	99.9	94.5
1973	69.4	65.1	63.8	67.1	68.0	103.6	101.2
1974	80.5	77.9	78.4	79.1	77.4	101.5	101.8
1975	100.0	100.0	100.0	100.0	100.0	100.0	100.0
1976	116.5	120.4	116.2	115.6	120.5	102.6	105.1
1977	135.0	128.4	127.2	126.1	131.7	105.2	105.9
1978	146.2	146.4	145.8	142.4	147.9	108.1	107.1
1979	165.8	168.4	168.6	164.6	165.7	110.0	108.9
1980	195.6	198.7	203.1	198.6	–	109.2	107.3
1981	218.9	218.8	231.9	224.1	–	111.6	112.7

Sources: Column 1, *ET(AS)*, 1982 and *ET*, April 1982.

Columns 2, 3, 4, *NIER*, November 1979, and May 1982. Column 2 relates to manual workers only, the figure for 1969 is linked from the previous series. Column 3 relates to manual and non-manual workers and is based on *NIER* estimates, the figure for 1969 is linked from the previous series. Column 4 covers workers in all industries.

Column 5, *DEG*, October 1979 and March 1980. This series, now discontinued, related to GB and covered employees in all industries. The series was compiled on the basis of surveys for April of each year with a base year April 1970 = 100. For this table the figures have been recalculated to give 1975 = 100. The figure for 1969 is derived from the previous series relating to 'Salaries' of non-manual workers.

Column 6, *ET*, April 1982.

Column 7, *NIER*, November 1979 and May 1982. This is an estimate by the NIESR, based on output per person and the average weekly hours worked.

TABLE A-3

UK Personal Income, Expenditure and Saving 1969-81 (£m)

PERSONAL INCOME BEFORE TAX

Year	Wages and Salaries	Forces Pay	Employers Contributions	Current Grants from Public Authorities	Other Personal Income	Total[1]	Transfers Abroad (Net)	UK Taxes on Income (Payments)
	1	2	3	4	5	6	7	8
1969	24,254	539	2,428	3,937	8,084	39,242	29	5,178
1970	27,098	658	2,790	4,330	8,562	43,438	1	5,744
1971	29,644	748	3,079	4,780	9,605	47,866	−12	6,490
1972	33,312	862	3,662	5,845	10,992	54,673	34	6,623
1973	38,430	925	4,418	6,420	13,459	63,652	78	7,726
1974	45,478	1,071	5,714	7,876	15,428	75,567	97	10,419
1975	58,932	1,283	7,980	10,284	17,401	95,880	110	15,042
1976	66,161	1,474	9,963	12,765	20,289	110,652	−28	17,422
1977	78,379	1,506	11,152	15,108	22,945	124,032	−	18,164
1978	83,971	1,645	12,861	17,904	26,954	143,335	119	19,483
1979	98,519	2,020	14,931	20,980	33,598	170,048	232	21,644
1980	117,152	2,426	17,514	25,495	37,751	200,338	290	25,897
1981	125,934	2,619	19,292	31,374	40,119	219,338	239	28,942

Sources: NIBB, 1980, 1981; *ET*, April 1982.

Notes: 1 Before providing for depreciation and stock appreciation.
  2 Before providing for additions to tax reserves.
  Column 6 = 1 + 2 + 3 + 4 + 5   Column 13 = 14 − 11
  Column 10 = 6 − 7 − 8 − 9   Column 15 = 10 − 14

National Insurance and Health Contributions	Total Personal Disposable Income[2]	CONSUMERS' EXPENDITURE					PERSONAL SAVINGS		
		Durable Goods		Other			Amount (£m)	As % of P.D.I.	Year
		Amount (£m)	As % of P.D.I.	Amount (£m)	Total				
9	10	11	12	13	14	15	16		
2,242	31,793	2,063	6.5	27,170	29,233	2,560	8.1		1969
2,655	35,038	2,394	6.8	29,384	31,778	3,260	9.3		1970
2,826	38,562	3,074	8.0	32,525	35,599	2,963	7.7		1971
3,337	44,679	3,862	8.6	36,321	40,183	4,496	10.1		1972
3,937	51,911	4,228	8.1	41,531	45,759	6,152	11.9		1973
5,000	60,051	4,274	7.1	48,394	52,668	7,383	12.3		1974
6,848	73,880	5,367	7.3	59,382	64,749	9,131	12.4		1975
8,426	84,832	6,396	7.5	68,556	74,952	9,880	11.6		1976
9,508	96,418	7,083	7.3	78,918	86,001	10,417	10.8		1977
10,107	113,626	9,082	8.0	89,865	98,947	14,679	12.9		1978
11,535	136,637	11,438	8.3	105,413	116,851	19,786	14.5		1979
14,028	160,123	12,052	7.5	123,391	135,443	24,680	15.4		1980
16,376	173,781	12,663	7.3	137,302	149,965	23,816	13.7		1981

TABLE A-4

UK Population, Working Population, Unemployment; GB Unemployment and Vacancies, 1969–81 (thousands)

Year	Total Population (Mid-year estimate) (UK)	Working Population[1,2] (UK)	Unemployed[1] (including school-leavers) (UK)	Registered Unemployment (GB) Monthly Average	Unemployment Rate[3] (GB) %	Unfilled[4] Vacancies (GB) 'A' (monthly average)	Unfilled[4] Vacancies (GB) 'B' (monthly average)
	1	2	3	4	5	6	7
1969	55,263	25,375	518	539	2.3	285	—
1970	55,421	25,308	555	577	2.5	260	—
1971	55,610	25,123	724	752	3.4	176	—
1972	55,781	25,195	804	835	3.7	189	—
1973	55,913	25,547	575	588	2.6	398	—
1974	55,922	25,601	542	591	2.6	294	91
1975	55,900	25,849	866	936	4.1	151	33
1976	55,886	26,120	1,332	1,305	5.6	120	23
1977	55,852	26,276	1,450	1,423	6.0	153	21
1978	55,836	26,389	1,446	1,410	6.0	209	26
1979	55,881	26,434	1,344	1,325	5.6	240	30
1980	55,945	26,350	1,660	1,716	7.3	142	14
1981	n.a.	26,069	2,681	2,628	11.1	97	5

Sources: Column 1, *MDS*, April 1982; Column 2 and 3, *MDS*, April 1982; Columns 4-7, *AAS*, 1982 and previous issues *MDS*, April 1982.

Notes:

1 Estimates are for June of each year.

2 The Working Population includes employees in employment, self-employed persons, HM Forces and the registered unemployed. Numbers in the sub-aggregates may be found in the listed sources.

3 The unemployment rate is obtained by dividing the relevant monthly average unemployment figure by the relevant total employees (including unemployed) for June of that year. Self-employed and HM Forces are excluded from the figure for total employees.

4 For 1969 to 1973 Column 'A' relates to total vacancies. After 1973 Column 'A' relates to vacancies notified to employment offices and Column 'B' to vacancies notified to careers offices. These columns should not be added because of duplication in the series. Figures for 1974, 1975, 1976 and 1977 are based on estimates for some of the months.

UK Money Stock, Domestic Credit Expansion and Public Sector Borrowing Requirement (£m) and Interest Rates, 1969-81

Year	Money Stock[1,4] (M_1)	Money Stock[2,4] (Sterling M_3)	Money Stock[3,4] (M_3)	Change in Money Stock[5] (Sterling M_3)	Domestic Credit Expansion[6]	Public Sector Borrowing Requirement[7]	Yield on UK Treasury bills (%)	Yield on 2½% Consols (%)
	1	2	3	4	5	6	7	8
1969	9,647	16,339	16,919	374	−226	−449	7.8	8.88
1970	10,554	17,893	18,529	1,541	742	−10	6.93	9.16
1971	11,707	20,372	20,944	2,459	1,177	1,364	4.46	9.05
1972	13,295	25,355	26,245	4,927	6,691	2,055	8.48	9.11
1973	13,967	32,029	33,466	6,702	8,066	4,200	12.82	10.85
1974	15,457	35,282	37,685	3,255	6,926	6,370	11.30	14.95
1975	17,483	37,595	40,573	2,331	4,531	10,505	10.93	14.66
1976	19,467	41,160	45,129	3,565	7,474	9,187	13.98	14.25
1977	23,659	45,290	49,565	4,130	1,128	5,993	6.39	12.32
1978	27,535	52,062	56,963	6,772	8,069	8,332	11.91	11.92
1979	30,046	58,677	63,996	6,615	10,256	12,564	16.49	11.38
1980	31,230	69,591	75,934	10,914	15,656	12,289	13.45	11.86
1981	34,301	79,021	89,592	9,430	14,079	10,658	15.39	13.00

Sources: Cols. 1-6: Figures kindly supplied by the Bank of England. More recent figures may be found in *ET*, *FS* and *BEQB*. All cols. based on seasonally unadjusted data. Cols. 7-8: *ET(AS)*, 1981, *FS*, April 1982.

Notes:
1 M_1 consists of notes and coin in circulation plus sterling sight (or demand) deposits held by the private sector. Totals refer to amounts outstanding at the year end.

2 Sterling M_3 is a wide definition of the sterling money stock. It includes notes and coin together with all sterling deposits (including certificates of deposit) held by residents in the private and public sectors. Totals refer to amounts outstanding at the year-end.

3 This is col. 2 plus all deposits held by UK residents in other currencies. Totals refer to amounts outstanding at the year-end.

4 Cols. 1-3 are not necessarily the amounts outstanding as given in published series. The money stock series contains a number of breaks caused by the introduction of new banking statistics in mid-May 1975 and the re-classification of institutions as banks. The figures given here are smoothed series produced by the Bank of England, which should give a more accurate indication of the trend growth of the money stocks. Actual year-end data may be found in the publications listed above. Data for 1982 onwards will be based on the new 'Monetary Sector' and will not be comparable with data presented here. See *BEQB*, December 1981, p. 531.

5 Figures relate to the sum of quarterly changes in £M_3 (unadjusted). For reasons partly explained in Note 4 the annual change given in col. 4 is not equivalent to the first difference in col. 2.

6 DCE is the increase in the domestic money stock (£M_3) after adjustment for any change in money balances caused directly by an external surplus or deficit. See chapter 2 and *BEQB*, March 1977.

7 The public sector includes the central government, the local authorities and public corporations. The borrowing requirement is discussed in chapter 2.

TABLE A-6

UK General Government: Current Account, 1968-80 (£m)

	1968	1969	1970	1971	1972	1973	1974	1975	1976	1977	1978	1979	1980
RECEIPTS													
Taxes on income	5,846	6,489	7,388	8,003	8,100	9,164	12,589	16,657	18,864	20,333	22,461	25,098	30,888
Taxes on expenditure	6,809	7,782	8,417	8,788	9,267	10,121	11,457	14,134	16,532	20,261	23,221	30,254	37,287
National Insurance, etc. contributions	2,161	2,242	2,655	2,826	3,337	3,937	5,000	6,848	8,426	9,508	10,107	11,533	13,977
Gross Trading Surplus	132	153	152	177	146	139	148	141	110	147	163	186	170
Rent	546	623	703	737	770	922	1,243	1,523	1,849	2,012	2,171	2,617	3,092
Interest, dividends, etc.[1]	711	809	899	1,030	1,171	1,374	1,775	2,027	2,363	2,710	2,922	3,344	3,836
Imputed charge for consumption of non-trading capital	246	268	301	349	402	497	599	763	908	1,030	1,170	1,399	1,775
Total	16,451	18,366	20,515	21,910	23,193	26,154	32,811	42,093	49,052	56,001	62,215	74,431	91,025
EXPENDITURE													
Current expenditure on goods and services	7,416	7,729	8,690	9,901	11,273	12,883	16,019	22,276	25,868	28,207	31,799	36,842	46,562
Non-trading capital consumption	224	268	301	349	402	497	599	763	908	1,030	1,170	1,399	1,775
Subsidies	895	842	884	939	1,153	1,443	3,004	3,702	3,461	3,293	3,624	4,389	5,215
Current grants to personal sector	3,678	3,937	4,330	4,780	4,845	6,420	7,876	10,284	12,765	15,108	17,905	20,977	25,476
Current grants abroad	179	177	177	205	210	360	323	370	788	1,115	1,703	2,058	1,832
Total expenditure excluding debt interest	12,392	12,953	14,382	16,174	18,883	21,603	27,821	37,395	43,790	48,753	56,201	65,665	80,860
Debt interest[1]	1,794	1,929	2,025	2,089	2,286	2,738	3,607	4,211	5,394	6,373	7,227	8,950	11,285
Total current expenditure	14,186	14,882	16,407	18,263	21,169	24,341	31,428	41,606	49,184	55,126	63,428	74,615	92,145
Balance: Current surplus before providing for depreciation	2,243	3,484	4,108	3,647	2,024	1,813	1,383	487	-132	875	-1,213	-184	-1,120
TOTAL	16,429	18,366	20,515	21,910	23,193	26,154	32,811	42,093	49,052	56,001	62,215	74,431	91,025

Sources: NIBB, 1980, 1981.   *Note:* 1 Excluding interest on loans from central government to local authorities.

TABLE A-7

UK Balance of Payments, 1969-81 (£m)

CURRENT ACCOUNT[1]

	Visible Trade			Invisibles			
				Government Services and	Private Services and	Interest Profits and	
Year	Exports (f.o.b.)	Imports (f.o.b.)	Visible Balance	Transfers (net)	Transfers (net)	Dividends (net)	Invisible Balance
	1	2	3	4	5	6	7
1969	7,269	−7,478	−209	−467	683	498	714
1970	8,150	−8,184	−34	−486	789	554	857
1971	9,043	−8,853	+190	−520	952	502	934
1972	9,437	−10,185	−748	−561	1,018	538	995
1973	11,937	−14,523	−2,586	−769	1,117	1,257	1,605
1974	16,394	−21,745	−5,351	−842	1,505	1,415	2,078
1975	19,330	−22,663	−3,333	−940	1,979	773	1,812
1976	25,191	−29,120	−3,929	−1,455	3,138	1,365	3,048
1977	31,728	−34,012	−2,284	−1,839	3,978	104	2,243
1978	35,063	−36,605	−1,542	−2,401	4,296	592	2,487
1979	40,687	−44,136	−3,449	−2,855	4,522	846	2,513
1980	47,396	−46,211	+1,185	−2,620	4,605	−112	1,873
1981[4]	n.a.	n.a.	n.a.	−2,432	4,631	1,148	3,347

Sources: ET, December 1981 and March 1982.

Notes: 1 All items listed represent a positive flow if unsigned. Negative flows are indicated by a − sign preceding the figure. For capital account items a positive flow represents an increase in liabilities or a reduction in assets, whilst a negative flow indicates an increase in assets or a reduction in liabilities.

2 Includes Capital Transfers for 1972 (−£59m) and 1974 (−£75m).

3 The sum of Columns 8, 13 and 14 is defined in official sources as 'Balance for Official Financing'. The balance is normally the negative of the item shown in Column 15. For certain years this relationship is disturbed by special items which should be added to the sum of columns 8, 13 and 14 in order to get the appropriate figure for column 15. The special items are 1970, allocation of SDRs, +171, gold subscription to the IMF −38; 1971, allocation of SDRs, +125; 1972, allocation of SDRs, +124; 1979, allocation of SDRs, +195; 1980, allocation of SDRs, +180; 1981, allocation of SDRs, +158.

4 Figures for columns 1, 2, 3, 8 and 14 were not available at the time of printing because of delays in the release of statistical data caused by industrial action.

INVESTMENT AND OTHER CAPITAL TRANSACTIONS[1]

Current Balance	Official Long-term Capital	Overseas Long-term Investment in UK Private and Public Sectors	UK Private Long-term Investment Overseas	Other Capital Flows Mainly Short-term	Total Investment and Other Capital Trans-actions[2]	Balancing Item	Total Official Financing[3]
8	9	10	11	12	13	14	15
505	−100	517	−693	100	−176	358	−687
823	−206	703	−829	877	545	−81	−1,420
1,124	−274	1,015	−860	1,909	1,790	232	−3,271
247	−254	772	−1,402	200	−684	−828	1,141
−981	−255	1,497	−1,760	684	107	103	771
−3,273	−287	2,204	−1,148	825	1,519	108	1,646
−1,521	−291	1,514	−1,367	278	134	−78	1,465
−881	−160	2,088	−2,269	−2,747	−3,088	341	3,628
−41	−303	4,399	−2,334	2,415	4,177	3,225	−7,361
945	−336	1,908	−4,634	−1,180	−4,242	2,171	1,126
−936	−401	4,307	−6,555	4,819	2,170	476	−1,905
3,058	−91	4,779	−7,103	997	−1,418	−448	−1,372
n.a.	−339	3,668	−9,470	−132	−6,273	n.a.	687

Index